Inside the IBM PC

Revised and Enlarged

Peter Norton

A Brady Book
Published by Prentice Hall Press
New York, NY 10023

Inside the IBM PC, Revised and Enlarged

A Brady Book
Published by Prentice Hall Press
A Division of Simon & Schuster, Inc.

Gulf + Western Building
One Gulf + Western Plaza
New York, NY 10023

PRENTICE HALL PRESS is a trademark of Simon & Schuster, Inc.

Library of Congress Cataloging in Publication Data

Norton, Peter, 1943-
    Inside the IBM PC.

        Bibliography: p. 361
        Includes index.
        1. IBM microcomputers.   I. Title.
QA76.8.I2594N67   1985   004.165   85-25562
ISBN 0-89303-583-1

Printed in the United States of America

86 87 88 89 90 91 92 93 94 95 96   3 4 5 6 7 8 9 10

Contents

About the Author

Peter Norton was born in Seattle, Washington, and educated at Reed College in Portland, Oregon. During the past 20 years, he has worked with a wide variety of computer equipment from personal computers to the largest main-frames, and he has worked on every kind of software from the most intricate system programming to thoroughly mundane commercial applications.

Shortly after he began working with microcomputers, he created, for the IBM PC family of computers, the now-legendary Norton Utilities software package.

Although Mr. Norton continues to develop software for small computers, his work now concentrates on writing about the use of personal computing.

Limits of Liability and Disclaimer of Warranty

The author and publisher of this book have used their best efforts in preparing this book and the programs contained in it. These efforts include the development, research, and testing of the theories and programs to determine their effectiveness. The author and publisher make no warrantyof any kind, expressed or implied, with regard to these programs or the documentation contained in this book. The author and publisher shall not be liable in any event for incidental or consequential damages in connection with, or arising out of, the furnishing, performance, or use of these programs.

Note to Authors

Have you written a book related to personal computers? Do you have an idea for developing such a project? If so, we would like to hear from you. Brady produces a complete range of books for the personal computer market. We invite you to write to Editorial Department, Brady Communications, Inc., General Reference Group, Simon&Schuster Building, 1230 Avenue of the Americas, New York, New York 10020.

Introduction

T his is the beginning of a marvelous voyage of discovery into the secrets, wonders, and mysteries of the IBM Personal Computer and the family of computers that has grown up around it.

From the day it first appeared, the IBM Personal Computer has been stirring up excitement and fascination, because the PC—as everyone calls it—marked the coming of age of personal computing. Today, the PC is solidly established as the power tool without equal for helping business and professional people improve their performance and the quality of their work. The PC has also spawned a great many other computers—some from IBM, and some from the makers of "PC compatible" computers—that have become what we call "the PC family."

This book is designed to help you understand the remarkable PC and its entire family. In this book, we—you and I—will set off to discover the mysteries and wonders of what the PC is and what marvels it can perform. I am excited and enthused about the PC and the PC family, and I want to lead you into understanding the workings of this marvel and sharing with me the excitement of knowing what it is, how it works, and what it can do.

As you must have already realized, this isn't a book for people who are having trouble finding the On/Off switch on their computers. Instead, it's for people like you who have both the intelligence *and* the curiosity to comprehend this wonderful family of machines. My goal is to make understanding the PC easy for you and fun as well.

This is, more than anything else, a book of understanding, written to help you learn what you really need to know about the PC. You can very successfully use a PC without really understanding it. However, the better you understand your PC, the better equipped you are to realize the potential in the machine, to recognize the best software and hardware for your machine, and—*let's not forget this*—to deal with emergencies that might arise when working with a PC. After all, when something goes wrong in your PC, the better you understand the machine the more likely you are to make the right moves to fix the problem, rather than goof up and make things worse.

There are a lot of reasons why we might want to understand the inner workings of our PCs. One reason, a really good one, is simply for the intellectual satisfaction and sense of mastery that comes with understanding the tools that you work with. Another reason is to open up new realms for yourself. After all, there is plenty of demand these days for people who have PC savvy. But perhaps the most practical reason is the one that I suggested above. By analogy, we might think back to the early days of the automobile, when you had to be an amateur mechanic to safely set out on a journey by car. It doesn't take the skills of a mechanic to drive a car today, because cars have been tamed for everyday use. We'd like it to be that way with computers, but frankly computing hasn't progressed that far yet. Today, to safely and successfully use a personal computer you need some degree of expertise—and the more expert you are, the better you can deal with the practical crises that sometimes arise.

This book is here to help you, to take you as far as possible into the realm of expertise, to help you join that select band of wizards who *really* know how to make the PC perform its magic.

If you know anything about me, Peter Norton, or about the first edition of this book, you know that I made my reputation, and this book became a best-seller, by explaining the technical wizardry of the PC. In the early days of the PC, that was what PC users needed most—an inside technical explanation of how the PC worked. The world of the PC has matured and changed since then, and so have the needs of the mainstream of PC users. Today people *still* need to understand their machines, how they work, and what it takes to make them sing, but the focus of people's needs has changed, so this new edition of *Inside the IBM PC* has changed as well.

You will still find in here lots and lots of interesting and useful technical information that will help you understand what makes the PC tick. But now, I'm drawing a dividing line between two kinds of material that you'll be seeing here. The first and main part of this book explains the basic principles of the PC and the PC family covering all those elements that you need to comprehend the PC *without* having to plow through a great deal of technical information; that part of the book is for all readers, and you can easily identify it because it appears as normal text.

For readers who want to go further, dig deeper, and understand more technical details, the second phase of the book, identified by this head:

TECHNICAL BACKGROUND ▮ ▮ ▮ ▮ ▮ ▮ ▬▬▬▬▬▬▬▬▬▬

will cover the heavier stuff. In these sections, we'll go into the hardware and programming details that show the underlying engineering that gets things done in the PC family. These more advanced sections are for anyone who wants to have more than simply a *practical* understanding of the PC— this part is for anyone who wants to actually wear the wizard's cap and perform, or at the least know how to perform, the *real* magic that the PC can be made to do. When you see this head, you'll know we're going into deeper country, and you should stay back or come along, as suits your needs.

Another thing that you'll find in this book are some sample programs that we can use to show off some of the PC's capabilities, to illustrate and exercise features of the machine, or just to have some fun. These programs will generally use the BASIC programming language, so that it will be relatively easy for you to try out what they have to show you by simply keying them in from the listings that appear here. You'll also find, at the end of each chapter, a few things to do that you can use to test your understanding or a few exercises that you can perform to develop your PC skills. Along those lines, we have a bit of fun for you.

A Maze to Think About

For the fun of it, I wrote a little program in BASIC that illustrates what a lot of life is like, including the process of learning to fully understand our PCs. (You'll find the listing for the program, called MAZE, in Appendix A, where we've placed all the longer programming examples.) In Figure I-1, you will see what it looks like in the middle portion of a program. The program has drawn two boxes marked START and FINISH, and it's started working a path from one to the other. In this case the program doesn't know where it's going, so it winds a random path until it stumbles onto the goal; but when it gets there it rewards you with some fanfare (as you'll see if you try running the full program).

Fortunately this book isn't like that. We'll be working our way in a purposeful fashion toward our goal of understanding the PC. Sometimes, though, it can feel like the path from START to FINISH is as aimless as the operation of this particular program.

I'm offering this toy program to you for two reasons. The first is that you might actually find a use for it—for example, if you ever have to convince someone just how circuitous the path to success can be, you can use this program to make the point. You can use it to tell your boss why results haven't been appearing instantly and to explain to your friends the easy path you took to mastery of personal computing. The second reason is to provide a little food for thought.

One of the most important and valuable things for us to learn about our computers is just how complex a task it is to add polish and refinement to computer programs. If you understand that, then you're better prepared to

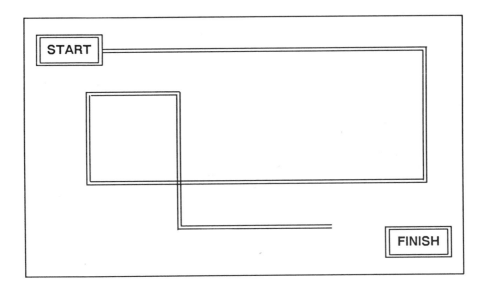

Figure I-1. The start-to-finish maze in progress.

understand the realities of the program you work with (or any programs you might want to design and build). So, here are some questions to ponder about our toy MAZE program before we plunge into the Chapter 1 and explore the basic ideas of computers.

Some Things to Try

1. If you haven't already taken a peek at the MAZE program listing in Appendix A, ask yourself how complex a task it is to write a program that draws a random path from START to FINISH and recognizes when it gets there. Write an outline—in English or in any programming language that you're familiar with—of a program to do what this program does. How would you make sure that the lines don't run off the edge of the screen? How would you know when the program reaches its goal?

2. Take a look at the MAZE program listing in Appendix A. Is it longer and more complex than you thought it would be, or less? If you know how to "read" a BASIC program, or if you can puzzle your way through it, check to see if my version of the program includes any important details that yours didn't or vice versa; did you cover any significant details that I missed?

3. As the MAZE program draws its path, it just writes over any lines that have already been drawn. What if we want to recognize when we cross an old line, or to avoid retracing along an existing line? Without getting into the programming specifics, try to work out the *logical* details that have to be added to the program. What details are most important? Which details might just be called icing on the cake? Does adding a feature like this make the program much more complex? What does that suggest to you about the overall character of computer programs?

1

A Family Tree

One of the most important—and interesting—things about the IBM Personal Computer family is that it *is* a family, a group of related computers instead of a single computer. This makes the story of the PC a richer and more fascinating one, and it makes the PC more important and more useful to us, because, as a family, the PC gives us a wide selection of computers differing in features, price, and performance.

In this chapter we're going to take a look at the PC family tree. It's a multi-dimensioned story, because there are several different ways to view the PC family. One dimension of the story is historical—it covers the chronological unfolding of the original IBM PC and its relatives. Another dimension—another way of analyzing the PC family—looks at the different models of PC. This aspect of the story, the model-by-model aspect, emphasizes the range of computing power and the range of features in the PC family. A sidelight to both of those dimensions is the role that non-IBM members of the family play. These are the so-called *PC clones,* distant relatives of the PC and members of the extended family. And still another dimension to the story is the tale of the family of microprocessors that power the PC and that will lead it into the future.

We'll take a look at all that in this chapter, so that we have a good overall understanding of what the PC family is, and where it's going.

1.1 Some Family History

The public history of the PC began in August 1981, when IBM first announced "The IBM Personal Computer," what we all know as the original PC. The behind-the-scenes story began earlier, of course, but not as long before as one might guess. From the decision to try to make an IBM Personal Computer to the day of announcement took, we're told, just about a year—a remarkably short time for so large and so deliberately-acting an institution as IBM. The prehistory of the PC, as interesting as it may be,

1

really isn't our concern here (but I'll pass on to you one fascinating tid-bit, in the sidebar *How the PC Became a 16-Bit Computer*). What is of real interest and use to us is a brief history of how each model of PC appeared, so that we can better understand how the PC family came to be, and where it is headed.

How the PC Became a 16-Bit Computer

At the time that the PC was being planned, all personal computers belonged to a now-obsolete category called 8-bit computers. (For more on 8- and 16-bit computers, see the last section of this chapter, and Chapter 3, titled *Data!*)

According to one legend, the PC almost became an 8-bit computer, which would have severely reduced its capabilities compared to what it was to become, and would have made the growth of the original PC into a PC family much more difficult.

As the story goes, IBM was planning to make the PC an 8-bit computer because that was the clear standard of the time. But one of the industry experts that IBM consulted in the planning of the PC was Bill Gates, the legendary founder of Microsoft Corporation. Bill understood that although 8-bit computing was strong at the time, its days were numbered. For the IBM PC to be really successful, it had to lead the way into the much more powerful realm of 16-bit computing. Bill knew this and talked IBM into changing its plans.

Whether this story is truth or legend, the decision to make the PC a 16-bit computer was extremely important in making the IBM PC the dominant desktop computer it is today.

The history outlined here is necessarily incomplete, because there are many details that I don't have space to relate and because the history of the PC family continues to unfold even as I'm writing this. But here is the main story.

The IBM PC made its first appearance in the fall of 1981. By spring of 1982, PCs were being shipped in volume, but to everyone's amazement demand far exceeded the supply. The PC was clearly ''an overnight success.'' While this success may have caught IBM and the rest of the computer industry off guard, everyone quickly woke up to the possibilities that this created.

During the earliest days of the PC, a number of experienced computer executives and engineers realized that there was a real need for a version of the PC that could be carried around—that idea turned into Compaq Computer Corporation. Their first addition to the PC family (the first addition by IBM or anyone else) was the computer known as the Compaq. The Compaq was announced in the fall of 1982, just over a year after the original PC was announced.

The following spring, in 1983, saw IBM's first addition to the PC family—the XT model, which added a high-capacity hard disk storage facility to the PC. Compaq matched the XT with a portable version in the fall of 1983 called the Compaq Plus.

In 1983 word began leaking out that IBM was planning a less-expensive scaled-down version of the PC that could be used as a home computer or just a more economical model of PC for business and professional use. This machine was the PC*jr*, widely known as "the Peanut."

Nearly everyone expected the PC*jr* to be an even bigger hit than the original PC, but when it first appeared at the end of 1983, it was an enormous disappointment. The PC*jr* was doomed to a short life, thanks to a hard-to-use keyboard, seemingly limited expandability, and other problems—such as interference between the keyboard and diskette drive that made the *jr* annoying to use—combined with less-than-expected interest in home computers in the *jr*'s price range. Throughout 1984 the *jr* limped along, despite several heroic attempts on IBM's part to make it a success. In 1985 the *jr* was discreetly allowed to die, awaiting IBM's revised plans for the low end of the PC family.

But if 1984 was a year of disappointment for the low-end PC*jr*, it was an exciting year for the high end of the PC family. The summer of 1984 saw two high-powered models of PC appear. First there was Compaq Desk-Pro, the first member of the PC family to have more basic computing power than the original PC. Shortly after that, IBM introduced the AT model, which had a much greater computing speed than the PC and XT or even the new DeskPro.

All during this time, IBM was adjusting to the remarkable success of the PC family and the growing importance of personal computing. This led to a gradual and subtle change of philosophy in IBM's management of the PC family, which I call "mainstreaming." This is a tendency to change the focus of the PC family away from isolated and individual personal computing into a more institutionalized approach that fit the PC family better into the central parts of IBM's computing business. This marked the end of some of the wild-and-woolly days of the PC, and passed into an era of somewhat less *personal* personal computing.

That's a short summary of the main points of the history of the PC family. But there's another way to view the chronology of the PC family that's less detailed and precise, and which gives us a sweeping overview and analysis of the PC's history. It's a summary of what has characterized each of the first six years of the PC:

- 1980—planning:
  IBM decides to make a PC, and begins design.

- 1981—announcement:
  The PC design is finished and, in August, the PC is announced, surprising everybody.

- 1982—runaway success:
  The PC appears in stores, and is wildly successful, beyond anyone's expectations, including IBM's.

- 1983—hard disks and home thrills:
  Early in the year the XT is introduced, adding a hard disk to the PC line; at the end of the year after overblown anticipation and speculation, the PC*jr* is announced.

- 1984—*jr* fades and Sr appears:
  The PC*jr* passes through the main period of its disappointing history; in the summer the AT is announced, pointing the way toward the new generation of PCs.

- 1985—the changing of the guard:
  IBM consolidates and refines the PC line, preparing to replace old models with a second generation; the PC family is redirected into the mainstream of IBM's products.

In summary, that's the history of the PC family. Now let's take a closer look at the various models of PC to see how they relate to each other.

1.2 The PC family

The historical perspective that we've just gone through gives you some sense of how the PC family as we know it today has evolved, and it should give you a feeling for the irregular fits and starts that naturally accompany computer family life. But it doesn't make coherent sense of the various members and how they relate to each other, in power and in features. That's what we're going to take a look at now.

As I did in the last section, I have to offer a disclaimer here to alert you to the limitations in this family outline. Three factors constrain how complete our view of the family can be. The first is a constraint of passing time: no sooner can I describe the current state of things than new developments arise. What we'll find here is as complete as it could be when I wrote these words. The second constraint is space: if we tried to mention every obscure and distant relative of the extended PC family, the family tree would spread out wider than you or I are likely to have patience to comprehend. Finally the third constraint is my own judgment, in deciding which elements of the family tree are most important and most worth discussing.

With those honest limitations in mind, let's take a look at the main models of computer that make up the PC family tree. Figure 1-1 gives you a rough sketch of the family. The line in the center indicates the main trunk of the PC family, arranged in the order of how powerful each model is, from the least powerful PC*jr* at the top to the most powerful AT at the bottom. Spreading to the sides are the models with diverging features. Figure 1-1 gives a rough sense of just how unusual, strange, or maverick each model is by how far away from the main trunk it appears.

Let's begin by talking our way down the main trunk of the tree, from top to bottom. The first, and least powerful member of the family is the ill-fated PC*jr*. To give some measure to the idea of how powerful and capable each model is, we'll compare them to a more-or-less standard PC,

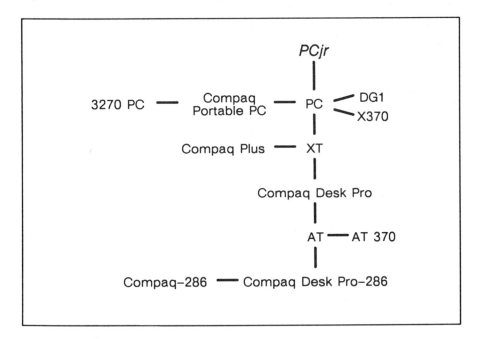

Figure 1-1. The main PC family tree.

in terms of computing speed and disk storage capacity. By both measures, the PC*jr* is about half of a standard PC; by another measure, internal memory capacity (which doesn't vary between most other models), the PC*jr* is also about half a standard PC's memory.

Next in scale comes the original PC—by its own standard, it's 100 percent of what a PC should be. It has the computing power to perform roughly a quarter-million instructions per second; in computer jargon, that's ¼ ''mips.'' Its disk storage capacity is typically 360,000 characters (bytes) in each of two ''floppy''diskette drives—for a total of almost ¾ of a million bytes. Its internal memory capacity (which is, in effect, the workspace where the computing activity takes place) is typically a quarter million bytes, but it can be increased to two and a half times that much.

The next step in succession is the XT model. The XT exactly matches the PC in both computing speed and internal storage. What sets it apart is a much larger (and also faster working) disk; this kind of disk is called a *hard disk* (or a *fixed disk*) as opposed to the conventional *floppy diskettes* that the PC uses. A computer's disk acts as a combination of file drawer and working library, and so a larger and faster disk significantly increases the practical working capabilities of the computer, even though the XT has the same computing speed and the same internal working memory space as the PC. The size of the XT disk is ten million characters, over a dozen times as much as a PC; and the effective working speed of the XT's hard disk is about five times as fast as the PC's floppy diskettes.

A small step further down the line comes the Compaq DeskPro model. The DeskPro uses a different and faster microprocessor than the PC and XT, so it has a faster computing speed; relative to a PC, the DeskPro has about 50 percent more computing power. (In Section 1.3 we'll see what this faster microprocessor is.) The disk capacity is also greater in the Desk-Pro, with up to 20 million bytes, twice what the XT has. Thanks to the faster computing speed and the bigger disk, the DeskPro seems to be an even bigger jump beyond the XT than the XT was beyond the PC. But in practice it's a much smaller step; nevertheless, an important step.

The next big jump in capacity comes with IBM's AT model. Like the DeskPro, the AT uses a different microprocessor engine to gain extra speed over the PC; but the AT's is faster still, *much* faster. That gives the AT the computing power of about *five* PCs or more than three DeskPros—that's a lot more computing power. To go along with that computing power, the AT has a 20-million byte disk, twice the XTs, and it can accommodate even larger disks if needed. Just to sweeten the cake even further, the AT can take on more internal working memory than any of the previous models, as much as three or more million bytes; under ordinary circumstances, though, we can't take advantage of this extra working storage, so we've got to discount its importance.

The final step (so far) in the main trunk of the PC family is the Compaq Deskpro-286 model. The Deskpro-286 is much like IBM's AT model, but its engine revs one-third faster than the AT's, giving it a third more raw computing power; it comes equipped with a hard disk that holds 30 million bytes.

Scattered along this main part of the PC family are a number of PC clones, which aren't of any special interest by themselves, though some of them can be distinct bargains when it comes to buying. Among the many that fall into this category are the Tandy models 1000 (equivalent to a PC) and 1200 (equivalent to an XT); the NCR PC-4 and the Zenith 150 (PCs); and the Texas Instruments Business Pro (an AT class of machine).

Branching off the main trunk, we find a number of very interesting variations on the PC mainstream. The first branch consists of the portables (also called transportables or "luggable" since they can be carried, but not easily). The portables bring together the main computer and a display screen into one rugged case—which makes it practical to carry them around, check them as airline luggage, or even ship them. Four portables are noteworthy: the original Compaq (the first, and some consider the best of the PC clones) and the IBM Portable PC model, both of which are equivalent to a standard PC; the Compaq Plus, a portable that's equivalent to the XT; and finally the Compaq Portable-286, a portable mate to the Deskpro-286, more than equivalent to the standard IBM AT model.

Also in the broad category of portables, but a in a distinct class by itself (at least for a while) is the lap-sized Data General One, or DG-1. The DG-1 is a partly failed attempt to take the "lug" out of portable computing by making a PC that's small and light enough to carry easily. Due to its unique design, the DG-1 has 85 percent of the computing power of a PC— slightly less than standard—but twice the disk space. The DG-1 was a heroic but unsuccessful attempt to make a truly portable PC; it's sure to be followed by more successful ones as the advance of technology permits. By itself the DG-1 isn't an important member of our PC family, but it represents a class of machines that are likely to become important.

Finally we get to the most exotic realm of PC family members, the ones that have truly unusual capabilities. There are three models from IBM worth mentioning; all of them are essentially PCs that can also do double duty as something else. The 3270-PC acts as an XT-class of PC, and it also serves as a standard-type terminal (called a 3270) that can talk to and work with a large "mainframe" IBM computer. The other two exotics in the line are the XT-370 and the AT-370. These little wonders can function as an XT or AT, and also carry out much of the work of a full-sized mainframe computer. These three, needless to say, are quite special machines, but they are part of our PC family.

The last category of computers for us to discuss are the distant relatives of the PC, computers that are similar to, and partly—but only partly—compatible with the IBM PC. Notable among these are the Tandy model 2000, the Texas Instruments Professional Computer, the Wang PC, the DEC Rainbow, and the NEC APC-III. Frankly, there are more of these sometimes-oddball distant relatives than anyone can keep track of. They're not of a great deal of interest to us, but I'm mentioning some of the more widely known ones so that if you hear of them, and wonder where they fit into the PC family portrait, you'll know.

1.3 The 8086 Family

One of the keys to understanding the PC family is understanding the microprocessor that acts as the working "brains" of the computer. Unlike the mainframe computer tradition, microcomputers like our PC aren't designed and built in an independent way. Instead, nearly all microcomputers incorporate many standard components that are designed independently of the computers in which they are used.

If a computer maker, such as IBM, designs a computer from scratch, then they can determine what the features and capabilities of the computer will be. This includes the instruction set, or internal language, that the computer will have. However, most microcomputers, including our PC, aren't made that way. Instead, they get their thinking power (and instruction set) from one of several standard microprocessors offered by computer chip makers. IBM could have chosen from several possible microprocessors to serve as the brains of the PC. The one they chose would both define the current instruction set, or language, for the PC, and also define a great many things about the direction the computer could take in the future.

IBM chose the Intel 8088 microprocessor as the brains or engine inside the PC. The 8088 is just one member of a whole family of microprocessors, called the *8086* family, that was designed by the pioneering silicon chip maker, Intel. By choosing the 8088 for the original PC, IBM committed the PC family to live within the range of possibilities that are defined by its microprocessor family. To understand what the PC family is (and can become), we need to understand the main points of its microprocessor family, the 8086 family.

Before I cause any confusion, I need to make clear that while each member of the PC family of computers uses a member of the 8086 microprocessor family for its brain, there isn't any direct correspondence between the PC family and the 8086 family. There isn't a separate member of the PC family for each member of the 8086 family. Since each PC includes something from the 8086 family, knowing about this family can help us understand the directions that the PC family can take.

The founding member of the Intel 8086 family is the 8086 chip itself, the chip that the whole family is named after. The 8086 was designed to introduce the concept of 16-bit computing, which means that the computer can deal with 16 bits of information at a time (we'll get a clearer idea of what that means when we discuss bits and our computer's data in Chapter 3). The previous generation of Intel microprocessors, the 8080, were 8-bit computers.

The 8086, as a 16-bit microprocessor, had a much greater range of capabilities than its predecessors. The power of a microprocessor is only very loosely implied by describing it as "8-bit" or "16-bit" or "32-bit"; the features of each new generation of computer chips go far beyond what the bit rating suggests. But this bit rating does at least tell us how much data the computer can sling around at a time, and the 8086 could sling twice as much as the 8080 that went before it.

There was an inherent practical problem, though, in using the 8086 as the base of a computer design. While the 8086 had 16-bit capabilities internally—which is very good—it also had to work exclusively with other computer components that handle 16 bits at a time as well. When the PC was being designed, 8-bit parts were plentiful and cheap; 16-bit parts were more expensive and in shorter supply. This presented an obstacle to anyone designing a computer around the 8086.

Intel found a simple, practical solution to this problem with the 8088 chip. The 8088 *internally* has all the 16-bit skills of the 8086, but when it communicates with other circuitry around it, it talks only 8 bits at a time; this slightly reduces the speed of the 8088, but it makes it possible for the 8088 to work with other components that are cheap and plentiful.

For practical reasons, IBM designed the original model of PC around the 8088—a microprocessor with 16-bit power, but 8-bit economy. The 8088 formed the heart of the first four models of PC from IBM—the PC, the XT, the Portable PC, and the PC*jr*—as well as the first two Compaq contributions to the family—the Compaq and the Compaq Plus. Most other "PC clones" also used the 8088. However, when Compaq wanted to add more computing power to their third model, the DeskPro, they used the 8086 for its greater speed.

After designing the 8086 and its junior brother the 8088, Intel began working on some improvements and extensions to this family of microprocessors. Up to this time, all microprocessors, including these two, relied on the assistance of other related computer chips which played a supporting role in getting the computer's work done. Intel realized that there were two important disadvantages in having these support functions performed by separate circuit chips: working with separate chips slowed down the operation of the computer, and increased the total cost of making a computer. If many of the support functions were incorporated into the same chip as the microprocessor, it could work faster, and using fewer chips would reduce the cost.

This thinking led to the development of the Intel 80186 and 80188 (which are usually called the 186 and the 188 for short). These two new microprocessors had some extra instructions and capabilities that their predecessors didn't have, but their main feature was that they integrated several support functions into the microprocessor. As you've probably guessed from the model numbers, the 186 is like the 8086 in being 16-bits inside and out, while the 188, like the 8088, has an 8-bit external face with 16-bit internal skills.

Either of these 18x chips could be used to power major members of the PC family, but that hasn't happened. They have been used in quite a number of distant relatives of the PC, including the near-PC-compatible Tandy 2000 computer. Neither IBM nor Compaq has used either of these two chips, even though the 188 would have been a natural for the PCjr and the 186 would have been perfect for the Compaq DeskPro. The reason why is very simple: when the 18x's were the hottest thing around, they weren't available in large enough quantities to safely design a best-selling computer around. By the time they were plentiful, there was something much more exciting to design a computer around.

While the 18x's were an important (if little-used) extension to the 8086 family, they didn't really add dramatically to the capabilities of the chips that went before them. To do that, Intel labored mightily and came up with its proudest achievement to date, the 80286 (or 286 for short).

The 286 goes enormously beyond the capabilities of its predecessors in three main ways. First, it can accommodate much more working memory than the previous chips; the others were limited to a million bytes, or characters, of memory. The 286 can have up to 16 million bytes—a major addition. Second, the 286 can perform an important computer trick known as *virtual memory*, which allows it to appear to have even more memory than it actually does. Both of these memory extensions greatly increase the scale of the work that the 286 can undertake. The third new feature of the

286 is something known as *hardware multitasking;* this feature lets the computer work on more than one problem at a time in a safe and reliable way. (The previous chips could attempt multitasking, but without hardware support, it isn't completely reliable and it's subject to unexpected breakdowns.)

IBM introduced the 286 to the PC family with the appearance of the AT model in the summer of 1984. This was followed by a number of AT-clones, most notably the Compaq Deskpro-286 and the Compaq Portable-286. Like the Compaq models before them, these 286 models matched IBM's machines and added some small but important extras. The most interesting is a "power switch" that allows the Compaq-286s to either run at the same speed as an AT (for pure speed compatibility) or one-third faster for greater computing power.

Like the 18*x*'s before it, the 286 features the integration of support chips and faster speeds than previous chips. Initially the 286-based machines didn't take significant advantage of the powerful new capabilities that were inherent in them. Instead they were treated simply as faster PCs, very much as if they had been designed around the 186 instead of the 286.

Needless to say, the Intel 8086 family doesn't end with the 286. By the time the 286 saw commercial success in the AT, Intel was busy planning the next major extension of the family, the 386. Among the new skills that the 386 will bring to the 8086 family, and our PC family, is the ability to work with data 32 bits at a time.

However the 8086 family evolves, you can be sure that our PC family will also evolve to take advantage of the additional power that any new chips provide.

Some Things to Try

1. Do you see any gaps in the PC family tree? Discuss what you think might be the most sensible spectrum of computers in this family.

2. Does adding a hard disk to a PC—making it an XT—actually add to the computer's ability to work for us? What sort of computer work would be easier to perform on an XT than a PC? What sort of work can an XT perform that a PC cannot?

3. Is computing speed important all the time? Is there computing work for which the AT's speed is no advantage over the PC, or even the PC*jr*?

2

Fundamentals:
What a Computer Is

oday, computers are something familiar to everyone, since they are used so much in our lives. Increasingly those computers are *personal* computers, like our IBM PC. Having them as an everyday thing in our lives makes them something we're comfortable with, and that's very good; but it doesn't mean that we understand them, or know how they work.

This book is written to make it easy for you to understand the ins and outs of the IBM PC. But before we get into the PC specifics, we need to make sure that we understand the basic ideas that underlie *all* computers, so that we know what a computer is and isn't, and we know in a general sort of way how computers work. That's what this chapter is for: to explain the basic, fundamental ideas about computers.

2.1 My Computer, the Model

Computers are based on the simple idea of modeling or imitation. Radios and phonographs work that way too, and if we pause to think about them we'll understand our computers more easily.

When we play a record on a phonograph, we hear music—but there isn't a musician inside the phonograph. Instead, the phonograph contains an electronic *model* or imitation of what sound is like. Our radios and phonographs are possible because we discovered a way to capture the essence of sound, to create a mechanical or electronic imitation of sound, and to build machines that will reproduce the sounds we want. The same sort of thing goes on with the visual images provided by television and motion pictures.

Our computers do essentially the same thing, but they do it with numbers and arithmetic. The most fundamental thing that goes on within a computer is that electronically the computer imitates and creates a *working model* of numbers and arithmetic.

If we set out to invent a machine that can do arithmetic, we need to find a way to match what machines can *do* with whatever the essence of arithmetic *is*. Needless to say, accomplishing this calls for a great deal of intellectual creativity and some heavy-duty theory in mathematics. Essentially a meeting ground had to be found where math and machines could merge, and it was found in the idea of *binary arithmetic*.

The numbers that you and I work with are based on the number ten: we use the *decimal* number system, which works with ten symbols, 0,1, 2, and so on through 9, and builds all our numbers using those ten symbols. However, there is nothing fundamental about the decimal system; we can base our numbers on eight symbols, or three, or two. Math theory, and some simple exercises demonstrate that you can write the same numbers and do the same arithmetic operations in any number system, whether it's based on ten, three, or two. The mathematical theory of information, however, has proven that you can't go smaller than two—the *binary*, or base 2, number system captures the smallest essence of what information fundamentally is.

That's something of a lucky break. It is very easy to make a machine, particularly an electronic machine, that represents, or models, binary numbers. A binary number is written with two symbols, 0 and 1 (just like our decimal numbers are written with ten symbols 0-9) and electric parts—such as switches—naturally have two states: a switch can be either on or off. Once we see that, it's easy for us to make the leap of imagination to see that an On-Off switch can represent, model, or imitate a binary 0 or 1. In fact, it's such a natural connection, that you'll see the power switches on many appliances and machines labeled 0 and 1 meaning off and on.

Of course it's a giant step between seeing that a switch or an electric current on or off can represent a number 1 or 0 and having a computer that can perform marvels of calculation. It's a very big step indeed. But it shouldn't be too hard for us to see how this electronic model of a simple binary number can be elaborated, or built up into something much larger. It's like knowing that once children have learned to write simple sentences, they can grow up to write essays, term papers, and books. There's a lot of work in between and a lot of complicated steps involved, but the idea, the basic principle, is clear enough.

That's the foundation on which our computers are built. Information, including numbers and arithmetic, can be represented in a binary form; electronic parts, such as switches that are turned on and off, are binary at heart. Using switches and other parts, an electronic machine can imitate, or model, numbers and all other forms of information.

What we've discussed so far is good enough to give us an idea of how it's at all possible to make such a thing as a computer. But that hasn't yet told us a great deal about computers. So that you can understand a building made of bricks, we've talked about what bricks are. That doesn't tell us much about architecture, though, or what a finished building looks like. That's what we'll do next.

2.2 An Outline of the Computer

There are five key parts to a computer: the processor, the memory, the Input/Output (I/O, as it's almost always called), disk storage, and the programs. We'll take a quick look at each of these key parts here and then in a little more detail that will fill up this chapter. The rest of the book will be devoted to burrowing into the really fascinating deeper details.

The *processor* is the "brains" of the computer, the engine, the main working heart of this marvelous machine. It's the processor that has the ability to carry out our instructions (our programs) to the computer. The processor is the part that knows how to add and subtract and to carry out simple logical operations. In a big mainframe computer the processor is often called a *Central Processing Unit*, or *CPU*. In a miniaturized or "micro" computer, like our IBM PC family, the processor is usually called a *micro*processor. That's the term we'll be using almost exclusively in this book. You already know, from our discussion of the PC family history in Chapter 1, that our PC family is powered by the 8086 family of microprocessors. Later in this chapter we'll learn more about what processors do, and in Chapter 6 we'll cover the specifics of what the PC's microprocessors can do.

The *memory* is the computer's work area: its desktop, its playing field. A computer's memory is nothing like our own memory, so the term can be misleading until you understand what a computer's memory is and what it's used for. The memory is the computer's *workplace*. It's analogous to the desktop of an office worker, the workbench of a carpenter, or the playing field of a sports team. The computer's memory is where all activity takes place. The analogy with a workbench is particularly good, because it helps us understand when the amount of memory is important and also when it's not. Like the size of a workbench, the size of a computer's memory sets a practical limit on the kinds of work that the computer can undertake. A handyman's skills and other factors are really

15

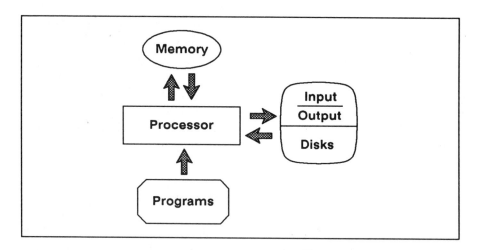

Figure 2-1. The five parts of the computer.

the most important things that determine what the handyman can and can't do, but the size of the workplace matters as well. This is true with our computers. That's while you'll often hear of computers rated by the amount of memory they have, usually in kilobytes (thousands of bytes which we'll learn more about in Chapter 3). For example, a fully-loaded PC has 640 kilobytes of memory.

Input/Output, or *I/O*, are all the means that the computer uses to take in or spit out data. It includes *input* that we type in on the keyboard and *output* that the computer shows on the video display screen or prints on the printer. Every time the computer is taking in or putting out data, it's doing I/O using *I/O devices*, which are also called *peripheral devices* in computer jargon. Among the many kinds of I/O devices is one that's so important and critical to the successful operation of the computer that we single it out as the next of the five key parts of a computer.

Disk storage is a very important kind of I/O—it's the computer's reference library, filing cabinet, and tool box all rolled into one. Disk storage is where the computer keeps *its* data when it's not in use inside the computer's memory. Data can be stored in other ways besides disk, but disks are the most practical and most important way of storing data. In fact, as we saw in the outline of the PC family in Chapter 1, a big increase in disk storage is enough to mark the difference between a member of the family that's considered high-powered (the XT) and one that's not (the original PC).

Programs are the last of the five key parts of a computer—they are what makes the computer go, what brings it to life, what turns it from a heap of fancy parts into a powerful working tool. Programs are the instructions that tell the computer what to do.

With that simple summary out of the way, let's take a slightly more detailed look at each of these key parts, bearing in mind that we're still providing brief descriptions. The real details will come in the following chapters.

The microprocessor is the part of our computer designed to carry out or execute our programs. The whole point of the entire computer is to make a machine that can perform, execute, or carry out the series of steps that we call a program. So both the purpose and the internal organization of the computer come together in this one key component, the microprocessor. In order to be able to perform this ingenious miracle, the microprocessor has to have some particular skills that it calls on to perform its work. The first skill is the ability to read and write information in the computer's memory. This is a critical skill, because both the program instructions that the microprocessor is to carry out and the data that the microprocessor is to work on are temporarily stored in the computer's memory. The next skill is the ability to recognize and perform a series of very simple commands or instructions so that our programs are carried out. The last skill is for the microprocessor to know how to tell the other parts of the computer what to do, so that the microprocessor can orchestrate the entire operation of the computer.

As you might imagine, there is a lot to how a microprocessor can carry out its assigned task, and how it gets these skills that we've been mentioning. Later we'll get into the details of the microprocessor. Chapter 6 is devoted to telling you how the microprocessor performs *its* magic.

Throughout this book we'll be talking constantly about programs and data: programs that the microprocessor carries out and data that the programs act on. To the microprocessor, the distinction between programs and data is vital—one indicates what the microprocessor is to do, and the other is what the doing is done to. Not every part of our computer makes this distinction, which we'll see shortly.

The memory, as we've already seen, is where the computer's microprocessor finds its programs and data, when the microprocessor is actually doing its assigned task. As we've mentioned, the memory is the activity center, the place where everything is kept when it's being worked on. For us to understand our computers it's important to understand that the computer's memory is just a temporary space, a scratch pad, a workbench, a black board where the computer scribbles while work is being done. The computer's memory is not a permanent repository of anything, unlike the memory inside our own brains. Instead, the computer's memory simply provides a place where computing can happen. It's the playing field where the game of computing is played. After each game, the memory playing field is relinquished to the next team and the next game.

While the computer's microprocessor makes a vital distinction between program and data, the computer's memory does *not*. To the computer's memory (and to many other parts of the computer) there is no difference between programs and data—both are just information that can be recorded, temporarily, in the memory. A piece of paper neither knows nor cares what we write on it—whether it's a love poem, the figures from our bank balance, or instructions to a friend. So it is with the computer's memory. Only the microprocessor knows—or has the ability to tell the difference—between programs and data. To the computer's memory and also to the I/O devices and disk storage, a program is just some more data, some more information that can be stored.

The computer's memory is more like a chalkboard than a piece of paper in that nothing is permanently recorded on it. Anything can be written on any part of the memory, and the writing can be changed in a wink by writing over it. Unlike a chalkboard, the computer's memory doesn't have to be erased before anything new can be written down; the mere act of writing information into the computer's memory automatically erases what was there before. Reading information out of the memory is as simple and as straightforward as reading anything written on paper or a chalkboard. Both the microprocessor and all the computer's I/O devices have the natural ability to read (and write) data from or to the memory.

Together the microprocessor and the memory are the actors and the stage on which the drama of computing is performed. But by themselves they make up a closed world. *Input/output devices* open up that world and allow it to communicate with us. An input/output device is anything that the computer communicates with other than its memory. As we've mention, these devices include the keyboard that we type on, the display screen that we stare at, the printer, a telephone line that's connected to the computer, and any other channel of communications into or out of the computer. Taken together the I/O is the computer's window on the world— what keeps the microprocessor and memory from being a closed and useless circle. We devote plenty of time and effort to understanding the PC's various I/O devices in later chapters of the book.

In general we can say that all the I/O devices that the computer can work with have us as their real target. One way or another, everything that the computer takes in (particularly from the keyboard) comes from us. And everything that the computer puts out on the screen, on the printer, or wherever, is intended to be seen by us. But there is one special category of

I/O that is intended only for the computer's private use: the disk storage devices.

Disk storage, as we've said, is only one kind of I/O, one type of device that the computer can use to read data into its memory or write data out of its memory. There is one key difference, though, between disk storage devices and essentially all other devices—the information on the disk storage can't be read or written by us, and it's not for our use; it can only be read or written by the computer itself. The other I/O devices are an *interface* between us and the computer. The computer "sees" what we type on the keyboard, we see what the computer writes on the printer or display screen. This is true with the disk storage devices. Instead, the disk storage is the computer's library, toolbox, and lumberyard. It's where the computer keeps its instruction manuals (our programs), its raw materials (our data), and any other information that it needs to have on tap. We'll be covering the PC's disk storage in lots of detail, so that you can understand how it works, what it does for the computer, and how we can help safeguard the information stored on our computer disks.

Finally, we have to consider programs. Programs tell the computer what to do. Programs are the hardest part of computing because computers "consume" programs, using them as fuel. That's not exactly true, because unlike an engine that burns fuel it can't use again, a computer can use a program over and over again. But even if a computer doesn't consume or burn up programs, our computers do have an endless appetite for programs, the way we have an endless appetite for newspapers, magazines, and books. Once a book is written, any number of people can read and enjoy them, endlessly. So it is with programs for computers. But we also have an unending need for new books, new magazines and new newspapers; so it goes with programs for computers. There is always something new that we want to do with our computers, so there is always a need for new programs.

As it turns out, there are two very different kinds of programs, and we need to learn about the difference right from the start. These two kinds of programs are called *systems programs* and *applications programs*. All programs do something, accomplish some kind of work. *Systems* programs work to help operate the computer; in fact, the inner workings of a computer are so complex that we cannot get them to work without the help of programs. *Applications* programs carry out the tasks that we want done, whether it's adding up a column of numbers or checking the spelling of something we've written on the computer. In summary, *applications programs* get our work done and *systems programs* help the computer manage itself (and carry out our work).

Some of the systems programs that the IBM PC needs to manage its operations are permanently built into it. This is a part of the computer called the *ROM* programs, because they are permanently stored in *Read-Only Memory* (unlike the reusable main memory that we've been talking about). These kinds of systems programs do the most fundamental kind of supervisory and support work, which include providing essential services that all the application programs use. These service programs are called the *Basic Input/Output Services*, or *BIOS* for short. You'll often hear them referred to as the BIOS, or as the *ROM-BIOS*, since they reside in ready-only memory, or ROM.

Other systems programs build on the foundation of the ROM-BIOS programs, and provide a higher level of support services. Operating systems, such as the PC's familiar DOS (Disk Operating System), are examples of these higher-level systems programs, which aren't built into the computer. Systems programs are one of the major topics that we discuss in the rest of this book. Although applications programs are very important, and we'll discuss them and learn how they are put together, systems programs are a more important topic for us. That's because our goal is to understand the workings and the potential of the PC—and both are closely tied to the PC's systems programs.

The outline of the computer that we've been looking at here gives us a good basis to start with, a springboard for diving into the details of computing power. Before we proceed, though, we ought to pause to consider just what it is that the computer—particularly the computer's microprocessor—can do for us and what it can't.

Some Things to Try

1. We've said computers "model" arithmetic just as radios or phonographs "model" sound. Are there other machines that work by "modeling?" We could say that television models both sight and sound. Do our computers model more than numbers?

2. Suppose that electrical switches were somehow completely different than they are. Instead of having two settings or states (On and Off) they always had three states. Would it still be possible to make a calculating machine out of them? Would anything be fundamentally different, or would the details just change, but the principles stay the same?

3. List any computer programs that you're familiar with. Which ones would you categorize as *systems programs* and which as *applications programs*? Do you think that there is a strict dividing line between the two groups? Are there programs that have both characteristics?

3

Data!

In this chapter we're going to introduce ourselves to the basics of computer data and the main data formats that the PC uses. When we're done, we'll have a clear foundation for understanding what the PC really works with: data!

3.1 Bits, Bytes, and Characters

The starting point of computer data—the smallest, most fundamental unit—is called the *bit*. The word "bit" is a charming contraction for a longer and clumsier expression, *binary digit*. We're all familiar with the ten decimal digits, 0 through 9, that are used to express the numbers that we work with. Binary digits, bits, are similar, but while there are ten distinct decimal digits, there are only two different bit values, zero and one, which are written, naturally enough, as 0 and 1.

The bits 0 and 1 represent Off and On, False and True, No and Yes. They have the obvious numerical meaning that you'd assume they do: the bit value 0 really does mean zero, or nothing, and 1 does mean one. As we mentioned in Chapter 2, it is the concept of the bit that makes information-handling machines—computers—possible. Because it's practical to make electronic machines that work with On/Off signals at great speed, it's possible to make machines that actually *work with information,* that actually process data. It all depends, however, on our ability to match information that's meaningful to us with the "model" of information that the computer can work with—and that depends on our ability to construct real information out of the simple bits of 0 and 1.

Common sense and some heavy mathematical theory both tell us that a bit is the smallest possible chunk of information. Bits serve as building blocks with which we can construct and work with larger and more meaningful amounts of information. By themselves bits usually aren't of much interest and only on occasion will we be talking about bits, individual bits, in the course of this book. It's when we string bits together, into larger patterns, that we get something more useful and interesting.

The most important and the most interesting collection of bits is the *byte*. A byte is eight bits, taken together as a single unit. Bytes are important to us because they are the main practical unit of computer data. You're undoubtedly used to hearing of the memory capacity of a computer or the storage capacity of a disk measured in bytes (or in kilobytes, which we'll be discussing shortly). That's because the byte is really the main unit of data; a bit may be the atom, the smallest grain of sand of computer data, but the byte is the brick, the real building block of data.

Our computers work mostly with bytes. They can work with larger aggregates of bytes, and they can get into the bits inside a byte, but our computers are designed mostly to manipulate and work with bytes.

As we mentioned, there are eight bits in a byte. That means that there are eight individual 0 or 1, Off or On, settings inside a byte. The math of combinations tells us that if we have more right here.

will be times when we need to refer to the individual bits inside of a byte—particularly when we get into some of the more technical matters. To learn about how we refer to individual bits, see *The Bits Inside Bytes and Words* sidebar.

TECHNICAL BACKGROUND ▌ ▌ ▌ ■ ■ ■ ▬▬▬▬▬▬

The Bits Inside Bytes and Words

When we want to look at the bits inside a byte, we need a way of referring to them. This is done by numbering them from the right-most (or least significant byte) starting with the number zero, as shown in the table at the end of this sidebar.

It may seem screwy to number the bits from the right and to start numbering them from zero, but there is a fundamental reason for doing it this way. The identifying bit number is also the power of 2 that represents the numeric value of the bit in that place (when we interpret the byte, and the bits in it, as a number). For example, bit 3 has a numeric value of 8, and 2 to the third power is 8.

A similar scheme applies when we're looking at two bytes together as a word. Instead of numbering the bits in the individual bytes separately, we number them all together, from 0 through 15. But this is only done when we're looking at a pair of bytes and treating them as a single unit, a 16-bit word.

Bit number 76543210	Numeric value
. . . . 1	1
. . . . . . 1 .	2
. . . . . 1 . .	4
. . . . 1 . . .	8
. . . 1	16
. . 1	32
. 1	64
1	128

A byte inside our computer is raw data, which can be used for anything. Two of the most important things that we do with our computers is to work with numbers and to manipulate written text (such as the words you are reading here). Bytes are used as the building blocks of both numbers and text (character) data.

There is nothing fundamental about a byte, or any other collection of data, that makes it either numeric or text. Instead, it is simply a matter of what we want to do with our computers. If we're working with numbers, then the bytes in our computer are treated as numbers, and the bit patterns inside the bytes are given a numerical interpretation. On the other hand, when we want to work with character text information, the bytes are interpreted as characters that make up the written text information. Each byte represents one character of text.

Basically, we (through the programs we use) put bytes to work as either numbers or characters, depending on what we need them for at the time. In effect, bytes are raw clay that we can mold into numbers or text characters to suit our purposes. To do this, a meaning is assigned to each pattern of bits in our bytes. The patterns aren't unique, though, and there is nothing intrinsic about the meaning that we give to these patterns. The same pattern of bits could be, for example, the letter A or the number 65, depending upon what we were using them for.

We'll be seeing how bytes can be used as numbers and characters, and how several bytes taken together can be treated as more complicated numbers or strings of text characters. That will occupy us for most of the rest of this chapter. The business of how bytes are interpreted as individual charac ters, and all the fascinating characters that our PCs can work with, will covered separately in Chapter 4. It's such an interesting and rich topic we need to give it a chapter of its own.

Before we go on to more details about interpreting data, we ne discuss a special term that will be cropping up now and again—that is *word*. While the byte is the most basic and convenient unit om- puter's data, sometimes our computers need to work s, so that they're handling not eight bits but 16 bi name for a pair of bytes that are handled together at name, in computer terminology, is *word*. "We it here, is a

en all together. It eryday meaning of the by it. We won't be talking it when we do, take care that

computers being referred to as it, or even 32-bit—that's talking th in one gulp. Our PC family computers, because they can, in many of the things that they do, process data 16 bits at a time; 16 bits is the "word size" of our computers—that's what makes them 16-bit computers. Despite this, most of the time our computers and the programs that make them go will be handling data in individual bytes, one at a time.

Finally, there is one more piece of basic terminology concerning com- puter data that we need to cover—the kilobyte, commonly called a *K*.

It's always handy to be able to talk about things in round numbers, particularly when we're dealing with large quantities. Our computers deal with large numbers of bytes, and so people have become accustomed to handy ways of dealing with computer data in round numbers. But, com- puters being what they are—binary critters—the round number that's used is a round number in binary, and only roughly a round number in our familiar decimal numbers. This mysterious round number is 1024; that happens to be 2 raised to the tenth power, so it actually is a round number in binary. It's also reasonably close to a round number, 1000, in decimal, which is one reason why it's used so much.

This number, 1024, is called a K, or sometimes kilo (borrowing the metric term for one thousand). So 1024 bytes are referred to as a kilobyte, or 1Kb, or sometimes just 1K. When you hear people talking about 64K, they mean 64 times 1024, or exactly 65,536.

Table 3-1. The sixteen hex digits.

Hex Digit	Decimal Equivalent	Bit Equivalent	Value
0	0	0000	Zero
1	1	0001	One
2	2	0010	Two
3	3	0011	Three
4	4	0100	Four
5	5	0101	Five
6	6	0110	Six
7	7	0111	Seven
8	8	1000	Eight
9	9	1001	Nine
A	10	1010	Ten
B	11	1011	Eleven
C	12	1100	Twelve
D	13	1101	Thirteen
E	14	1110	Fourteen
F	15	1111	Fifteen

with. Since the most common unit of computer data is the byte, hex can conveniently represent all the bits in a byte with two hex digits, each one representing four of the byte's eight bits. Hex fits neatly into the fundamental scheme of our computer's data.

So far we've talked about individual hex digits, but we also need to work with larger numbers expressed in hex. Particularly, later in the book, we'll be talking about the memory addresses used in the PC family that take us into four-, and even five-digit hex numbers. Therefore, we need to have a sense of the size of larger hex numbers and we need to be able to do some arithmetic with them.

Hex arithmetic, of course, works just like decimal arithmetic, but the value of the numbers is different. The largest decimal number is 9 (nine) and the number after it is ten, which is written, in decimal, as 10. The same principle applies in hex (or any other number base): the largest hex digit is F (which has a value of 15) and the number after it is written 10, which has a value of 16; next comes 11 (which is 17) and so on.

Two hex digits are all we need to express all the possible bit combinations in a byte. With eight bits in a byte, there are two to the eighth power different combinations, or 256 different bit patterns to a byte from 00000000 to 11111111. In hex, 00000000 is 00 and 11111111 is FF. The first four bits are represented by the first hex digit, the last four by the second hex digit.

We can use Table 3-2 to translate between any pattern of bits and their hex equivalents. That's what we do when we're just looking at hex and bits as arbitrary data. When we want to interpret some hex digits as a number (which we'll be doing from time to time in this book) we need to know how to convert between hex and decimal, and we need to know how to do simple arithmetic in hex.

First let's see how to evaluate a hex number. It helps to pause and think of how we evaluate decimal numbers, say the number 123. 123 really means 100 plus 20 plus 3. Each position over to the left has a value that's ten times higher than the place just to the right. The same principle works in hex, but the multiplier is 16, not ten. So, if we interpret "123" as a hex number, it's 3 + 2 times 16 + 1 times 16 squared (which is 256): that totals up to 291 in decimal. In Table 3-2 the value of hex digits is in the first five places.

If you want to manually convert between decimal and hex, you can use the numbers in Table 3-2 to look up the equivalents. For example, to convert the hex number F3A into decimal, we'll look up the value of A in the first column (it's decimal 10), 30 in the second column (48), and F00 in the third column (3,840). Totaling them up, we get 3,898 as the decimal equivalent of hex F3A.

Table 3-2. Hex value table.

Hex	Dec	Hex	Dec	Hex	Dec	Hex	Dec	Hex	Dec
1	1	10	16	100	256	1000	4,096	10000	65,536
2	2	20	32	200	512	2000	8,192	20000	131,072
3	3	30	48	300	768	3000	12,288	30000	196,608
4	4	40	64	400	1,024	4000	16,384	40000	262,144
5	5	50	80	500	1,280	5000	20,480	50000	327,680
6	6	60	96	600	1,536	6000	24,576	60000	393,216
7	7	70	112	700	1,792	7000	28,672	70000	458,752
8	8	80	128	800	2,048	8000	32,768	80000	524,288
9	9	90	144	900	2,304	9000	36,864	90000	589,824
A	10	A0	160	A00	2,560	A000	40,960	A0000	655,360
B	11	B0	176	B00	2,816	B000	45,056	B0000	720,896
C	12	C0	192	C00	3,072	C000	49,152	C0000	786,432
D	13	D0	208	D00	3,328	D000	53,248	D0000	851,968
E	14	E0	224	E00	3,584	E000	57,344	E0000	917,504
F	15	F0	240	F00	3,840	F000	61,440	F0000	983,040

To convert decimal into hex, we work the other way, subtracting as we go. For example, to convert the decimal number 1,000,000 we look up the largest entry in the hex table that's not over our decimal number. In this case, it's F0000 at the end of the last column. We subtract its decimal value (983,040) from our starting number and continue the process until there's nothing left—then the series of hex numbers we subtracted out combine to make the hex equivalent of our decimal number. In this case it is hex F4240.

Fortunately, there are some tools that do the work of hex-decimal conversion for us, so we don't have to resort to this manual process. One of them is the Sidekick program, by Borland International, which includes a calculator that converts from hex to decimal and does arithmetic in either form. Another is BASIC. Here are two little programs that demonstrate BASIC's ability to easily convert numbers between hex and decimal:

```
10 ' Convert hex to decimal
20 '
30 INPUT "Enter a hex number ", X$
40 PRINT "The decimal equivalent is "; VAL("&H"+X$)
50 GOTO 30
```

```
10 ' Convert decimal to hex
20 '
30 INPUT "Enter a decimal number ", X
40 PRINT "The hex equivalent is "; HEX$(X)
50 GOTO 30
```

If you ever need to do any arithmetic on hex numbers you can use Sidekick's calculator feature, or use BASIC's ability both to do arithmetic and, as illustrated in the short programs above, convert between decimal and hex. If you're forced to do hex arithmetic the hard way, or just want to try your hand at it, you'll find tables to do hex addition or subtraction and multiplication in Appendix B. The HEXTABLE program in Appendix A generates these tables.)

3.3 Standard Numbers

Since numbers are so important to computers, we're going to look here at the kinds of numbers our PCs can work with. We're going to start this section with the simple number formats that are part of the PC's basic repertoire of numbers—the numbers that the PC has a native ability to work with. Later, in the next section, we'll look at some more exotic types of numbers that the PC can use when we stretch its skills in a couple of ways. But for now, we'll just look at the kinds of numbers that come most naturally to the PC.

You might be surprised to realize that the PC's natural skills only allow it to work with whole numbers—called *integers* in the terminology of math—and with rather small numbers at that.

There are basically only two varieties of numbers that the PC has an inherent, built-in ability to work with—integers that are one byte in size, and integers that are two bytes, or a word, in size.

The PC, as you may already be aware, is called a 16-bit computer. What that means in practical terms is that the fundamental design of the PC (and of the microprocessor that provides the brain or working engine of the PC) is structured to work with information up to 16 bits (two bytes) at a time. All of the PC's inherent skills at doing arithmetic can only be applied to either single 8-bit bytes or to 16-bit (two-byte) words. With the assistance of clever programs, the PC can work with larger numbers; for example, by combining two 16-bit words into a larger 32-bit number. But this can only be done with special software. When we're talking about the PC's natural skills, we're talking about only 8- and 16- bit arithmetic.

Just how big can 8- and 16-bit numbers be? Not very big really. As we already know from looking at 8-bit bytes, there are only 256 distinct values that an 8-bit byte can have—2 raised to the eighth power, which is 256. A 16-bit, two-byte word can have 2 distinct values of sixteenth power: 65,536 in all. That sets a rather small limit on the range of numbers that we can work with using bytes and words. (If you want to explore 2-byte words or other longer integer formats inside your computers, you need to know about "back-words" storage—see the *How Words are Stored* sidebar in Chapter 7.)

Each of these two sizes of integer can be interpreted in two ways, which doubles the number of different numeric formats that we can have. The two interpretations depend upon whether we want to allow for negative numbers or not. If we don't need to work with negative numbers, then the entire range of values of each of these two sizes of integers can be devoted to positive numbers. For a byte-sized integer, the range of numbers can run from 0 up to 255, using all the 256 distinct bit patterns in a byte; for a 2-byte word, the range of positive integers is 0 through 65,535.

On the other hand, if we need to have negative numbers as well, half the range of values is devoted to negatives, and we can only have numbers half as large. In the case of bytes, the range of values is from -128 through

0 to +127; for words the range is from -32,768 through 0 to +32,767. We don't get to choose the range, so we can't get a wider range of positive numbers by giving up some of the negative range. For more on negative numbers, see the *How Negatives are Represented* sidebar. You'll notice that the range of negative numbers is one greater than the range of positives: there is a -128, but there isn't a +128; that's just an odd byproduct of the way negative numbers are handled.

Table 3-3 summarizes the range of numbers handled by the four integer formats.

Table 3-3. Range of integer formats.

	1 byte			2 bytes		
Unsigned Integer		0 to 255			0 to 65,535	
Signed Integer	−128 to	0 to +127		−32,768 to	0 to +32,767	

As I mentioned before, the microprocessor inside our PCs can do all of its standard arithmetic—add, subtract, multiply, and divide—on these four integer formats, but that is the extent of all the basic calculating that the PC can do.

As you might imagine, most programs can't get along with just those four simple integer formats for their numbers. For example, BASIC uses three kinds of numbers. Only one of them, called *integer* in BASIC's terminology, is one of these four formats (it's our signed 2-byte word format). The other two, which BASIC calls *single-* and *double-precision* have to be created by going beyond the PC's ordinary skills. We discuss this in Section 3.4.

How Negatives are Represented

Negative integers are represented inside the PC in a form known as *two's-complement*. It's a commonly-used scheme in computers and closely related to the borrow-and-carry tricks we were taught when we first learned to add and subtract. It's easiest to explain with an example done with decimal numbers that we'll make three digits long; that's analogous to the fixed length one- or two-byte binary numbers that the PC calculates with.

In our 3-digit decimal numbers, zero is written 000 and one as 001. If we subtract 001 from 001, we get 000. How can we subtract 001 again to get minus one? We can do it by borrowing from an imaginary 1 in the fourth place. We think of 000 (and all other positive numbers) as having a 1 in front that can be borrowed from like this:

```
    (1)000   zero
  −    001   subtract one
     ──────       gives us
       999   minus one
```

So minus one is represented as 999; minus two is 998, and so on.

The positive numbers start at 000, 001, 002 and go on up to 499. The negatives go 999 (that's -1), 998 (-2), and so on down to 500 which really means minus five hundred. The same trick works with the binary numbers inside our computer.

Notice that the value of a number can depend on whether we interpret it as signed or unsigned. As a signed number 999 means minus one; as an unsigned number it means nine hundred and ninety nine.

3.4 Hot Numbers

Most of our computing needs go beyond the simple integers that are native to the PC. Whether we're doing financial planning with a spreadsheet program, performing engineering calculations, or just balancing our checkbooks, we need numbers more powerful than the integers we've looked at so far. Just dealing with money, the integers we've discussed so far couldn't handle anything more than $655.35, when we figure down to the penny. So we need some hotter numbers.

There are two ways that the PC can give us a wider range of numbers, and two ways to calculate with those numbers. Let's look at the kinds of numbers first, and then how those numbers can be calculated.

The first way to extend the range of numbers that our PCs can deal with is to simply make longer integers. We've already seen one- and two-byte integers. We can press on with that idea and use integers of three, four, or more bytes. Anything is possible, but the most practical extra length of integer is four bytes, and that gives us a much wider range of numbers, to over plus or minus 2,000,000,000. That does a lot for us, but it doesn't do everything.

To handle fractional amounts, and to handle extremely long numbers, our computers use a concept known as *floating point*. Floating point works in a way similar to something you may have learned about in school called scientific or engineering notation. In this scheme, numbers are represented in two parts—one part represents the digits that make up the number; the other part indicates where the decimal point is located. Since the decimal point can be moved around freely, floating-point numbers can become very, very large—astronomical, as they say—or very small fractions. No matter how large or small the number becomes, it is just as accurate, because the digits that determine the number's accuracy, or precision, are independent of the numbers that specify where the decimal point is.

In the BASIC programming language, the style of numbers known as *single-* and *double-precision* are both floating-point formats. The difference between them is that double-precision has more digits of accuracy. Other programming languages make use of floating point, too.

Spreadsheet programs, like Lotus 1-2-3, also use floating point to represent their numbers, because it gives them greater flexibility and greater precision in the calculations that they perform.

These are the two ways that the PC's number scheme can be extended—longer integers and floating point. But, as we mentioned, the PC's microprocessor, the PC's "brain," only has the natural ability to work with the four simple integer formats we covered in Section 3.3. How do we get any arithmetic done in these extended formats? There are two ways, through software and through hardware.

Software is the most common solution. Every programming language, including BASIC, and nearly every calculating program, including 1-2-3, contains program routines that can do the work of performing calculations on floating-point numbers or long integer formats. These subroutines use the PC's basic arithmetic and logic skills as building blocks to perform the more complex calculations necessary to work with these other number formats. This goes on at a cost, though. While the PC can perform its own integer calculations very fast—typically in a few millionths of a second—a floating-point subroutine takes perhaps a hundred times as long to do an equivalent calculation, simply because the subroutine has to perform its work using a hundred elementary steps.

For many purposes the speed of these software-based calculations is still fast enough, but it isn't as fast as it could be. To get more speed there is another way, a hardware solution.

As we'll learn more about in following chapters, the microprocessor inside our PC has a companion designed for one task alone: fast floating-point calculations. These companion chips are called *numeric coprocessors*. There are two of them for different models of PC: one is known as the 8087 chip, and the other is the 80287—for simplicity, most people simply call them the 87s. Most models in the PC family are designed to use an 87. When an 87 is installed, *and when a program knows how to make use of it* (which isn't often), the speed and accuracy of floating-point calculations can be enormously improved.

It's worth bearing in mind that many programs just don't do any floating-point calculations. Word processing programs, for example, have no use for floating-point numbers. These programs aren't slowed down by floating-point subroutines, or sped up by the presence of an 87 coprocessor. Even programs that *do* perform floating point don't all take advantage of an 87. For example, BASIC ignores any 87 that might be present; 1-2-3, on the other hand, uses the 87 whenever it would help.

Unlike the integer formats that we discussed before, and unlike the PC character set that we'll explore in Chapter 4, there aren't universal standards for what kinds of longer integers and floating-point numbers might be used by a program. We can't come up with a short summary of all of the extended number formats, but we can take a look at the most common ones.

First, let's look at longer integers. Our programs could work with any number of bytes to make a long integer, but one size is by far the most common—four-byte signed integers. These numbers can range to slightly over plus or minus two billion. The 87s are designed to work with four-byte integers and eight-byte integers as well; they get as large as nine billion billion. The 87s can also work with a special *decimal* integer format that holds 18 decimal digits, which is also in the billion billion range. This special decimal format that the 87s use is a unique example of a decimal orientation; everything else that our computers do is essentially binary in nature and not decimal.

Next, let's look at what floating point can do for us. The two most common sizes of floating-point numbers occupy four or eight bytes of storage, like BASIC's single and double precision formats. Four-byte floating-point formats give us the equivalent of about six decimal digits of accuracy, and eight-byte formats give us about 16 digits of accuracy. The range—how large numbers can get—is in the neighborhood of 10 to the 38th power. Because there are several different ways to code a floating-point number, there is some variety in the amount of precision and range that we can get in the same general size of floating-point numbers, so the figures that I've given you here are only rough ones. The 87s can also work with a slightly larger format that occupies ten bytes; it gives about 18 digits of accuracy.

The kind of numbers that we can work with depends on the kind of program that we are using. What we've described here applies to most programming languages, but specialty programs may have their own unique number formats. For example, it's common for spreadsheet programs to use their own variations on the idea of floating-point numbers. But what we've talked about here gives you a clear idea of the kinds of hot numbers that can be at our disposal when we work with our computers.

3.5 Stringing Along

Character or text data—letters of the alphabet and so forth—are very important in our use of the computer. In fact, our computers are used more for working with text data than with numeric data, which is ironic because computers are first and foremost fancy calculators. But we've learned how to make these fancy calculators do lots of useful work for us in manipulating written text, like the very words you are reading (which of course have been handled by a computer from the moment they were written). It's important to understand some of the fundamentals of how computers handle text data.

Text data is made up of individual characters, like the letter A. As we saw earlier in this chapter, each letter is represented by a particular pattern of bits and occupies a byte of storage. The ASCII coding scheme is used to define the standard way, common to most computers, of determining which pattern of bits represents which letter. In Chapter 4, we'll take a more detailed look at all of the individual characters that our PCs can work with. What we want to talk about now is how we work with more than one character at a time.

By themselves characters aren't of a great deal to use, until we put them together to form words and sentences. Similarly, inside our computer's groups of character bytes are more significant than individual bytes by themselves. There is a technical term in computing used to describe a bunch of characters handled as a single entity, and that term is *string*. A string is a group of bytes, one right after another, that are treated as a combined unit.

All of our computer's programming languages, and many of the most important kinds of software—such as spreadsheet programs like Lotus 1-2-3—work with strings of character data. Word processing programs—such as WordStar, Volkswriter, Multimate, Microsoft Word—are primarily designed to work with character strings. Strings are a very important part of the computer data that we need to understand, which is why we're devoting this section of the book to making you aware of strings.

Even though strings are important there isn't a great deal to say about them. But there are a few key things that you ought to know, particularly about how they are stored and the limitations that are sometimes placed on what sort of string data we can use.

Inside the computer's memory and on the computer's disks, strings are stored in just the way common sense would have it: the character bytes are recorded one right after another. That's nothing special. However, what is special about strings is that something has to tie them together. When we discussed numerical data earlier in this chapter, every kind of data had its own specific format that rigidly defined how big the data was, how many bytes it occupied. Strings, however, are special because they don't have any fixed length—some are long, some are short. And something has to define that length, to tie together the characters that make up a string.

As it turns out, there isn't any one, universal way that it's done. Different programs use their own methods and rules to define what a string is and what holds it together. We can't lay out any universal rules that say exactly how strings are defined—but we can look at some of the most common methods, and that will give us some insight into how our programs work with strings and how the limitations on strings come about.

There are two main ways used by programs to define how big a string is, where its end is. One is to simply keep track of the length of the string as a number that's recorded separately from the string (usually this length-of-string number is placed just before the beginning of the string). Here's a hypothetical example:

4This2is1a6string2of5words

As you can see, each word in the example is a separate string, and the number of character bytes in each word is recorded just before it. This is a very common technique for dealing with strings and determining how long they are. If you think about it, you'll realize that this method places an inherent limit on how big any individual string can be. The number that represents the length of the string is recorded in some numerical format, such as the ones we've discussed. The maximum number which that format allows sets a limit on how long the string can be.

It's very common for the length of a string to be recorded as a single unsigned byte—which can't be larger than 255. So many programs that work with strings have a limit of 255 as the longest string they can work with. (Sometimes the limit is a few less than 255, because a byte or two may be needed for some overhead requirement.) The ordinary BASIC in our computers works this way, so strings in BASIC can't be over 255 characters; but compiled BASIC happens to record its string lengths as 2-byte words, so the string length for compiled BASIC can be over 32,000. Many word processing programs hold each line as a separate string and use a 1-byte string length counter; that's why so many of them have the limitation that a line can't be over 255 characters.

There is another way to determine the size of a string that doesn't place any arbitrary limit on how long a string can be. With this technique the length of the string isn't recorded, but instead the end of the string is marked off with some sort of *delimiter*. Here's another hypothetical example, using asterisks as delimiters:

This*is*a*string*of*words*

The delimiter is used to mark the end of the string, but it's not considered part of the string itself. There are two delimiters that are widely used: one is a 0-byte, a byte with all the bits off. (As you'll see in Chapter 4, a 0-byte isn't a bad choice of delimiter, since a 0-byte is normally never used as an ordinary text character.) The other commonly used delimiter is a byte with a numeric code of 13. Thirteen is the code for a carriage-return character, which is normally used to mark the end of a line of text. Since it's common to treat each line of text as a separate string, it makes sense to use the same byte code to mean both end-of-line and end-of-string. (We'll learn more about this when we cover text file formats in Chapter 9.)

There is one obvious disadvantage to using a special end-of-string delimiter code—it means that the string can't include that code value inside the string. This may not be a major problem in most circumstances, but still it is a disadvantage and a limitation that we need to be aware of.

Some Things to Try

1.   BASIC can easily convert numbers between hex and decimal as long as the numbers aren't any bigger than the equivalent of four hex digits. Try writing a program that works with larger numbers, converting between hex and decimal.

2.   Try your hand at some hex arithmetic. Add 1234 to ABCD. Subtract 1A2B from A1B2. Multiply 2A by 2 and by 3.

3.   Can you figure out a way to test either the accuracy or range of numbers that a program can handle? Try writing a BASIC pro-

gram that tests how large a number can become, or how precisely a number is represented.

4. Analyze the problems inherent in the two ways of defining a string. Think of practical situations where the limitations might matter. Can you think of a scheme that would place no limit on the length or contents of a string? Are there any disadvantages to your scheme? Write a program in BASIC (or any other programmable software, such as 1-2-3) that finds out how long a string can be by increasing a string character by character.

4

The PC Character Set

I n Chapter 3, we took an overall look at the form data takes inside our PCs, and what different kinds of data we can have. But we only looked briefly at the PC's character set. That was because there is so much that's interesting to know about the PC character set that we've set aside this chapter to take a deeper look at these characters. We'll get an overview of the whole character set, see how the PC's characters relate to a widespread standard known as ASCII, and we'll particularly dig into and analyze the PC's full set of special characters.

4.1 A Character Set Overview

Characters in the PC, as in most modern computers, occupy an 8-bit byte, so that there can be as many as 2 to the eighth power, or 256, distinct characters. We begin by looking at them all (see Figure 4-1).

There are two easy ways for you to see all the characters on the screen of your own computer. One is to use the simple BASIC program called ALL-CHAR found in Appendix A; this ALL-CHAR program was used to create Figure 4-1. The other way is to use the popular program called Sidekick. One of Sidekick's many features is a quick and handy display of the PC's full character set. When you use ALL-CHAR, or Sidekick, you'll see the PC character set in exactly the way your computer's screen shows them, which can vary somewhat depending on the type of display screen you have (we'll learn more about that when we come to the chapters on the video display). Figure 4-1 shows the characters in more-or-less their ideal form (as printed by IBM's Quietwriter printer) and gives you a quick and accurate way of seeing just what each character is like for close comparison to all the other characters.

For reference, we need another chart of the PC character set that shows each character's appearance together with the numeric character codes in decimal and hex. You'll find that in Figure 4-2. We'll be referring to this figure a lot through the rest of this chapter. If you want to see the information from Figure 4-2 on your own computer's screen, you can use either the REF-CHAR program that's listed in Appendix A or the Sidekick program.

Figure 4-2 lists each of the 256 characters and their decimal character codes, followed by the same code in hex (it's the same code because the two codes have the same numerical value, they're just being expressed two different ways) followed by a picture of what the character looks like. As you'll notice, Figures 4-1 and 4-2 are laid out in the same order, in columns reading top to bottom, so it'll be easy to match them up for comparison whenever you want to.

Surprisingly, there is an awful lot to say about these characters, because they are designed to do so many things and because some of them take on a different quality, depending upon how they are being used. We will discuss that in this chapter. We'll begin with a quick overview.

If you glance at Figure 4-1, you'll see that it begins with two columns of very curious characters (the first 32 characters, with decimal codes 0 through 31) followed by six columns of the characters we're most familiar with: the digits 0-9, the letters of the alphabet in upper- and lowercase, and a lot of punctuation characters. These eight columns are the first half of the PC's character set, and they are called the *ASCII characters,* because they follow a widespread standard that is used in most computers called ASCII—the American Standard Code for Information Interchange.

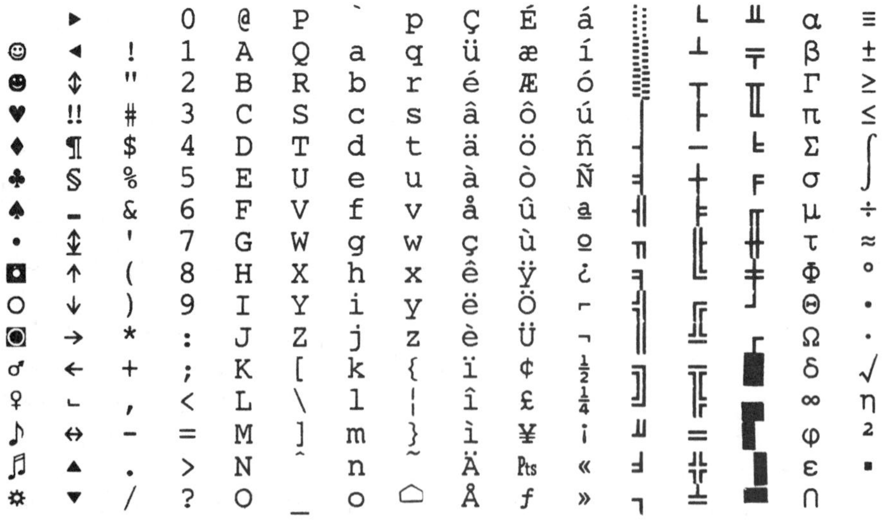

Figure 4-1. The full PC character set.

ASCII proper has only 128 characters in it, the characters with decimal codes 0-127. Our PC character set has twice as many entries, including the codes that go from 128 through 255. These higher codes, which make up the other half of the PC character set, are usually called the *extended* ASCII characters. Strictly speaking, only the first half, the codes 0-127, are ASCII characters, but you'll often find people using the term ASCII to mean just any character or to mean the coding scheme that defines how characters are represented in patterns of bits. There's no harm in that, but you ought to be aware that, depending on how it's used, the term ASCII can have a precise technical meaning or a broader meaning.

The ASCII half of our character set has an official meaning and definition that ranges far beyond our PC family—it's a universal code used by many computers and other electronic equipment as well. The *extended* ASCII characters, however, are another story. There is no universal convention for what these character codes 128-255 will be used for, and these characters were specially designed for the PC. Because of the importance and popularity of the PC, these particular extended ASCII characters have been used not only by the entire PC family, but have also been adopted into the character set of many computers that are only very distant relatives of the PC.

This particular group of characters is on its way to becoming something of an *un*official standard; but it's only that, unofficial. Because of that, you'll find that there are many computers and lots of computer equipment—particularly printers—that know nothing about our PC's extended ASCII characters. In fact, one of the reasons why some of the illustrations for this book have been prepared using the IBM Quietwriter is that it is one of the few printers that can display almost the entire PC character set; that's something you'll want to keep in mind. After all, one of the main reasons why we're poring over the PC character set in detail is so you will know how to use this rich collection to your full advantage—and that includes knowing that some parts of the character set can't be used as easily and as widely as other parts.

Now it's time for us to dig into the details of our PC's character set. We'll do it in three parts—two covering the ASCII characters (first the most ordinary ASCII characters and then some special ASCII control characters), and finally a section discussing the extended ASCII characters and some other unique characteristics of the PC character set.

4.2 The Ordinary ASCII Characters

The ASCII character set, character codes 0-127, breaks into two very different parts that can be readily seen by a glance at Figures 4-1 and 4-2.

Dec	Hex	Char		Dec	Hex	Char		Dec	Hex	Char		Dec	Hex	Char
0	00			32	20			64	40	@		96	60	`
1	01	☺		33	21	!		65	41	A		97	61	a
2	02	☻		34	22	"		66	42	B		98	62	b
3	03	♥		35	23	#		67	43	C		99	63	c
4	04	♦		36	24	$		68	44	D		100	64	d
5	05	♣		37	25	%		69	45	E		101	65	e
6	06	♠		38	26	&		70	46	F		102	66	f
7	07	•		39	27	'		71	47	G		103	67	g
8	08	◘		40	28	(		72	48	H		104	68	h
9	09	○		41	29	)		73	49	I		105	69	i
10	0A	◙		42	2A	*		74	4A	J		106	6A	j
11	0B	♂		43	2B	+		75	4B	K		107	6B	k
12	0C	♀		44	2C	,		76	4C	L		108	6C	l
13	0D	♪		45	2D	-		77	4D	M		109	6D	m
14	0E	♫		46	2E	.		78	4E	N		110	6E	n
15	0F	☼		47	2F	/		79	4F	O		111	6F	o
16	10	►		48	30	0		80	50	P		112	70	p
17	11	◄		49	31	1		81	51	Q		113	71	q
18	12	↕		50	32	2		82	52	R		114	72	r
19	13	‼		51	33	3		83	53	S		115	73	s
20	14	¶		52	34	4		84	54	T		116	74	t
21	15	§		53	35	5		85	55	U		117	75	u
22	16	▬		54	36	6		86	56	V		118	76	v
23	17	↨		55	37	7		87	57	W		119	77	w
24	18	↑		56	38	8		88	58	X		120	78	x
25	19	↓		57	39	9		89	59	Y		121	79	y
26	1A	→		58	3A	:		90	5A	Z		122	7A	z
27	1B	←		59	3B	;		91	5B	[		123	7B	{
28	1C	∟		60	3C	<		92	5C	\		124	7C	|
29	1D	↔		61	3D	=		93	5D	]		125	7D	}
30	1E	▲		62	3E	>		94	5E	^		126	7E	~
31	1F	▼		63	3F	?		95	5F	_		127	7F	⌂

Figure 4-2. The PC character set with decimal and hex codes.

Dec	Hex	Char	Dec	Hex	Char	Dec	Hex	Char	Dec	Hex	Char	Dec	Hex	Char	Dec	Hex	Char	Dec	Hex	Char	Dec	Hex	Char
128	80	Ç	144	90	É	160	A0	á	176	B0	░	192	C0	└	208	D0	╨	224	E0	α	240	F0	≡
129	81	ü	145	91	æ	161	A1	í	177	B1	▒	193	C1	┴	209	D1	╤	225	E1	ß	241	F1	±
130	82	é	146	92	Æ	162	A2	ó	178	B2	▓	194	C2	┬	210	D2	╥	226	E2	Γ	242	F2	≥
131	83	â	147	93	ô	163	A3	ú	179	B3	│	195	C3	├	211	D3	╙	227	E3	π	243	F3	≤
132	84	ä	148	94	ö	164	A4	ñ	180	B4	┤	196	C4	─	212	D4	╘	228	E4	Σ	244	F4	⌠
133	85	à	149	95	ò	165	A5	Ñ	181	B5	╡	197	C5	┼	213	D5	╒	229	E5	σ	245	F5	⌡
134	86	å	150	96	û	166	A6	ª	182	B6	╢	198	C6	╞	214	D6	╓	230	E6	µ	246	F6	÷
135	87	ç	151	97	ù	167	A7	º	183	B7	╖	199	C7	╟	215	D7	╫	231	E7	τ	247	F7	≈
136	88	ê	152	98	ÿ	168	A8	¿	184	B8	╕	200	C8	╚	216	D8	╪	232	E8	Φ	248	F8	°
137	89	ë	153	99	Ö	169	A9	⌐	185	B9	╣	201	C9	╔	217	D9	┘	233	E9	Θ	249	F9	∙
138	8A	è	154	9A	Ü	170	AA	¬	186	BA	║	202	CA	╩	218	DA	┌	234	EA	Ω	250	FA	·
139	8B	ï	155	9B	¢	171	AB	½	187	BB	╗	203	CB	╦	219	DB	█	235	EB	δ	251	FB	√
140	8C	î	156	9C	£	172	AC	¼	188	BC	╝	204	CC	╠	220	DC	▄	236	EC	∞	252	FC	ⁿ
141	8D	ì	157	9D	¥	173	AD	¡	189	BD	╜	205	CD	═	221	DD	▌	237	ED	φ	253	FD	²
142	8E	Ä	158	9E	₧	174	AE	«	190	BE	╛	206	CE	╬	222	DE	▐	238	EE	ε	254	FE	■
143	8F	Å	159	9F	ƒ	175	AF	»	191	BF	┐	207	CF	╧	223	DF	▀	239	EF	∩	255	FF	

Figure 4-2. The PC character set with decimal and hex codes (continued).

45

The first part, which we'll discuss separately in Section 4.3, are the first 32 characters, codes 0-31. These are called the ASCII *control characters* and they are something quite different from what they appear to be in Figures 4-1 and 4-2. We'll come back to them after we've talked about the more conventional characters, codes 32-127.

If you look at the third through eighth columns of Figures 4-1 and 4-2, you'll see what we usually think about when we think of characters: they are the everyday letters of the alphabet, digits, and punctuation. Although it might seem that there's little to discuss in these ordinary characters, there are actually quite a few subtle details that we ought to run through, if you really want to understand the ins and outs and tricks of these characters.

It seems all too obvious to point out that there are separate characters for upper- and lowercase, that A isn't the same thing as a, but there is something here you shouldn't miss. Whenever you're using any program that arranges data into alphabetical order (sorts data) or that searches for data, this will matter, unless the program takes special pains to treat upper- and lowercase the same (some programs do, some don't, and some let us choose). This means that a search for the letter a may not match the letter A; and it means that, in alphabetical order, a comes after A and after Z as well. We also should note that the number-digits come before the alphabet.

The next thing we need to consider are the punctuation and other special symbols. There are lots of little points to see about these characters. One thing to note is that they are scattered all around the digits and upper- and lowercase letters: before, after, and in between. This means that the punctuation characters as a group won't sort into any one place relative to the alphabet and digits. Some will come before, some after; sometimes that's important to know. There are some interesting and useful details about these punctuation characters that you need to know.

The blank-space character has a decimal character code of 32—the lowest of all the punctuation characters, so it appears at the beginning of any alphabetic sort. (In the character charts in Figures 4-1 and 4-2 you'll see three different characters that appear to be a blank space—see the sidebar *Spaces and Nulls* for more about that.) You'll notice that besides parentheses ( ), there are also two other pairs of characters that can be used to enclose things: the brackets [] and the braces {}; people also use the greater-than and less-than characters, ⟨⟩, as a way of enclosing things, like ⟨this⟩. It's good to know about all four of these embracing pairs, because they can come in handy at times.

Let's consider quotes. In the type styles used in a book you'll find that there are left and right quote marks, but ordinary typewriters don't have them; neither does our PC character set. Our PC set has only one double-quote mark and one single-quote mark that are used on both the left and the right hand side of a quotation. But there is also a curious character known as a reverse-quote—it's the one just before the lowercase a, with a decimal character code of 96. But you shouldn't think of it as something to be paired with the ordinary single-quote character. It's used to produce foreign (that is, non-English) characters. It's used in combination with letters of the alphabet to form a letter with a diacritical mark. There are several other characters that are used this way: the carat, ˆ, code 94; the tilde, ˜, code 126; the single-quote, ', code 39; and the comma, code 44. This idea of combining characters only works when you can overstrike one character on top of another—which you can do on a computer printer or on a typewriter, but not on the computer's display screen. To properly handle these non-English characters of the alphabet the PC has them incorporated into the extended ASCII characters, as you'll see by a glance at the latter half of the character tables. We'll talk more about them in Section 4.4.

There are other characters that call for a brief mention. Besides the regular slash character, /, code 47, there is a reverse slash, \, code 92. As far as I know this has no ordinary use, but only some special uses in computing. For example, in the BASIC programming language it indicates whole-number division (the slash indicates regular division, which includes a fractional result) and when working with DOS, it indicates directory paths (which we'll be discussing in a later chapter). Also take care not to confuse the hyphen character, -, code 45, with the underscore character, _, code 95. Finally, the carat character, ˆ, code 94, is sometimes used to indicate special "control characters" (which we'll cover in Section 4.3) rather than being an independent character in itself. This can cause confusion so when you see a carat, check carefully to see if it indicates the carat character is meant or these special control characters.

TECHNICAL BACKGROUND ▎ ▎ ▎ ■ ■ ■ ▬▬▬▬▬▬▬▬▬

Spaces and Nulls

In the character tables in Figures 4-1 and 4-2 you'll find three or four characters that appear to be blank. Only one of them actually is the proper blank character—the one with character code 32. Character codes 0 and 255 are called "nulls" or null characters. They aren't supposed to be treated as true characters at all, but as inactive nothings. For example, if we send code 32 (the true space character) to a computer printer, it prints a space and moves on to the next location. But the null characters are supposed to be ignored, so that a printer won't move to the next location, leaving a blank space.

In the proper ASCII character set, there are two nulls—codes 0 and 127. In our PC character set, code 127 is a real, visible character with an appearance something like a little house. To substitute for the ASCII null-127, our PC character set treats code 255 as a null.

Null characters don't have any everyday use—they are mostly used in communications, to mark time: transmitting nulls is a way of keeping a line active while not actually sending any real data.

4.3 The ASCII Control Characters

The first 32 places in the ASCII character set, codes 0 through 31, have a very special use that has nothing to do with the appearance of these characters as they look in Figures 4-1 and 4-2. For the moment, ignore what appears in those two illustrations, because in this section we'll be looking at these characters from an entirely different perspective.

When a computer "talks" to a printer, it needs to tell the printer what to print and also how to print it—it has to indicate, for example, where the ends of the lines are, and when to skip to the top of a new page. The ordinary ASCII characters, which we discussed in Section 4.2, are the "what to print" part of the ASCII character set. The "how to print it" part is the subject of this section—the ASCII control characters.

The first 32 codes in the ASCII character set are reserved to pass special information to a printer, or to another computer through a telephone line, and so forth. These codes aren't used to pass information or data itself, but to provide action commands, formatting signals, and communication control codes. There is a wide variety of different things that these 32 codes are used for, and the uses can vary in different circumstances. We'll cover the main items here, to give you a broad perspective on what these characters are for.

First off, I need to tell you that these 32 codes have special names when they are used (as we're discussing here) as ASCII control characters, and not as the pretty picture characters that you see in Figures 4-1 and 4-2. Table 4-1 gives you a summary of these codes, and the names that they have.

Before we go into any explanations of the details of these control characters, there are a few things about Table 4-1 that should be mentioned. The first two columns of Table 4-1 are, of course, the numeric character codes in decimal and in hex. The third column shows some special control key codes that are used in connection with these characters. Each of these

Table 4-1. ASCII control characters.

Dec code	Hex code	Control-key	Name	Description
0	00	ˆ@	NUL	null character
1	01	ˆA	SOH	start of header
2	02	ˆB	STX	start of text
3	03	ˆC	ETX	end of text
4	04	ˆD	EOT	end of transmission
5	05	ˆE	ENQ	enquire
6	06	ˆF	ACK	acknowledge
7	07	ˆG	BEL	bell
8	08	ˆH	BS	backspace
9	09	ˆI	HT	horizontal tab
10	0A	ˆJ	LF	line feed
11	0B	ˆK	VT	vertical tab
12	0C	ˆL	FF	form feed (new page)
13	0D	ˆM	CR	carriage return
14	0E	ˆN	SO	shift out
15	0F	ˆO	SI	shift in
16	10	ˆP	DEL	delete
17	11	ˆQ	DC1	device control 1
18	12	ˆR	DC2	device control 2
19	13	ˆS	DC3	device control 3
20	14	ˆT	DC4	device control 4
21	15	ˆU	NAK	negative acknowledge
22	16	ˆV	SYN	synchronize
23	17	ˆW	ETB	end of text block
24	18	ˆX	CAN	cancel
25	19	ˆY	EM	end of medium
26	1A	ˆZ	SUB	substitute
27	1B	ˆ[	ESC	escape
28	1C	ˆ/	FS	file separator
29	1D	ˆ]	GS	group separator
30	1E	ˆˆ	RS	record separator
31	1F	ˆ_	US	unit separator

characters can be keyed in directly on our keyboards by simply holding down the "Ctrl" control shift key and pressing A (for code 1) or B (for code 2) and so on. There is a conventional way of indicating these control-shift codes, by writing a carat, ˆ, before the name of the key we press, and that's what is shown in the third column of this table. When we write ˆA we *don't* mean the carat character (ˆ) followed by the character A—

we mean Control-A—the character that is keyed in on the keyboard by holding down the control key and pressing the A key.

It's worth remembering that this "carat notation" is used quite often. In your reading you might run across ˆZ or ˆC, which we know mean Control-Z or Control-C: two special codes that have a real meaning to the PC, as we'll see shortly.

In the last column of Table 4-1 is a descriptive name for each of these 32 special codes, and in the fourth column just before the description you'll find a two- or three-letter code, which is a standard abbreviation for the full descriptive name of the control code character. You'll find these short codes sometimes used in writing about computers and communications.

Some of these ASCII control characters are very interesting and useful to us, and others are rather obscure and technical in their use. Instead of discussing them from first to last, let me cover them in a way that's closer to how important they are to us.

First let's talk about the ones that are on our keyboard. As we mentioned, any of these characters can be keyed in with a Control-and-key combination. But some of these characters actually have regular keys dedicated to them so that we don't have to use the control combination for them. These are characters that are definitely important to our use of the computer. There are four of them: backspace (BS, code 8), tab (HT, 9), the Enter key or carriage return (CR, 13), and the escape key (ESC, 27). (Don't think that the Del key on your keyboard keys in the ASCII DEL, 16, code: it doesn't.)

A whole group of these control codes is used to indicate the basic formatting of written material. These codes function as both logical formatting codes (which help our programs make sense out of our data) and printer control codes (which tell our printers just what to do). The most common ones are some we've already discussed, such as backspace (BS), tab (HT), and carriage return (CR). Others are line-feed (LF, code 10), which is used in conjunction with carriage return, form feed (FF, 12) which skips to a new page, and vertical tab (VT, 11).

There are more characters that are of general interest and use. The bell character (BEL, 7) sounds a warning bell or beep. If we send this character to a printer or to our computer's display screen, we'll get an audible signal as a result. The Control-C character (ETX, 3) is also known as the break character, and keying Control-C on the keyboard usually has the same effect as pressing the BREAK key. The Control-S and Control-Q characters (DC3, 19 and DC1, 17) can often be used as a pause command and a restart command, particularly when we're working with a communications service (such as The Source, CompuServe, or MCI Mail)—it can be handy to know about them. The Control-S "pause" command is not, however, the same as the PAUSE key on our computer (which we'll learn more about in Chapter 14). (If you don't find the PAUSE key on your keyboard, that's because it's not marked, but it's there; it's Control-NumLock, just as BREAK is Control-ScrollLock.) The PAUSE key actually stops our computer, while this Control-S "pause" command just asks the program we're working with to pause (but our PC computer keeps right on working).

Then there is the Control-Z key combination (SUB, 26). This control code is used to mark the end of text files stored on our computer's disks. We'll learn more about this code, and the carriage return and line feed codes in Chapter 9, when we discuss file formats.

Those are the ASCII control characters that are of the widest interest. We'll finish this section with an overview of some of the more technically-oriented control characters. You can skip over the following paragraphs if you're not interested.

TECHNICAL BACKGROUND I I I ■ ■ ■ ▬▬▬▬▬▬▬▬▬▬▬

The rest of the ASCII control characters are used for a variety of purposes that assist in communications, data formatting, and the control of printers (and other devices). We can't really cover this topic exhaustively here, but we can give you an idea of what some of the details are like.

Codes 1-4 (SOH, STX, ETX, EOT) are used in communications transmissions to indicate the boundaries of header (descriptive) information and actual text data and the end of an entire transmission. Those codes are oriented particularly to text data. Other codes, such as 28-31 (FS, GS, RS, US) are used as punctuation marks in other forms of data, to mark the boundaries of files—"groups," records, and "units"—which take on different meanings depending upon the type of data that is being transmitted.

Other codes are used for the control of communications—for example, acknowledge (ACK, 6) and negative-acknowledge (NAK, 21) are used to indicate if data is passing successfully. ENQ, SYN, ETB, CAN, and other codes are also used in the control of communications (which is much too deep and specialized a subject for us to get into here). At least you might want to know what these control codes are used for in general.

A number of our ASCII control codes are used to control printers and other devices. Although the exact control codes vary widely from printer to printer, there are some commonly used codes which are worth mentioning. The shift-out and shift-in codes (SO, 14 and SI, 15) are commonly used to instruct a printer to print double-wide or compressed-width characters. The four device control codes, DC1-4, 17-20) are set aside for uses such as controlling printers, and many printers use them for such commands as turning off double-width printing.

However, because most printers have more formatting and control commands than there are ASCII control characters available, it is normal for the escape character (ESC, 27) to be used as a catch-all command prefix. When a printer receives an escape character from our computers, it knows that a special command follows, and instead of printing the next few characters, the printer interprets them as a control command; for example, a command to set the location of the tab stops, or a command to turn on underscoring of all the characters that follow.

If you want to learn more about these control characters, see *Communications and Networking with the IBM PC* (Brady Communications, 1983). For details of printer control codes, you'll need to turn to the reference manual that comes with the printer you are interested in.

4.4 A Cast of Odd Characters

Now it's time for us to look at all of the PC's special characters—that's the entire second half of the character set: the extended ASCII characters with character codes 128 through 255, plus the PC-specific character pictures for the first 32 ASCII characters. We'll be discussing them in groups, pausing to make comments and point out interesting highlights as they appear.

Before we proceed, I need to discuss again a major source of confusion, the first 32 characters, codes 0-31. There are two *completely* different ways of viewing these characters. We discussed one way in Section 4.3—interpreting them as ASCII control characters. When these characters are interpreted as ASCII control characters, *they do not have any appearance.* There is no picture of them—because they are not characters that look like something (the way an A looks like an A), they are basically commands. That's the interpretation of these characters which we discussed in Section 4.3. In this section, we'll be looking at the other interpretation of these character codes: as characters, like any other, that have an appearance (an appearance shown in Figures 4-1 and 4-2).

What determines whether the same character code is interpreted as an ASCII control command or as one of these visible characters? Basically it all depends on how the code is used. In most circumstances these codes are treated as ASCII control characters. But if we manage—by one means or another—to get them to appear on our PC's display screen, then they take on their other interpretation, which is as part of the PC's very special character set.

If you look at the pictures of the first 32 characters (in Figures 4-1 and 4-2) you'll see that they form a fascinating hodge-podge of graphic characters that can be used for a variety of purposes, none of them really essential. Since the use of these character codes is relatively restricted (they are usually interpreted as control characters, and so won't be shown as we see them in Figure 4-1), IBM decided to put the most important special characters into the extended ASCII area, and use this section of characters for some of the more amusing and dispensable characters.

Nevertheless, you will find some worthwhile and useful characters here, such as the card-suit group (codes 3-6), the paragraph and section marks (codes 20 and 21), the arrow group (16-31) and the "have a nice day" group (1 and 2). There are real uses for these characters, but they are mostly frivolous. It's nice that something as serious as the IBM Personal Computer family has a frivolous element to it.

When we move on to the extended ASCII characters, codes 128-255, we find more serious special characters. They are organized into three main groups: the foreign characters, the drawing characters, and the scientific characters.

The foreign characters use codes 128 through 175, and they include essentially everything that is needed to accommodate all of the major European languages other than English. (ASCII, as the *American* Standard Code, is oriented to the needs of the English language and American punctuation symbols.)

There are three main subparts to this foreign character group. One part, using codes 128-154 and 160-167, provides the special alphabetic characters (with diacritical marks) that are used in various European languages. We mentioned earlier that the regular ASCII character set contains most (but not all) of the diacritical marks needed for European languages. They can only be used, as on a printer, when you can backspace and overstrike them onto letters of the alphabet. That doesn't work on the PC's display screen. These European characters solve that problem in an attractive way.

The second part of the European set provides currency symbols: the cent sign (code 155), the pound sign (156), the Japanese Yen (157), the Spanish peseta (158), and the franc (159). (The dollar sign (36) is part of the regular ASCII set.)

The third part of the European set provides some special punctuation: Spanish inverted question marks and exclamation point (codes 168 and 173) and French-style quotation marks (codes 174 and 175). These French quotes are worth noting, for they can be used for many graphic purposes as well as for their intended use.

Buried among the European characters are four symbols that have general use: the ½ and ¼ symbols (codes 171 and 172) and two angle marks (169 and 170). Look them up in case you might have any use for them.

The next major section of the extended ASCII characters are the drawing or graphics characters. These are characters that are designed to make it possible for our programs to produce drawings just using the PC's character set. There are three subgroups of drawing characters.

The most interesting and most widely-used part of the drawing characters are what I call the box-drawing characters. These characters allow us to draw precise rectangular outlines—boxes—on the computer's display screen. These box-drawing characters are sophisticated enough to allow us to draw vertical and horizontal dividing lines within an outline, and they allow us to draw with either single or double lines. There are actually four sets of characters for box drawing: a set for double lines, another for single lines, and then two mixed sets, for double-horizontal single-vertical lines, and vice versa. Figure 4-3 illustrates all four sets and shows the character codes that are used as well. If you want to see the boxes in action on the screen of your computer, the program called BOXES, listed in Appendix A, reproduces Figure 4-3.

Practically every important and impressive program for the PC makes heavy use of these box-drawing characters, because they look so good on the computer's display screen. That's why I've taken the trouble to produce Figure 4-3 and the program that draws it, to make it as easy as possible to look up the codes for these box-drawing characters and use them in your own work.

The next group of drawing characters is used to provide shaded areas of varying degrees of "solidness." Code 176 is ¼ dense, filling the entire character space (so that two next to each other blend together); code 177 is ½ dense; code 178 is ¾ dense; and code 219 is completely solid. Together with the blank character, they provide a range of four or five "shades of grey" that can be used either to fill an area on the screen or to produce bar-charts of distinctly different appearance.

The final group of drawing characters consists of codes 220-223. Each of them is half of the all-solid character (219) that we just mentioned. One is the top half, another the bottom, the right, and the left. They can be used to draw solid, filled-in shapes that are twice as fine-grained as could be drawn with the all-solid character alone. For example, they can be used to make bar graphs that are detailed to half a character length instead of full character size.

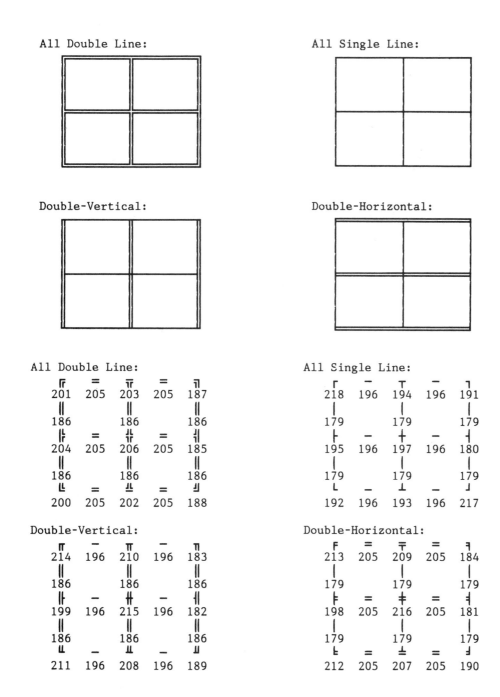

Figure 4-3. The box-drawing characters.

There are incredibly many amazing drawings that can be produced on the screen of the PC using just the PC's standard characters—including all the drawing characters that I've mentioned and also using some of the regular characters as well (for example, using the lowercase o for the wheels of a train). With some imagination you can do wonders this way.

The final part of the PC's extended ASCII special character set consists of the scientific character group, in codes 224-254. These include Greek letters commonly used in math and science, the infinity knot (code 236), various special mathematical symbols, including two (244 and 245) which, when stacked together, form a large integral sign. There is even a square and square-root symbol (253 and 251). While these symbols don't cover everything that might be needed for mathematics, science, and engineering, they do take care of some of the greatest needs.

Some Things to Try

1. Experiment to find out how your computer's screen and printer respond to the 32 ASCII control characters. Write a program in BASIC, or use any other handy means, to send these characters one-by-one to the computer's screen and printer. (Hint: if you precede and follow each control character by an X, you can get a clearer idea of what the response is to each control character.)

2. Do your computer's printer and display screen respond differently to the same control characters? Try to explain why.

3. Look at the BASIC programs called ALL-CHAR and REF-CHAR in Appendix A that generate Figures 4-1 and 4-2 on your computer's screen. Find how they write the characters onto the screen. Why don't they use the ordinary PRINT command?

4. If a program sorts data treating upper- and lowercase letters alike (which is often what we want) it will either treat both as uppercase or both as lowercase. Does it matter which way it's done? What effect does that have on punctuation?

5. The design of the PC's drawing characters was limited by the number of character codes available. Suppose there were another 50 or more codes available. What sort of additional drawing capabilities might have been added? Try to produce your own extensions to the PC's set of drawing characters.

5

Hardware:
The Parts of the PCs

I

t's time to start looking at the guts of the PC family, the hardware parts that make up our computers. We'll be looking at the PC's hardware from three angles: first we'll go through a basic breakdown of how the PC is organized into mechanical and electrical modules, each a major component of our PC. Next, we'll look at some of those components to see how they present us with options to assemble different kinds of PCs. Finally, on a more technical level, we'll look at the specific circuit chips that make the PC work.

5.1 The Breakdown

When we look at our PCs, we see three physical parts. First, there is the main box, called the *system unit,* that holds most of the computer. In front of it is the *keyboard* that we type on. And finally, there's the *display screen,* usually perched on top of the system unit. That's what the PC looks like from the outside. But when we dig inside the PC, we see that it's built around a modular design, that breaks the computer down into electronic components. You can see a logical diagram of these components in Figure 5-1.

The dotted line in Figure 5-1 represents the case that encloses the PC's system unit, and you'll see that just about everything is inside it. For portable members of the PC family, such as the Compaq and the Portable PC, the system unit also embraces the display screen; that only changes a detail of how the computer is physically built, but it doesn't change anything fundamental in the design.

To learn the basics of the design of the PC and how the parts fit together, we're going to talk our way through Figure 5-1. To help make things more concrete, we'll be describing where each of the components that we talk about is physically located, which is the same for most of the main models of the PC family. While the physical layout may vary (particularly for some of the more remote relatives of the family), the logical organization, and the function of each of the components that we talk about is the same for every member of the PC family. You can also match the parts we'll be discussing with the actual PC shown in Figure 5-2. Better yet, if you take the cover off a PC's system unit, you can follow along by matching what we discuss with your computer's own parts.

At the right rear of the system unit is the power supply. The power supply uses alternating current (AC) and converts it into the direct current (DC) voltages that the computer's parts need. The power unit supplies four different DC voltages: +12 volts, -12 volts, +5, and -5 volts. Besides converting the electricity from high-voltage alternating current to low-voltage direct current, the power supply also grooms the power, smoothing out unevenness in the electricity. The capacity of the power supply sets a limit on how many options can be installed in the computer. The original PC model supplied about 65 watts of power, not really a generous amount. Later models have more, for example, the XT provides about 130 watts, and the AT about 200 watts of power.

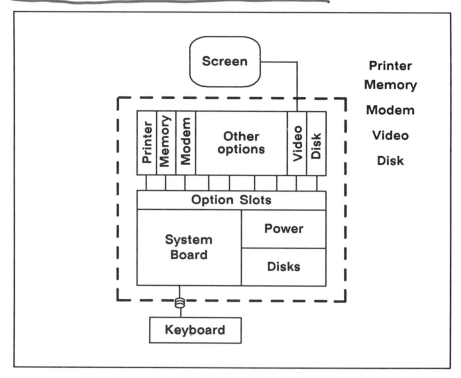

Figure 5-1. Components of the PC.

The first and primary part of a PC is the *system board*. This is a large printed circuit board that holds most of the main electronic parts, the key silicon chips that make the PC go. These include the computer's microprocessor and also the supporting chips that the microprocessor needs to help it perform its tasks, such as the ''clock'' chip that acts as a metronome setting the pace of work for the whole computer. Also on the system board is the computer's basic complement of working memory and the special read-only memory chips that hold the computer's complement of built-in programs. The system board is also sometimes called the *mother board*—you'll find both terms used.

The system board is the largest single electronic component of the whole computer and by far the largest of all the printed circuit boards in the machine. It fills practically the whole bottom of the system unit box. The space above the system board is where all the other components inside the system unit are placed.

If you pick up a PC system unit, you'll discover that it's heaviest at the right rear corner, where the power supply is. That's because the power supply includes a heavy transformer, which is used to lower the voltage level. In the PC*jr*, the transformer part of the power supply is in a separate

Figure 5-2. Inside the system unit.

external case; this reduces the weight of the *jr's* system unit and ensures that there's only low voltage inside it.

Besides supplying converted power to the rest of the computer's components, the power supply also provides an external power socket that we can plug a display screen into, and it contains a fan that provides a cooling air flow for all the parts inside the system unit.

At the right front of the system unit are the disk drives, nestled next to the power supply. Different members of the PC family feature different sizes and types of disk storage drives, as we'll see in Section 5.2 where we discuss various options in the PC. Part of the reason why the disk drives are placed here, in the right front corner, is to provide a short, easy connection to the power supply. The disk drives are the only mechanical part inside the system unit. They use more power than most of the electronic parts so they have their own direct connections to the power supply. All of the other components inside the system unit get their power indirectly from the power supply, passed through the system board.

The power supply and the disk drives take up the righthand side of the computer. The lefthand side, over the system board, is set aside for a number of optional parts known as *option boards*. These plug into a row of sockets at the left rear of the system board. The sockets are called *option slots*, or *bus connectors*, and they represent one of the most important things about the PC, its open design.

The designers of the PC had to allow a way to connect various optional parts such as printers, telephone modems, and so forth. They could have made special-purpose connections for each option, but if they had, they would have reduced the flexibility of the PC and restricted the variety of things that we can add to our PCs. That would have made the PC something of a *closed* system, with only predefined possibilities. Instead, the connections inside the PC—like many aspects of the PC's overall design—are "open," meaning that their use isn't defined and limited in advance. What makes this possible is an engineering concept known as a *bus*, and it's important enough to discuss here.

The various silicon chips and other parts of the computer have to be connected to one another so that they can pass signals back and forth, or "talk" to each other. If the connections are made with individual wires, going from part to part as needed, then only those parts that have been wired to each other can communicate. There is another way to make these connections, that allows any part—particularly new parts that are added to the computer—to talk to any other part. This is done by setting up a common communication channel, a set of wires that act as a common carrier for signals passing from any part to any other. It's called a *bus* since all the signals ride on it.

The sockets at the back of the PC's system board are connected to all the lines of the PC's bus, so that anything we plug into these option slots can talk to every part of the PC that uses the bus, including the memory and the microprocessor. These option slots, or bus connectors, give us a way to plug in optional, additional equipment freely. This allows us to plug in practically any combination of equipment we want, plugging them in wherever we want. (You need to know that, for obscure technical reasons, some option boards work best in particular slots; in theory, all slots are equally good connections to the bus.) For some technical information on the bus, see the sidebar *What's in a Bus*.

TECHNICAL BACKGROUND ❘ ❘ ❘ ■ ■ ■ ▬▬▬▬▬▬▬▬

What's in a Bus

The bus used by the PC has a total of 62 separate lines, or wires, to it. They are identified by the codes A1 through A31 and B1 through B31; the numbering scheme corresponds to the physical layout of the lines on the option boards: the A side is on the right, the B on left, with the numbers running from back to front.

There is quite a variety of signals that are passed in all these lines. Five of them are used to pass the four different power voltages, with one voltage duplicated. Another three are used as ground lines to be used along with the power lines.

Eight of the lines are used to pass the eight bits of data in a byte, so that the PC bus can transfer data a byte at a time. Twenty of the lines are used for addressing, to indicate what part of the computer is being talked to. The addressing is used two ways: one is as a memory address and the other is as an I/O port address (which we'll discuss in Chapter 6). Whichever mode is being used, the address is signaled on these lines, while data passes on the eight data lines.

The remaining lines of the PC bus are used for a variety of control purposes. One indicates whether the bus is busy or free for use. Another set of lines handles *interrupt requests,* which are basically hardware signals indicating that one part of the computer or another needs attention. A pair of these interrupt lines, for example, are set aside to indicate activity on the first and second serial ports, known as COM1 and COM2.

The AT bus uses the standard PC bus and adds another 36 lines. The physical and electrical layout of the AT bus is designed to be compatible with the PC bus, so that the AT-class of machines can use as many PC option boards as possible. The 36 new lines are numbered C1 through C18 and D1 through D18, similar to the PC bus numbers. These extra lines provide more of what we've already seen: eight more data lines (since the AT has a 16-bit data path, over the PC's 8-bit data path), eight more address lines to extend the range of addressing, and five more interrupt request lines.

As you might imagine, there are many more technical details of the buses than we've covered here, but we've seen the essential parts.

Among the various models of PC there are some differences in the number and size of the slots and also the type of bus. There are actually three different buses used in the PC family. The main, or PC, bus is the bus used in the original PC, the XT, the Compaq, and most other models. The AT bus is an *extension* of the PC bus; it contains exactly the same connection lines as the PC bus *plus* some additional ones that are needed for the AT's 286 microprocessor. As an extension, the AT bus is a "superset" of the PC bus, and it can accommodate most option boards that were designed for the PC bus.

The third bus is peculiar to the PC*jr*. It's equivalent to the PC bus, with the addition of some *jr*-specific features such as a sound channel. The physical shape of the *jr* bus is different, and so is its location: the *jr* bus connection is out the right side of the system unit, instead of inside as it is for other PC models.

Option boards for the PC plug into the option bus connector slots and extend forward over the system board. The amount of space available inside the system unit determines how many slots there can be and how long each one is. The original PC had five slots, all the standard full-length (about 13 inches, 33 cm). The XT model increased the number of slots to eight, partly by squeezing them more closely together, and partly by tucking another slot next to the power supply. Because the disk drive sticks out in the way of this slot, only half-length short option cards can be fitted into this slot space. Some other models, such as the Portable PC, also have some slots that are too short to accommodate a full-length option card.

The next thing we come to in our logical diagram of the PC are the option boards, which we'll cover in Section 5.2.

Before we look at the variety of options that can be installed in our computers, I want to say one more thing about our diagram in Figure 5-1 to help you have a concrete sense of how a PC is constructed. The diagram in Figure 5-1 is a logical schematic that portrays in a block diagram the main parts of a PC; it isn't a true picture of what a PC is physically like. But I did draw this diagram so that it's not too much different from the actual layout of a PC. If you compare the diagram in Figure 5-1 with Figure 5-2, you'll easily see the correspondence between the logical parts of a PC and the actual physical form of a PC.

5.2 Options and Adapters

The option and adapter boards that can be plugged into the option slots in the PC allow us to create a wide variety of differently configured PCs. They give us great flexibility in creating just the kind of PC that we need. In this section we'll cover both the various option boards that we can use in the PC and also other optional equipment that goes along with them, such as different types of disk drives and display screens.

When we're talking about the *option boards* that are plugged into the expansion slots, it sounds as though we're only talking about extra features that we might or might not install in our PCs. That creates a false impression. Actually there are two standard option boards that normally are plugged into every PC: a disk drive adapter and a display screen adapter. Except under usual circumstances every PC has both of those. The disk drive adapter and the display screen adapter are key parts of a PC, and you'll find them both inside your PC.

Let's consider them separately, starting with the display adapter. The display adapter provides all the control circuitry necessary to convert the computer's commands to ''show this'' as a visible picture on the display screen. In essence the display adapter acts as a translator, converting computer-signals into video-signals.

The display adapter has two key components to it: one is a special silicon chip called a *video controller,* which has the special command skills needed to regulate a display screen. The other component is *memory.* As we'll see in more detail in later chapters, the information that appears on our display screens needs to be recorded in memory that's set aside just for that purpose. Although this memory operates like the computer's main working memory, the amount (and addressing) of the memory depends on the type of display adapter, so the display memory is made an integral part of the adapter.

There are many kinds of display adapters that can be used with the PC family. We'll summarize the five main ones, and then we'll leave more detail for later chapters that are devoted to video information.

The two dominant video adapters are the two that were introduced with the original PC: the *monochrome adapter* and the *color-graphics adapter* (CGA). The monochrome adapter is the most popular, even though it has the most limited capabilities. It can only show text characters (the full PC character set we covered in Chapter 4) and only in one color (although it provides some variety in how those characters are shown: it can display bright or dim characters, underlined, or in reverse image). The monochrome adapter has been the most popular because it creates much more legible characters on the screen than the color-graphics adapter. There is only one choice of display screen for the monochrome adapter, the monochrome display that was specially designed for use with the monochrome adapter.

The color graphics adapter is the second of the original two display adapters. It is designed to show both text characters and pictures (graphics) drawn from a series of fine dots. The color graphics adapter is able to show as many as 16 colors and it has several display modes (which we'll cover in later chapters) that provide a variety of combinations of color and screen resolution (which is how finely or crudely the picture is drawn). Although the CGA has a wider variety of skills than the monochrome adapter, it can't show ordinary text characters as clearly as the monochrome. The CGA can work with quite a few different display screens, including ordinary TV sets. Usually it's connected to a special-purpose color computer display known as an RGB monitor.

The portable versions of the PC have built-in display screens, so we don't have a choice of display adapters or screens for them. The IBM Portable PC comes with the color graphics adapter, and a single-color graphics screen. The Compaq comes with a similar single-color graphics screen, but its display adapter can simulate both the CGA and the monochrome adapter, giving it most of the best of both worlds.

After the original two video adapters, others were developed that provided better features, particularly higher resolution. The most popular one, by far, is the Hercules Graphics Adapter, made by Hercules Computer Technologies; it's popularly called "the Herc card." The Herc card connects only to a monochrome display screen, and it provides both the high-quality monochrome text image, and also a very high-resolution one-color graphics mode. The result is similar to what the Compaq provides, but with better quality graphics.

The other two display adapters that we need to mention are two advanced ones from IBM. The first is called the Enhanced Graphics Adapter (EGA for short). This is a do-anything board, which can be connected to a monochrome display, an RGB color display, or a special Enhanced Color Display (ECD). The EGA can act as either a monochrome adapter, or simulate the color graphics adapter, or it can perform its own special magic, which includes monochrome graphics (similar to the Herc card) and 64-color high-resolution text and graphics when it's used with the ECD. The other special display adapter is the high quality and very high priced Professional Graphics Adapter, which connects to an equally pricey Professional Graphics Display; this combination is intended for special-purpose graphics work that needs very high resolution and hundreds of colors.

That's the situation with the PC family's display adapters, which are the most complicated part of the options. The next standard part, which is also complex, is the disk drive adapter.

Disk drive adapters provide the same kind of service for disk drives that display adapters do for the display screen—they provide a control service, translating between the worlds of the disk drives and the rest of the computer. Like the display adapters, the complex circuitry in the disk adapter is based around one special chip, a special-purpose disk controller chip. Unlike the display adapters, the disk adapter does not have or need any special memory built into it.

There are two main types of disk drives—floppy disks and hard disks—and there are three kinds of drive adapters for them: adapters that handle one type or the other, and adapters that handle both. Unlike the display adapters, there's not much of interest to discuss about the disk adapters—but there are interesting things to know about the varieties of disk drives.

There are many, many kinds of disk drives. The best way to consider them is to divide them into simple categories. First, there are diskette drives that use the most common and standard 5¼-inch flexible (''floppy'') diskettes. (There are other sizes of floppies, larger *and* smaller, but they are rarely used with our PC family.) These are the standard diskette drives that nearly every member of the PC family includes. Even for these common drives there are two varieties: the now-obsolete single-sided drives (which only record on one side of a diskette) and double-sided drives. Next, there are high-capacity diskette drives, introduced with the AT, which can work with standard diskettes or special high-capacity (*hi-cap*) diskettes that hold over three times as much data. The final category of diskettes are 3½-inch micro diskettes; these are smaller and have more capacity than regular diskettes, and they come in a rigid (non-floppy) case, that protects them better.

The storage capacity of diskettes ranges from a low of 160K for single-sided diskettes to 1,200K, for high-capacity diskettes.

The next major type of disk is a *hard disk,* called a *fixed disk* by IBM. Hard disks have rigid, nonflexible magnetic platters, and they are able to store much more data and work much faster than a diskette. Unlike floppy diskettes, which can be taken in and out of their diskette drives, hard disks are permanently installed, which is why IBM calls them "fixed" disks. Hard disks have a capacity that ranges from a low of 5 or 10 megabytes up to hundreds of megabytes. The most common sizes are 10, 20, and 32 megabytes. The XT features a 10-meg disk, and the AT a 20-meg disk.

There is also a hybrid type of disk that you ought to know about, called a *disk cartridge*. This is a disk that can be removed like a floppy diskette, but it has most of the speed and capacity of a hard disk.

All these kinds of disks are so important to understanding and using our computers that we'll be devoting several chapters to them, digging into all their fascinating details.

The display and disk adapters that we've covered so far are only the beginning of the options that can be attached to our PCs. Now we'll start looking at the other main kinds of option boards.

One important kind is memory boards. While the computer's system board holds the computer's basic complement of memory, it doesn't hold all the memory that the computer can use. The amount of memory that can be placed on the system board varies from model to model—it might be as little as 64K or as much as 512K. Additional memory is added on with memory expansion boards. Most PCs will have a memory expansion board in them.

The next type of option boards are a pair called *parallel* and *serial ports*. A parallel port is designed specifically to work with a printer. A serial port is normally used to connect to either a telephone line (through a modem) or to a printer. Most computer printers are set up either to be connected to a serial port or to a parallel port. The parallel port is specialized for controlling a printer, but a serial port is more generalized and it can be used for a variety of purposes (though printers and telephones are the most common things to connect to it).

The options we've seen so far are the most common and the most important types of option boards. But there are many others that can be used as well. Among them are light pens, game adapters (which work with joystick controls for video games), mice (which are small hand controls used to provide a precise way of pointing on the display screen), and modems. Modems deserve a special mention.

For our computers to work with most devices (disks, printers, display screens), only one kind of translating circuit is needed. To connect a computer to a telephone, we need two; one is a serial port (which we've already mentioned) and the other is a modem. The job of a modem is to translate computer signals into telephone signals. Our computers can use an external modem connected to a serial port adapter card, or they can have an internal modem. An internal modem—such as the popular Hayes 1200B modem—combines a serial port and a modem translator into a single option board that can be plugged right into one of the computer's option slots.

The final kind of option board we need to mention is a kind that's suggested by the internal modem (which really combines a serial port and a modem), and that's a multi-function board. It's quite efficient to combine several option features into a single board; that's quite efficient—it uses one of the option slots, and typically it's much cheaper than separate single-purpose boards. There are many kinds of multi-function boards. Some combine a display adapter with a single parallel port; others provide several ports, serial and parallel. The most popular kind, though, are what I call kitchen-sink boards: they provide memory, serial ports, parallel ports, permanent clocks, game adapters, and perhaps even a comb and a shoe-shine rag.

This quick overview of the options that can be installed in a PC's bus connector slots should give you some idea of the range of possibilities that a PC can provide with the right equipment installed. In later chapters we'll cover the many features of the PC so we'll get a better understanding of how each of these optional parts works, and what they can do for us. Before we continue, we'll finish this discussion of the PC's hardware parts with some technical discussion of the chips that are the key working parts of the system board (and some of the option boards).

TECHNICAL BACKGROUND | | | ■ ■ ■ ▬▬▬▬▬▬▬▬▬

5.3 Key Chips

If you're interested in the details of electronic circuit design, or if you're just hungry for more of the fascinating details about the inner workings of the PC, you'll want to know about some of the key chips used in the design of the PC family.

One of the first things that you need to know is that there are very few custom chips in the PC: that was one of the biggest surprises that electronics experts and microcomputer buffs discovered when IBM first unveiled the original PC. Essentially, the entire design of the PC was accomplished using industry-standard circuit chips. Not just the microprocessor "brain" in the PC, but the *entire* PC was made from readily-available chips that had been used in other computer designs. That was quite a radical change for an IBM product. IBM usually goes its own way in the internal design of its computers. But the PC was a very different product for IBM, a product that ended up changing many things about the way IBM did business. A full discussion of that is a story for another time, but one aspect of it is a key part of our story here: all the parts that we discuss here are microcomputer parts that are familiar to circuit designers everywhere.

We'll concentrate on the two central models of the PC family, the original PC, the father of the PC wing of the family, and the original AT, the first of the AT-series. We'll begin with the main chips on the system boards of these two machines, which are outlined in Figures 5-3 and 5-4.

The primary chip is the microprocessor itself, which is an Intel 8088 in the PC (and the XT, the Portable PC, the Compaq and Compaq-Plus, and nearly all others in the PC branch of the family), and an Intel 80286 in the AT (and all the other members of the AT-branch). Other microprocessors are used in other family members: the 8086, the 80188, and the 80186.

Nestled next to the microprocessor is a socket space for an 87 chip, the numerical coprocessor, or Numeric Data Processor (NDP), with its special abilities to perform very fast and extra-accurate floating-point calculations. Relatively few PCs have the numeric coprocessor installed, but almost all members of the family have a socket to accommodate them.

The first pair of chips we're interested in has to do with the internal timing operations of the computer. One of them is called the *clock generator,* and it's primarily used to create the metronome beat that drives the basic operating cycle of the computer. In a PC the ID number of this chip is the 8284; in an AT it's the 88284. In either case, this chip provides the timing signal used by the rest of the computer to set the fundamental working pace. The clock generator chip uses a quartz crystal, like those in ''quartz'' watches, as the accurate basis for its timing. Our clock generator subdivides the crystal's ultra-fast beat into the fast beat needed by the computer, and puts it out in a form that other parts of the circuitry can use.

Closely related to the clock generator is the *programmable timer* chip, identified by the number 8253. The programmable timer is able to produce other timing signals that occur every so many clock cycles. The rate can be changed, which is what makes this chip ''programmable.'' If the computer's main clock runs at six million beats a second (which is the AT's actual clock rate), and we want something else to happen at six thousand times a second, we can program the timer chip with a count of 1000. This means that every thousand clock cycles, the programmable timer will put out a signal that will turn out to be six million divided by a thousand, or six thousand times a second. This facility of the timer chip can be used to produce regular timing signals for many purposes, including generating sounds on the speaker, as we'll see in a later chapter.

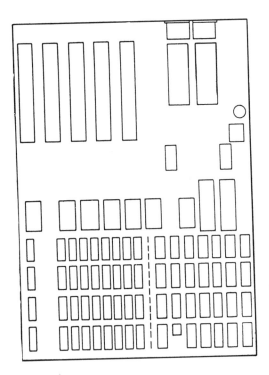

Figure 5-3. The PC system board.

We've mentioned how information signals flow among parts of the PC through a *bus*, and we looked at what the main bus channels are. To act as a traffic cop on the bus, to regulate the flow of information, our computers have a *bus controller* chip. On a PC this chip is known as the 8288; on an AT it's a 82288. The bus controller's job is to make sure the operation of the bus goes smoothly.

As we'll learn in more detail later in the book, some parts of the computer—particularly the disk drives—can exchange data directly with the computer's memory, without the data having to pass through the micro-processor. This helps keep the microprocessor free to get more work done. This process is called Direct Memory Access, or DMA. There is a special chip to facilitate this, called the DMA controller; its chip number is 8237.

Similarly, interrupts—which are a key feature of the PCs that we'll be discussing in Chapter 6—are supervised by a special circuit chip, the 8259. In computers, as in real life, interruptions come in varying degrees of importance, and one of the tasks of the 8259 interrupt con-

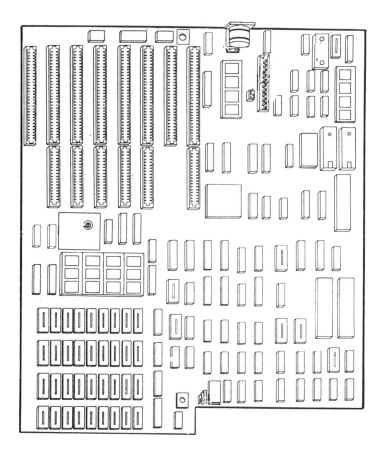

Figure 5-4. The AT system board.

troller is to keep them in priority order, and to hold any pending interrupts.

Another key chip is the *Programmable Peripheral Interface,* or PPI, the 8255 chip. The PPI supervises the operation of some of the computer's simpler peripheral devices, such as the PC's cassette tape port. Most computer peripheral devices, however, are much too complex to be regulated with a simple, common circuit.

Among them are the diskette drives. A key chip to facilitate the computer's working with diskette drives is the PD765 *Floppy Disk Controller,* commonly called the FDC. For the display screens, there is a commonly used chip called the 6845 CRT (cathode ray tube) controller. Both the standard monochrome display adapter and the original color graphics adapter (CGA) contain a 6845 as their key component. Later, more advanced display adapters usually have more custom components.

There are, of course, a great many other important chips used in the PC family, on the system boards, on the option boards, and also inside the peripheral parts (such as disk drives) themselves. But the chips we've briefly discussed are the most important ones, and the ones that you are most likely to read about if you dig into any of the technical publications for the PC family.

Some Things to Try

1. Why is the PC divided into three main parts,—the system unit, the keyboard, and the display screen? Some computers have the keyboard rigidly attached to the system unit. What are the advantages and disadvantages of building a computer this way? Some computers— including the portable members of our family, such as the Compaq and the Portable PC—have the display screen integral with the system unit. What are the advantages and disadvantages of building a computer this way?

2. The main family members have bus connectors for options located inside the computer's case. The PC*jr* has it coming out the right side, so that options are plugged in *externally*. For more than one option on a *jr*, they are plugged into each other, serially. How does that make things different for the *jr*? What are the advantages and disadvantages of the two ways of connecting options?

3. Several of the key chips mentioned in Section 5.3 are referred to as "programmable." What does this mean? What makes anything—one of these circuit chips, your TV set, or anything else—"programmable?" What might be the benefits of having some parts of the PC's circuits programmable? Are there any disadvantages?

6

Brains:
Our Microprocessors

Since the microprocessor is the key working part of a personal computer, if we want to understand our PCs, we need to understand the capabilities of the microprocessors that power them. As we saw in Chapter 1, the PC computer family is based on the Intel 8086 microprocessor family, and most members of the PC family specifically use the 8088 chip—so that's the microprocessor that we'll be talking the most about.

What we'll learn about the 8088, though, is pretty much universal to the whole 8086 family of microprocessors. In Section 6.5 we'll look into the special powers of the 286 microprocessor, which powers the AT branch of the PC family.

If you're deeply interested in the inner workings of your computer, or if you expect to be working at all with the PC's intimate assembly language instruction set, you already realize that you need to know the details of the PC's microprocessor that we'll be discussing here. If not, you might be wondering if it's worthwhile learning about such technical information. Frankly, for the day-to-day PC user who'll never even glance at any assembly language program code, there's no real need to learn what we'll be covering here. This chapter is for those who have an intellectual hunger to comprehend what's going on inside their PCs. The benefit from this chapter—besides the pure satisfaction of it—is that you'll have a better grasp of what the PC's powers are, including the important matter of understanding the limitations on that power.

6.1 What the Microprocessor Can Do

The best place for us to start is to take a look at what our microprocessor can do, its fundamental instruction set.

73

When *we* ask our computers to do anything, no matter what it is, it's a complex task from the computer's viewpoint. What the computer actually does is perform a series of steps built out of the computer's own instruction set. These basic instructions are called *machine language* or *assembly language*. (When it's in the form that programmers write it, it's called *assembly language*, and when it's in the form that the computer works with it's called *machine language*; either way, we're talking about the same thing.) One of the best ways to grasp the power of a computer is to see what its basic machine language instructions can do (and how quickly they can do them).

If we tried to look at them in depth, we'd get bogged down in lots of tedious details, the details that assembly language programmers have to work with. That isn't what we're after here; what we want to do is get a good working idea of what the computer's skills are. We'll start with simple arithmetic since arithmetic forms the basis for a great deal of what the computer does for us.

Our PC's microprocessors can perform the four basic operations of arithmetic: add, subtract, multiply, and divide. Addition and subtraction are the simplest operations, and by far the most common, particularly since they are used for many purposes besides the obvious ones (as we'll see shortly). Since our microprocessors are what's called 16-bit processors, we know that they can do their adding and subtracting on 16-bit numbers; but they can also perform arithmetic on individual 8-bit bytes. You might wonder why our computers can do both 8-bit and 16-bit operations. Since 16-bit operations are inherently more powerful, why bother with 8-bit numbers?

There are at least three good reasons for using 8-bit arithmetic instead of 16-bit. One is that if we know we'll be working with numbers that aren't any bigger than can be accommodated in an 8-bit byte, why use twice as much storage as is really needed? When we're working with lots and lots of numbers that could be stored in 8-bit bytes, the added efficiency of only using single bytes can be very worthwhile. Another reason for using 8-bit arithmetic appears when we want to work on individual bytes.

Here's an example. Sometimes we need to convert alphabetic character data to all uppercase; this is something that's needed more often than you might imagine inside the program we use. You'll recall from our discussion of the PC's character set in Chapter 4 that the lowercase letters are each 32 places above the uppercase letters in the ASCII coding scheme. A program can convert a lowercase letter into uppercase simply by subtracting 32 from the byte that holds the lowercase letter—and that's done with an

8-bit subtraction command. You can demonstrate this for yourself, by trying this simple command in BASIC:

```
PRINT "a", ASC ("a"), ASC ("a") - 32, CHR$( ASC ("a") - 32 )
```

Finally, there's a third good reason why our computers can do 8-bit arithmetic in addition to 16-bit arithmetic: it can be easily used as the building blocks of more powerful operations. For example, suppose we want to add and subtract numbers that are larger than 16 bits can handle. Say we need to work with numbers that are as large as 24 bits, or three bytes. We can see how the computer can do this by looking at how we ourselves add numbers together, say by adding 123 to 456. When we add numbers like that, we do it digit by digit, starting on the righthand side: so we add 3 to 6, getting 9, and then move left to the next place. If any pair of digits gives us a sum over 10, we *carry* 1 to the next place. Our computers can do the same thing using 8-bit arithmetic. With 8-bit addition and subtraction operations, our microprocessors can work with numbers of *any size*, byte-by-byte. Carries from one byte position to the next are handled by a special feature (which we'll hear of from time to time) called a *carry flag*. (For more on flags, see the sidebar *The PC's Flags* in Section 6.3.)

When we discussed data formats in Chapter 3, we mentioned that our 8- and 16-bit numbers can be treated as *signed* or *unsigned;* the signed formats allow for negative numbers, and the unsigned formats allow for bigger numbers. Our microprocessors have variations on the basic addition and subtraction operations that allow our programs to choose between 8- and 16-bit size, signed or unsigned values, and using or ignoring carries from previous operations. All of these operations concern the computer's basic *binary* number system. There are also some auxiliary instructions that make it practical for the computer to work with *decimal* numbers.

While our microprocessors handle just about every possible variation on addition and subtraction, they take a slightly less complicated approach to multiplication and division. We can multiply 8- or 16-bit (byte or word) numbers, and treat them as signed or unsigned. For division, we always divide a 32-bit (or double-word) dividend by an 8- or 16-bit dividend, signed or unsigned.

That's the basic arithmetic that our computers can do. If we need anything richer—such as larger numbers or floating-point format—then the arithmetic is usually handled by special-purpose subroutines that build a larger operation out of simple arithmetic building-blocks. The math coprocessors, the 87s, can also be used for some sorts of special arithmetic, as we'll see in Section 6.2.

Snooping at Code

If you want to learn more about the power and features of the PC's instruction set, there are several ways you can do it without having to go through the often difficult and tedious details of learning assembly language programming. It will require some cleverness on your part in deciphering some of the cryptic codes used in assembly language, but the effort can be richly rewarded in the satisfaction of knowing some of the most intimate details of how the PC works.

The trick is to get your hands on some assembly language programs that you can read and inspect to see just how things are done directly with the PC's instruction set. The best of all is to see some assembly language programming complete with the programmer's comments that explain a great deal about what is going on.

As it happens, we have available a fully annotated listing of the intimate ROM-BIOS programs that are built into the PCs. You'll find these listings in the *Technical Reference* manuals that IBM publishes for each model in the PC family.

If you can't get your hands on IBM's *Technical Reference* manuals, there is another way to see how some skilled programs were written: that's by decoding them (from their unintelligible *machine language* into the slightly more readable *assembly language*) using an "unassembler." One crude but usable unassembler is available to us as a part of DOS. It's included in the DEBUG program.

You can use DEBUG to "unassemble" any programs that you have access to, including the PC's built-in ROM programs. You'll find an example of how to do this later in this chapter in the sidebar *Looking at an Interrupt Handler*.

Our computer's microprocessors can do more than arithmetic, though arithmetic forms a great deal of the important core of the computer's operations. If all the computer could do was arithmetic (and other straightforward manipulation of data, such as just moving it around) then our computers would be nothing more than glorified adding machines. What makes our computers much more powerful than simple calculators is a variety of instructions known as computer *logic*.

The computer's logic operations allow it to adjust what's being done to the situation at hand. There are three main kinds of logic operations that our computer has in its repertoire: *tests, conditional branches,* and *repeats.* As an example, I'll let our computer play the role of a parking lot attendant.

If a parking lot charges, say, $1 an hour with a $5 maximum, the parking lot attendant has to calculate our hourly charge and then check to see if it's over the maximum. The attendant multiplies $1 times the number of hours we were parked and then *compares* the amount to $5. In computer logic, that comparison is the *test*, and the result of the test is noted in some special-purpose *flags*, like the *carry flag* that we've already mentioned. Generally the test is some form of arithmetic (such as comparing two numbers, which is the equivalent of subtracting one from the other to see which is bigger or if they are equal), and the flags that are used have an arithmetic-style meaning: the *zero flag* means the result of an arithmetic operation was zero, or that a comparison of two numbers found them equal. Similarly, the *sign flag* means the result was negative. These flags, which are the result of any general arithmetic operation, or any test comparison operation, set the stage for the second part of computer logic: *conditional branches*.

Conditional branches let the computer adjust its operation to the situation. A "branch" means a change in the sequence of steps the computer is carrying out. A conditional branch skips from one set of commands to another based on a "condition," such as how the flags are set. Our parking lot attendant computer, after comparing our hourly parking charge to the $5 maximum, charges us only $5 if the hourly charge was higher.

Conditional branches are used in computer programs in two quite different ways; the instruction, the conditional branch, can be the same, but the use it's put to is quite different. One use, which we've already seen, is simply to select between two courses of operation, such as charging the hourly rate or the maximum limit. The other way to use a conditional branch instruction is to control *looping*, or the repetition of a series of instructions. Our parking lot attendant computer, for example, will repeatedly perform the operation of parking a car, as long there are parking spaces available and customers waiting to leave their cars. The parking attendant will "loop" through, or repeat, the process of parking a car, as long as the *test* and *conditional branch* instructions show that there are cars to park and places to put them.

A regular conditional branch instruction can be used for either purpose—selecting between two courses, or controlling a loop—in a computer program, but because loops are so important to computer work, there are also special-purpose instructions that are custom made for the needs of looping: these are the *repeat* instructions. Some of them are designed to repeat a series of instructions, and some repeat just a single instruction, a tightly-coupled operation that can be executed with amazing speed and efficiency.

What we've seen so far of the instructions that our computer's microprocessors can perform is really just a short sampler of their full repertoire of commands—but it is a summary of the most important things that the computer can do, and it should give you some feeling for the basic building blocks that our programs are constructed out of. We should also get some sense of just how quickly our computers can carry out these instructions.

Here's a sampler of the speed it takes our computers to perform some basic instructions. For a standard PC, using the 8088 microprocessor, to add two numbers together can be done about one million times in a second; to multiply two numbers can be done about 40,000 times a second; a conditional branch can be done about a half-million times a second. On the average, a standard PC can perform perhaps a quarter-million instructions each second. For the much faster AT, using the 286 microprocessor, adding two numbers can be done two million times a second, or roughly twice as fast as in a PC; multiplying can be done about 300,000 times a second, or over *seven* times faster than a PC; a conditional branch can be done about 600,000 times a second. On the average, an AT knocks down perhaps one and a half million instructions a second, about five or six times the power of a standard PC.

Whether we're looking at a PC or an AT, that's an impressive amount of computing that can be dispatched in a second. However, we need to be aware that even the simplest thing that we ask our computers to do involves hundreds and thousands of individual detailed instructions to be performed. Since the computer can perform millions of instructions in seconds, our work should get done pretty quickly.

6.2 Math Auxiliary: the 87s

The PC family's microprocessors are designed in a way that lets their computing power be augmented with other processors, in two key ways. One—which we haven't yet seen in the PC family—allows several of the microprocessors (say two or more 8088s) to be tied together and work on the computing in cooperation. The other adds specialized "coprocessors" or auxiliary processors to perform work that the main microprocessor can't do well. There are actually two different types of coprocessors available for use with our PC's microprocessors. One type is specialized to take on much of the burden of I/O processing, and it *isn't* used in the PC family. The other type is specialized to perform extra-fast, extra high-precision floating-point arithmetic. These are the "87" chips—the 8087 for the regular PC branch of the PC family and the 80287 for the AT branch of the family—the Numeric Data Processor (NDP) or math coprocessor chips.

The 87 chips allow the main microprocessor to off-load appropriate number-crunching onto the 87's specialty circuits. But it can only happen, as we noted in Chapter 3, when there is an 87 installed in the PC, when we're using software that knows how to take advantage of the 87, and when there is suitable work for the 87 to do.

Nearly all members of the PC family are designed to accommodate an 87, but not many PCs have them installed. Usually they're installed only when there is a particular need for them: when there's a combination of heavy computational work to be done, and computer software that can take advantage of the 87.

On the subject of programs that know how to use the 87, it's worth knowing that there are two general categories of programs that use the 87: one is programs that *require* the 87 in order to be used, such as IBM's version of the APL programming language. Generally programs that require the 87 are oriented to engineering and scientific work. The other is programs that can take advantage of the 87 if one's installed. Many spreadsheet programs, such as 1-2-3 and Framework, are like this. Because more and more compilers for programming languages contain the ability to detect and use an 87—without any special effort needed on the part of the programmer—we're seeing an increase in the number of programs that benefit from an 87.

You should not expect, though, that installing an 87 in your computer will automatically accelerate the speed of the programs that you use. First, many programs simply have no use for an 87—for example, word processing programs. Second, even programs that we think could use the 87 heavily, don't. For example, Framework knows how to use an 87, but doesn't use it for routine spreadsheet calculations, rather only for exotic things like exponentiation.

What can an 87 math coprocessor, or Numeric Data Processor, do for us? Basically it can add both speed and accuracy to our calculations. The speed comes from the fact that the 87s produce their results roughly 50 to a 100 times faster than software subroutines can build the same calculation out of the regular microprocessor's conventional arithmetic commands. (That spectacular speed improvement is for the pure calculation itself. When you combine it with a program's routine operations, and some overhead that comes with using the 87, the advantage drops down to something in the five to twenty times range—less, but still very impressive.)

The added accuracy comes from the fact that the 87s do all their calculations with the 10-byte format that we briefly mentioned in Chapter 3. The main microprocessor can present data to the 87 in a variety of formats that we've mentioned—long and short integer, three sizes of floating point, and even a decimal format. The 87s actually do all their work in the longest 10-byte floating-point format (called, in computer jargon, *temporary real*), which means that any calculations done with the 87s are performed in the highest possible precision. Often that won't matter in the least, but in involved lengthy calculations, with demanding requirements for high precision, the 87 can add a great deal of accuracy to the results.

The 87s have one additional and curious benefit besides those we've mentioned. They offer some special features that go beyond the ordinary bounds of floating-point arithmetic in two ways. One is that the 87 has seven special constant values built into it, values such as *pi* that are commonly used in scientific calculations. Those built-in values are a convenience for programmers, and they provide a way to make sure that a standard, highly-accurate value is used to represent these seven mathematical quantities. The other special feature of the 87s is that besides the standard four arithmetic operations (add, subtract, multiply, and divide) the 87s have five other so-called *transcendental operations*, which are essential for performing trigonometric and logarithmic calculations. For scientific and engineering calculations, these special instructions reduce the burden of programming, and ensure that these calculations are performed in a standard way.

The 87s are called *coprocessors*, which means that they work as an auxiliary to the main microprocessor. It's interesting to know how this is done. The 87s act as a subsidiary of the microprocessor, and they only spring into action when the microprocessor generates a special signal for them. A special instruction, called ESCAPE, is used for the main microprocessor to pass a command to the 87 coprocessor. (By the way, don't confuse this special ESCAPE command with the escape character, decimal code 27, that we discussed in Chapter 4 as part of the PC's character set.) The main microprocessor's ESCAPE instruction includes in it the instruction code for whichever 87 instruction is to be performed. When the 87 receives its instruction, it begins performing independently of the main microprocessor (which is then free either to wait for the result from the 87 or to go on performing other tasks.) The sequence of steps involves a little dance of cooperation between the two chips, which is shown here in outline form:

- the microprocessor sets the 87 into action with an ESCAPE instruction

- the 87 swings into action leaving the main microprocessor free

- the microprocessor proceeds with other work (say preparing data for the next 87 instruction) if it has anything useful to do; otherwise, it proceeds to the next step

- when the microprocessor is ready for the results from the 87, it performs an FWAIT instruction, which waits for the completion of the 87's instruction (in case it's not yet done)

- after the FWAIT, the microprocessor can safely use the results of the 87's calculation

This sequence seems cumbersome, but it's easier than it looks. The only thing special about writing assembly language programs like this is that ESCAPE instructions are used instead of regular arithmetic instructions, and FWAIT instructions are added before using the results of the calculations. Of course only assembly language programmers have to bother with these details, anyway. For those of us who use programs that take advantage of the 87, all the fuss and bother is taken care of for us—we just get to enjoy the benefits the 87s provide.

TECHNICAL BACKGROUND | | ▮ ▮ ▮ ▮ ▬▬▬▬▬▬▬▬▬

The 87's Constants and Special Ops

As we mentioned, the 87s have built into them something more than just high-powered floating-point arithmetic: they also have a set of special constant values and transcendental operations that are especially useful for mathematics and engineering use. Here is what they are.

There are seven special constants. Two are quite ordinary: 0 and 1; they save us the trouble (and space) of storing these values in our program's data. One is familiar to everybody: *pi*, the ratio of the diameter to the circumference of a circle. The other four provide the basic values needed to work with logarithms, either in base 10 or the "natural" base mathematicians call *e*: $\log_2 10$ (the logarithm to the base 2 of 10); $\log_2 e$; $\log_{10} 2$; and $\log_e 2$.

The 87's special transcendental operations are needed to calculate functions that can't be built from ordinary, four-function arithmetic. Transcendental functions are usually calculated by approximate formulas, but these five built-in functions provide the basis for performing many different transcendental functions, without having to grind through an approximation formula (the standard approximations are built into the 87s). These are the five functions:

1. partial tangent
2. partial arctangent

3. $2^x - 1$ (2 raised to a power, minus one)

4. $Y * \log_2 X$

5. $Y * \log_2 (X + 1)$

These five functions may seem obscure to most readers—even those with vivid memories of mathematics classes—but we can rest assured that they do indeed provide the core of what is needed to calculate the most common transcendental functions.

6.3 Tools at Hand: Memory and Ports, Registers and Stacks

So far, we've talked about the kinds of operations our microprocessors can perform, by themselves and with the help of the 87 numeric coprocessors. Now it's time for us to take a look at the tools that the microprocessor has at its disposal to help it carry out these instructions and get useful work done. What we'll be looking at are how the microprocessor uses memory and ports, registers and stacks.

The computer's microprocessor has only three ways of talking to the world of circuitry outside of itself. One of the three is the special communication that it has with the 87 coprocessors through the ESCAPE command discussed in Section 6.2. The other two are much more ordinary, and they have a key role in the core of the computer's operation; these are the computer's *memory*, and the use of *ports*.

In Chapter 2 we saw that memory acts as the computer's desktop, its playing field, and workplace. The memory is the place where the microprocessor finds its program instructions, and where the microprocessor also finds its data. Both data and instructions are stored in memory, and the microprocessor picks them up from there. The memory is internal to the computer, and it's essential function is to provide a work space for the microprocessor. Since memory is so important, we'll take a deeper look at it in Chapter 7.

If memory is essential for the microprocessor's *internal* use, there has to be a way for the microprocessor to communicate with the world outside of it and its memory, and that is what *ports* are for. A port is something like a telephone line that the computer can call up on. Any part of the computer's circuitry that the microprocessor needs to talk to is given a port number, and the microprocessor uses that number like a telephone number to call up the particular part. For example, one port number is used to talk to the keyboard; another is used for the program-mable timer mentioned in Section 5.3. Controlling the disk drives and transferring data back and forth is also done through ports. The display screen is also controlled by using ports, but the data that appears on the display screen happens to be handled through memory, and not ports, as we'll see in Chapter 11.

The microprocessor has 65,536 port "telephone" numbers available for it to use. Not all of them are connected. The designers of any micro-computer, like our PC family, decide which port numbers to use for various purposes, and the circuit elements of the computer are wired up to respond to those port numbers. The computer's bus (which we covered in Chapter 5) is used something like a telephone party line, used in common by every part of the computer that is assigned a port number. When the microproces-sor needs to talk to one circuit part or another, it signals the port number on the bus, and the appropriate part responds.

The microprocessor has two special assembly language commands that are used to communicate with ports: the OUT command sends data to a port number, and the IN command requests data from a port number. Usually when we talk about assembly language instructions, such as these IN and OUT commands, there is nothing we can do to experiment with them unless we work directly with assembly language; but in the case of these two instructions, BASIC gives us two commands, called INP (*not* IN, but INP) and OUT, which do exactly what the assembly language instructions do. We can use them to experiment with our computer's ports, although it's very tricky to do. To give you a quick example, here is a short program that turns the PC's sound on and off, simply by using the ports (we'll learn more about how this works in a later chapter):

```
10 SOUND 500,1
20 X = (INP (97) \ 4) * 4
30 PRINT "Press any key to stop this infernal noise!"
40 OUT 97, X + 3 ' turn sound on
50 FOR I = 1 TO 250 : NEXT I ' kill time
60 OUT 97, X ' turn sound off
70 FOR I = 1 TO 250 : NEXT I ' kill time
80 IF INKEY$ = "" THEN GOTO 40
```

Give this program a try, and you'll have some firsthand experience in toying with the PC's ports!

Unless we're doing some very special and unusual kinds of program-ming, we'll never have any reason to do anything directly with ports. Ports are almost exclusively reserved for use by the computer's most intimate controlling programs, the BIOS. Our main interest in ports is to understand that they are the mechanism the microprocessor uses to talk with other parts of the computer's circuitry.

Here we'll discuss *registers* and *stacks*, the tools available to our computer's microprocessor to carry out its work. We'll start with the registers.

Registers are basically a small special-purpose kind of memory that the microprocessor has available for some particular uses. Registers are similar to the computer's main memory in one way: they are a set of places where data can be stored while the microprocessor is working on it. But the computer's main memory is large; it's located outside the microprocessor. It can be used for just about anything, and it's referred to through memory addresses; the registers are different in each of these respects.

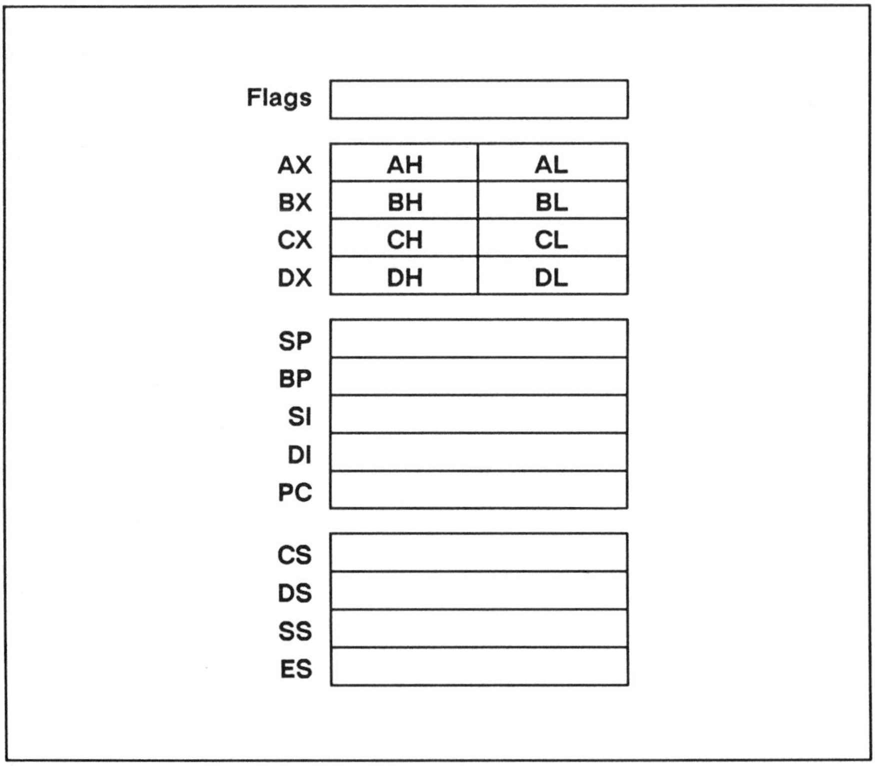

Flags		
AX	AH	AL
BX	BH	BL
CX	CH	CL
DX	DH	DL
SP		
BP		
SI		
DI		
PC		
CS		
DS		
SS		
ES		

Figure 6-1. The PC's registers.

The registers are a series of fourteen small 16-bit places where numbers can be stored. They are each an integral, internal part of the microprocessor. In effect, each of them is a small scratchpad that the microprocessor uses for calculations and record keeping. Some of them are dedicated to one special use, while others have a broad, general use. We'll take a quick overview of them all, so that you're familiar with them, and so you'll know what they are when you see them referred to. Their actual use, however, really only matters to assembly language programmers.

The first group of registers is called the *general-purpose registers*, and they are truly used as scratchpads for calculations. There are four of them, known as AX, BX, CX, and DX. Each of them can be used by our programs as a temporary storage area and scratchpad for calculations. Each of these registers is 16 bits in size. If we want to work with just half of any of these registers, we can easily do so, because they are divided into high- and low-order halves, called AH and AL, BH and BL, and so forth. A great deal of the work that goes on inside our computers takes place in these general-purpose registers.

The next group of four registers is used to assist the microprocessor in finding its way through the computer's memory. These are called the *segment registers*. Each one is used to help gain access to a section, or *segment* of memory, 64K bytes big. The *Code Segment*, or CS register, indicates where in memory a program is located. The *Data Segment*, or DS register, locates data that a program is using; the *Extra Segment*, or ES register, supplements the data segment. The *Stack Segment*, or SS register, locates the computer's stack, which we'll discuss shortly. We'll get a clearer idea of the use of these registers in Chapter 7 when we take a closer look at memory.

While the segment registers are used to gain general access to large 64K chunks of memory, the last group of registers is used to help find our way to specific bytes in memory. They are used, in conjunction with a segment register, to point to an exact place in memory. There are five of these registers, each used for a particular purpose. The *Instruction Pointer*, IP, also called the *Program Counter*, PC, tells the microprocessor just where its place is in the program being executed. The *Stack Pointer*, SP, and the *Base Pointer*, BP, are used to help keep track of work in progress that's stored on the stack (coming shortly). The *Source Index*, SI, and *Destination Index*, DI, are used to help our programs move large amounts of data from one place to another.

Finally there is one remaining register, called the *Flag Register*, that is used to hold the condition flags that we talked about earlier. The various flags tell our programs just what state the computer is in: the results of arithmetic operations, whether interruptions are allowed, and similar status conditions.

TECHNICAL BACKGROUND | | █ ■ ■ ■ ▐▀▀▀▀▀▀▀▀▀▀▀▀▀▀▀▀▀

The PC's Flags

The PC's microprocessors are largely controlled through a series of 1-bit flags, each of which signals or sets a particular state in the computer. The flags operate independently of each other, but they are, for convenience, gathered together into the *Flag Register*. Individual flags can be tested and set with special-purpose instructions, and the entire group of flags can be read out or set with a pair of instructions that read or set the entire flag register.

Here is what the individual flags are used for: There are nine standard flags in all. Six are used to indicate the results of arithmetic and similar operations: the Zero Flag, ZF, indicates a zero result (or equal comparison); the Sign Flag, SF, indicates a negative result; the Carry Flag, CF, indicates a carry out to the next position; the Auxiliary Carry Flag, AF, indicates a carry from the first four bits (which is needed for simulating decimal operations); the Overflow Flag, OF, indicates a too-large result; and finally, the Parity Flag, PF, indicates the odd or even parity of the result.

The three other flags are used for control purposes. The Direction Flag, DF, controls which way repeated operations (such as a byte-by-byte data move) go, right to left or left to right. The Interrupt Flag, IF, controls whether or not interrupts are allowed or temporarily suspended. The Trap Flag, TF, causes the computer to generate a special "trap" interrupt after executing a single instruction. This makes it possible to single-step through a program, tracing the results of each individual instruction.

In addition to these nine flags, the advanced 286 microprocessor used in the AT branch of the PC family adds two more special flags. One, called NT, is used for nested tasks, and the other, a two-bit flag called IOPL, controls the I/O privilege level.

You can see and tinker with the flags, and all the other registers, by using the **R** command of DOS's DEBUG program. For example, if you activate DEBUG, then press R and ⟨*enter*⟩, DEBUG displays the current register contents and the setting of all the flags.

There is one remaining tool at the command of the microprocessor which allows it to perform the complicated juggling act needed for the computer to do all the things that we want it to do. As the computer is working, it gets buried in an increasingly complicated stack of work, and it needs a way to keep track of where it is and what it's doing. To switch from one part of the computer's work to another, the computer needs a way to put work on hold, not lose sight of it. The *stack* serves as a computerized holding area that records all the information that's current about what the computer has been doing. When the computer passes into a subroutine, or temporarily interrupts one task to look after another, the stack is used to take note of "where was I and what was I doing" so that the computer can return to it with no difficulty. As the computer switches to something new, information about it is placed on *top* of the stack, indicating what's current. Later, when the computer returns to prior work, the other information is removed from the stack, and the prior work now reappears as the first thing on the stack.

We've looked at what our microprocessors can do—the general power and features of their instruction set—and some of the tools that they have to help them do it—the memory and the stacks and so forth—but we have barely mentioned a key driving force to make our computers work: interrupts. That's what we'll look at next.

6.4 Interrupts: The Driving Force

One of the key things that makes a computer different from any other kind of machine that mankind has built, is that computers have the ability to respond to an unpredictable variety of work that comes to them. The key to this ability is a feature known as *interrupts*.

The interrupt feature allows the computer to suspend whatever it is doing, and switch to something else, based on something that causes the interruption—such as our pressing a key on the computer's keyboard.

The ability to be interrupted solves what would otherwise be a very difficult problem in getting the computer to work effectively for us. On the one hand, we'd like the computer to be busy doing whatever work we've given it; on the other hand, we'd like it to instantly respond to any request for its attention, such as our pressing keys on the keyboard. If the computer could only slog along doing just what it's been told to do in advance, it couldn't respond promptly to our keystrokes unless it was constantly checking the keyboard for activity. Interrupts, however, make it possible for the microprocessor to respond to keystrokes—or anything else that needs attention—even though it's busy working on something else.

The computer's microprocessor has built into it the ability to be interrupted, combined with a convenient way of putting the work that's been interrupted on hold while the interrupt is being processed. The microprocessor's stack, which we looked at in Section 6.3, is used for this: when an interruption occurs, a record of what the microprocessor was doing at the time is stored on the stack, so that when the interruption is finished work can resume exactly where it left off. This is one of several uses the stack is put to, and it's a very key one. Without the stack as a place to put work on hold, the whole idea of interrupts couldn't work.

Every part of the computer which might need to request the microprocessor's attention is given its own special interrupt number to use. The keyboard has its own interrupt, so that every time we press a key on the keyboard (or, interestingly enough, *release* a key we've pressed), the microprocessor finds out about it, thanks to the keyboard interrupt. The PC's internal clock also has its own interrupt to let the computer's time-keeping program know each time the clock has ticked—which is about 18 times each second. That sounds like a lot of interruptions, and we'd be inclined to think that being interrupted 18 times a second would harass the computer to death. However, the microprocessor can perform tens of thousands of instructions between each clock tick, the clock interrupts don't take up much of the microprocessor's time. Our computer's disk drives and printers have their own dedicated interrupt numbers, too. The disks use theirs to signal that they have finished some work the program asked to be done; the printers use theirs to signal when they are out of paper.

It's an interesting and curious fact about the history of computers that interrupts were not part of the original concept of a computer. In fact computers had been used for decades before the interrupt feature came into widespread use. Today it's hard to imagine a computer doing much of anything useful without the interrupts that make it possible for the computer to respond to demands for its attention.

Although interrupts are used to make the microprocessor respond to outside events—such as the printer running out of paper—that isn't the only thing that they are used for. The concept of an interrupt has turned out to be so useful that it has been adapted to serve a variety of purposes inside the computer. There are essentially three different kinds of interrupts that are used in our PC computers. The first is the kind we've already discussed: an interrupt that comes from another part of the computer's circuitry reporting something that needs attention. This is called a *hardware interrupt*. But there are two other kinds of interrupts relating to software programming.

Sometimes, while the computer is running one of our programs, something goes wrong with either the program itself or with the program's data. It's as if you were just reading along on this sentence then suddenly you found yourself reading glepty murph bofa—some jibberish that didn't make any sense. That can happen to the computer too, although it's not supposed to. The microprocessor might run into some instructions that don't make any sense, or some data that drives it wild (such as trying to divide a number by zero). When this happens, the microprocessor generates what I call an *exception interrupt*.

The last category of interrupt, unlike the others, doesn't occur unexpectedly. The whole idea of interrupts is so powerful, that they have been put to use as a way of letting programs signal that they want some service to be performed by another part of the computer's programs. This type is called a *software interrupt*. We've mentioned before that our PCs come equipped with built-in service programs called the ROM-BIOS. Our computer's application programs need a way to request the services that the BIOS provides, and software interrupts are the means that are used. Software interrupts function in exactly the same way as the other kinds of interrupts. The only thing that's different about them is what causes the interrupt. In this case, instead of happening unexpectedly, software interrupts are intentionally generated by our programs. There is a special assembly language instruction, called INT, that is used by our programs to request an interrupt. (To learn more about the surprisingly wide variety of uses for interrupts, see the sidebar *Another Look at Types of Interrupts*.)

Another Look at Types of Interrupts

There is a wider variety of types and uses for interrupts than you might imagine. In the text I outline three categories of interrupt: *hardware, exception,* and *software*. But there is another way of looking at interrupts that cuts closer to the way they are used in the PC family. By this analysis, there are *six* different kinds of interrupts.

First, there are the *Intel hardware interrupts*. These are the interrupts that are defined into the microprocessor by its designer, Intel. These interrupts include the divide-by-zero interrupt we mentioned before, a power-failure interrupt, and others. These interrupts are universal to any computer using the Intel 8088 microprocessor, no matter how unlike the PC family the computer might be.

Next are the *IBM-defined PC hardware interrupts*. These are interrupts that report hardware events (e.g., ''printer out of paper'' or ''disk action completed'') to the microprocessor. The PC hardware interrupts are essentially universal to the PC family.

Then there are the *PC software interrupts*. These are also defined by IBM and universal to the whole PC family. They are used to activate parts of the PC's built-in ROM-BIOS software, for example, to display a message on the computer's screen.

Then there are *DOS software interrupts*. Unlike the previous three types, these interrupts aren't built into the computer, they are added on by software: in this case by the DOS operating system. Since we normally use the same operating system all the time, these interrupts are, in reality, there all the time, even though they aren't fundamental to the computer's operation. These interrupts are defined and handled by routines internal to DOS (or any other operating system that we might be using.)

Next are the *application software interrupts,* which are established temporarily by the program we run (including BASIC, which uses quite a few of its own special interrupts). These interrupts are defined (and handled) by the application program that we use.

The sixth and final category is an odd one, because it doesn't truly involve interrupts at all. These are the so-called *table interrupts*. As we'll see in Chapter 7, part of the interrupt mechanism involves a "vector table" which holds the memory addresses of the interrupt handlers. There are some addresses in this table, however, that have nothing to do with interrupts. Instead, the address table is used as a convenient place to store some important addresses which actually have nothing to do with interrupts. For each of these, there's a corresponding interrupt number, but one that can never be used, since there's no interrupt handling routine for it.

Just how does an interrupt work? Let's take a look, in outline form, to see what the interrupt mechanism does. Each distinct interrupt is identified by an interrupt number, which identifies the type of interrupt. For example, one interrupt number is used for the disk drives (all the drives share the same interrupt). The clock, the keyboard, and the printers each have their own. For the BIOS services, they are grouped by category; for example, there are over a dozen different BIOS services for different operations on the display screen, but they all share one interrupt number.

For each different interrupt number that's been established for the computer there is a special program, called an *interrupt handler*, that performs whatever work the interrupt requires. A special table is kept at the very beginning of the computer's memory that records the location of each interrupt handler. When an interrupt occurs, the interrupt number is used to look up the proper interrupt-handling program. Before the interrupt handler begins work, however, the microprocessor's interrupt-processing mechanism saves a record (on the stack) of what work was in progress. After that is done, control of the microprocessor switches over to the interrupt-handling routine.

The interrupt handler begins its operation temporarily protected from further interruptions, in case it has to perform any critical or delicate operations that must not be disrupted. Usually this involves changing the *segment registers* that control memory access, and saving on the stack any further status information that's needed besides what is automatically saved when the interrupt begins. Once that's done, the interrupt handler can safely reactivate further interrupts (of other types) and do whatever work the interrupt calls for. When the work is done, the interrupt-handling routine restores the status of the machine to what it was before the interrupt occurred, and finally the computer carries on with the work it was doing. If you'd like to have a look at part of an interrupt handler, see the sidebar *Looking at an Interrupt Handler*.

TECHNICAL BACKGROUND | ▪ ▪ ▪ ▪ ▪

Looking at an Interrupt Handler

To give you an idea of what some of the program code in an interrupt handler looks like, we'll show you some of it here. This fragment is ''unassembled'' from the ROM-BIOS of an AT model. The particular code we'll show you is taken from the beginning of the routine that handles requests for video (or display screen) services.

We begin by activating the DEBUG program, like this:

DEBUG

Then we tell DEBUG to ''unassemble'' some program code, which translates the computer's machine language into the slightly more readable assembly language format. I happen to know where to find the routine I want to show you, so I tell DEBUG to unassemble it at the hex address where I know it is:

U F000:3605

In response, DEBUG gives us an unassembled listing, which looks like this (I'll talk our way through it in a moment):

```
F000:3605 FB          STI
F000:3606 FC          CLD
F000:3607 06          PUSH    ES
F000:3608 1E          PUSH    DS
F000:3609 52          PUSH    DX
F000:360A 51          PUSH    CX
F000:360B 53          PUSH    BX
F000:360C 56          PUSH    SI
F000:360D 57          PUSH    DI
F000:360E 55          PUSH    BP
```

```
F000:360F 50        PUSH   AX
F000:3610 8AC4      MOV    AL,AH
F000:3612 32E4      XOR    AH,AH
F000:3614 D1E0      SHL    AX,1
F000:3616 8BF0      MOV    SI,AX
F000:3618 3D2800    CMP    AX,0028
```

The very first column (F000:3605, etc.) is a set of reference addresses, which we can ignore. The next column of information (FB FC 06, etc.) is the actual machine language code, in hex. Following this is what we're interested in: the assembly language equivalent of the program code we've unassembled. I want to give you a short running narrative on this, so that you get an idea of what assembly language code, particularly the code inside an interrupt handler, is like.

It begins with the instruction STI, which reactivates interrupts. When an interrupt occurs, further interrupts are suspended in case the handler needs to do anything critical. In this case, there's nothing important to do, so the handling of other interrupts is turned on first.

The next instruction, CLD, sets the direction flag (which we discussed in *The PC's Flags* sidebar) to its normal, forward state. This makes sure that any data movement the program performs goes forward, not backward. This isn't a particularly important operation to us, but it's interesting to see that the programmer took the time to make sure the direction flag was set forward before anything else was done.

Following that is something much more interesting to us: a series of nine PUSH instructions. The PUSH instruction saves data on the computer's stack. You'll see that each of these nine PUSH instructions names a register (ES, DS, etc) that is being saved. These register values are being saved on the stack, so that this interrupt handler can be sure they are safeguarded. When the interrupt handler is done, it restores these values from the stack to the registers, so that no matter how the registers have been used in the interim, they are returned to their former state.

Following the register-saving PUSH operations, we find four data manipulating instructions (MOV, XOR, SHL, MOV) which do one simple thing: they grab a number and prepare it for comparison. Although it's not easy to tell just by looking at these instructions, what is going on here is fairly simple: there are a variety of display screen services which this interrupt handler can provide, and they are identified by a request code number. Before proceeding, the program gets its hands on that code number and puts it into the form that this program wants it in. That's what these four instructions do.

Having done that, the interrupt handler needs to make sure that the service code requested is a proper one, and that's what our last instruction does. Using the CMP (compare) instruction it compares the number with the value 28, which is the highest number corresponding to a proper service request. After that, the program goes on to branch on the basis of that test, either performing the service requested, or rejecting the invalid service number.

This isn't an in-depth look at assembly language code, but it should give you a sampling of what assembly language looks like, and how to go about decoding some. You can use the same techniques shown here to inspect other parts of your computer's ROM-BIOS or other programs.

Interrupt handlers, for the most part, appear in the computer's built-in ROM-BIOS programs or as a part of the operating system, like DOS. But they aren't restricted to just those *systems* programs. Our *applications* programs—word processors, spreadsheets, and the like—can also have their own interrupt-handling routines, if they have a need for them. Any program can create an interrupt handler, and use it either to replace a standard interrupt handler (so that its interrupts are handled in some special way) or to create a new kind of interrupt.

In the heading of this section, I described interrupts as the *driving force* of the PC. This is actually a very accurate characterization. Modern computers like our PCs, which are designed to use interrupts, are called, in the terminology of circuit designers, "interrupt driven." That's because interrupts are used as the mechanism that connects the computer to the world around it (including us). Interrupts *drive* the computer, because, one way or another, all the work that comes to the computer comes to it in the form of interrupts. More importantly, the whole internal organization of the computer is designed around interrupts as the controlling factor that determines just where the microprocessor will turn its attention. Since the flow of interrupts directs the computer's attention to where it's needed, it's quite accurate to think of them as the *driving force* behind the whole machine.

Now that we've seen interrupts, we've looked at all the basics that concern our PC's microprocessors. We've covered the key things that are common to every member of the Intel 8086 microprocessor family, which our PC computer family is based on. But, as we've been mentioning, the AT branch of the PC family uses the Intel 286 microprocessor, the most advanced member of the 8086 family, and the 286 has some special features that don't come with the standard PC's 8088 microprocessor. To finish up our discussion of the PC family's microprocessors, we'll see what's special about the 286 "super chip."

6.5 Special Features of the 286

The Intel 286 microprocessor chip, which powers all the members of the AT branch of the PC family—including the IBM AT and the Compaq Deskpro-286, among others—has two personalities, and that is the key to its special power. One personality makes it act like the 8088 microprocessor that powers a standard PC; the other personality allows the 286 to take on extra powers and features that set it completely apart from anything else. These two personalities are known as the *real mode* and the *protected mode*.

In its "real" mode, the 286 acts very much like the 8088 microprocessor that's inside a standard PC. (To be more precise, the 286 acts like an 8086, since it works with a 16-bit external memory bus, rather than an 8-bit bus, which is the difference between the PC's 8088 and the Compaq Deskpro's 8086. That's a minor point; the key thing about the 286's real mode is that it has the same features and carries out programs in the same way as the 8088 inside a standard PC.) In real mode, the 286's special features and special powers are in disguise, so that a computer with a 286 running in real mode can be fully compatible with a normal PC.

Don't think that the 286 in real mode is nothing to be interested in. The 286 in real mode is inherently much more powerful than a 8088 simply because it can execute programs much faster. The 286 is faster for a combination of two reasons: First, its internal design is more streamlined, so that it performs its instructions in fewer steps, fewer clock cycles. For example, a basic multiply operation takes about 120 clock cycles on a 8088, but only about 20 cycles for a 286, a very dramatic difference. The 286 is internally much more efficient, so it gets its work done faster. The other reason for the increased speed is simply that the 286 can run with a faster clock cycle. A standard PC uses a 4.77 Mhz clock—in plain English this means that the clock that drives the microprocessor like a metronome clicks 4.77 million times each second. A 286, on the other hand, can run faster. In the case of the IBM AT model, the clock speed is 6 Mhz, a 25 percent faster clock speed than the PC's; in the case of the Compaq Deskpro-286, the clock can run at 8 Mhz, 67 percent faster than the PC. When we combine the 286's greater efficiency in using clock cycles with a faster clock, we get a much faster overall speed. In my own experience, using a performance testing program that is a part of my Norton Utilities program set, a 286-based member of the PC family is roughly 5 to 8 times faster than a standard PC.

So we know that the 286 microprocessor working in real mode is nothing to sneer at. But it also doesn't offer anything (other than speed) that the standard PC's 8088 offers. For extra features, we have to switch into *protected* mode.

In protected mode, the 286 adds a series of features that allow it to safely and reliably expand the number of programs the computer can be working on at one time. This is accomplished through four main facilities: *protection* (which gives protected mode its name), *extended memory*, *virtual memory*, and *multi-tasking*.

Protection allows the operating system (such as DOS) to erect barriers to prevent a program from interfering with the operation of other programs or of the operating system itself. In a standard PC, or with a 286 running in real mode, a rogue program can mess up the workings of the operating system or any other program that's using the computer, or it can even lock up the computer entirely, halting its operation. The 286's protected mode makes it possible for the operating system to prevent any program from "crashing" the computer or even tampering with any part of memory that doesn't properly belong to it. When we use our computers for just one program at a time, it doesn't matter a great deal if a program runs wild and locks up the machine. But if we want to have several things going on in the computer at one time, it becomes much more important to protect the computer's operation from rogue programs. The protection feature makes that possible.

The standard PC—as we'll see in more detail in Chapter 7—can only work with a million bytes of memory (and about 40 percent of that is set aside for special uses, and not available for general use). A million bytes may sound like a lot (and it is), but with computers, people always need more. The 286's protected mode provides more memory, in two ways. First, with *extended memory*, the 286 allows up to sixteen million bytes of working memory to be installed in the computer. Second, with *virtual memory*, the 286 can simulate—or appear to have—even more memory than is actually present. Virtual memory allows the computer to give each program as much as one billion bytes (one *giga*byte, in computer jargon) to work with. That's a lot of memory.

Finally, with hardware-supported *multi-tasking*, the 286 can swiftly and reliably switch among several programs that are running at the same time. Multi-tasking is involved when a computer is working on more than one program (task) at a time. In actual fact, in each instant the computer is only carrying out the instructions of one program at a time, but with multi-tasking all the programs are kept in progress, much the same way that a juggler can keep many balls in the air at one time. Any computer can attempt to do multi-tasking, but it can't be done well without some special hardware features (such as memory protection). The protected mode of the 286 provides a variety of features that make it practical for the computer to do multi-tasking work.

While these special features of the 286 are very important, and represent a real breakthrough in what our PC computers can do, they aren't quite as beneficial as they might seem to be. Basically that's because the use of protected mode requires that programs work in a fairly cooperative way. Because the features of protected mode were not present in the standard PC, most of the popular programs for the PC family were designed and written without any regard for the ground rules that protected mode requires. Many of the most important PC programs assume that they have the exclusive use of the computer, and so they do things that can't be done when several programs share the computer (as they do with multi-tasking). In addition, the main operating system for the PC, DOS, was not designed with the 286's protected mode in mind.

What all of this means is that the popular programs and operating systems for the PC aren't really compatible with the 286's protected mode, and in many cases it won't be easy to adapt them to work in a protected environment. As long as the important majority of programs for the PC family aren't compatible with the protected mode, there will be a serious obstacle to the widespread use of the protected mode's advantages.

Some Things to Try

1. We've discussed how our PC's microprocessors can do both 8- and 16-bit arithmetic. Is it really necessary to have both? What might be the benefit and cost of only having one or the other? What would be the benefit and cost of adding 24-bit or 32-bit arithmetic?

2. We've seen, in the PC's arithmetic and in its logic looping instructions, some duplication: a variety of instructions that could be simplified into fewer instructions. What might be the advantages and disadvantages—both for the computer's designers and programmers—of making a computer with lots of instructions (that provide many different ways of doing roughly the same thing) or with very few instructions (which allow for just one way of doing things)?

3. Few PCs have the 87 numeric coprocessor installed, and few programs can take advantage of the 87. Why do you think that came about? What might have made the 87 more popular?

4. Using BASIC's INP and OUT commands, write a program to blindly explore the PC's ports. Do you find anything interesting?

5. In the *Looking at an Interrupt Handler* sidebar, we show how to use the DEBUG U (unassemble) command. Try using it on the PC's built-in BASIC language, which is located at memory address F600:0. (Note: this works on IBM models of the PC family, but not on compatibles.)

7

The Memory Workbench

Now it's time for us to get to know our computer's memory. In this chapter we'll quickly look at what memory is and how data is stored in it. Then we'll look into the complex but fascinating details of how our programs gain access to the memory. We'll see how the PC's designers subdivided the memory into different uses, and then we'll take a look at two different kinds of additions to the PC's memory. Sounds like a lot—but it's all intriguing.

7.1 Memory Overview

We already know, from earlier parts of this book, most of the underlying ideas about our PC computer's memory, so we really don't need to introduce you to the fundamentals of computer memory. But, to help make sure that we're on the right track, let's pause briefly to summarize the key things that we know about computer memory. Then we'll be ready to dive into the really interesting details of the memory's ins and outs.

The computer's memory is a scratchpad where working information—which includes both program instructions and data—is kept while it is being worked on. For the most part what's in the computer's memory is temporary working information, nothing permanent (for the exception, see the discussion of read-only memory later in the chapter).

Our computer's memory is organized into units of bytes, each made up of eight bits. With eight On-Off, Yes-No bits in a byte, each byte can take on 256 distinct values. No matter what kind of information we are storing in the memory, it is coded in some particular pattern of bits, which are interpreted in whatever way is appropriate to the kind of data. The same bit pattern can be seen as a number, or a letter of the alphabet, or as a particular machine language instruction, depending upon how we interpret it. The same memory bytes are used to record program instruction codes, numeric data, or alphabetic data.

While the computer's memory is divided into bytes as its basic unit, the bytes can be combined in any way that is needed to create larger aggregates of information. One of the most important is called a *word*, which is two bytes taken together to form a single 16-bit number. (For an interesting side-light on that, see the sidebar *How Words are Stored*.) When we interpret a series of bytes together as alphabetic text, it's called a *character string*. There are endless ways to combine bytes into meaningful data, but these are some of the most important.

In order to be able to work with the computer's memory, each byte of the memory has an *address*, a number that uniquely identifies it. Most of what we'll be concerned with in this chapter is really just one aspect or another of the memory's addressing. The memory addresses are numbered one by one, beginning with zero as the first address. The same numbers that are used as computer data can also be used to specify memory addresses, so that the computer can use its ability to do arithmetic to find its way through its own memory. This integration of arithmetic, data, and memory addressing gives the computer an astonishingly compact and flexible power to perform work for our benefit.

That's the essence of the computer's memory. Now, let's uncover the amazing workings of our PC family's memory.

How Words are Stored

If you plan to do any exploring of the computer's memory, or you're going to be working with assembly language, or if, like me, you just want to know everything about your computer, you need to know about what's whimsically called *back-words* storage.

When we write down either numbers or names, we write it with what's called the *most significant* part first. That's the part that matters the most when we arrange names or numbers in order. In the number "1776", the "1" is the most significant, or high-order part; in the name "California," the "C" is the most significant letter.

In our PC computers, it doesn't go exactly that way. For character string data, which is the format we'd use to store names like "California"—the most significant letter is stored first, in the left-most byte (the byte with the lowest address), just the way we write names. However, numbers are stored the other way around. For numbers that take up more than one byte (such as a 16-bit, 2-byte *word* number), the *least* significant byte is stored first. In effect, the number we know as 1776 is stored in the computer as "6771."

(Please don't take that example too literally for reasons we'll see in a moment.)

This way of storing numbers has been called "back-*words*," to indicate that a *word* (a 16-bit, 2-byte integer) has its bytes stored backwards from what we might expect. This doesn't just apply to 2-byte words; it also applies to longer integer formats, such as 32-bit, 4-byte "long" integers. And it also applies inside the complex bit-coding that's used to represent floating-point numbers.

While our PCs can work with any numerical format, the one that they use the most is the *word* format that occupies two bytes. That's because 16-bit words are used in every aspect of the PC's memory addressing (as we'll see in more detail in Section 7.2) and because 16-bit words are the largest numbers that the PC's instruction set handles.

To explain the idea of back-words storage, I gave the example of the (decimal) number 1776 written back-words as 6771. But that doesn't exactly tell us what's going on. Back-words storage concerns *binary integers* stored in reverse order *byte-by-byte*. When we see binary integers written down, we see them in hex notation, which uses two hex digits for each byte. For example, our decimal number 1776 in hex is 06F0, when we write it front-wards. To write the same hex number back-words, we don't reverse the order of the individual hex digits, we reverse the bytes (which are represented by *pairs* of digits). Hex 06F0 back-words is F006 with the two hex pairs (06 and F0) reversed.

Knowing about this back-words storage is more that just a matter of simple intellectual curiosity. Anytime you may be working with computer data represented in hexadecimal, you have to be alert to whether you're seeing numbers represented front-wards (the way we write them) or back-words (the way they are actually stored). Generally speaking, whenever data is formatted for our consumption, it will be in front-wards order; but whenever it's being shown *as stored in the machine*, it will be back-words. We have to be careful that we don't get confused about which way we're seeing it.

Here's an example of how we'd be shown a number in both forms. If we work with some assembly language, using either DEBUG or the Assembler, and we have an instruction to move the hex value 1234 into the AX register, we'd see something like this:

```
B8 3412        MOV  AX, 1234H
```

On the right-hand side we see the number in human-oriented form, frontwards (1234); on the left-hand side, we see the number as it's actually stored, back-words.

7.2 Getting Into Memory

There's a messy little problem inside the PC's microprocessors, a problem that makes it complicated for our programs to find their way around the computer's memory. The problem centers around 16-bit arithmetic.

As we've seen, our PC's microprocessor works best with 16-bit numbers that can range no larger than 65536, or 64K. Since the computer uses numeric addresses to find its way through the memory, that suggests that the memory can't be bigger than 64K bytes. Experience has shown that 64K bytes is laughably too little memory for serious computer applications; as we know, many of our PCs are equipped with ten times that amount, 640K. So how can we work our way into a bigger memory and still use 16-bit numbers to access it?

The solution that Intel designed into the 8086 microprocessor family involves what are called *segmented addresses*. Segmented addresses are built with *two* 16-bit words, combined in a way that allows them to address 1,048,576 (or roughly a million) bytes of memory. To see how it's done, we have to look at two things: the arithmetic that's involved in combining the two words of a segmented address, and the way these segmented addresses are handled inside the microprocessor.

The arithmetic involves what we can call "shifted addition," which allows us to create a 20-bit binary number (which goes up to 1,048,578) from two 16-bit numbers. Suppose we have two 16-bit words, which, in hexadecimal, have the values ABCD and 1234. Remember that each hex digit represents four bits, so four hex digits (ABCD or 1234) represent 16 bits altogether. We take one of these two numbers, say ABCD, and put a 0 on its end, like this: ABCD0. In effect this shifts the number over one hex place (or four binary places), or we can say that it has multiplied the value of the number by sixteen. The number is now five hex digits (or 20 bits) long, which brings it up to the million range that we're after. But, unfortunately, it can't serve as a complete 20-bit memory address, because it has a 0 at its end: it can only represent addresses that end in 0, which are only every sixteenth byte.

To complete the segmented addressing scheme, we take the other 16-bit number (1234 in our example) and add it to the shifted number, like this:

```
  ABCD0
+  1234
  ACF04
```

When we combine these two 16-bit numbers like that, we end up with a 20-bit number that can take on any value from 0 through 1,048,577. And that's the arithmetic scheme that underlies the PC's ability to work with a million bytes of memory, using 16-bit numbers.

The two parts of this addressing scheme are called the *segment* part and the *offset* part. In our example, ABCD is the segment value, and 1234 is the offset value. The segment part specifies a memory address that is a multiple of 16, an address that has a hex 0 in its last place. These memory addresses that are a multiple of 16 are called *paragraph* boundaries, or *segment* paragraphs.

The offset part of a segmented address specifies some exact byte location following the segment paragraph location. Since the 16-bit offset word can range from 0 through 65,535 (or 64K), the offset part of the segmented address allows us to work with 64K bytes of memory, all based on the same segment address.

There is a standard way of writing down these segmented addresses, which you will encounter often when you're dealing with technical material about the PC. It's done like this: ABCD:1234. The segment part appears first, then a colon, and then the offset part. If you do anything with assembly language, or use the DEBUG program, you'll see plenty of segmented addresses written this way. If you look at the DEBUG listing that appears in the sidebar *The Interrupt Vector Table* later in this chapter, you'll find them in the right-hand column.

Almost always when we talk about addresses inside our computer's memory, we'll refer to them in their segmented form. But occasionally we'll need to see them in their final form, with the two parts of the segmented address combined; whenever we need to do that, I'll be careful to call them *absolute addresses* so that there is no confusion about what they represent. In our example of combining ABCD and 1234, ACF04 is the resulting absolute address.

That's the arithmetic behind our computer's segmented addressing scheme. Now, how does it work inside the computer?

The segment part of segmented addresses is handled entirely by a set of four special *segment registers*, which we mentioned in Chapter 6. Each of the four is dedicated to locating the segment paragraph for a particular purpose. The CS code segment register indicates where the program code is. The DS data segment register locates the program's main data. The ES extra segment register supplements the DS data segment, so that data can be shifted between two widely separated parts of memory. And the SS stack segment register provides a base address for the computer's stack.

Most of the time these segment registers are left unchanged, while our programs waltz around within the base that's set by the segment paragraph.

Detailed addressing is done by working with the offset part of the address. While the segment part of an address can only be used when it's loaded into one of the four segment registers, there is much greater flexibility in how offsets can be used. Our programs can get their address offsets from a variety of registers (such as the general-purpose registers AX, BX, etc, or the indexing registers SI and DI). Offsets can also be embedded in the program's actual machine language instructions; or offsets can be calculated by combining the contents of registers and the machine language instructions. There is a great deal of flexibility in the way offsets can be handled.

The way that our PC's microprocessor uses segmented addresses has plenty of practical implications for the way our programs work. For an important sidelight on that, see the sidebar *Banging into 64K Limits*.

Fortunately, the tedious details of working with segmented addresses are kept out of our way as much as possible. For the most part only if we're doing assembly language programming will we have to bother ourselves with the tricky problems of segmented addressing. However, if we want to explore the idea of segmented addressing, BASIC gives us a way to do it. The DEF SEG statement in BASIC gives us a way of specifying the segment part of a segmented address, and the number that's used with the PEEK and POKE statements provides an offset part that's combined with the DEF SEG's segment part. So, if you want to try your hand at tinkering with segmented addresses, you can do it with these features of BASIC. For some examples of how it's done, see some of the program listings in Appendix A, particularly the ALL-CHAR program.

Banging into 64K Limits

Now and again you'll encounter what are called 64K limits. For example, when we use BASIC, we're limited to a maximum of 64K of combined program and data memory. Some other programs that we use mention that they can handle no more than 64K of data at one time. Some programming languages can't build programs with more than 64K of program code.

We know, of course, where the 64K number comes from: it's the maximum amount of memory that can be addressed with one unchanging segment register value. The question is, why are we restricted to one fixed segment pointer, and why do we encounter such different types of 64K limitations?

The answer lies in something called the *memory model*, and it's all based on the degree of sophistication that a program has in manipulating the segment registers.

When a program is running in the computer, it has to find its way to both parts of the program and to its data. In simplified terms, each program uses the CS *code segment* register to locate parts of the program, and uses the DS *data segment* register to locate the data. While the program is running, these registers can be treated as fixed or changeable, independently. If either of them is fixed (that is, not being changed by the program while it's running), then that component (program code, or data) can't be any bigger than the 64K that a single segment value can address. But if either can be dynamically changed during the program's operation, then there is no such limit on the size of that component. If both are fixed, we have the *small* memory model—which limits a program to 64K of code and another 64K of data; with both changeable, we have the large model, without the limits. In between we have two more models, with one segment fixed and the other changeable.

The advantage of changing the segment registers (no 64K limits) is obvious; the price isn't so obvious, but it's quite real. When a program undertakes to manipulate the segment registers, it takes on both an extra work load (which slows down the operation) and an extra degree of memory management (which can complicate the program's logic). There is a clear tradeoff to be made between speed, size, and simplicity on the one hand, and power on the other.

As it turns out, the design of our microprocessor's instruction set makes it relatively easy and efficient to change the CS register that controls the program code, and relatively clumsy to control the data's DS register. So we find a fair number of programs that themselves are bigger than 64K, but still work with only 64K of data at a time.

Fortunately for us all, both the art of programming the PC and the PC's programming languages are becoming increasingly sophisticated, so less and less often do we hit the 64K limit.

And what about BASIC? Why does it have a single limit of 64K for program and data, combined? BASIC is a special case. When we use BASIC, the actual program that's running in the computer is the BASIC interpreter. To the BASIC interpreter, our BASIC "program" and its data are accessed with one 64K data segment. That's why BASIC has a quite distinct kind of size limit.

7.3 The PC's Memory Organization

One of the most useful things we can learn about the inner workings of our PCs is how the memory is organized and used. Knowing this helps us understand how the PC works, comprehend what many of the practical limits are on the kinds of work the PC can undertake, know how the display screens work, and also learn the basis for the often-mentioned but little-understood 640K memory limit in the PC. All of that, and more, will become clear when we take a look at the basic organization of the PC's memory space.

We know, from seeing how the PC addresses memory through its segment registers, that there is a fundamental limit on the range of memory addresses that the PC can work with: a million different addresses, each representing a distinct byte of memory. That means that the PC has an *address space* of a million bytes.

A computer's address space is its potential for using memory, which isn't the same thing as the memory that the computer actually has. However, the basic address space provides a framework for the organization of the computer's workings. When the designers of a computer figure out how it's going to be laid out, the scheme for the address space is a very important part of it. So let's see how the PC's designers laid out the use of the PC's address space.

The easiest way to see it is to start by dividing the entire 1 megabyte address space into 16 blocks of 64K each. We can identify each of these blocks of memory by the high-order hex digit that all addresses in that block share. So, the first 64K of memory we can call the 0 block, since all addresses in that block are like this 0xxxx (in five-digit absolute address notation) or like this 0xxx:xxxx (in segmented address notation). Likewise, the second block is the 1-block, since all addresses in that 64K begin with 1. In the 1 meg address space, there are 16 blocks of 64K, which we'll call the 0-block through the F-block.

It's very important to note, when we're talking about these blocks, that there is not a barrier of any kind between the blocks. Memory addresses and data flow in smooth succession through all of memory, and across the artificial boundaries that separate these blocks. We refer to them as distinct blocks partly for convenience, but mostly because the overall scheme for the use of the PC's one megabyte of memory is organized in terms of these blocks.

Low-Memory Goodies

The very lowest part of our computer's memory is set aside for some important uses that are fundamental to the operation of the computer. There are three main divisions to this special use of low memory.

The first is the *interrupt vector tables*, which define where interrupt-handling routines are located. The first 1024 bytes of memory is set aside for the interrupt vector tables, with room for 256 distinct interrupts—quite a few more than are routinely used. This occupies absolute memory addresses 0 to hex 400. (You can learn more about this area in *The Interrupt Vector Table* sidebar later in this chapter.)

The second area is used as a workplace for the ROM-BIOS routines. Since the ROM-BIOS supervises the fundamental operation of the computer and its parts, it needs some memory area for its own record-keeping. This is the *ROM-BIOS data area*, one of the most fascinating parts of the computer's memory. Among the many things stored in the ROM-BIOS data area is a buffer that holds keystrokes we've typed before our programs are ready to receive them, a note of how much memory the computer has, a record of the main equipment installed in the computer, and also an indicator of the display screen mode, which we'll cover in a later chapter (if you take a close look at the ALL-CHAR program in Appendix A, you'll find the program inspecting and using the display mode).

An area of 256 bytes is set aside for the ROM-BIOS data area in absolute memory addresses hex 400 to 500. There are amazing things to find inside this area. If you want to learn more about them, there are three places you can look: one is in the ROM-BIOS listing that's a part of IBM's *Technical Reference* manual for the PCs; another, where you'll find a detailed discussion of virtually every byte, is my *Programmer's Guide to the PC Family*; the third is Brett Salter's *Peeks 'n' Pokes*.

The third part of the special low memory area is the *DOS and BASIC work area*, which extends for 256 bytes from absolute address hex 500 to 600. This region is shared by both DOS and BASIC as a work area, similar to the ROM-BIOS work area that precedes it. You'll find some facts about the contents of this area in the same three sources I mentioned before, but the information that's available is not as complete as it is for the ROM-BIOS.

This low memory area is just loaded with goodies for the interested explorer. Anyone who wants to know a lot about the inner workings of the PC can get a graduate education in PC tinkering simply by digging deeply into this part of memory.

The key working area of memory is the part that's used for our programs and their data: that's the area made up of the first ten blocks, the 0-through 9-blocks. This area is often called the *user memory area*, to distinguish it from the rest of the address space, which is, one way or another, at the service of the computer system itself. When we talk about the amount of memory that our PC computers have, what we're really talking about is the amount of user memory that's installed in this area. In theory it could be as little as just 16K (a quarter of the first 64K block) or as much as 640K with all ten blocks of memory installed. Whatever amount of memory is installed in our computers forms one contiguous chunk, from the 0-block to wherever the end of the memory is.

There are actually several different kinds of memory (as we'll learn more about later), and the kind that's installed here is regular read/write Random Access Memory, which is often called simply *RAM*. Two things characterize RAM memory: first, as read/write memory it can have the data in it inspected (read) and changed (written); second, it is volatile, which means that the data in it is preserved only as long as the computer is running.

```
0-block    1st 64K   Ordinary user memory to   64K
1-block    2nd 64K   Ordinary user memory to  128K
2-block    3rd 64K   Ordinary user memory to  192K
3-block    4th 64K   Ordinary user memory to  256K
4-block    5th 64K   Ordinary user memory to  320K
5-block    6th 64K   Ordinary user memory to  384K
6-block    7th 64K   Ordinary user memory to  448K
7-block    8th 64K   Ordinary user memory to  512K
8-block    9th 64K   Ordinary user memory to  576K
9-block   10th 64K   Ordinary user memory to  640K
A-block   11th 64K   Extended video memory
B-block   12th 64K   Standard video memory
C-block   13th 64K   ROM expansion (XT, EGA, 3270 PC)
D-block   14th 64K   other use (PCjr cartridges)
E-block   15th 64K   other use (PCjr cartridges)
F-block   16th 64K   System ROM-BIOS and ROM-BASIC
```

Figure 7-1. The PC's memory blocks.

This memory is dedicated to holding our programs and data while the computer is working with them. The amount of RAM memory installed here in many ways determines the size and scope of the problems that our computers can undertake.

The basic design of the PC family sets aside only ten of the total sixteen blocks in the address space for this main working memory area. That's just over 60 percent of the total. Today, that 640K area seems much too small for the problems we want to hand our PCs, but at the time that the PC was being designed it seemed like a very generous amount. At that time, typical personal computers were limited to perhaps 64 or 128K total memory, and the PC's 640K seemed enormous then. (This is a mistake that has occurred over and over again in the history of computing: underestimating the need for growth and expansion in the computer.)

It is possible to expand the 640K user memory area slightly by encroaching on some of the system area that follows, but that isn't really wise because the memory blocks that come after the 640K user area are reserved for some special uses, which we'll see shortly, that should not be sabotaged.

Not every single bit of the user memory area is actually available for our programs to use. The very first part of it, beginning at memory address 0, is set aside for some essential record-keeping that the computer has to have. You find a discussion of that in the *Low-Memory Goodies* sidebar, and some deeper technical information about one part of it in *The Interrupt Vector Table* sidebar. But, except for that small (and interesting) part, this entire 640K section of memory is set aside for use by our programs—and, as such, there's really not much to say about it. On the other hand, the rest of the memory blocks have some very fascinating details for us to discuss.

TECHNICAL BACKGROUND | | | ▌ ▌ ▌

The Interrupt Vector Table

When we introduced interrupts in Chapter 6, I explained that the interrupt mechanism causes the current program to be put on hold, while an interrupt-handling program is activated. The microprocessor needs a simple and straightforward way to find where the interrupt handler is, and that's accomplished using the *interrupt vector table*. It's a very simple table of the addresses of the interrupt-handling routines stored beginning with the "vector" for interrupt number 0 at memory location 0. Each vector address is four bytes long; the vector for any interrupt number x is simply found at memory location *x* times 4.

The "vectors" are simply the complete memory address, in segmented form, of the routine to be activated when the interrupt occurs. A segmented address is made up of a pair of 2-byte words, so we can see why the vectors are four bytes each.

You can inspect the interrupt vector table in your computer very easily by using DEBUG. Use the D-display command to show the beginning of memory like this: D 0:0. DEBUG will show you the first 128 bytes, or 32 vectors, which look something like this:

```
0000:0000   E8 4E 9A 01 00 00 00 00-C3 E2 00 F0 00 00 00 00
0000:0010   F0 01 70 00 54 FF 00 F0-05 18 00 F0 05 18 00 F0
0000:0020   2C 08 51 17 D0 0A 51 17-AD 08 54 08 E8 05 01 2F
0000:0030   FA 05 01 2F 05 18 00 F0-57 EF 00 F0 F0 01 70 00
0000:0040   90 13 C7 13 4D F8 00 F0-41 F8 00 F0 3E 0A 51 17
```

```
0000:0050   5C 00 B7 25 59 F8 00 F0-E2 0A 51 17 9C 00 B7 25
0000:0060   00 00 00 F6 8E 00 DE 09-6E FE 00 F0 F2 00 7B 09
0000:0070   27 08 51 17 A4 F0 00 F0-22 05 00 00 00 00 00 F0
```

The vectors are stored back-words, the offset followed by the segment. For example, the first four bytes that DEBUG shows above (E8 4E 9A 01) can be translated into the segmented address 019A:4EE8.

Generally we'll find three kinds of addresses in the vector table. They'll be ones that point to the ROM-BIOS, which we can identify by a hex F leading the segment number. They'll be ones that point into main memory, like our example of 019A:4EE8. These may be pointing to routines in DOS, or in a resident program (e.g., Sidekick or Prokey), or they may point into DEBUG itself (because DEBUG needs to have temporary control of the interrupt). Finally, the vectors may be all 0, because that interrupt number is not currently being handled. You'll notice that the second interrupt vector (for interrupt number 1) in our display above is like that.

If you want to, you can chase down any of the interrupt-handling routines by first decoding their interrupt vectors (as we showed above), and then feeding that segmented address to DEBUG's U-unassemble command in order to inspect the program code inside the interrupt handler.

Immediately following the user memory area is a 128K area, consisting of the A- and B-blocks, that is set aside for use by the display screens. The data that appears on the screens of our computers has to be stored somewhere, and the best place to store it turns out to be in our computer's own memory address space. The reason why that's such a good idea is that it makes it possible for our programs to very quickly and easily manipulate the display screen data. So, to make that possible, the 128K area of the A- and B-blocks is set aside for the display screen's own data. (In Chapters 11-14 we'll take an in-depth look at the how the display screens work, and how they use this memory. Until then, it's enough for us to know that what appears on our screens is recorded in this part of memory.)

In the original PC design, only part of the B-block was actually used for the display screens; the A-block was reserved but not used. This is why it has been possible for some PCs to have an additional 64K of user memory installed, encroaching on the A-block. This has never been a wise thing to do, though, because it broke an important design convention of the PC family. The first official use of the A-block came with the appearance of the IBM Enhanced Graphics Adapter, which needed more working display memory than the previous display adapters.

The memory that is installed for use by the display screens operates just like the conventional RAM user memory. Normally, it has one extra feature which helps speed the operation of our computer: there are two circuit doorways into it, so that both our programs (using the microprocessor) and the display screen can simultaneously work with it, without interfering with each other.

After the display memory area comes three blocks, C through E, which are set aside for some special uses. They are rather nebulously called the "ROM extension area." There is no hard-and-fast assignment for this memory area. Instead, it is used for a variety of purposes that have arisen in the evolving history of the PC family. One use, which gives this section its name, is as a growth area for the very last section of memory, the ROM-BIOS which occupies the final F-block. When new equipment is added to the PC family and it requires built-in software support, the additional ROM-BIOS programs are added here. That, for example, is how the XT model's hard disk was accommodated, using a small part of the C-block.

Another use for the ROM extension area, which we have only seen in the PC*jr*, is as a home for removable software cartridges. Software cartridges have programs recorded on them, and when they are plugged into the computer they have to appear somewhere in memory. In the PC*jr* the D- and E-blocks are used for this purpose.

A third use for the ROM extension area, one which was not designed by IBM, is to support "extended memory," which we'll discuss shortly in Section 7.4.

The final part of the PC family's memory address space is the F-block, which is used to hold the computer's built-in ROM-BIOS programs. The memory used here (and in the PC*jr*'s software cartridges) is a special kind known as Read-Only-Memory, or ROM. ROM memory is permanently recorded, so that it can't be *written to* or *changed by* our programs, and it isn't volatile so turning off the computer does not disturb it. As you can see, ROM is very different than the RAM we discussed earlier, although their names are all too easy to confuse.

The ROM-BIOS holds a key set of programs that provide very essential support for the whole operation of the computer. There are three main parts to the ROM-BIOS programs. The first part is used only when the computer is turned on: these are test and initialization programs that make sure our computer is in good working order. The delay between when we turn on the computer and when it starts working for us is mostly taken up by the operation of these test and initialization programs, which are sometimes called the *POST*, Power-On Self-Test.

The second and most interesting part of the ROM-BIOS are the routines that are properly called the Basic Input/Output Services, or BIOS. These programs provide the detailed and intimate control of the various parts of the computer, particularly the I/O peripherals, such as the disk drives, which require careful supervision (including exhaustive checking for errors). The ROM-BIOS, to help support the whole operation of the computer, provides a very long list of services that are available for use both by the computer's operating system (DOS) and by our application programs. We'll have much to say about this part of the ROM-BIOS throughout the rest of the book.

The third part of the ROM-BIOS, which applies only to the members of the PC family made by IBM, is the built-in ROM-BASIC (also called Cassette BASIC). This is the core of the BASIC programming language, and it can be used either by itself, or it can serve (invisibly to us) as part of the disk-oriented BASIC that comes with DOS.

All of the ROM-BIOS routines are contained very compactly within the 64K F-block of memory. The amount of this block that is used varies from model to model in the PC family, since some of them require more program support than others. For example, the PC*jr* probably has the most programming packed into this area, because the *jr* uses inexpensive software to perform tasks that other models handle with more costly hardware. Generally the more complex the model, the more software gets crammed into the ROM-BIOS; so the advanced AT has quite a bit more than the original PC.

If we care to, we can explore and experiment with any and all of these sections of memory. For example, I happen to know that the ROM-BASIC program is located at the segmented memory address F600:0000 in all the IBM models of the PC family. Knowing this, we can use the DEBUG program to display some of the program code, and see the messages that are hidden inside of BASIC. To do this, we can just fire up DEBUG, and give it the command D F600:0000. That will show us the first part of BASIC's code; if we give DEBUG the command D (without typing anything else), DEBUG will show us successive chunks of BASIC until it starts to reveal BASIC's hidden messages.

In fact, if we want to, we can write a short BASIC program that will hunt through all of the ROM-BIOS looking for messages. In Appendix A you'll find the listing for a short program called MSG-HUNT that hunts through the whole F-block, looking for a string of five letters or punctuation characters in a row; when it finds them, it displays them, and goes on hunting. If you'd like to learn more about what's inside your computer's ROM-BIOS, try MSG-HUNT.

There's one final and quite interesting thing to know about the ROM-BIOS. IBM places an identifying date at the end of the BIOS. We can inspect that date if we want to. It's interesting to see because it tells us essentially when the ROM-BIOS for our machine was finished. It can also be used to identify the revisions to the ROM-BIOS that IBM makes on rare occasions. This simple BASIC program will root out the date stamp, and show it to us, if it is there:

```
10 ' Display ROM-BIOS date
20 DEF SEG = &HFFFF
30 DATE.$ = ""
40 FOR I = 5 TO 12
50    DATE.$ = DATE.$ + CHR$(PEEK(I))
60 NEXT
70 IF PEEK (7) <> ASC("/") THEN DATE.$ = "missing"
80 PRINT "The ROM-BIOS date is ";DATE.$
```

While all of the IBM-made members of the PC family have this date stamp, most of the non-IBM family members do not, including the Compaq models. However, you'll find that some makers of PC-compatible computers have been nice enough to include the date stamp in their machines. Panasonic's Senior Partner is one such computer.

In addition to the date stamp, IBM has created a loosely defined model ID code, which can be used by programs that need to know when they are running on some of the more different models of the family. This simple BASIC program displays the ID byte:

```
10 ' Display machine id byte
20 DEF SEG = &HFFFF
30 ID = PEEK (14)
40 PRINT "The id byte is";ID;"hex ";HEX$(ID)
```

The original PC model had an ID byte of hex FF. The FE code is sometimes called the XT code, but it can be found on a variety of models, including the XT and the Portable PC. The distinct PC*jr* has an ID byte of FD; the PC*jr* is sufficiently different from the other models that some programs identify the *jr*'s ID byte, and adjust their operation to be more ideal for the *jr*. Likewise, the AT model is identified by a byte code of FC.

Since each model of computer has its own subtle but distinct characteristics, it can be beneficial for programs to make appropriate adjustments in the way they operate based on the machine ID. From this point of view, it's unfortunate that the most important of the non-IBM members of the family cannot be easily identified by either a model ID byte or by the ROM-BIOS date. But, that's the way things go.

7.4 Into Extended Memory

While the regular members of the PC family are limited to addressing only one megabyte of memory by the fundamental design of the 8088 microprocessor that they are based on, the AT branch of the family, which uses the 286 microprocessor, can work with much more memory.

As we mentioned in our discussion of the 286 at the end of Chapter 6, 286-based computers can have up to 16 megabytes of actual memory in them. Interestingly enough, that is exactly the same memory limit applied for many years to IBM's huge multimillion-dollar mainframe computers. It's amazing to think that IBM's mighty mainframes had no more capacity than our little microprocessors.

In addition to the ability to accommodate large amounts of real working memory, the AT's 286 can also provide vast amounts of *virtual memory*, a clever simulation of more memory than is actually present. (See the *How Virtual Memory Works* sidebar.) The AT's virtual memory can provide up to one *gigabyte* (1024 megabytes) of virtual memory for each and every program that's running in the computer.

Bear in mind that the address space designed into a microprocessor, like the 286, is one thing, and a specific computer's ability to use that address space is another thing. While the 286 allows for 16 megs of memory, the IBM AT model has an official limit of 3 megs of actual memory.

To take full advantage of either the AT's extended memory or virtual memory requires an operating system environment (and accompanying programs) that is designed for those features. Since the original PC and the PC's mainstream operating system DOS were not developed with extended and virtual memory in mind, the potential of these features will remain largely untapped, until we see a new generation of operating system and application software built with the AT in mind.

However, it is still possible for a program to make some use of the AT extended memory. The standard way to do that is for a program to use some of the services provided by the computer's built-in ROM-BIOS programs. One of these services transfers blocks of data, in whatever size we need, between the special extended memory and the conventional memory. It's also possible for a program to switch the 286 microprocessor from *real* mode (in which it acts like a regular 8088) into its *protected* mode. However, a program has to be more sophisticated to successfully manipulate protected mode. If all a program wants to do is to benefit from the extended memory, it can just use the memory transfer service that the BIOS provides, and avoid all the complications of protected mode.

We have an example readily at hand of a program that uses the BIOS's transfer service to use an AT's extended memory: the virtual disk utility called VDISK, which has been a part of DOS since version 3.0. When VDISK is activated with the extended memory, it uses the BIOS transfer service to move data into and out of extended memory without VDISK needing to work in protected mode or directly manipulate the extended memory area. If you want to see how VDISK accesses and manages the

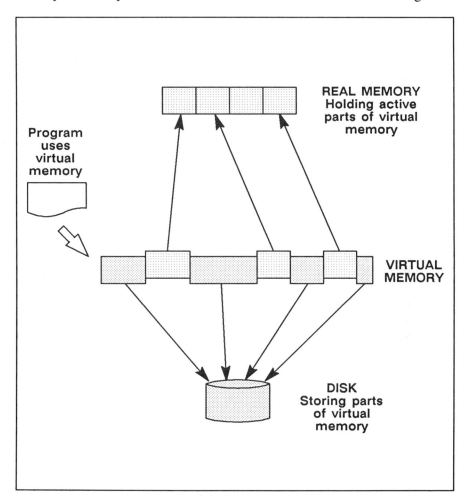

Figure 7-2. Virtual memory.

extended memory, you can find out by looking at the assembler listing of the program, which comes with the DOS diskettes.

How Virtual Memory Works

Virtual memory is a sleight-of-hand operation that involves some carefully orchestrated cooperation between the microprocessor, a virtual memory support program, and the computer's disk. It essentially works like this.

When a program is being set up to run in the computer, the operating system creates a "virtual memory space," which is a model of the amount of memory and the memory addresses that the program has at its disposal. Then, a portion of the computer's "real" or actual, physical memory is given over to the sleight-of-hand operation that is the core of the virtual memory concept. Using a feature that's an integral part of the 286 microprocessor, the operating system's virtual memory support program tells the 286 to make the real memory that's being assigned to the program *appear to be* at some other address, the virtual address that the program will be using. A "memory mapping" feature in the 286 makes the real memory appear to have a different working memory address than its true, real address.

So far what we've described is just a shuffling act, a trick that makes some real memory addresses appear to be, and work as, some other virtual addresses. The most important part of virtual memory comes in the next step, when our programs try to use more virtual memory than there is real memory.

A program starts out with some of its (large) virtual memory space mapped into a part of the computer's (smaller) real memory. As long as the program is only working with that part of its virtual memory, all goes well. The program is actually using different locations in memory than it thinks it is, but that doesn't matter. What happens when the program tries to use some of the large virtual memory that hasn't been assigned a part of the smaller real memory? When that occurs, the microprocessor's mapping table discovers that the program is trying to use an address that doesn't currently exist; the microprocessor generates what is called a *page fault*.

When there is a page fault—indicating that a program is trying to use a virtual address that isn't actively mapped into real memory—a special virtual memory support program swings into action. It temporarily places the program on hold while it deals with this crisis. The support program chooses some part of the virtual memory that is currently in real memory, and saves its contents temporarily onto the disk; that's called *swapping out*. That part of the real memory is recycled to act as the newly-needed part of the virtual memory.

When the swapped-out part of memory is needed again, it's *swapped-in*, copied back from disk.

As you can see, the computer's disk is used as a warehouse to store the parts of virtual memory that aren't in current use.

Depending upon how things go, the virtual memory operation can either run very smoothly, or it can involve so much swapping in and out of memory that too much time is spent waiting to swap between memory and disk. When this happens, it's called *thrashing*; when a virtual memory system starts thrashing, very little work gets done.

The practical operation of a virtual memory system can involve a very sensitive balancing act known as *system tuning*. Our microcomputers can benefit from a moderate and careful use of virtual memory, but they are too small and too slow to get into the heavy use of this powerful concept.

7.5 Memory Banks and Expanded Memory

While the future of the PC family's evolution belongs to the 286 microprocessor-based AT branch of the family, the past and present are dominated by the literally millions of 8088-based PCs. The ATs may have access to vast amounts of extended memory, but a PC is limited to only addressing one million bytes of storage, and only using 640K of that for working programs and data. When PCs get into heavy-duty use, that's just too little memory.

Fortunately there is a solution to the problem of the PC's memory limitation, based on an idea called *bank-switched memory*.

Bank-switching allows the computer to actually have more memory than it has room for in the microprocessor's 1-meg memory address space. The memory is *physically* in the computer, but it's not firmly assigned any place in the microprocessor's address space. Instead, the memory is in a kind of limbo, without an address, inaccessible to our programs until it is switched on.

The circuit boards for this special kind of bank-switched memory allow the addressing of the memory to be turned on and off at will, and moved around at will. For example, a bank-switched memory board might contain eight "banks" of memory, each of them 64K (for a total of 512K). All of these 64K blocks share a single 64K address block in the computer's memory. At any instant, only one of eight banks can be active, with its data accessible, while the others will be on hold.

The benefit of bank-switching is that it allows more memory to be attached to the computer, memory that is instantly accessible. All that it takes to switch a bank into place is to send a command to the memory circuit board, telling it to change the addressing of the banks. The switch takes place as quickly as an instruction can execute—with no delay at all.

There are complications, though, in using bank-switched memory. Unlike the computer's conventional memory, bank-switched memory requires active management, to make sure that the right pieces are available at the right times. The need for that management—and a standard way of performing it—held back the use of bank-switching until the software giant Lotus and the microprocessor chip wizards at Intel teamed up to define a standard way of working with bank-switched memory. Officially this bank-switched approach is called the Lotus/Intel/Microsoft Expanded Memory Specification, but many people refer to it by the name of Intel's own memory board design for the specification, "Above Board."

(To avoid problems, let me pause to note that the variety of bank-switched memory we're talking about here is called *expanded* memory, while the AT's special memory that goes beyond 1 megabyte is called *extended* memory. The two terms *expanded* and *extended* are easy to confuse, so be careful.)

Here's how the expanded memory works. It operates in three parts: one piece of hardware (the bank-switched memory board), and two pieces of software (the expanded memory manager—known as the EMM—and the application program that uses the memory). The bank-switched memory board—which could be Intel's Above Board or any similar memory board—provides anywhere from 64K up to 8 megabytes of memory, subdivided into small 16K pages that can be individually readdressed through bank-switching.

The EMM memory manager program is activated when the computer is first started up, and it lays the groundwork for the expanded memory's operation. A key part of its task is to find an unused area in the PC's memory space, which it can use to map the bank-switched memory into. It requires a full 64K work area, called a *page frame*, but it's flexible about where the page frame is located. As we can readily see from looking at the PC's general memory allocation (see Figure 7-1), the D and E blocks of memory are obviously good candidates; however, the EMM can place the page frame in the C block as well. The exact location doesn't matter, as long as it doesn't interfere with any other use of the memory address space. Also, the 64K page frame doesn't have to be placed on a memory block boundary. For example, it can begin at the segment address C400 and extend up through the rest of the C block and into the first 16K of the D block.

Once the EMM has established where its 64K page frame will be located, it divides the frame into four 16K *windows*. After that, it's ready for action, ready to supply any application program that knows how to use it with the service of swapping memory data in and out of the 16K windows.

To use the expanded memory, an application program tells the EMM that it needs to use one or more of the four available windows. The application can ask the EMM supervisor to assign memory pages to it, and then to make those pages accessible by bank-switching them into the window area. As the application program needs to work with different 16K pages of data, it asks the EMM to switch different pages into place. Figure 7-3 illustrates how this works.

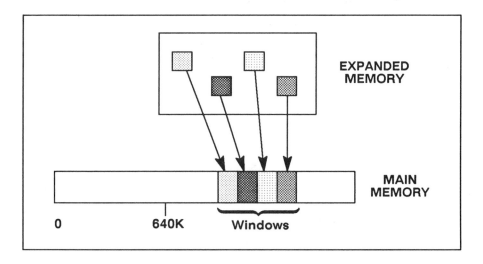

Figure 7-3. Expanded memory.

While this scheme is very powerful and also very fast, it does have some obvious limitations. One is that it can only be used for a program's data, and not for the program code itself. DOS still has to find sufficient room in the conventional memory area to hold large programs, but once those programs are running in conventional memory, they can take advantage of expanded memory to work with more data than can be accommodated in the conventional memory. Another obvious drawback to expanded memory is that to use it a program must know how to work together with the expanded memory manager, EMM, and it must know how to conveniently work with its data fragmented into 16K pages. Within these limitations, though, the expanded memory scheme can greatly enhance our computer's ability to work with large amounts of data.

This expanded memory scheme can be added to any regular member of the PC family, including the AT wing of the family. While the ATs can have their own extended memory that goes beyond the PC's 1-meg limit, they can also use expanded memory within the regular 1-meg address space.

Some Things To Try

1. Explain why the segmented addresses 1234:0005, 1230:0045, 1200:0345, and 1000:2345 all refer to the same memory location. Which of these refers to a different location than the other two: A321:789A, A657:453A, and A296:824A? Is there an ideal way to divide up the two halves of a segmented address?

2. Using the DEBUG program's U-unassemble instruction, unassemble some of your computer's ROM-BIOS (for example, like this: U F000:A000 L 100); then pick out the examples of back-words storage that appear.

3. How could you write a program in BASIC that will find out how much memory is installed in the computer by experimental means? Can this operation disrupt the computer? Write such a program and see what happens. (Incidentally, you'll find a very fast version of such a test in the "System Information" program that is a part of my Norton Utilities program set.)

4. What do you think are the advantages and limitations of the Above Board approach to bank-switched memory? What does a program have to do to take advantage of it? What might the problems be for a program to work with windows of data that are 16K bytes each?

5. If you try using the MSG-HUNT program, which searches through the ROM-BIOS looking for messages, you'll find that it gives some false alarms; for example, one "message" that it detects on my computer is "t'⟨.u"—nothing very fascinating or meaningful. That's because the program accepts as candidate message characters anything from a blank to a lowercase z. That allows us to capture punctuation inside of a message, but it also finds spurious messages, like the one above, that are mostly punctuation characters. What sort of test can we add to the program to filter out this nonsense? Try adding such a filter to MSG-HUNT; experiment with making your rules for an acceptable message tighter or looser, and see what the result is.

8

Disks:
The Basic Story

Here we're going to begin a three-chapter odyssey exploring our computer's disks. Only one other aspect of our computers (the display screen) is as richly varied and has as many fascinating aspects as the disks.

Since everything we use on our computers—all our programs and all our data—makes its home on our disks, understanding the disk storage in our computers has a great deal of practical importance to us besides just being so downright interesting.

It's worth knowing, at this point, how we'll be dividing up the subject of disks into these three chapters. Here we'll get the basics down so that we have a clear idea of just what a disk is. Since we use our disks under the supervision of DOS, the *Disk* Operating System, in Chapter 9, we'll look at our disks from the DOS perspective, seeing how DOS views them. In Chapter 10, we'll wrap up our discussion by inspecting some of the deeper details of disks.

We begin now with the basics of disk storage.

8.1 Basic Disk Ideas

The disk storage that our computers use is based on two things: a recording technology and a quick-access design scheme.

The technology is magnetic recording, the same method that's used in all the various forms of magnetic tape that we know about—from music cassettes to video cassette recorders (VCRs). The basis of magnetic recording lies in the fact that iron, and some other materials, can be magnetized. You probably remember from childhood science lessons in school how an iron bar becomes magnetized if we direct a magnetic field over it. The magnetic field is, in a crude sense, *recorded* on the iron. All of our sophisticated magnetic recording is nothing more than a refinement of that simple science lesson.

Magnetic recording was first and most widely used to record sound, which is an analog form of information. Only later was magnetic recording adapted for the *digital* recording that our computers require. That's ironic, because magnetic recording is essentially binary (magnetized or not), or digital in nature.

Digital magnetic recording is done on a surface of magnetically sensitive material, usually a form of iron oxide that gives magnetic media their characteristic rust-brown color. The magnetic coating is quite thin—in fact, the thinner it is, the better it works. It's coated onto some supporting material, usually flexible mylar plastic for recording tape and diskettes, or rigid aluminum platters for so-called hard disks.

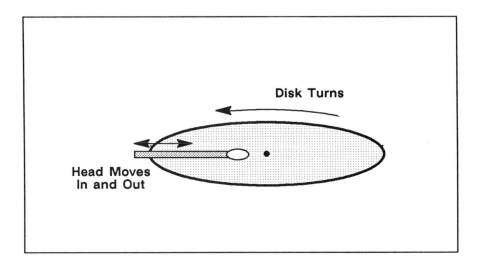

Figure 8-1. Disk direct access.

Whether we're talking about tapes or disks, the way the information is recorded onto the magnetic surface is the same. The surface is treated as an array of dot positions, each of which is treated as a bit that will be set to the magnetic equivalent of 0 or 1. Since the location of these dot positions isn't precisely determined, the recording scheme involves some "ready-set-go" markings that help the recorder to find and match up with the recording positions. The need for these synchronizing marks is part of the reason why our disks have to be "formatted" before we can use them.

That's the essence of the recording technology that I said was one of the two things that formed the basis for our computer's disk storage. The other is the quick-access design scheme of a disk.

A magnetic tape is essentially *linear* because information has to be recorded on it front to back; there's no quick and easy way to skip to the middle of a tape, short of just running through the length of it. A rotating disk, however, is another matter.

There are two things about a disk that make it possible to get to any part of the surface quickly. The first is the disk's rotation. In a very short time the disk spins around so that any part of its circumference passes by without much delay. It's quicker than you might think. A diskette spins at 300 RPM, which means it takes at most one-fifth of a second for any desired part to swing into place; for a hard disk it's about 3600 RPM, or one-sixtieth of a second per rotation.

The other part of finding our way on the surface of a disk is the movement of the magnetic recording head, which corresponds to the tone arm of a phonograph player, across the disk from outside to inside. For a diskette it takes an average of about one-sixth of a second to move to any desired location; for a hard disk, around 1/25th of a second.

When we combine the two factors—moving the read/write magnetic recording head across the disk surface, and rotating the disk into position under the head—we see that we can get to any part of the disk very quickly. That's why computer disks are called *random access storage*, because we can get to (access) any part of the recorded data directly, randomly, without having to pass through the whole set of information sequentially, as we would with a tape recording.

If you want to *roughly* understand how computer data is stored on a disk, the analogy of a phonograph record and player gives you an approximate idea of what it's like. But there are some important differences that make the analogy only a crude one.

On a phonograph record, the sound is recorded in one continuous spiral groove. That makes it, like a tape, actually a linear medium, although we can easily skip from one part of the record to another. Our magnetic disks, on the other hand, are actually recorded in a series of concentric circles, unconnected to each other.

In computer terminology, each of the concentric circles of a disk is called a *track*. The disk surface is divided into these distinct track/circles, starting from the outer edge of the disk, where the first track is located, to the innermost track. The number of tracks varies with the type of disk. Conventional diskettes, of the type that's called *double-density*, have 40 tracks; *quad-density* diskettes, including the AT's high-capacity diskettes and other quad-density types, have 80 tracks. Hard disks typically have around 300 to 600 tracks. The tracks, however many there are, are identified by number, starting with track zero as the outermost track.

You might expect that the tracks spread across most of the width of the recording surface, but they don't; they cover a surprisingly small area. For both double- and quad-density diskettes, the space between the first and last track is just over three-quarters of an inch (or almost exactly 2 CM). In technical terms, a double-density diskette is recorded with 48 tracks per inch, and quad-density is recorded at 96 tracks per inch. (In the technical literature, *tracks per inch* is often abbreviated TPI; if you run into that term, you'll now know what it is.)

Just as the width of a disk surface is divided into distinct tracks, so the circumference of a track is divided into parts, called *sectors*. The type of the disk and its format determine how many sectors there are in a circular track: usually it's eight or nine for regular diskettes, 15 for high-capacity diskettes, and 17 for the hard disks that are normally used with the PC family.

Sectors are all a fixed size on any given disk. Our PCs can handle a variety of sector sizes, from ones as small as 128 bytes to as large as 1024 bytes; however, 512-byte sectors have become a fixed standard size that is all-but-never deviated from.

All of the reading and writing of data that our computers perform with disks is done in terms of complete sectors. As we'll see later, our data can

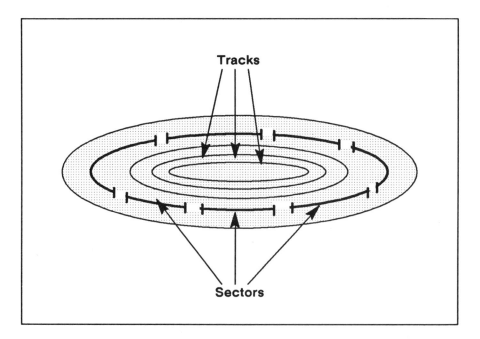

Figure 8-2. The tracks and sectors of a disk.

be any size and it's made to fit snugly into the fixed storage size of sectors. But the actual disk I/O that the computer performs is only done in full, complete sectors.

The sectors in a track, like the tracks on the side of a disk, are identified by numbers that are assigned to them, starting not with zero, but with one (sector number zero on each track is reserved for identification purposes, rather than for storing our data).

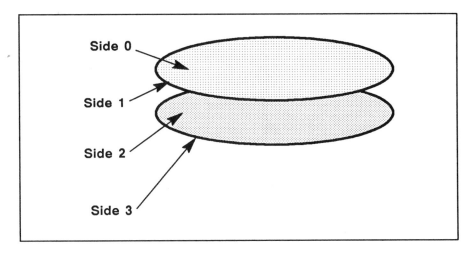

Figure 8-3. The sides of a disk.

There is one final dimension to a disk which we haven't mentioned so far: the number of sides. A diskette might be recorded on both of its sides or only on one (more about that in Section 8.2). While a diskette, like anything that's flat, has only two sides, hard disk systems often contain more than one disk platter inside them, so they can have more than two sides. The sides of a disk, as you'd expect by now, are identified by number; as it is with tracks, the sides are numbered starting with zero for the first side.

When we combine all these dimensions, we arrive at the size, or storage capacity, of a disk. Multiplying the number of sides by the number of tracks per side by the number of sectors per track gives us the total number of sectors per disk. Multiply that by the number of bytes per sector—which is normally 512 bytes, or ½K—gives us the raw capacity of the disk. Naturally some of that total capacity is taken up, when we use the disk, with overhead of one kind or another, as we'll see in Chapter 9. But the number that we can calculate this way is essentially the storage capacity of the disk; it should be the same, or close to the capacity that's reported to us by the DOS utility program CHKDSK (check-disk).

If you're interested in learning more about the dimensions of your disks, and if you have my Norton Utilities programs, you can use the program called NU to show the full dimensions of any disk you have. Go to menu 2.2, called Display Disk Technical Information, and you'll be shown the four dimensions of your disk's storage (together with some DOS-related information that we'll learn about in Chapter 9).

There's one more thing we should cover in this section on basic disk ideas: that's what disks look like physically, how they are packaged and protected. But that varies with different types of disks, so we'll defer it just briefly until after we describe the main varieties of disks.

8.2 Varieties of Disks

At times it seems that there are more varieties of disks that can be used with our PC family than we can shake a finger at. It certainly isn't practical for us to undertake an exhaustive discussion of all the types of disks that there are, but we can see the principle types, outline the more exotic varieties, and look more deeply at the most important kinds. That's what we'll do here. In this discussion we need to keep clearly in mind that there are varying degrees of difference between the types; some differences are quite fundamental and others are important but not major differences. Finally, some are purely minor variations. We'll see the distinctions as we go along.

(Keep in mind that disk storage technology moves forward rather rapidly, and advances in disks come all the time. Between the time I wrote this and you read it, it's likely that the PC family will have gained some new disk formats. It's certain that more will appear in the future.)

The place to begin our discussion is where the PC family began, with the most common type of disk, the 5¼-inch floppy diskette. You'll see a picture of one in Figure 8-4.

There are a lot of variations on this diskette, but before we get into them, we will look at the common characteristics of this type of diskette. The circular diskette itself is made of very soft flexible material, mylar plastic with a magnetically sensitive iron-oxide coating. The coating is the same on both sides, even for "single-sided" diskettes that are intended to be recorded on only one side. The second side of a single-sided diskette may not have its second side finished, polished, and tested, but it still has the same coating. Incidentally, not many people know it, but the first side of a diskette, the active side on a single-sided diskette, is on the bottom of the diskette, opposite the diskette label, not the top.

The diskette has two holes in it. One is the hub where the disk drive grabs it. This hub may have a reinforcing hub ring on it, to help make sure that the diskette is properly centered. The other hole is just outside the hub. It provides a reference point that defines the beginning of a track.

Surrounding and holding the circular diskette is the diskette *jacket*, which is usually black. On the inside surface of the jacket, almost completely out of sight, is a white felt liner. The liner is specially designed to help the diskette slide smoothly around, and wipe it clean at the same time. A large oval slot provides the opening where the diskette drive's read/write head reaches in to touch the diskette. The two small cuts to either side of the read/write slot are called *stress relief notches*; they help make sure that the jacket doesn't warp. Near the hub opening is an *index hole*, which allows the diskette drive to see the diskette's own index hole. And, finally, on one side there is a *write-protect notch*. If this notch is covered over, you cannot write onto the diskette.

There are some possible variations that you might encounter in the holes and notches that appear on a disk jacket. You'll see some disks that don't have a write-protect notch, which means that they are always protected against being written over. These diskettes are used for the original copies of programs that we buy, such as the diskette that DOS comes on. You may also see some diskettes that have two write-protect notches and two index holes; these are "*flippies*," diskettes that are reversible (turn it over and use the other side) diskettes.

That's the physical layout of a 5¼-inch diskette. Now let's look at the surprising variety of distinctly different diskette types that all look as if they are the same. We begin with *single*- versus *double*-sided.

In the early days of the PC family diskettes were recorded on only one of the two sides of the disk, which saved a small part of the cost of the disk drive (at the expense of halving the potential storage capacity of the diskettes). Today it's almost unheard-of for a computer to have single sided drives in them, yet it's common for programs to come to us on single-sided diskettes. Let's pause to talk about the why and wherefore of that, because it's important if you're not going to trip your feet over the matter.

A diskette *drive* that's single-sided can only read or write diskettes in single-sided format; on the other hand, a double-sided *drive* can read and write either way, single or double. A diskette that's *manufactured* as double-sided can be *used* either way. A diskette that's *manufactured* as single-sided is only supposed to be used that way, because the second side isn't necessarily usable. However, a single-sided diskette can often be

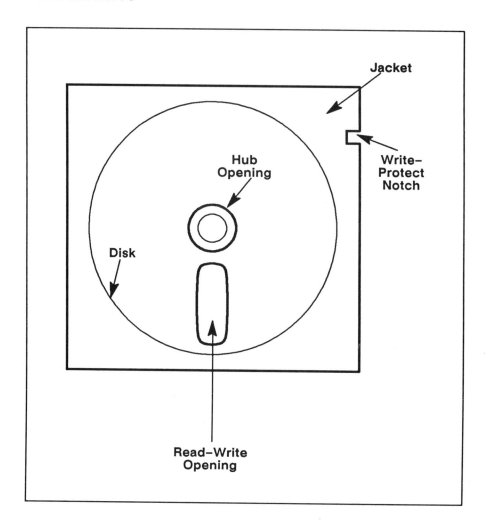

Figure 8-4. A 5¼-inch floppy diskette (top view).

formatted and used as a double-sided diskette with no problems at all—and that fact ends up making a lot of people confused about the matter.

OK. Suppose we have diskettes and drives that are both made to be double sided. What determines whether we're actually *using* them as single or double? That turns out to be a question of software. When a diskette is being formatted, the FORMAT program marks the diskette as to how it should be used. After that, any time the diskette is used, the marking is checked to see how the diskette should be used.

We can understand this better through an analogy. A completely new blank diskette is like a blank piece of paper. Let's imagine that we can not write on the paper until it has been ruled with guidelines. When we format a diskette, we're recording on it something very much like ruled guidelines, which provide a framework for what will later be written on the diskette. In addition, formatting a diskette has a second element to it that's something like writing a note at the top of the page that says whether or not it's OK to turn the page over and use the other side. At the beginning of a diskette the FORMAT program records how the diskette can be used, single- or double-sided.

Unlike a piece of paper, a diskette can be formatted over and over again. Each time a diskette is reformatted, any previous information is erased and overwritten, and the type of formatting can be changed as well.

With that background established, we're ready to learn more about the variety of formats that a conventional 5¼-inch diskette can take on. There are quite a few variations. First, a diskette can be single- or double-sided. Next, it can be formatted with either eight or nine sectors squeezed into a track. Just considering those two parameters, we have four different possible formats. The single-sided 8-sector format was the original PC format, and it was all that the first version of DOS, version 1.0, could use. Because the single-sided 8-sector format was the earliest format, it has the dubious honor of being the lowest common denominator, the one format that is universally usable on all PC models and all versions of DOS. That's why we see a great deal of software delivered in this format, even though it's a long-obsolete format. The next release of DOS, version 1.10, added the double-sided 8-sector format. Next came DOS 2.0, where it was decided that putting only eight sectors on a diskette track was overly conservative, and that nine per track could be safely and reliably used. So, with DOS 2.0 the single- and double-sided 9 sector formats were introduced.

While those four are the standard 5¼-inch diskette formats, there are actually more. Although IBM has used only double-density (40 track) standard diskette drives, some folks have installed in PCs quad-density drives (which have 80 tracks). There are also a variety of (nonstandard) quad-density formats as well.

For extra variety, there is the high-capacity format, which was introduced with the AT model. High-capacity diskettes have a special magnetic coating on them that allows a track to hold an amazing 15 sectors, rather than just 8 or 9. In addition, the hi-cap drives are quad-density, which means that they can put 80 tracks on a diskette side. Thankfully there is only one hi-cap format, so far, avoiding all this single-sided, double-sided, etc. nonsense.

It isn't quite accurate, however, to consider the hi-cap format as just an additional fifth addition to the standard four formats for 5¼-inch diskettes, because hi-cap diskettes have to have a special magnetic coating on them. The four standard 5¼-inch formats can be thought of as minor variations in the use of the same kind of diskette, while the hi-cap format requires a special (and much more expensive) diskette, even though it looks identical to the other garden-variety diskettes.

That finishes our discussion of the varieties of 5¼-inch floppy diskette, but before we pass on to other kinds of disks, I should briefly mention that there are other sizes of diskettes, even though they are rarely used within the PC family. There is an 8-inch diameter format that has mostly been used with an older generation of personal and word-processing computers. Also, there is a little-known 3½-inch size of floppy diskette which looks just like a miniature version of the 5¼-inch diskette.

The next basic kind of disks that we need to consider are the 3½-inch microdiskettes; one is diagrammed in Figure 8-5.

Microdiskettes are much smaller than floppy diskettes, and they are enclosed in a rigid protective case. Thanks to the smaller size and hard case, they are much easier and safer to mail and carry around (they fit nicely into a pocket). Inside, a micro diskette is the same familiar soft, flexible plastic, with a metal hub piece. Outside, the jacket is rigid, and it protects the disk from outside damage: the hub opening is nearly covered by a hub piece, and the read-write opening is sealed by a spring-loaded sliding metal protector. There's one further difference in the case: write-protection is signaled by a sliding plastic tab, rather than by a notch cut.

Standard microdiskettes are recorded in quad-density format, so that they have exactly twice the storage capacity of conventional diskettes. Their small size, protected case, and larger storage capacity have made them the disk of choice for newly-designed computers (such as Apple's Macintosh and numerous Japanese machines). However, the weight of tradition, the problems of incompatibility, and the PC users' huge collective investment in conventional 5¼-inch floppy diskettes have together retarded the use of this improved diskette format within the PC family.

That finishes our tour through the land of diskettes; hard disks are the next variety of disk for us to consider.

Hard disks get their name from the fact that the magnetically-coated disks themselves are rigid platters, made of an aluminum alloy. Because of many factors, including the much faster speed of rotation and the higher recording density, hard disks need to be in an atmosphere that's carefully protected against dust and other contamination. So hard disks are sealed inside the disk drive, and not removable like a diskette. It's because of this that IBM uses the term *fixed disk* for what everyone else calls a hard disk.

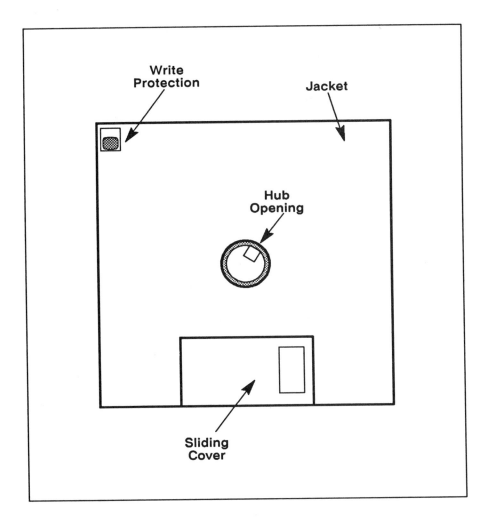

Figure 8-5. A 3½-inch microdiskette (bottom view).

There are many varieties of hard disks, differing in the number of platters and active recording sides, number of cylinders, number of sectors per track, speed, and other characteristics. We generally lump them all together into the collective category of hard disk. Two varieties are best known in the PC family.

The first is the 10-megabyte disk, which is used by the XT model, the Compaq Plus, and many other similar PC family members. The XT's disk has four sides, 305 *cylinders* (as track locations are called on hard disks), and 17 sectors per track. The second best-known variety of hard disk is the one introduced with the first AT models. This disk has four sides, 615 cylinders, 17 sectors per track, and a capacity of 20 megabytes. These two, however, are only typical of the many varieties of hard disk that can be used in the PC family. The AT model alone has a built-in capability to accommodate no fewer than 14 different hard disks, and others can be easily added.

There is one final basic variety of disk storage that we need to know about, *cartridge disks*. These are a hybrid type, combining the characteristics of hard disks (particularly the large storage capacity) and removable diskettes. There are quite a few varieties of cartridge disks, but probably the best known is the one called the "Bernoulli box," made by IOMega Corporation. Typically, cartridge disks have a capacity of five or ten megabytes, and they operate at a speed that is similar to a conventional sealed hard disk. But, like diskettes, cartridge disks can be removed, which makes it possible for data to be exchanged, shipped through the mail, or simply locked up for security.

That finishes our basic tour of disks and disk formats. It gives us the foundation of information that we'll need to understand the next stage in our journey through disks, where we explore how DOS views disks.

Some Things to Try

1. It's a mystery to me why the original PC ever had single-sided diskette drives, instead of double-sided. I wouldn't expect you to know why either, but see how many reasonable theories you can come up with. The exercise may help you understand a great deal about the realities that underlie personal computing.

2. In one of the IBM *Technical Reference* manuals, it states that for a regular diskette drive, which has 40 tracks, moving the read/write head takes five milliseconds per track. The average move, we're told, takes 81 milliseconds; why? What does that tell us?

3. There are hard disks that have the same capacity as each other, but they are "shaped" differently. For example, among the disk types that the AT can automatically accommodate, there is one with four sides and 614 cylinders and another with eight sides and 307 cylinders. The capacity of the two is identical. Is there any practical difference between them?

9

Disks:
The DOS Perspective

I
n this the second of our three chapters on disks, we'll take a look at our computers' disks from the DOS perspective, as DOS lays them out and uses them. Our disks, by themselves, are a kind of raw, unsurveyed land. It's only when an operating system, such as DOS, creates a map of how they are to be used that disks take on a useful form. Each operating system—and the PC family has several, in theory—has its own plan for how the unbroken land of a disk should be turned into productive fields. Since DOS is the only operating system that most PC users encounter, DOS's way of organizing a disk is the only one that we'll cover.

First we'll look at the basics of how DOS uses a disk, followed by the technical specifics that underlie a DOS disk. Then we'll explore key elements of what DOS data files look like, so that we have a better understanding of the working contents of our disks. Particularly, we'll focus on the most universal data format, ASCII text files.

This chapter will give us most of what we need to know about our disks. What's missing here, we'll find in Chapter 10, the final installment of this three-chapter series, which covers deeper details of our disks.

9.1 DOS Disk Overview

In Chapter 8, when we looked at the basics of our computer's disks, we saw how a disk is intrinsically a three- or four-dimensional object. The three dimensions—of track or cylinder, the radial dimension; of side, the vertical dimension; and sector within a track, the circular dimension—locate the position of each sector on the disk. The size of each sector, how much data can be stored inside it, is the fourth dimension. Multiplying the first three dimensions gives us the total number of sectors on a disk, the number of working pieces that DOS has at its disposal when it uses the disk. Multiplying the number of sectors by the sector size gives us the data capacity of the disk, the number of bytes that DOS has to tuck data away in.

The sectors on a disk are the fundamental units of disk activity. All reading and writing on a disk is done with full sectors, and not any smaller amount of data. An important part of understanding how DOS looks at a disk is seeing how DOS handles sectors. A key part of this is that DOS "flattens" a disk, by ignoring the inherently three-dimensional shape of a disk. Of course DOS can't completely ignore the three-dimensional shape of a disk. To actually read and write disk sectors, DOS has to work with sectors in terms of the dimensions that locate and identify each sector. That, however, is just to accommodate the physical nature of the disk. For its own purposes, DOS thinks of a disk as a one-dimensional object.

This means that DOS treats the sectors of a disk as just a sequential list of sectors, from the first sector on a disk to the last. The diagram in Figure 9-1 draws a picture of how this is done. For its own purposes, DOS numbers the sectors on a disk sequentially, starting at 0 (for the first sector on the first side of the first cylinder of a disk), to 1 (for the second sector on

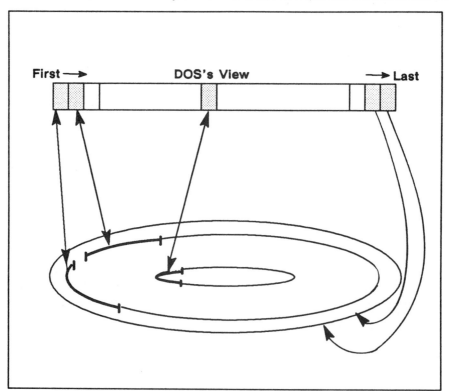

Figure 9-1. A three-dimensional disk meets a one-dimensional DOS.

the first side, etc.) and on to the last sector in sequence (which is the last sector of the last side of the last cylinder). Everything that DOS does in working with and planning the use of disk sectors is done in terms of these sequential sector numbers. Only at the last moment, when information is actually read or written on the disk, does DOS translate between its internal notation (the sequential numbers) and the disk's own three-dimensional notation.

This linear, sequential approach to a disk greatly simplifies DOS's job of organizing a disk. But it does have a price to it. One part of the price is that DOS can't take advantage of the fact that it takes quite a bit longer to go from one sector to another when they are located on different cylinders than between sectors in the same cylinder—that's because, to switch cylinders, the disk drive's read/write heads have to move from place to place. Basically DOS doesn't know which sectors are on the same cylinder because it ignores the disk's division into cylinders. There is another price too: the traditional way DOS handles disks sets a limit on how large a disk we can use with our PC computers. For more on that, see the sidebar *The 32-Megabyte Limit*.

The 32-Megabyte Limit

The linear, sequential approach that DOS uses to organize disks led to a limitation that wasn't expected in the early days of DOS: a limit of 32 megabytes in the size of disk that DOS could use.

This limitation comes about as the natural result of two simple things: first, that the standard size of a disk sector for DOS is 512 bytes. Second, that DOS numbers diskette sectors sequentially, and holds those numbers in the PC's most natural data format, as a 16-bit integer. There are only 64K (or 65,536) different 16-bit numbers; so, using this scheme, DOS can only work with 64K distinct sectors. If the sectors are 512 bytes big, that sets a limit of 32 megabytes (64K times 512, roughly 32 million) as the largest disk that this scheme can handle.

In the early days of DOS and the PC family, few imagined that anyone would want a disk that big on a computer this small. But the history of computing has one truism: however much you have, it's not enough.

There are ways around this limit: sectors can be made bigger (say 1024 bytes each), or DOS could use more bits to number the disk sectors with. One way or another the "32-meg barrier" will be broken—perhaps by the time you read this it will already be done, since the PC family is continually growing and expanding. But the original design of DOS was created with this inherent limit on how large a disk could be.

DOS takes a similar approach when it comes to storing our data on the disk. As we've mentioned, all reading and writing of data on a disk is done in terms of complete sectors. But when we work with data—or our programs, acting on our behalf, work with data—it may be read or written in any amount. We can work with our disk data byte by individual byte, or we can have DOS transfer huge amounts of it at one time. This points to one of the main jobs that DOS performs in managing our disks: it acts as a translator between the way the disk works with data (which is a 512-byte sector at a time) and the way we want to work with it (which can be any of a hundred ways). DOS's disk management routines handle the conversion between the amounts of data that we want, and the amounts of data that the disk stores. In effect DOS does it by running a warehouse operation. It packages and unpackages our data, so that the data is bundled in appropriate-sized quantities—the size we want when we use it, and the size of sectors when it's transferred to the disk.

TECHNICAL BACKGROUND

Physical and Logical Formatting

The formatting of a disk actually has two parts to it—which I call *physical* and *logical* formatting—and if we don't want to be confused about what's going on with our disks, we need to be aware of the distinction.

Physical formatting involves the creation of sectors on a disk, complete with their address markings (which are used like name tags to identify the sectors after the formatting is done) and with the data portion of the sector (the part we and our programs know about) established and filled in with some dummy data. A brand-new, unused diskette normally comes to us *without* the physical formatting done, while a new hard disk will *already* be physically formatted.

Logical formatting is essentially the adoption of a disk to the standards of our operating system. When a disk is formatted for DOS, the DOS-style logical structure (discussed in Section 9.2) of the disk is created. The logical formatting is the road map that DOS, or any other operating system, uses to navigate through and make sense out of a disk.

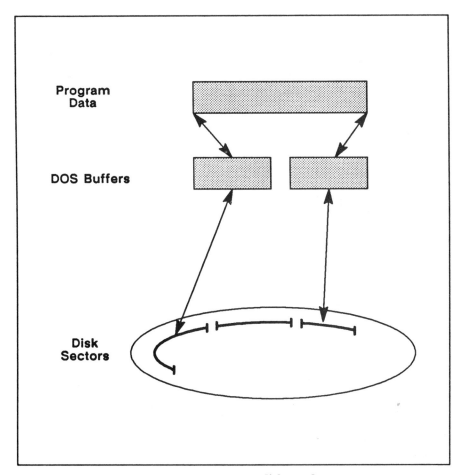

Figure 9-2. DOS repackages data between disks and our programs.

In terms of physical and logical formatting, the FORMAT command of DOS acts differently on diskettes and hard disks, which is why the distinction between logical and physical formatting is important to know about. Since the logical formatting is essential to DOS's use of a disk, naturally the FORMAT command always does that. What differs between diskettes and hard disks is whether or not DOS is free to perform the physical formatting.

For a diskette, the FORMAT command performs the physical formatting as well as the logical. That's because a diskette completely "belongs" to the operating system that formats it, while a hard disk may be *partitioned* into sections that can belong to differing operating systems (we'll see more about that in Chapter 10). On a hard disk, the FORMAT command does not dare perform the

137

physical formatting, even within a partition that DOS "owns," since that might well interfere with the rest of the disk.

While DOS doesn't provide us with a program to physically format a hard disk, you'll find one on the IBM Advanced Diagnostics diskette. There are some unusual circumstances in which we might want to get a fresh, from-scratch start on a hard disk, and it's good to know how to get our hands on a program that will do the physical formatting.

The DOS FORMAT program uses a special BIOS command (see Chapter 18) to format diskettes track by track. The mechanism of physical formatting requires that the formatting for all the sectors in each track be laid down in one coordinated operation. This track-by-track diskette formatting feature can be used as the basis of a copy-protection scheme, as we'll see more about in Chapter 10.

When FORMAT formats a diskette, it sets the sector data to a default value, hex F6, in each byte. Since the FORMAT command overwrites each byte of the diskette, all old data on the diskette is completely obliterated. That eliminates any hope of recovering any previous data after a diskette is formatted. However, FORMAT does *not* overwrite the old data on a hard disk, so it is possible to recover data from a reformatted hard disk.

Before DOS can use a disk, the disk has to be *formatted*, which means marked off and organized the way DOS likes to work with its disks. We use the DOS utility program FORMAT to do that. The FORMAT command does whatever is necessary to put a disk into the state that DOS expects it to be in (which varies, depending upon the type of disk—see the sidebar *Physical and Logical Formatting* for more details). After that's done, FORMAT lays out the DOS structure on the disk, the structure that establishes how and where files can be stored. We'll see how that works in Section 9.2.

9.2 The Structure of a DOS Disk

In order to organize our disks, DOS divides them into two parts: a small system area that DOS uses to keep track of key information about the disk, and the data area, the bulk of the disk, where our file data is stored. The system area uses up only a quite small portion of a disk: at most it's just two percent of the total space (that's on the very smallest 160K diskette format), and on a hard disk it's quite a bit less—for example just 3/10 of one percent on the AT model's 20-megabyte hard disk.

The system area that DOS uses is itself divided into three parts, called the *boot*, the *FAT*, and the *root directory*. Let's explore them one by one.

The *boot*, or *boot record* is the very first part of a DOS disk. It holds a very short program—one that's only a few hundred bytes long—that performs the job of beginning the loading of DOS into the computer's memory. The start-up procedure is called *booting* (because the computer is "pulling itself up by the bootstraps"—loading the programs that are necessary for the computer to carry on its work). When we have a DOS *system* disk (one that's been formatted with the /S system option) the disk contains a full copy of DOS. The job of this boot record program is to begin the process of starting DOS from a disk reading from disk to memory the first part of the DOS programs. Interestingly enough, the boot record doesn't just appear on a *system* formatted disk. It's on every disk, and it's clever enough to report the error if we try to boot up from a disk that isn't system formatted (doesn't include a copy of DOS on it).

The boot portion of a disk is very small—only a single 512-byte sector, so it takes up practically none of the space in a disk. Incidentally, there is some very interesting information that's recorded on some disks' boot records. We'll look into that in Chapter 10, when we dig into some of the more technical information about our disks.

The next part of the system portion of a disk is called the *File Allocation Table,* or *FAT* for short. DOS needs a way to keep track of the big data portion of a disk, to tell what's in use and what's available for new data storage. The FAT is used to record the status of each part of the disk. In order to manage the data space on a disk, DOS divides it up into logical units called *clusters*. When a file is being recorded on the data portion of our disks, disk space is assigned to the file in these clusters. How big a cluster is varies from one disk format to another; it can be as small as an

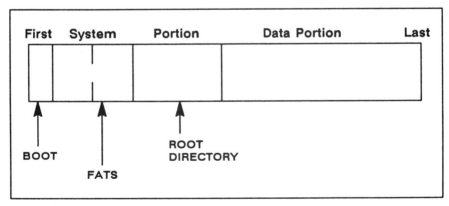

Figure 9-3. The parts of a DOS diskette.

individual sector or much bigger. On the largely-obsolete single-sided diskettes, each sector is its own cluster; on double-sided diskettes, clusters are two sectors each, 1024 bytes. On the XT model's 10-megabyte disk, the cluster size is usually eight sectors, 4096 bytes. There's an obvious pattern here—the bigger the disk, the bigger the cluster size, generally; but it's far from a strict rule. On the AT model's larger 20-megabyte disk the cluster size is half that of the XT: four sectors, 2048 bytes.

Whatever the cluster size, DOS carves up the data portion of the disk into these relatively small clusters and then uses them as the unit of space that it allocates to the disk files. This allocation is managed by using the File Allocation Table. The FAT is simply a table of numbers, with one place in the table for each cluster on the disk. The number that's recorded in each cluster's FAT entry indicates if the cluster is in use by a file or available for new data. A zero in the cluster's FAT entry means the cluster is free. Any other number indicates it's in use (and the number is used to link together the different clusters that make up one file's data; we'll see more of these technical details in Chapter 10).

The essence of the FAT is that it gives DOS a distinct and separate place to keep track of the allocation of the disk's data space. This isolates the space and record-keeping function, which helps protect it from possible damage. If you think about it, you'll see why the FAT is the most critical part of a disk, the part that most needs to be protected. In fact, the FAT is so critical that DOS usually records two separate copies of the FAT on each disk. Only the first copy is actually used, but the second copy is made to help make it possible to perform emergency repairs on damaged disks.

The last part of the disk's system area is the *root directory*. This is the file directory that every disk has—it's the basic, built-in directory for the disk. (Disks can also have subdirectories added to them, but subdirectories are an optional part of a disk that we can create as we need. The root directory isn't an optional part of the disk.)

The directory, of course, records the files that are stored on the disk. For each file, there is a directory entry that records the file's 8-character filename, the 3-character extension to the filename, the size of the file, and a date and time stamp that records when the file was last changed. All those parts of a file's directory entry are known to us, because they're shown in the DIR listing that we're used to seeing. There are also two other pieces of information that are recorded about a file in its directory entry. One is called the *starting cluster number*—which indicates which cluster in the disk's data space holds the first portion of the file. The other item in the directory entry is called the *file attribute*—it's used to record a number of things about the file. For example, subdirectories have a particular *direc-*

tory attribute marking; DOS's so-called system files have a special pair of attributes called *system* and *hidden*. There are also two attributes that serve us more directly: the *read-only* attribute protects our files from being changed or deleted; the *archive* attribute is used to help keep track of which files on our disk already have or need backup copies.

The root directory of each disk, like the other items in the system portion of a disk, is a fixed size for each disk format. This size determines how many entries there are for files in the root directory. Each directory entry occupies 32 bytes, so 16 of them fit into a single sector. The smallest diskette format, the single-sided 160K format, has four sectors set aside for the root directory, so it has room for 64 files in the directory. A double-sided diskette has seven directory sectors, making room for 112 files. Hard disks have more: for example, the AT's 20-meg disk has 32 sectors, making room for 512 file directory entries.

I mentioned before that the FAT is used to chain together a record of where a file's data is stored. Here is how it works. As we saw, each file's directory entry includes a field which gives the cluster number where the first part of the file's data is stored. The FAT table has a number entry for each cluster. If we look up the FAT entry for the first cluster in a file, it will contain the number of the next cluster in the file—and the FAT entry for that cluster will point to the next one. This way, the FAT entries are chained together to provide DOS with a way of tracing through the entire contents of a file. When the end of the file is reached, the FAT entry for the last cluster doesn't hold the number of another cluster. Instead, it contains a special code number marking the end of the file's space allocation chain.

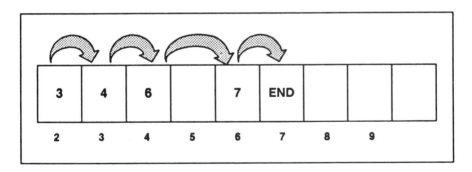

Figure 9-4. A file's space allocation in the FAT.

That finishes our survey of the system portion of a disk. What remains is the majority of the disk, the data portion. But we already pretty much know everything basic there is to know about this part of a disk. The data portion is used to record the actual data contents of the disk files. The data space, as we've seen, is divided up into units called clusters (which are made up of one or more sectors; on each disk the clusters are all the same size, but between disk formats the cluster size will vary). Each file's data is recorded on one or more clusters (and the record of which clusters, in which order, is kept in the disk's File Allocation Table). It's worth noting that a file's data can be scattered all over a disk in disjointed clusters. DOS generally tries to keep a file's data gathered together into contiguous sequential clusters, but with varying activity in the disk's space allocation files can end up being stored scattered around different parts of the disk.

We've mentioned subdirectories, and at this point I should explain that each subdirectory acts like a mixture of a data file and the disk's root directory. As far as how a subdirectory is recorded on the disk, it's no different than any other disk file: the subdirectory is stored in disk's data space, and a record of where the subdirectory is located is kept in the FAT, exactly like any other file. But when it comes to using the contents of a subdirectory, it acts like the disk's root directory: it holds a record of files and other subdirectories that are stored on the disk, and DOS works with subdirectories just like it works with the main, root directory. There are two major differences between subdirectories and root directories. One is that there is only one root on each disk, but there can be numerous subdirectories. The other is that each root directory has a fixed size and capacity, while subdirectories, like files, can grow to any size that the disk can accommodate.

What we've seen so far gives us all the fundamental information that we need to understand the basics of the structure of DOS disks. There is more to know about them, of course; there are plenty of fascinating technical details left to explore. We'll get into that in Chapter 10 when we dig into deeper disk details.

9.3 Learning About File Formats

Each file that we have stored on our disk potentially has its own unique data format—the structure of the data that's recorded inside the file. It would seem that there is little that we can say about the format of our disk files; and in many ways that is true. However, there are a number of important observations that we can make about files which will deepen our understanding of what's going on inside our disks.

First, we should note that the three-character extension part of a filename is intended to be used as an indication of the format and use of a file.

Some of these filename extensions are standard and must be used to correctly identify the file type; most, though, don't have a strict use, just a conventional one.

The strictly enforced extensions mostly have to do with programs: DOS requires that all programs be recorded in one of two special program formats, and they must be identified by the standard extension names of COM and EXE. Batch command files also must be named BAT. Most other filename extensions are optional, but each application program system is usually designed to work more easily with files that have extensions that are standard for the system. For example, the BASIC interpreter expects that BASIC program files will be named BAS. Other programming languages also expect this: Pascal expects program source files to be named PAS, and so forth. Likewise, programs like 1-2-3, Word, and so forth, all have their conventional extension names.

The contents of data files can be very interesting to us, but we have to make a special effort to look inside our files—using snooping tools like DEBUG or NU, both described in Chapter 22—and often it's hard to decode, or otherwise make much sense of what we can see inside a data file. However, by looking, we can sometimes find some very interesting things.

There is one very good reason for taking a look at and learning about the data formats created by the programs we use: if we ever need to do any repair work on our disks, such as "unerasing" deleted files or other such file recovery operations. If we learn what our data looks like in advance, we have a better chance of recognizing it in an emergency.

As a general rule, the data files created by our programs have an internal structure that is completely jumbled to the human eye. Certain parts can be easily recognized if we take a look at them: character text data, such as the names and addresses in a mailing list database, are easy to recognize. But the parts of the data which hold numbers and formatting information describing the layout of the data are usually recorded in a form that is thoroughly cryptic, and can only be deciphered by the programs that work with the data.

One special kind of file, though, has a pattern to it that we should be able to recognize fairly well: these are data files made up of what are called "fixed length records"—a repeated pattern of data where content of the data varies, but each element has the same length, so that we can notice a repeated pattern, even when the actual data itself isn't recognizable. This is the kind of data that BASIC uses for its *random files*. Since the data records in this kind of file are all the same length, BASIC can calculate its way to the location of any randomly specified record number without having to search through the file from the beginning. Whenever we look at one of these data files that is built from fixed-sized elements, we may be able to recognize the pattern in it and decode some of the file's data.

By exploring and digging through our files data, we can learn a great deal about how our computers and programs work with disk data.

9.4 ASCII Text Files

There is one particular file format that every PC user needs to know about, the *ASCII text file* format. ASCII text files—which are also called *ASCII files* or *text files* for short—are the closest thing the PC family has to a universal format for data files. While most programs have their own special way of recording data, the ASCII text file is a common format that can be used by any program, and *is* used by very many of them.

ASCII text files are designed to hold ordinary text data, like the words that you are reading. ASCII text files are used by many simple text editing programs (such as the EDLIN editor program that is a part of DOS), and some word-processing programs also work directly with ASCII text files. However, most programs, including word processors, the BASIC interpreter, spreadsheet programs, and many others, use the ASCII text file format as an alternative to their own "native" data formats. These programs are prepared to work with ASCII text files simply because the ASCII text file format is something of a last resort way of transferring data from one program to another. Often, in fact, more than a last resort, it's often the only way to get data from here to there.

ASCII text file data is rather nude—it isn't clothed in the rich formatting that most programs use for their data. But, when we need to pass data from one place to another, it's often the only reasonable way to get it done.

When I said that most programs have their own special data formats that are different than ASCII text files, I was really referring to applications programs such as databases, spreadsheets, and so forth. There are also many programs which expect to work *only* with the simple and common data format of ASCII text files. Programming language compilers and assemblers expect to read their program source code from plain ASCII text files. Some other programs too are intended to work primarily with ASCII text files, such as IBM's spelling checker WordProof. Among programs that are, one way or another, writing tools, there is an informal division between the simple ones which use ASCII text files (e.g., many text-editing programs and spelling checkers) and the complex ones that use their own custom data formats (e.g., most word-processing programs). Finally, there is one further and very important use for ASCII text files which I need to mention: batch command files, which allow DOS to carry out a series of commands together as a single unit; these batch files are kept in the text file format.

The data in a text file is composed of two character types: ordinary ASCII text characters—letters of the alphabet and so forth—which we learned about in Section 4.2 and the ASCII control characters, covered in Section 4.3. The regular *text* characters are the principle data in an ASCII text file, while the ASCII *control* characters tell how the text is formatted: they mark its division into lines and paragraphs and so forth.

There is no strict definition about how our programs and computers are supposed to make use of ASCII text files. Instead, all the programs that work with ASCII text files use the most basic elements of this file format, and some programs go further and make use of some of the less-common formatting control characters. Let's start by describing the most common elements.

- A pair of ASCII control characters are used to mark the end of each line: the characters *carriage-return* and *line-feed* (known in ASCII terminology as CR and LF; they are character codes 13 and 10, or hex 0D and 0A). These two, together as a pair, are the standard way to mark the end of a line of text.

- One ASCII control character is used to mark the end of the file of text data. It's the Control-Z character, code 26 or hex 1A. In most tables of ASCII control characters this code is called SUB, but since it's used here to mean *End-Of-File,* it's also called EOF. Normally an ASCII text file has this *End-of-File* character to mark the end of the text data.

- The *tab* character is used as a substitute for repeated spaces; its character code 9, and the ASCII term for it is HT, short for horizontal tab. *Tab* appears in many ASCII files, even though there is no universal agreement about just where the tab stops are. Most programs (but, unfortunately far from all) handle tabs on the assumption that there is a tab stop every eight positions (at the 9th, 17th, etc., columns).

- The *form-feed* character is used to mark the end of one page and the beginning of the next; the character code is 12, hex 0C, and the ASCII name is FF. This control character is also called *page eject.*

An ASCII text file can contain any of the control characters that you saw in Section 4.2 (they're summarized in Table 4-1, on page 49), but most often the only ones used are the five I just described, and in many cases even the last two—tab and form-feed—aren't used, to keep the coding as simple as possible.

There are several commonly used ways to indicate the division of text data into paragraphs. The most common form marks the end of each line of text with a carriage-return/line-feed pair. This is the form that compilers expect to find their program source code in. When this form is used to mark words, sentences, and paragraphs, it's common to indicate the end of a paragraph by a blank line (that is, two pairs of carriage-return/line-feeds in a row, with no other data in between). Sometimes, though, we'll see ASCII text files in which each paragraph is treated as a single, very long line, with a carriage-return/line-feed pair at the end of the paragraph, but nowhere inside the paragraph. Some word-processing programs like to create ASCII text files like this.

Because there are these different ways of laying out an ASCII text file, there can often be conflicts between the way one program expects a text file to be and the way another program expects it. We often find that different programs are at odds with each other when we try to use ASCII text files as a way of transferring data between them. For example, if we try to use ASCII text files to pass something we've written from one word-processing program to another, we may find that what one program considered to be just lines that make up a paragraph the other program considers to be separate paragraphs. This sort of nonsense can be very annoying to deal with. Nevertheless, ASCII text files are the closest thing our computers have to a universal language which every program can speak. That's why you may find yourself working with ASCII text files more often than you expect to.

We usually think of ASCII text files as containing either words, like the sentences and paragraphs you are reading here, or program source code, like the programming examples that you have seen throughout this book. But any form of data can be translated into an ASCII text format, one way or another. So, we might find some text files that consist only of numbers, written out in ASCII characters. This is the way that programs can use ASCII text files to exchange data that isn't made up of words. For example, the *Data Interchange File,* or DIF, standard uses ASCII text files to transfer data between spreadsheets and other programs that know how to interpret "DIF" data. These DIF files are simply ASCII text files whose text describes, for example, the contents of a spreadsheet, all expressed in ASCII text characters rather than the internal coded format that the spreadsheet program uses for itself.

To get a more concrete idea of what an ASCII text file looks like, let's create an example. Suppose we had a text file with these two lines in it:

```
Columbus sailed the ocean blue
In fourteen hundred and ninety two.
```

To see what that looks like inside an ASCII text file, I'll write it out again in a way that represents what would be in the text file's data. To do that, I'll indicate the control code characters with ⟨CR⟩ for carriage return and so forth. Here's what our two-line rhyme looks like:

```
Columbus sailed the ocean blue⟨CR⟩⟨LF⟩
In fourteen hundred and ninety two.⟨CR⟩⟨LF⟩⟨EOF⟩
```

The more advanced tinkering you do with your computer, the more likely it is that you will find yourself working with, or looking at, ASCII text files. When you do, there is one anomaly that you may run into that you should know about so that it doesn't confuse you. It has to do with the way ASCII text files are ended and the size of the file.

I mentioned earlier that the Control-Z end-of-file character, code 26, is normally used to mark the end of a text file's data. There are several variations on just how that is done. The cleanest and strictest form has the Control-Z end-of-file character stored right after the last line of text (the way I show in our example above). The length of the file, as recorded in the file's disk directory, includes the end-of-file character in the size of the file. Sometimes though, a file may appear to be bigger, judging from the size recorded in the disk directory. This is because some programs work with text files not byte by byte, but in chunks of, say, 128 bytes at a time. When this kind of program creates a text file, the Control-Z end-of-file character will show where the true end of the file is, but the file's disk directory entry will show a length that's been rounded up to the next higher multiple of 128. In cases like that, the real length of the file is slightly smaller than what we would expect it to be, based on the size in the directory. There is another way that an ASCII text file might appear odd to us: it could be recorded without a Control-Z end-of-file character marking the end. In this case, the file size recorded in the directory indicates the true size of the file, and there's no end-of-file marker, on theory that none is needed, since the size tells us where the end is. Any time we take a close look at the insides of an ASCII text file, or any time we write a program to read them, we need to be prepared for variations like this in the way the end of the file is indicated.

147

Some Things to Try

1. If you have the NU program, use it to explore the dimensions of your disks and see the size of the clusters which DOS creates on your disks. You'll find the cluster information displayed in NU's menu selection 2.2.

2. Why is the FAT the most critical part of a disk? What makes it more important than the directory portion? There is a DOS file recovery utility called RECOVER that can recreate a disk's directory if the directory is damaged but the FAT is not. How do you think this is this possible? Could there be a similar program that will recreate a damaged FAT if the directory was intact?

3. To see how BASIC can record its program files in two forms, in BASIC's own coded format or in the ASCII text file format, enter a short BASIC program (just a line or two of any BASIC program) and then save it to disk in both formats, using these commands: SAVE ''BASFORM'' and SAVE ''TEXTFORM'',A. Then see the differences between the two files: compare their sizes using the DIR command. See how their contents differ by using the TYPE command to print them on your computer's display screen. If you know how to snoop in files using DEBUG or NU (see Chapter 23 to learn how if you don't), inspect the contents of the two files with either of these two snooping tools.

10

Disks:
Deeper Details

This is the last leg of our three-chapter journey though the PC family's disk storage. Here we'll move into some of the deeper and more technical details of how our computers use their disks. We'll be covering what's special about hard disks and the way that our computers work with them. Then we'll see the details of how DOS works with our disks, expanding on what we covered in Chapter 9. Finally, we'll close our treatment by looking at some special disk peculiarities, including copy protection and nonstandard disk formats.

As you've seen so far, this book is divided, in an informal way, into two parts, with the more technical information separately identified, so that readers who want to focus on understanding the PC could easily pass over the technical parts. Most of this chapter falls into that category, but there is one part that I don't want you to miss: that's the discussion of hard disks and particularly hard disk partitions. If you want to understand all the most important practical things about the PC family, you need to be sure to know what's what with hard disks.

10.1 Hard Disk Features and Partitions

Hard disks present some special challenges to the designers of computers that just don't apply to diskettes. The most obvious thing that's different about a hard disk is that it has a storage capacity that's much bigger than a diskette. In nearly everything in life there comes a point when a quantitative difference becomes a qualitative difference—when more isn't just more, it's also different. That's the case with our computer's hard disks: their storage capacity is so much more than a diskette's that it also has to be treated differently than a diskette. A hard disk's greater capacity, and also its much faster speed, is part of what's special about a hard disk, but oddly enough it isn't the most critical difference. What's most different about a hard disk is that it isn't removable.

I've been using the term "hard disk" because that's what nearly everybody likes to call them. But IBM's own term for them is "fixed disk"—a name that emphasizes the key fact that, unlike a diskette, a (fixed) hard disk is built into the machine and can't be casually switched to change the data that's on-line to our computer.

(We should note here that there are some hard disk systems that have removable disk cartridges, so that they aren't fixed; they are as changeable as a floppy diskette. One widely known brand of cartridge disk system is the *Bernoulli Box*. This type of disk combines the size and speed of a conventional hard disk with the removability of a diskette. Our discussion of hard disks (or more properly fixed disks) here mostly does not apply to these cartridge hard disk systems.)

The fact that a fixed hard disk is fixed presents a special problem: we're stuck with the disk in our computer, we can't switch it for another one in a different format or set it up to accommodate another operating system. While most of us work exclusively within the framework that DOS creates for our computers, DOS isn't the only operating system around— there are others for the PC family, including *CP/M-86,* the *UCSD p-System, Xenix,* and *PC-IX* (a pair of operating systems derived from the well-regarded UNIX system) and others.

The idea here is that there is no problem with a diskette being "owned" by an operating system like our DOS—owned in the sense that the diskette has a format and logical structure that only applies to the program (DOS) which works with the disk. Likewise, there's no fundamental problem with a game program using its own peculiar diskette format if it wants to (which many games do, just for copy-protection reasons). Although odd diskette formats can be a nuisance for us, it's not any fundamental problem for our use of our PCs, simply because our machines aren't *committed* in any sense to always using these odd formats, since we can just switch our diskettes around, take one out, and put another on it.

With a (fixed) hard disk the situation is completely different. If our hard disk is "owned" by one operating system (say our DOS), then we can't use it with another operating system (say any of the increasingly popular UNIX-type systems). Since almost everything that we do with our PCs is based on DOS, we'd be tempted to say "So what?" But that is a very short-sighted view. The world of computing is always changing, and it's quite likely that the operating system that we use for our computers today isn't the one we'll use a few years hence. Even today, there are PC users who find good reasons to use systems besides DOS. How do we accommodate different operating systems, with incompatible ways of structuring the use of a disk, all on one hard disk?

The answer, of course, is partitioning: dividing a hard disk into areas which can be ''owned'' by different operating systems. Within the confines of each partition, the disk can be formatted and logically structured to meet whatever the needs are of the operating system that ''owns'' the partition.

This arrangement allows for a great deal of flexibility in the use of our hard disks, but it relies on some across-the-board standards that every program using the disk must follow. There has to be a variety of master format that the disk has which all the operating systems on the disk must live within. Part of this common ground is the actual physical formatting of the disk, which sets, among other things, the sector size that will apply in every partition on the disk. This points up the distinction between physical and logical formatting that we discussed in Chapter 9. But a common sector size isn't all there is to the common ground and rules of coexistence that apply to a partitioned hard disk. There also has to be standard way of marking off the boundaries of a disk's partitions; and each operating system using a partitioned disk has to agree to stay within its own bounds and not poach on another partition's territory.

Here is how it's done. The very first sector of a hard disk is set aside for a special master record, which contains a partition table describing the layout of the disk. This table shows what the dimensions of the disk are, and shows how many partitions there are, and what the size and location of each is. Now a disk doesn't have to be divided into more than one partition—in fact, the most common thing on our PCs is to have only one partition, a DOS partition, which takes up the entire disk. However many partitions there are on the disk—from one to four—and whether they take up the whole disk or leave part of it for future use, this master disk record, stored on the first sector of the disk, shows how many there are, and where they are located in the hard disk. Figure 10-1 gives you a picture representing what this is like.

By far the most common thing that PC owners do is to ignore the extra possibilities and complexity that disk partitioning brings us. Instead, most of us simply create a single DOS partition that fills the entire hard disk, and use it as if DOS owned the whole disk and as if there were no such thing as partitioning. This, in fact is the most sensible thing to do. Until you have a need for another partition, which may never happen, there is no reason to set aside hard disk space in case you might need another partition in the future. We can take care of that problem when the time comes.

To deal with partitions on our hard disks, DOS has a program called

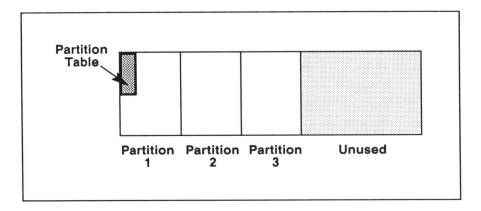

Figure 10-1. A partitioned hard disk.

FDISK, which can display and change partition data. Figure 10-2 shows a typical display of partition data, for a disk that's devoted entirely to DOS. There can be up to four partitions in the list that FDISK displays. Each will have its own starting and ending location and size in disk cylinders. Together they can take up the entire disk (as you see in Figure 10-2) or leave parts of the disk open.

The FDISK program allows us to manipulate the disk partitions while we're working with DOS. If we're working with other operating systems, they should have equivalent programs. DOS's FDISK allows us to create or delete a DOS-owned partition, but it doesn't allow us to remove a partition that belongs to another operating system. This seems like a good safety feature, but it has its disadvantages: if we end up with an unwanted partition from another system, we can't blow it away from DOS, so we could end up being stuck with a bum partition (this has happened to acquaintances of mine).

Suppose we've devoted our entire hard disk to DOS and now we want to surrender some of the space to make room for another partition? Can we simply give up the space? Unfortunately not. The way DOS structures it's disk partitions, it can't just simply shrink the partition. If we need to resize a DOS partition (to make it smaller *or* larger), we need to unload all the contents of the partition (say with the DOS utility BACKUP), delete the partition (with FDISK), create a new partition, format it (with FORMAT) and reload the data (with RESTORE). That can be a laborious process, which we can avoid by leaving room for new partitions when we first start using our hard disks. We could leave room, but I don't recommend it. I think that unless we know for sure that we'll be needing another partition, we're better off letting DOS use all of our hard disks, and face the chore of repartitioning when the need arises.

```
Display Partition Information


Partition    Status    Type    Start    End    Size
    1           A       DOS       0      613    614



Total disk space is 614 cylinders.




Press Esc to return to FDISK Options
```

Figure 10-2. Hard disk partition data.

In Figure 10-2 you'll notice that the sole partition is marked with status ''A'': that means that it is the *active* partition. On any partitioned disk, one partition at a time is marked as active. This has to do with the start-up, or booting, process. We know that every ordinary disk has a boot program on its first disk sector, which begins the process of starting up or booting the operating system. The same thing applies to a partitioned hard disk, but there is an extra set involved. The first sector of a partitioned hard disk contains a ''master boot program'' along with the table that describes the partitions. This master boot program looks at the partition table to see which partition is active. Then it fires up the boot program starting that partition. Each partition has its own boot program (just as each diskette has a boot record) that is tailored to the needs of the particular operating system which owns that partition. The master boot record does the job of finding the right partition boot record and getting it going.

We've spoken of disk partitions as belonging to distinct operating systems, but that isn't always the case. Officially there can be only one DOS partition on a hard disk, but sometimes there are actually two or more, and for an important reason. As we saw in Chapter 9, DOS ordinarily has a

32-megabyte limit to the size of the disks it can work with. What if we have a larger disk, say a 70 meg disk? The DOS partition that we create on such a disk ordinarily couldn't be bigger than 32 megs, leaving the rest of the disk unavailable to DOS. But, we can create other DOS-style partitions on the disk, and access them through a special DOS device driver. Using this trick, we can use the entire disk for DOS data, although it would be divided up into separate partitions (which we would treat as if they were separate disks).

You can see from all this that partitions are a special key to making the large storage space of hard disks work for us, with an extra flexibility that just doesn't apply to our diskettes. With this large size and extra flexibility, though, comes an additional degree of complexity that we have to master, if we want to get the full benefit from our computer's hard disks.

Next, we're going to look inside the structure that DOS places on our disks, and see some of the fascinating technical details of how DOS manages our disks.

TECHNICAL BACKGROUND ▌ ▎ ▎ ▌ ▌ ▌ ▬▬▬▬▬▬▬▬▬▬

10.2 Detailed Disk Structure

In this section we're going to take a deeper look at the way DOS structures a disk, so we can better understand what's going on with our disks. That will help us appreciate and use our disks when everything is going right with them, and it may help us work our way out of trouble when something goes wrong.

As we saw in Chapter 9, DOS divides each disk into two parts: the system part, used for DOS's record-keeping, and the data part, where our files are stored. The system portion itself has three parts: the boot record, the FAT (File Allocation Table), and the root directory. Now we'll get a closer look at what's stored inside each one.

The boot record is always the very first part of each disk. As we learned before, it's used to hold a short program which begins the process of starting up ("booting") DOS. The boot record is present on every disk, even those we can't boot from (because they don't contain a copy of the DOS system files).

The boot program is small enough to easily fit into a single disk sector, so it isn't necessary for the boot portion to take up more than one sector. But in case some future circumstance does make it necessary to have a larger boot program, DOS's method of handling disks allows for the possibility that the boot area might have to become larger.

There are more interesting things inside the boot record of a disk than you might imagine. We can use the DOS DEBUG program to inspect the contents of a boot record; it only takes two simple DEBUG commands: L 0 0 0 1, which reads into memory the boot record from a disk in the A drive, and D 0 L 200, which displays the boot record's data in hex and ASCII. Figure 10-3 shows what this information looks like for DOS version 3.10.

```
2B35:0000  EB 29 90 49 42 4D 20 20-33 2E 31 00 02 02 01 00   .).IBM  3.1.....
2B35:0010  02 70 00 D0 02 FD 02 00-09 00 02 00 00 00 00 00   .p..............
2B35:0020  00 00 00 00 0F 00 00 00-00 01 00 FA 33 C0 8E D0   ...........3...
2B35:0030  BC 00 7C 16 07 BB 78 00-36 C5 37 1E 56 16 53 BF   ..|..x.6.7.V.S.
2B35:0040  20 7C B9 0B 00 FC AC 26-80 3D 00 74 03 26 8A 05    |.....&.=.t.&..
2B35:0050  AA 8A C4 E2 F1 06 1F 89-47 02 C7 07 20 7C FB CD   ........G... |..
2B35:0060  13 72 67 A0 10 7C 98 F7-26 16 7C 03 06 1C 7C 03   .rg..|..&.|...|.
2B35:0070  06 0E 7C A3 34 7C A3 2C-7C B8 20 00 F7 26 11 7C   ..|.4|.,|. ..&.|
2B35:0080  8B 1E 0B 7C 03 C3 48 F7-F3 01 06 2C 7C BB 00 05   ...|..H...,|...
2B35:0090  A1 34 7C E8 96 00 B8 01-02 E8 AA 00 72 19 8B FB   .4|.........r...
2B35:00A0  B9 0B 00 BE BE 7D F3 A6-75 0D 8D 7F 20 BE C9 7D   .....}..u... ..}
2B35:00B0  B9 0B 00 F3 A6 74 18 BE-5F 7D E8 61 00 32 E4 CD   .....t.._}.a.2..
2B35:00C0  16 5E 1F 8F 04 8F 44 02-CD 19 BE A8 7D EB EB A1   .^....D....}...
2B35:00D0  1C 05 33 D2 F7 36 0B 7C-FE C0 A2 31 7C A1 2C 7C   ..3..6.|...1|.,|
2B35:00E0  A3 32 7C BB 00 07 A1 2C-7C E8 40 00 A1 18 7C 2A   .2|....,|.@...|*
2B35:00F0  06 30 7C 40 50 E8 4E 00-58 72 CF 28 06 31 7C 76   .0|@P.N.Xr.(.1|v
2B35:0100  0C 01 06 2C 7C F7 26 0B-7C 03 D8 EB D9 8A 2E 15   ...,|.&.|.......
2B35:0110  7C 8A 16 1E 7C 8B 1E 32-7C EA 00 00 70 00 AC 0A   |...|..2|...p...
2B35:0120  C0 74 22 B4 0E BB 07 00-CD 10 EB F2 33 D2 F7 36   .t".........3..6
2B35:0130  18 7C FE C2 88 16 30 7C-33 D2 F7 36 1A 7C 88 16   .|....0|3..6.|..
2B35:0140  1F 7C A3 2E 7C C3 B4 02-8B 16 2E 7C B1 06 D2 E6   .|..|......|....
2B35:0150  0A 36 30 7C 8B CA 86 E9-8B 16 1E 7C CD 13 C3 0D   .60|.......|....
2B35:0160  0A 4E 6F 6E 2D 53 79 73-74 65 6D 20 64 69 73 6B   .Non-System disk
2B35:0170  20 6F 72 20 64 69 73 6B-20 65 72 72 6F 72 0D 0A    or disk error..
2B35:0180  52 65 70 6C 61 63 65 20-61 6E 64 20 73 74 72 69   Replace and stri
2B35:0190  6B 65 20 61 6E 79 20 6B-65 79 20 77 68 65 6E 20   ke any key when
2B35:01A0  72 65 61 64 79 0D 0A 00-0D 0A 44 69 73 6B 20 42   ready.....Disk B
2B35:01B0  6F 6F 74 20 66 61 69 6C-75 72 65 0D 0A 00 49 42   oot failure...IB
2B35:01C0  4D 42 49 4F 20 20 43 4F-4D 49 42 4D 44 4F 53 20   MBIO  COMIBMDOS
2B35:01D0  20 43 4F 4D 00 00 00 00-00 00 00 00 00 00 00 00    COM...........
2B35:01E0  00 00 00 00 00 00 00 00-00 00 00 00 00 00 00 00   ...............
2B35:01F0  00 00 00 00 00 00 00 00-00 00 00 00 00 00 55 AA   ..............U.
```

Figure 10-3. A boot record displayed.

There are several obvious things that we can see looking at this boot record. The error messages, and the names of the two DOS system files (IBMBIO.COM and IBMDOS.COM) give us an idea of some of the things that can go wrong during the boot process, and it also, indirectly, tells us that the boot program checks for these two names in the disk's directory, to see that it is a system disk. You'll also see, near the beginning, a version marker that reads "IBM 3.1". Not so obvious, but quite interesting, is that this version marker is just the first element in a table describing the characteristics of the disk to DOS. The table includes key information such as the number of bytes per sector, sectors per track, and so on (the physical dimensions of the disk), and also the size of the FAT and the directory (the logical dimensions of the DOS structure on the disk). This table, and also an identifying signature at the end of the record, (hex 55 AA) are included in all disks except those formatted for versions of DOS earlier than version 2.0.

DOS needs to identify all the characteristics of each disk that it works with. In the earliest versions of DOS, when there were only a few disk formats, knowledge of those characteristics was built into DOS, and all DOS needed from a disk was a single-byte ID code (which is stored in the FAT) to know everything it needed about a disk. That approach isn't really flexible enough, though, so now DOS learns what it needs to know about a disk from the information table in the boot record.

If you want to decode the boot program to study it, you can use DEBUG's U-unassemble command. To see all of it, you'll have to unassemble it in pieces, and look to the addresses used in any "jump" commands to see where other parts of the program code begin. For the boot record shown in Figure 10-3, these two unassemble commands will get you started: U 0 L 2 and U 2B.

Immediately following the boot record on each disk is the File Allocation Table, or FAT, which controls the use of file space on the disk. As we discussed in Chapter 9, the data portion of a disk is divided into *clusters* of segments, and the clusters are the units of space that are allocated to files. Each cluster is identified by a sequential number, beginning with number 2 for the first cluster on a disk (cluster numbers 0 and 1 are reserved for the convenience of DOS). Regardless of the cluster size (which might be a single sector, or as much as eight sectors or more) each cluster has an entry in the FAT which records its status.

Since what's stored in each cluster's FAT entry is the identifying number of another cluster, the total number of clusters identifies how big a FAT entries need to be. Originally the FAT entries were stored as 12-bit numbers, which could accommodate numbers as large as 4K—and that set a limit of about 4,000 on the possible number of clusters. However, the design of the AT model's 20-meg hard disk called for over 10,000 clusters; that, in turn, required a larger FAT design. So, now there are two FAT formats: one, for smaller disks, with entries 12 bits in size, and one with entries 16 bits in size. The difference between the two is only in how the FAT itself is stored; the way the FAT is used is the same for both sizes.

If a FAT entry is zero, that indicates that the corresponding cluster is not in use—it's free for allocation to any file that needs it. For clusters that hold file data, the FAT entry contains either the identifying number of the next cluster or a special number which marks the end of a file's space allocation chain. The clusters where a file is stored are "chained" together by the numeric links that are stored in the FAT. The file's directory entry indicates the first cluster number, and each cluster points to the next cluster, or indicates the end of the chain (the end marker is hex FFF for a 12-bit FAT, FFFF for a 16-bit FAT). This allows DOS to trace the location of a file's data from front to back. Portions of a disk which are defective and shouldn't be used—so-called "bad track" areas—are identified by a FAT entry of FF7 (or FFF7 for a 16-bit FAT). Other special FAT codes, FF0 through FFF or FFF0 through FFFF, are reserved for any needs that may arise in the future.

You'll note that the special FAT codes are kept to the 16 highest values (for either FAT format), so that there are as many usable cluster numbers as possible: up to 4078 for 12-bit FATs and 65,518 for 16-bit FATs. As we know, the number 0 is used to identify available clusters, and the number 1 is also reserved for a technical reason.

Both 12-bit and 16-bit FATs are used the same, but each is recorded in its own way, to take account of the difference in the size of the entries. There's nothing special about how a 16-bit FAT is stored: 16-bit numbers are part of the PC's natural scheme, and so the numbers in a 16-bit FAT are simply stored as a list of 2-byte words. For 12-bit FATs, things are more complicated. The PC's microprocessors don't have any natural and convenient way to record numbers that are 1½ bytes long. To deal with this problem, the FAT entries are paired, so that two FAT entries take up three bytes with no wasted space. The method of coding two 12-bit numbers in three bytes is set up to be as convenient as possible to handle with assembly language instructions, but it's rather difficult for us to make sense of it if we look at the hex coding for this kind of FAT.

Each FAT table actually begins with the entry for cluster number 0, even though the first actual cluster is number 2. The first two FAT entries are dummies, and they are used to provide a place to store an ID byte that helps DOS identify the disk format. The very first byte of the FAT contains this code. For example, the hex code FE identifies the PC's original 160K single-sided diskette format.

To help safeguard the FAT, DOS can record more than one copy of the FAT. Usually disks have two copies of the FAT stored on them, although it's possible for a disk to have only one copy, or more than two. However many copies of the FAT there are, they are stored one after another. To the best of my knowledge DOS does not make any use of the second copy of the FAT, although it carefully records it each time the FAT is changed.

The next and final element of the system portion of each disk is the root directory, which is stored immediately following the disk's FATs. The directory works as a simple table of 32-byte entries that describe the files (and other directory entries such as a volume label) on the disk.

The directory entries record, as we noted in Chapter 9, the 8-byte filename, the 3-byte filename extension, the file's size, the date and time stamp, the starting cluster number of the file, and the file attribute codes. There is also an unused 10-byte field in each directory entry that can be used to take care of future needs. There are a lot of interesting things for us to discover in these directory entries. For example, in the filename field, there are two special codes that are used in the first byte of the filename. If this byte is 0, it indicates that the directory entry (and any following entries in this directory) has never been used; this gives DOS a way of knowing when it's seen all the active entries in a directory without having to search to the end. Another code, hex E5, is used to mark entries that have been erased. That's why, whenever we work with erased files (using my UnErase program or any similar program) we don't see the first character of the erased file's name; that's because when a file is erased, the first character of the filename is overwritten with this hex E5 erasure code. Incidentally, when a file is erased (or a subdirectory removed) nothing else in the directory entry is changed: all the information is retained. The only thing that's done when a file is erased is that the filename is marked as erased, and the file's space allocation in the FAT is released.

There's one more special and interesting thing to know about the filename and extension fields. For files and subdirectories, these two are treated as separate fields. But when a directory entry is used as a disk's volume label, the two together are treated as a single unified 11-character field. When a disk's volume label is displayed (as it is by the DIR and CHKDSK commands) the label isn't punctuated with a period the way filenames are.

The size of each file is stored in the file's directory entry as a 4-byte integer, which accommodates file sizes much larger than any disk we could use—this guarantees that our files won't be limited by the size that can be recorded in the file directory. Incidentally, the file size is recorded only for true files. Other types of directory entries have their file size entered as zero. That makes sense for the directory entry which serves as a volume label, but it's a little surprising for subdirectories. Even though subdirectories are stored in the data portion of a disk the same way files are, and even though a subdirectory *has* a size to it, it's not recorded in the subdirectory's own directory entry.

The date and time stamp in each directory entry is formatted in a way that can record any date from January 1, 1980, through the end of 2099; the time stamp records times to an accuracy of two seconds, although when DOS shows us the time stamp it only displays the time to the minute. The date and the time are separately recorded in two adjacent 16-bit words, and each is coded according to its own formula. However, the way they are stored allows the two together to be treated as a single 4-byte field that can be compared in a single assembly language instruction to learn if one stamp is earlier or later than another. The date and time are coded into 2-byte numbers by these formulas:

$$DATE = DAY + 32 * MONTH + 512 * (YEAR - 1980)$$

$$TIME = SECONDS / 2 + 32 * MINUTES + 1024 * HOURS$$

The final item of interest to us inside a directory entry is the file attribute byte. This single byte is treated as a collection of eight flags, each controlled by a single bit. Six of the eight are currently in use, while the other two are available for future use. Two of the six attribute bits are special and are used by themselves, without any other bits set: one marks a disk's volume label directory entry; the other marks a subdirectory entry, so that DOS knows to treat it not as a file but as a subdirectory. The other four attributes are used to mark files, and they can be set in any combination. One marks a file as read-only, not to be modified or erased; another marks a file as having been changed. This is used by the BACKUP program (and similar programs) to indicate which files need to have backup copies made. The final two attributes are called "hidden" and "system"; they are used to make a file invisible to most DOS commands. There is essentially no difference between hidden and system status. The two DOS system files that are on every bootable system disk are both marked as hidden and system. As an interesting oddity, hidden or system files are invisible to the DOS commands DIR, COPY, and DEL, but they *are* seen by the TYPE command; you can verify that for yourself by entering the command TYPE IBMDOS.COM on a system disk.

Like the other elements of the system portion of a disk, the root directory has a fixed size for each disk, so that DOS knows exactly where to find the beginning of the directory, and the beginning of the data area that follows it. This means that the root directory can only hold so many entries, which is a rigid limit. Subdirectories, on the other hand, don't have that problem. While subdirectories work essentially just like the root directory, they are stored in the data portion of the disk—just as though they were ordinary files—and they can grow to any size that the disk can accommodate. Using subdirectories, which were introduced with DOS version 2.00, avoids any arbitrary limit on the number of files that a disk can hold.

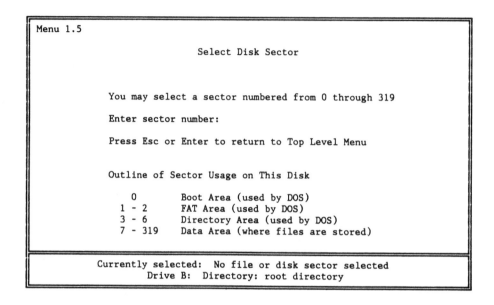

```
Menu 1.5

                        Select Disk Sector


          You may select a sector numbered from 0 through 319

          Enter sector number:

          Press Esc or Enter to return to Top Level Menu


          Outline of Sector Usage on This Disk

              0          Boot Area (used by DOS)
            1 - 2        FAT Area (used by DOS)
            3 - 6        Directory Area (used by DOS)
            7 - 319      Data Area (where files are stored)


            Currently selected:  No file or disk sector selected
                    Drive B:  Directory: root directory
```

Figure 10-4. Showing the sizes of parts of the disk.

As we've mentioned, each element of the system portion of a disk has a fixed size for that particular disk format. The boot record is always one sector. The FAT varies from as little as two sectors on a 160 kilobyte diskette to much larger sizes, such as 82 sectors on the AT's 20-meg hard disk. The root directory also varies, so that on a 160K byte diskette it has 64 entries and occupies four sectors, and on a 20-meg disk it has 512 entries and fills 32 sectors. If you have my NU program, you can see the size of each part of the disk, using menu selection 1.5. Figure 10-4 shows an example of this information for a standard 160K diskette.

The final and largest part of each disk is the data space. As you can imagine, there aren't quite as many fascinating details to discover about this part compared to the system part of the disk, but there are interesting things there. We know that our file data can have any length, but the file data is always stored on complete 512-byte disk sectors, and the sectors are allocated to files in complete clusters. So at the end of most files there is some slack filling out the last sector that's used, and there may even be completely unused slack sectors at the end of the last cluster assigned to a file.

When DOS writes file data out to the disk, it doesn't do anything to clean up these slack areas. Any slack sectors are just left undisturbed from whatever was recorded there before. In the case of any slack bytes at the end of the last sector of a file, we'll pick up whatever was stored in the computer's memory area where DOS was putting the sector's data together; usually it's a small fragment of other disk data—part of another file, or part of a directory. If you inspect the slack area at the end of a file, you'll find these odds and ends.

10.3 Nonstandard Formats and Copy Protection

Nearly everything that we've learned so far about our disks has to do with the standard way that DOS formats and structures a disk. But our computer's disks aren't bound by the rules that DOS follows; there are many other possible ways of handling a disk.

Some of the ways that we may encounter have to do with other operating systems, as we've mentioned—operating systems like CP/M-86, the p-System, and others. Also, there are a few programs that create their own operating system environments to suit their special needs. To see why, consider the limitation that DOS places on filenames: no more than 11 characters including the extension. If a program wants to have longer, more meaningful names for its data files, it needs to break out of the DOS mold. And that is one of the reasons why we sometimes find programs that use their own special disk formats.

However, when we encounter nonstandard disk formats it's usually for only one reason: copy-protection. If a program has its own peculiarities in the way its disks are formatted, then it has at least some resistance to being copied. Unfortunately for us, any nonstandard disk format presents us with special problems in using and protecting our programs and data, which has little to do with copy-protection. Discussing the matter here can only do very little to reduce the difficulties that copy-protection can impose. It's worthwhile to have a basic idea of what is going on with these nonstandard disk formats, so that we have the least possible difficulty with them.

The first thing that we need to know is that there are two distinct categories of nonstandard disks—one of disks that are totally different than the DOS format, and the other of disks that we might call *tampered-with*, but otherwise in DOS format.

161

Some copy-protected programs really have nothing to do with the ordinary uses that we put our computers to, and they have no reason to exchange data with other programs that use DOS. These are often game programs, such as the Flight Simulator program. Programs like this are usually designed to be self-loading from disk: they boot up the same way that DOS boots up. But while DOS goes into action to create an environment to help other programs run, these self-loading programs are booted up strictly to run themselves. Game programs like this have no need to exchange disk data with other programs, and so there is no compelling reason for them to be stored on standard DOS disks. They could be, but they don't need to be, and by being stored in their own unique self-loading formats, they can resist ordinary efforts to be copied.

In contrast, there are many programs that are copy-protected which also need to work with DOS so that they can fit into the overall DOS scheme of using our computers, including exchanging data files stored in the standard DOS manner. The best-known example of this type of program is Lotus' 1-2-3. These programs completely make use of standard DOS disk formats, with one exception, which forms the basis of their copy-protection. Typically these programs make use of a special master or key diskette, which has some special marking on it that resists conventional copying. When we begin using a program like this, the program inspects the key disk to see that the special copy-resistant marking is there—if it doesn't find the special marking then the program refuses to continue working.

How is it possible for these nonstandard formats to be created, and what makes them resist copying? As we saw in Chapter 8, our disks can be formatted with a variety of sizes of sectors, number of sectors per track, and so forth. DOS uses only a very simple variety of disk formats. For example, DOS only uses sectors of 512 bytes, even though our disks can have sectors of different sizes. The standard copy routines in DOS, including the COPY and DISKCOPY commands, only handle the standard forms of disk. Anything unusual—an odd-size sector, an oddly numbered sector, a missing sector, an extra sector, and so on—can't be properly handled by DOS. However, a smart program can work with these oddities to create and maintain copy-protection. Special copy programs, which know about the usual schemes used, can often defeat copy-protection, but the standard DOS operations cannot.

When we encounter a completely non-DOS disk format—whether it's a copy-protected disk, or a disk from another operating system—the ordinary things that we might do with a disk (for example, use the DIR command to see a list of the files on the disk) just can't be done. Don't expect to do anything like that with a game program. On the other hand, disks such as the 1-2-3 key disk, which are mostly in DOS format, can be treated largely like any other disk that we use. We can get a directory listing of the disk, we can copy the files (but not the special copy-protected part of the disk), and so forth.

There's one additional thing that we need to know about copy-protection, and that's how it's accomplished on a hard disk. Most copy-protected programs require that we load their original diskettes into our computer's diskette drive, even if we can copy the programs to our hard disks. To run, these programs have to inspect their key diskettes to check the copy protection. This of course is a real nuisance, and defeats one of the greatest advantages of having a hard disk, which is to avoid playing around with diskettes. However, there are some copy-protected programs that are able to transfer their copy protection schemes onto a hard disk, so that we don't have to fiddle with a key diskette. How can this be done?

Fortunately for us, it's not done by tampering with the format of our hard disk in anything like the way that a copy-protected diskette has a specially tampered format. Instead, these hard-disk copy protection schemes are based on the unusual use of file formats. These methods can involve things like hidden files (which ordinarily can't be copied) and special encrypted data which records key information about the computer it's loaded on (so that if it is transferred to another computer that's even slightly different, the copy-protection scheme can detect it).

Because there are so many different ways of achieving copy protection, and so many possible oddities in copy protection, there is no way that I can explain all of them to you, or offer any tips on dealing with copy-protection that would apply all or even most of the time. But hopefully just a little understanding of the nature of copy-protection and non-standard disk formats will help you deal with any peculiarities that come the way of you and your computer.

Some Things to Try

1. Can you explain why a DOS partition on a hard disk can't be changed in size without reformatting it? Is it possible to write a conversion program that can resize a partition? Describe the steps that would be involved.

2. Using the techniques shown in Section 10.2, inspect a boot record from one of your own disks and compare it to the one shown.

Then, using the U-unassemble command of DEBUG, get an assembly language listing of the boot program and discover how it works.

3. For every diskette format that your computer handles (single-sided, double-sided, etc.), format a diskette with the DOS files, and then inspect the disk to see what the differences are in the boot record and other elements.

4. If you have my NU program, use it to inspect the slack area at the end of your disk files. Go to menu selection 1.3 to select a file, then go to selection 2.5 to display the file's data; press the *End* key to jump to the end of the file—and see what you can find.

11

Video:
An On-Screen Overview

In one odd sense I suppose we could say that the only part of our computer that really matters is the display screen. At least that's the way it can seem, since most of the time that we're using our computers it's the results that appear on the screen that we're interested in, and not the messy details of what it took to figure out those results.

In this chapter, and the next two, we're going to discover how our computer's display screens work, and learn what they can do and what the limits are on what they can do for us. To begin, our goal for this chapter is to simply understand the basics of how our computer screens work, so that we know fundamentally what they can do for us. Then, in the next two chapters, we'll cover what's special about the two main screen modes: text mode and graphics mode.

We begin with the basics.

11.1 How the Screen Works

The first thing that we ought to note about our computer's display screens is that they show information, and that information has to be recorded somewhere. To gain the maximum flexibility and speed, the PC keeps the data that's shown on the screen inside the computer, rather than inside the display screen. That's in contrast to the way many computer terminals work. Consider, for example, the terminals used by travel agents. There, the screens are located miles away from the computers that feed them. They must hold their own record of the data that's displayed, and talk to the computer far away only when new data is needed. That's an approach that tends to make response on the display screen sluggish. By contrast, the display screens in our PCs are so close by that the screen and the computer can work together very intimately.

The way that's done is to place the memory that holds the data appearing on the display screen inside the computer. The memory is inside the computer in two senses: it's there physically, because the memory chips are inside the computer's boxy system unit, but it's also there in a logical sense, because the display screen data is recorded in an integral part of the computer's memory space. In Chapter 7 we discussed how our PCs have a one-million byte "address space" of memory that they can work with. The very memory that the display screen needs to record its data is a part of the PC's address space, so that it's not in any way remote to our computers and the programs that we run in them. The display memory is very intimately connected with the computer, so there is no delay or inconvenience in getting to it. This helps make our PC computers very responsive.

The display memory is rather different than the rest of the computer's memory, though, because it has to serve two masters. On the one hand it must be accessible to the PC's microprocessor and programs, just like any other part of the memory. On the other hand, the display memory also has to be accessible to the display screen, so that the screen can see the information that it is supposed to display.

As a consequence, the display memory used by our PC has special circuitry working with it. In effect the display memory is a room with two doors into it. The rest of the computer's memory has only a single "door," a single way of being accessed, because only one thing uses that memory—the microprocessor. But two parts of the computer work with the display memory: the microprocessor places data into the display memory to make it visible; and the display screen looks at that data to know what to show on the screen. Both parts access the display memory, and each part has its own "doorway" into the memory so that the two do not get in each other's way.

The programs running in our computer's microprocessor only have to tap into the display memory when they need to change what's being shown. The display screen, however, is constantly reading the display memory and constantly creating a screen image that reflects the contents of the display memory. Roughly 50 times a second, the display screen's electronic circuitry reads the display memory and paints a new picture on the screen to reflect what's recorded in the memory. With the screen being repainted that often, new data can appear almost instantly. All a program has to do to make new information appear in the screen is to place the data in the display memory and right away it shows up on the screen.

The electronic work behind all this is found in an optional part of our computer called the *display adapter*. To allow the PC family to work in as many ways as possible, the PC's display adapter was made a changeable part, which plugs into the computer's option slots inside the system unit. This makes it possible for us to change the kind of display adapter we have to suit our needs. We can even have more than one type installed in our computers, to give us more than one type of display screen at once. In Section 11.2 we'll take a look at the various kinds of display adapters for the PC family and see what each one can do for us.

As part of the idea of making the PC family's display screens changeable, the PC's design has numerous *video modes,* or ways of presenting data on the display screen. Each display adapter has its own repertoire of video modes which it can use. The video modes define what kind (and quality) of information we can show on the screen, and we select the display adapter hardware for our PCs to get the video modes that we want to work with—although, when we select the hardware for our PCs, we may not think of it in exactly those terms, but that's basically what we're doing. We'll see an outline of the various video modes in Section 11.2, and the following two chapters are devoted to discovering the ins and outs of how these video modes work and what they can do for us.

Because each display adapter uses its own video modes and because each mode has its own particular memory requirements, the display memory that our computers use is physically located on the display adapter board itself—so that if we change from one adapter to another, we'll also change the memory. That way, we automatically get just the right amount and kind of display memory when we install a display adapter in our computers.

Our computer's display screens themselves work in a manner very much like a television set. The scheme is what's known as *raster scan,* and it works like this: the display screen is constantly being "painted" by a moving electron beam which traces a path through the entire screen roughly the way we read; it starts at the upper left, "scans" the first thin line of the image from left to right, lighting up the active parts of the screen, and then skips back to the left to trace the next fine line. It proceeds from top to bottom, painting the entire image. As the electron beam scans over the screen, the display adapter's circuitry continuously reads out data from the display memory and translates the data bits into the signals that control the electron beam. To minimize flicker on the screen, the image is actually painted in two interleaved halves: every other line is painted from top to bottom, and then the remaining lines are painted in a second scan; after two quick scans, the image is complete. Television sets use the same interleaved double scan.

The Screen and its Border

There is a border area on our computer's display screens that surrounds the working part of the screen where data is displayed.

This border is an inactive part of the screen, and our programs can't show any information there—but that doesn't mean that the border is necessarily blank.

The electron beam that traces out the working part of the screen's "raster scan" also passes beyond the working area into what's called an *overscan*—the border area of the screen.

While we can't put data into the border, we can, at times, set the border color. The results we get vary among the display adapters and screens that we use. The Monochrome Adapter doesn't generate a changeable border; the Color Graphics Adapter does and so does the Compaq adapter (though at times in a less satisfying way). The Enhanced Graphics Adapter sometimes does and sometimes doesn't, even when it's being used in a way in which the Color Graphics Adapter does provide color.

The PC's ROM-BIOS software provides a service that sets the border color when it's available. BASIC gives us access to this service through the COLOR statement. This little program demonstrates the border colors if they are active:

```
10 SCREEN 0,1 : WIDTH 80 : CLS
20 FOR BORDER.COLOR = 0 TO 15
30    COLOR ,,BORDER.COLOR
40    PRINT "Border color is "; BORDER.COLOR
50    PRINT "Press a key..."
60    WHILE INKEY$ = "" : WEND
70 NEXT
```

The main reason for setting a border color is to have it match the background color that's being used—that can make the screen much easier on the eyes. Often it's not a good idea for a program to use a background color if it can't be matched with a border color.

Those are the basic principles behind how our computer's display screens work. The fundamental ideas are very simple, and the interesting parts lie in the details of what our PC's display screens can do for us. We'll begin uncovering those details by looking at an overview of the various video modes that our PCs can show us.

11.2 Video Mode Overview

Just about the most important thing for us to know about our computer's display screens is the variety of modes that they can work in. We need to know the different stunts that our screens can perform, and that means understanding the video modes, the different ways that our display screens can operate.

There are two parts to that. First, we need to understand what the range of modes is on *our* computer's screen. We need the answer to the question, "What tricks can my computer do?" Second, we need to understand the full range of video modes. We need the answers to the two questions, "What tricks can the PC family do?" and, "Do I want to add new tricks to my machine?" We need to know what our machines *can* do, what they *could* do if we equipped them with different display options; and then we need to decide if we've got the wrong stuff.

We'll start on the analytic side, seeing what the basic differences are among the display modes, seeing how the video modes provide us with a *multi-dimensional* range of choices. Then we'll tidy up by listing all the modes and seeing which ones apply to which display adapters.

The first big division among the video modes, the first of two main dimensions for us to consider, is between text mode and graphics mode. In a *text mode* (and there are several distinct text modes), all the display screen can show is the PC family's basic character set, which we pored over in Chapter 4; only these characters can be shown and nothing more. It's worth pausing to note again that the PC's character set is a rich one, and it provides plenty of opportunities for showing more on the screen than just written text. The box-drawing characters and others that we saw in Chapter 4 make it possible to create impressive character-based drawings on the PC's screen. But still, in a text mode, the only thing that can be shown are these 256 PC characters. In the text modes, the PC's screen is divided up into specific character positions—usually 80 columns of characters across the width of the screen, and 25 lines of characters from top to bottom. Chapter 12 is devoted to covering the details of how our computers work with the text modes.

The alternative to the text modes are the *graphics modes*. In the graphics modes the screen is treated as an array of tiny dots, called *pixels* (which is short for *picture elements*), and anything that appears on the screen is shown by building up a drawing made up of these dots. The various graphics modes differ in how many dots there are on the screen, which is called the *resolution*; a typical high-resolution mode has 640 columns of dot positions across the screen, and 200 lines of dots down. Any kind of dot-drawing can be built up from these dots, including drawings of the PC's text characters, like the letter A. The PC's built-in ROM-BIOS programs do the work of drawing characters dot-by-dot, so that programs operating in a graphics mode don't have to take on that chore, if they don't want to (sometimes they do to draw the characters in special ways such as italic).

Chapter 13 is devoted to covering the details of how our computers work with the graphics modes.

Text versus graphics is one dimension of the video modes; color is the other main dimension. There are modes which have no color *range* at all. These are the black-and-white or two-color modes. There are the honest-to-gosh color modes, which provide us with as few as four or as many as 64 colors to choose from. Finally, there are the monochrome modes, which don't have color in the ordinary sense, but have *display attributes* which are the equivalent of a variety of colors. The monochrome display attributes include normal and bright high-intensity, reverse video (dark characters on a lit background instead of the other way around), underlined characters, and so forth. There are color and black-and-white video modes for both text and graphics modes.

Within the four main possibilities that these two dimensions describe—text or graphics, colored or not—there are a number of minor dimensions, lesser variations in the range of video possibilities. These variations include the resolution (how many dots or characters the display screen holds), the range of colors, and so forth. We'll see them as the details of the video modes unfold.

The next way that we need to view the PC family's video modes is to see them from the hardware angle: looking at the various display adapters (and the display screens which connect to them) that determine which of the video mode possibilities apply to our computer. We'll look at the four main display adapters that the PC family uses (and peek at a few others as well).

The first two display adapters that appeared for the PC family and the most important ones are the *IBM Monochrome Adapter* and the *IBM Color Graphics Adapter* (CGA). The Monochrome Adapter was intended as the PC family's standard professional choice, the display adapter for "serious" work. It's a text-only display adapter which generates very crisp, easy-to-read characters. As a "monochrome" option, it only shows one actual color, but the video mode for this display adapter and screen features the color-like display attributes we mentioned before: underlining, bright intensity, and so forth. The Monochrome Adapter only works with IBM's Monochrome Display Screen or its equivalent. The IBM Monochrome Display Screen glows in a soft green color, but there are equivalent screens available in amber color as well. The Monochrome Adapter has only a single video mode.

The other of the PC's original pair of display adapters is the Color Graphics Adapter. The Color Graphics Adapter works in both text modes and colored and colorless modes in various resolutions, a total of seven video modes in all. It also works with four different types of display screens, in contrast to the one type that can be used with the Monochrome Adapter. By these simple specifications, it sounds as though the Color Graphics Adapter completely has it over the Monochrome Adapter, and superficially that's true. Everything that the Monochrome Adapter can do, the Color Graphics Adapter can also show—with color and graphics in addition. However, the Color Graphics Adapter has serious drawbacks which led to most PCs being equipped with the Monochrome Adapter. The main problem with the CGA is its relatively poor display quality. Its screen images are not nearly as crisp and clear as the Monochrome Adapter's. In fact many people, me included, think that the Color Graphics Adapter is too fuzzy and hard on the eyes to work with for an extended period of time. But, fuzzy or not, the Color Graphics Adapter gives us color, graphics, a selection of resolutions, and a selection of display screens that goes far beyond what the Monochrome Adapter gives us.

As I mentioned, the Color Graphics Adapter is able to work with four different types of display screens. One—which is not often used—is a TV set. The picture quality with a TV set is poor, and using it requires one additional piece of equipment, a RF modulator, which translates the Color Graphics Adapter's signal into TV signals. The best type is called an *RGB monitor,* because it accepts the display adapter's Red-Green-Blue display signals, and produces the best possible picture image; the standard IBM Color Display is an RGB monitor. In between a TV and an RGB monitor are the other two types, known as *composite monitors.* They work with a lower quality image signal from the Color Graphics Adapter, so they don't produce as good a picture as an RGB monitor. There are two kinds of composite monitors, color and monochrome; the monochrome composite monitors do accept a color signal, but they show colors in the form of shades of the one color the screen can show.

There is a special variation on the Color Graphics Adapter we need to know about, although it is not part of the mainstream of the PC family. That is the display adapter that comes with each of the Compaq computer models. This Compaq display adapter functions just like the Color Graphics Adapter, with its full range of video modes, but it has a special feature that overcomes the main problem with the Color Graphics Adapter, its fuzzy text characters. When the Compaq display adapter is working in the standard text mode it's able to show its text characters with the same clarity and fine-drawing that the Monochrome Adapter uses. The Compaq display adapter effectively combines the virtues of both the Color Graphics Adapter and the Monochrome Adapter. However, the Compaq adapter is only available on the Compaq members of the PC family. Some people

171

find that sufficient reason to choose these models over other members of the PC family. The Compaq adapter can work with the same four types of display screen as the Color Graphics Adapter. Essentially everything that there is to say about the Color Graphics Adapter applies as well to the Compaq adapter. If you're using a Compaq computer, you can think of it as having a special and slightly better version of the Color Graphics Adapter.

The next display adapter for us to consider is the Hercules graphics adapter—popularly called the *Herc card*—and its equivalents. There are strong similarities between the Herc card and the Compaq adapter. While the Compaq adapter is essentially a Color Graphics Adapter with the main advantage of the Monochrome Adapter (clear text characters) added, the Herc card is essentially a Monochrome Adapter with the main advantage of the CGA (graphics) added. The Herc card acts exactly as a Monochrome Adapter, but it has an additional display mode which provides high-resolution monochrome graphics, very suitable for most important graphics applications. The Herc card's graphics mode is, in IBM's view, very much a nonstandard display format which we might not take too seriously. However, the PC community has taken so favorably to the Herc card's capabilities that I consider it to be a key part of the PC family's equipment, and one of the four main display adapters that we'll be covering in this chapter and the next two. The Herc card, like the Monochrome Adapter, only works with the Monochrome Display or its equivalent. Although the Herc card's graphic mode is not a standard display mode (as IBM sets the standards) it has been widely accepted by software developers, so that most important graphics-oriented software works with the Herc card.

The last of our four mainstream display adapters for the PC family is the *IBM Enhanced Graphics Adapter* (EGA). The Enhanced Graphics Adapter is IBM's effort to unify the variety of display adapters and extend the PC family's capabilities into new technology. The Enhanced Graphics Adapter essentially combines all the features of the Monochrome Adapter, the Color Graphics Adapter, and the Herc card, together with new video modes that can be used with higher-quality color monitors like the IBM Enhanced Color Display, which is essentially a technologically advanced version of an RGB monitor. The Enhanced Graphics Adapter clearly set out to be *the* wonder-board, a single display adapter which would combine *all* the advantages of the other boards, obsoleting each of them. The Enhanced Graphics Adapter would be a complete replacement for both of IBM's original display adapters if it weren't twice as expensive as either of them. It would also be a replacement for the

Herc card if it weren't for the fact that the EGA's monochrome graphics mode isn't compatible to the Herc card's, and for some time there will be more Herc software than EGA software, because the EGA is a relative late-comer.

While these four are what I consider to be the mainstream of the PC family's display adapters, there are others; we've already seen one, the Compaq display adapter. You also should know about the PC*jr*'s built-in display adapter, which acts very much like the Color Graphics Adapter, but adds to the CGA's skills some extra graphics modes. There is also the very special IBM Professional Graphics Adapter, which is intended for unusually demanding circumstances. The Professional Graphics Adapter is *so* special that it has its own microprocessor built into it, a microprocessor that is more powerful than the one in the PC that it is installed in. In this case, the accessory has more horsepower than the instrument it's designed for. Because the peculiar capabilities of the PC*jr* and the Professional Graphics Adapter are so removed from the heart of the PC family, we won't go into them in any detail.

Most PC computers have a single display adapter in them, but it is possible to install and use two display adapters in the same machine. Before we move on to summarize all the display modes that these display adapters provide, let's take a look at which combinations of display adapters we can use, and which we can't.

The Monochrome Adapter and the Color Graphics Adapter can be used together, and either can be combined with the Enhanced Graphics Adapter. So any two of these three can be together in the same machine. The Herc card can't be combined with any of the three IBM display adapters, but Hercules makes an equivalent to IBM's Color Graphics Adapter that can be combined with the Herc card (just as IBM's own CGA can be combined with IBM's Monochrome Adapter).

Now, how do we make sense of all the possibilities that these various display adapters present us with? The best way to see them is to list them out in the form that IBM's technical manuals see them, by the video mode numbers that identify them. We'll gloss over some of the more interesting details until we get to the next few chapters; what we'll see here are the main aspects of each mode. After we talk about these modes, I'll show you how you can determine which mode your computer is in, and do some exploring with them.

The first seven modes, numbered 0 through 6, apply to the Color Graphics Adapter and any equivalent display adapter (which includes the Enhanced Graphics Adapter, the Compaq adapter, and the PC*jr*'s built-in display adapter). Here's a list of them:

Mode	Type	Color?	Width	Description
0	Text	No	40	40-column text, no color
1	Text	16	40	40-column text, with color
2	Text	No	80	80-column text, no color
3	Text	16	80	80-column text, with color
4	Graphics	4	320	Medium-resolution graphics, with color
5	Graphics	No	320	Medium-resolution graphics, no color
6	Graphics	2	640	High-resolution graphics, no color

There are some easily identifiable patterns in these seven modes. You'll note that the first six modes are in pairs, one mode with color, the other without. For the colorless modes, colors appear as shades of grey when they appear on either a TV set or a composite monitor (on an RGB monitor, color still appears, regardless). You'll also notice an inconsistency in the order of the color and colorless mode for video modes 4 and 5, the graphics modes. For all these modes which have more than two colors, a colorless variation makes sense. Mode 6 has only two colors (black and white) to start with so there would be no distinction between a colored and colorless variation on this mode. In the text modes, there are two widths available (40 and 80 characters across). The 40-column mode was created to be more legible when a TV set is used as a display screen, but few PCs use TV sets or this mode. Most major programs for the PC family are not designed to work in 40-column mode. All the text modes have 25 lines of characters on the screen. In the graphics modes, there are also two widths and two resolutions. The high-resolution mode has 640 dots across and the medium-resolution modes have 320 dots across. All three of these graphics modes have 200 lines from top to bottom. You'll also note the progression of colors that's available: 16 in the text modes, 4 in medium-resolution graphics, and 2 (or, if you prefer, none) in high-resolution graphics.

Those seven modes are all used by the Color Graphics Adapter, and any other adapters which duplicate its features, including the Enhanced Graphics Adapter. The Monochrome Adapter, on the other hand, has a single video mode, in keeping with its single-minded focus on text applications. Here it is:

Mode	Type	Color?	Width	Description
7	Text	Special	80	Monochrome text

This monochrome text mode, video mode 7, is similar to the 80-column text modes that the Color Graphics Adapter provides, with 80 columns of characters across and 25 lines down. There are two important differences: one is that the characters themselves are drawn in a more detailed way that produces an easier-to-read character (we'll see the details of that in Chapter 12). The other is that the the Monochrome Adapter has a special concept of "color," which displays characters in a variety of ways: underlined, in reverse video, and so forth. The Monochrome Adapter only works with the Monochrome Display screen, which is specially designed for it.

The next three video modes were introduced with the PCjr and only apply to it. It is possible that we'll see them also in use by some future display adapters, but I think that isn't likely since they were not included in IBM's do-everything Enhanced Graphics Adapter. They are all special graphics modes which extended the range of graphics that the Color Graphics Adapter provides:

Mode	Type	Color?	Width	Description
8	Graphics	16	160	Low-resolution graphics
9	Graphics	16	320	Medium-resolution graphics
10	Graphics	4	640	High-resolution graphics

Each of these three modes is a natural extension of the graphics modes we've seen so far. Mode 8 introduces a low-resolution (160 dots across) mode. Modes 9 and 10 add more color to the existing medium- and high-resolution modes. The PCjr's built-in display adapter works in these three special modes, plus all eight of the conventional Color Graphics Adapter modes. Like the Color Graphics Adapter, the PCjr works with four different kinds of display screen (TV, color and monochrome composite, and RGB).

After these video modes there are a missing pair of mode numbers, 11 and 12. They probably belong to modes that IBM defined for the PC family, but decided not to introduce. There's little to say about them, except that they could possibly appear in a later IBM product.

The Enhanced Graphics Adapter works in all of the first nine standard modes (but not the three special PCjr modes. In addition, it adds these four modes:

Mode	Type	Color?	Width	Description
13	Graphics	16	320	Medium-resolution, high-color
14	Graphics	16	640	High-resolution, more color
15	Graphics	No	640	Monochrome graphics, 350 line
16	Graphics	64	640	High-resolution, 350 line

These four new modes have more that's special about them than is readily apparent from this short summary table, such as which display screens they apply to. The first two, 13 and 14, work with the four standard color-graphics types of displays. These modes are similar to the PC*jr*'s medium- and high-resolution modes 9 and 10, but the high-resolution mode here, mode 14, offers the PC's full complement of 16 colors, rather than just 4. Both of these new graphics modes, like all the ones we've seen so far, have 200 lines of dots up and down the screen, but the two following modes, 15-16, have nearly twice as many, 350 lines. Mode 15 is IBM's monochrome graphics mode, which is only used with the Monochrome Display screen. Mode 16 is a special high-color, high-resolution graphics mode that can only be used with the special Enhanced Color Display which was developed to accompany the Enhanced Graphics Adapter. Using the Enhanced Color Display, video mode 16 can provide the highest resolution we've seen so far (640 across, 350 down) and many more colors—64— than any other mode can provide.

Finally, there is one more mode for us to consider, the monochrome graphics mode that is used by the Hercules graphics adapter. Since this mode is not a part of IBM's own designs, it does not have an IBM video mode number; we'll call it the Herc mode. It is similar to IBM's monochrome graphics mode (mode 15), but it has different dimensions and a slightly higher resolution:

Mode	Type	Color?	Width	Description
Herc	Graphics	No	720	Monochrome graphics, 348 line

It's worth noting that the two monochrome graphics modes that we've seen, IBM's 640 by 350 mode, and Hercules 720 by 348 mode, are roughly equivalent. IBM's has the advantage of being "IBM standard" and also of having built-in support in the machines' ROM-BIOS. Hercules has the advantage of having a 17 percent higher horizontal resolution and the initial advantage of being more widely used and software-supported. Ultimately I expect that both modes will have equal software support.

Now that we've dug our way through an overview of the video modes, it's time for us to have a little fun with them.

11.3 Exploring Video Modes

It's relatively easy to explore and tinker around with most of the video modes.

To begin, let's see how we can discover the video mode that our computer is currently using. As we saw in Chapter 7, in the *Low-Memory Goodies* sidebar, the PC's ROM-BIOS programs use a low-memory area, starting at hex address 400, to store information that the ROM-BIOS needs to keep track of. Part of that information is current status information about the display screen, including the current video mode. The mode is recorded in a single byte located at hex address 449. Any tool that allows us to inspect data in memory can show us the video mode. We can easily do it with either BASIC or with DEBUG.

In BASIC it requires two simple commands: the first sets up BASIC to inspect low-memory locations: DEF SEG = 0; the second command extracts the byte where the video mode is, and displays it on the screen: PRINT PEEK (&H449). To try it yourself, fire up BASIC and give it those two commands, and you'll see your current mode.

To do the same thing with DEBUG, activate DEBUG and give it this command: D 0:449 L 1. That tells DEBUG to display (D) one byte (L 1) at the address we're interested in. DEBUG will show us the mode, displayed in hex form, something like this:

```
0000:0440                    07
```

That shows a video mode of 7, the standard Monochrome Adapter mode.

If you do either of those two experiments, you'll see what mode your computer is currently in. It's also possible to change the mode and then inspect it. We can only see some of the possible modes, because the tools that we'll be using—DOS, BASIC, and DEBUG—only operate in certain video modes. While a program—say Lotus 1-2-3—is running, it can change the mode to anything it wants; but the tools which we'll experiment with only work in certain modes. And, of course, you can only see the modes that your computer is equipped to use. If your computer only has the standard Monochrome Adapter, the only mode you can see is mode 7. Even though we won't be able to see every mode, the experiments I'll describe here will let you tinker a bit, and get a feeling for what it's like to be in control of the display screens different modes.

There are two ways that we can change the mode, just as there are two ways that we can detect what mode we're in. One uses the DOS command MODE to set the mode; we can use this together with DEBUG to display the mode. The other method uses BASIC both to set the mode and to show it.

We'll begin with MODE and DEBUG. These two commands work in the standard DOS way, which only accepts text modes so we won't be able to try any of the graphics modes.

To do this experiment, we enter a MODE command to set the mode, and then use DEBUG in the way we've already seen to show what mode we're in. The idea is that we try to switch to a new mode with the MODE command, and then use DEBUG to see if we actually got there. We set the mode like this: MODE X, where, for X we put MONO, CO80, BW80. CO40, BW40, 40, or 80. After we've done that, we try DEBUG to see what mode we're actually in.

If we use BASIC, we can perform the same sort of experiment, but in a way that also allows us to try the graphics modes. Here is an example, which switches us into a medium-resolution graphics mode (if our computer is equipped to do it):

```
10  SCREEN 1
20  DEF SEG = 0
30  PRINT PEEK (&H449)
```

You can tinker with this program by changing line 10 to any of the screen modes that are allowed for your computer's BASIC. (By the way, don't be confused by mode numbers that BASIC uses in the SCREEN command; they aren't the same as the fundamental video mode numbers we've been using in this chapter.) If BASIC reports an error when it tries to perform the SCREEN command, then that mode does not apply to your computer.

You'll see a more elaborate version of this program under the name VID-MODE in Appendix A. Try running that program to see more about the video modes, or just study the program to learn more about how BASIC interacts with the PC family's video modes.

Now that we've covered the fundamentals of our computer's display screens, it's time to move on to see the specific details. We'll begin in Chapter 12 with the text modes.

Some Things to Try

1. Try all the MODE commands suggested in Section 11.3. Also, check your DOS manual to see if there are any other MODE commands that apply to your display screen. New ones may have been added to the list.

2. Check your computer's BASIC manual to see if any new display modes have been added beyond the ones covered here. You can find out by comparing the description of the SCREEN command options with the SCREEN commands that appear in the VID-MODE listing in Appendix A.

12

Video: Text Fundamentals

n this chapter we're going to explore the inner workings of the PC's display screen text modes. Although there is a growing shift in the use of computers towards the extra appeal and benefit of graphics images, by far the majority of work that's done on our PCs is done entirely in text mode, with nothing appearing on the display screen but the PC family's text character set. In fact, most PCs are equipped only with the IBM Monochrome Adapter, which can only show text characters and nothing more.

No matter how you look at it, and even if you are a graphics enthusiast, the PC's text mode is very important. So, we're going to see how it works and what the capabilities and limitations of the text mode are. We'll begin with an outline of how the text modes are organized and the fundamentals of how they work. Then we'll look at more of the technical details underlying the text modes; and we'll finish up by exploring some tricks that can be used to add sizzle to a program's use of the text modes.

12.1 Text Mode Outline

Underlying the PC family's text screen modes is the division of the display screen into individual character positions, arranged in a grid of columns and lines. Each character position has two separate components: its data, which determines what character appears on the screen, and its attribute, which determines how that character is to appear (in color, or blinking, or whatever).

In the text modes, our programs have full control over both the data and the attributes, so that they can specify exactly what characters will appear, where they will appear among the predefined character positions, and how they will appear in terms of the predefined color attributes, which we'll be discussing shortly. However, our programs have no control over any other details, such as how the characters are drawn or the precise position of the character locations. That's all strictly defined by the capabilities of the display adapter and the display screen. (By contrast, as we'll see in Chapter 13, when characters are used in the graphics modes, some or all of these things can be controlled by our programs.)

In short, in the text modes, our programs work within a rigid framework of what can be shown on the screen. That predefined framework, though, frees our programs from a great deal of overhead work that they would otherwise have to take care of, directly or indirectly.

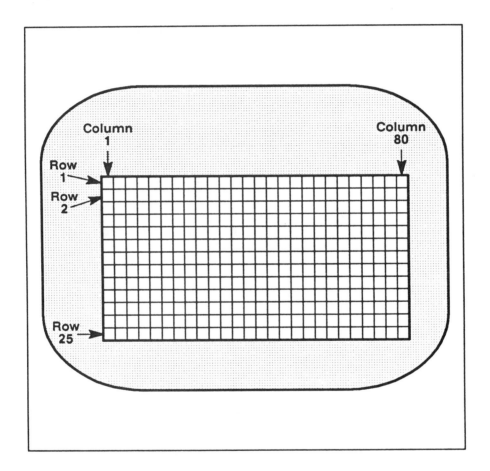

Figure 12-1. Display columns and rows.

The character positions on the screen are organized into 25 rows and usually 80 columns—but, as we saw in Chapter 11 there are two text video modes which have only 40 columns of characters across the screen. These 40-column modes were created to make it more practical to use a TV set as the display screen for a PC, since the resolution and picture quality on a TV screen is not good enough to show 80 characters clearly. The 40-column modes, together with a few other features (like the cassette tape link), were designed into the PC when it was thought that many people might want low-budget minimally equipped PCs. As it turned out, the 40-column modes are seldom used, and many programs do not accommodate them. Figure 12-1 shows how the display screen is organized into columns and rows for either 40- or 80-column widths.

We and our programs can treat the screen as either being divided into lines, or as a single continuous string of characters 2000 long (or 1000 for 40-column mode). The PC family's text mode is designed to work either way, in a neat and simple way. If our programs ask for their output to be placed on a particular row and column position, it will appear there. On the other hand, if our programs just pour out data onto the screen, it will be written out wrapping around from the end of one line to the beginning of the next. The PC's screen will work either way with equal ease, for maximum flexibility.

Our display screens are able to show all of the PC's character set that we learned about in Chapter 4, and saw demonstrated in the ALL-CHAR and REF-CHAR programs (see Appendix A). But to get some of the characters to appear on the screen can require special techniques such as the POKE statements used in those two programs. This is because the ASCII control characters, codes 0-31, have special meanings that are used to affect the way output appears, such as skipping to a new line. If any of these control characters are written to the screen—say with the PRINT statement in BASIC—generally they'll take action as control characters, but they may simply appear as ordinary PC characters. The results vary depending on which character codes are being written, and also they can vary depending on which programming language is being used.

Except for these ASCII control characters, though, all of the PC family's text character set can be easily shown on the display screen, placed in any of the screen's character positions.

The character that appears in each position is the data component of the character position. There is also an attribute component, which controls how the character appears, such as whether it's in color.

A character's attribute is a control code that determines how it is shown, and each position has its own attribute that's independent of all the others. There are basically two different sets of attribute codes, one designed for the Monochrome Adapter and one for the Color Graphics Adapter, but the two schemes are organized in a way that makes them as compatible as possible. Let's look at the Color Graphics Adapter's attributes first.

For the Color Graphics Adapter, each character position's attribute has three parts: one specifies the *foreground color* (the color of the character itself); the second controls the *background color* (the color around or "behind" the character); and whether or not the character blinks. There are 16 foreground colors, numbered 0 through 15, as listed in Figure 12-2. The colors are made up of the three component parts red, green, and blue. The various combinations of those three elements give us eight main colors, and with a normal or bright variation on each of the eight gives us a total of sixteen. There are eight background colors, just the main eight colors without their bright variations. The final part of the color attributes is a switch which allows the foreground character to either blink or appear solid and steady.

Code	Appearance
0	Black (nothing)
1	Blue
2	Green
3	Cyan (blue + green)
4	Red
5	Magenta (blue + red)
6	Light yellow or brown (green + red)
7	White (blue + green + red)
8	Grey (bright only)
9	Bright Blue (blue + bright)
10	Bright Green (green + bright)
11	Bright Cyan (blue + green + bright)
12	Bright Red (red + bright)
13	Bright Magenta (blue + red + bright)
14	Bright yellow (green + red + bright)
15	Bright White (blue + green + red + bright)

Figure 12-2. Color attributes.

What I've just described is the normal form of the color attributes, but some of the fancier display adapters can work variations on this scheme. For example, the PC*jr*'s built-in adapter is able to trade the blinking feature for bright background colors, allowing a full 16 background colors. And the PC*jr* and the Enhanced Graphics Adapter are able to remap the color palette, so that when we use the code for one color (say 1 for blue) another color actually appears. These are fancy features which are interesting and have their uses, but they're not a part of the PC family's standard repertoire of tricks.

The Monochrome Adapter also uses attributes to control how its characters will appear, but in a different way. The Monochrome Adapter doesn't have color at its command, but it can make its characters appear in bright or normal intensity, blinking, underlined, or in reverse video (black characters on a lit background). You'll see the various possibilities listed in Figure 12-3. Not all combinations of these features are possible; for example, there's no reverse underlined.

Code	Appearance
0	Invisible
1	Underline
7	Normal
9 (8 + 1)	Bright underline
15 (8 + 7)	Bright normal
112	Reverse
129 (128 + 1)	Blinking Underline
135 (128 + 7)	Binking Normal
137	Blinking Bright underline
(128 + 8 + 1)	
143	Blinking Bright normal
(128 + 8 + 7)	
240 (128 + 112)	Blinking Reverse

Figure 12-3. Monochrome attributes.

That's the essence of the features of the PC's text display modes. What's left to learn about them are the technical details of how the display data is laid out in memory, how the attributes are coded, and other fascinating details. We'll cover that next, in a more technical section.

TECHNICAL BACKGROUND ❘ ❘ ❙ ▪ ▪ ▪ ▬▬▬▬▬▬▬

12.2 Details of the Text Mode

Each display adapter contains its own memory chips which record the data that is displayed on the screen, and a special part of the PC's address space is set aside to hold this display memory. A 128K block of memory is available for use by the display adapters, filling the A- and B-blocks of memory (see Section 7.3).

The B block is the standard display memory area, where both the Monochrome Adapter and the Color Graphics Adapter place their memory. The Monochrome Adapter places its memory at the beginning of the B block, starting at hex paragraph address B000. The Color Graphics Adapter starts its memory at the middle of the B block, at hex paragraph address B800. (You'll see these addresses in some of the listings in Appendix A.)

Each of these two display adapters uses only part of the 32K of memory that's set aside for it. The Monochrome Adapter has only 4K of memory, while the Color Graphics Adapter has 16K. Each has just enough for the information that's displayed on the screen.

The Monochrome Adapter needs 4K, because the display screen has 2000 character positions (80 columns times 25 rows), and each position needs two bytes of memory to support it: one to hold the character data, and one to hold the display attributes. Exactly 4000 bytes used for the display data, and another, unused 96 bytes bring the total up to a round number in binary, 4096 or exactly 4K. The Color Graphics Adapter also needs 4000 bytes for its text mode, but more is needed for the graphics modes, as we'll see in Chapter 13, so the CGA has 16K of memory. In Section 12.3 we'll see how this extra memory is put to use.

The other display adapters are similar to these original two. The Compaq adapter works just like the Color Graphics Adapter, and the Hercules adapter, in text mode, works just like the Monochrome Adapter. Both have the same amount of memory and memory addressing as the adapters they mimic. The PC*jr*'s built-in display adapter acts as though it were a Color Graphics Adapter, and its display memory *appears* to be located at memory address B800, as it is for the CGA. In fact, the PC*jr* uses part of its standard memory for the display screen, and special addressing circuits make this ordinary memory appear to be located at B800.

The Enhanced Graphics Adapter can have even more memory, depending upon how much has been installed in it. Since the EGA is able to act like either a Monochrome Adapter or Color Graphics Adapter (or use its own special video modes), it's flexible about the memory addresses that it uses. Normally the EGA makes its memory appear in one of the two standard locations, B000 or B800. When the EGA switches into some of its special modes, it also makes use of the A-block of memory addresses. However, when it's functioning in an ordinary video mode, none of the EGA's display memory appears at A-block addresses, which is why we can't detect it with memory snooping tools, like DEBUG or the SI-System Information program that's part of my Norton Utilities set.

While different starting addresses are used for display memory of the Monochrome Adapter and Color Graphics Adapter, the layout of the text mode memory from there is the same. Memory is used in pairs of bytes, with two bytes for each text position on the screen. The very first byte of the display memory holds the character data for the top left-most screen position, and the next byte holds the display attribute for that position. The next pair of bytes are for the second column on the first line, and so on, continuously without any gap until we reach the last position on the screen. (See Figure 12-4.)

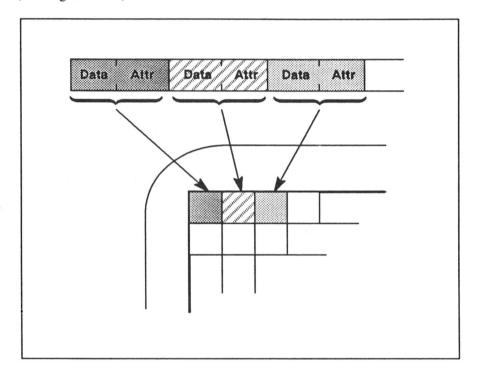

Figure 12-4. Display memory and the screen in text mode.

In the display memory, the screen is treated as a continuous string of 2000 pairs of bytes, and nothing indicates the division of the display into lines. So, if information is simply stored into the memory, byte after byte, it appears on the screen automatically wrapping around from one line to another. In the display memory, there are lines: only byte after byte of information. When the line and column positions matter to our programs, they calculate the relative position of the appropriate bytes, and set their data there.

We can calculate the relative memory location of any position on the screen, by using simple and obvious formulas. If we number the rows and columns on the screen starting with 0 (rather than 1), then this gives the location of a data byte:

$$\text{LOCATION} = (\text{ROW} * 80 + \text{COLUMN}) * 2$$

That location is relative to the beginning of the display memory, and the formula is for a 80-column mode; for a 40-column mode on the Color Graphics Adapter, we'd multiply the row by 40, not 80. The location of the attribute byte for the same screen position is just one higher.

The only way that information ever appears on the display screen is for it to be stuffed into the display memory by some program or other. It can be either done directly by the programs that we run, or it can be done by the computer's built-in ROM-BIOS services. There are two schools of thought about which way it should be done. If a program does this itself—by placing its data directly into the display memory— it can be done with great efficiency and impressive speed. Most or all of the snappy-appearing programs that you use work like this. When our programs work that way, they have to know how the display memory is laid out, and they have to incorporate a fair amount of knowledge about how the display adapters work. Programs like that wouldn't be able to work with any display adapter that placed its display memory at a new location. On the other hand, if our programs rely on the services of the ROM-BIOS to place data into the display memory, then it's easy to adjust to any changes in the display screen—whether it's a new location for the display memory, or a windowing environment like TopView that can move information around on the screen. Using the ROM-BIOS services decouples our programs from the peculiarities of the display screen and display memory, and that should make our programs more adaptable to changes in the computer they run on.

Seen from that point of view, it appears that all our programs should use the ROM-BIOS services for screen data, to get the maximum flexibility. But there is an enormous penalty in using the ROM-BIOS services: they take a surprising amount of time to work. (If you have my Norton Utilities program set, you can demonstrate this for yourself, because the NU program uses *both* methods of creating screen displays. Try the program with the ''/D0'' option to see how quickly it works with direct screen output, and try the ''/D1'' option to see how much slower it performs when it uses the ROM-BIOS services.) It's because of the heavy penalty in using the ROM-BIOS that so many programs perform their own screen output, moving their data directly into the screen buffer.

It's clear that IBM originally wanted all of our programs to route their display data through the ROM-BIOS, but things didn't work out that way. So many programs do their own screen output, using the two key display adapter memory addresses of B000 and B800, that it's become impossible for IBM to consider any radical change to the way the display memory works, at least for the text modes. That's why IBM has now announced that any future display adapters developed for the PC family will maintain compatibility with the original two adapters and continue using these two addresses. We can see that commitment in action in the Enhanced Graphics Adapter.

When people use their computers, they easily get the impression that there is a close link between the cursor and the information that gets displayed on the screen, as if information could only appear when it's painted there by the cursor. But we know that that's simply not true. Whatever information is placed in the display memory will appear on the screen, completely independent of the cursor. The cursor is simply a convenient way of indicating where the active part of the screen is, which can be very helpful for the person looking at the screen.

To reinforce that idea, the ROM-BIOS services that place information on the screen for our programs carefully match the writing of information with the placement of the cursor. For the ROM-BIOS, the cursor isn't only a visual clue for anyone looking at the screen, it's also a means of coordination between the screen, the ROM-BIOS, and the program that is generating information. The cursor lets both the program and the ROM-BIOS have one single way to indicate where information is to appear. For more information on the cursor, see the sidebar *The Cursor*.

The Cursor

The flashing cursor that we're accustomed to seeing on our screen is a hardware feature of the PC's display adapters, and it only applies to the text modes that we're covering here, and not to the graphics modes.

The flashing cursor is generated by the display adapter itself, which controls, among other things, the rate at which the cursor blinks on and off. The blink rate can't be changed, but the position of the cursor and the size of the cursor—which scans the lines it appears on—can be changed, and there are ROM-BIOS services built into the PC that control the cursor for our programs.

189

Normally the cursor blinks at the bottom of a character on the last two scan lines. But the lines the cursor appears on can be changed with a hardware command which is performed through the ROM-BIOS. We can experiment with changing the size of the cursor using BASIC's LOCATE statement. We can change the cursor to start and end on any pair of the scan lines that make up a character position (lines 0-13 for the Monochrome Adapter, 0-7 for the Color Graphics Adapter). One real curiosity is that if we start the cursor on a higher line number than we end it, we get a two-part wrap-around cursor. You can experiment with that using this BASIC statement:

LOCATE , , , 6, 1

The blinking cursor we've been describing is a *hardware* cursor that's an integral part of each display adapter. Many programs find that the hardware cursor doesn't suit their purposes, so they create their own logical cursor, typically by using reverse video to highlight the cursor area. One of the main reasons why programs create their own cursor is to extend the cursor to more than one character position on the screen (for example, the way a spreadsheet's cursor highlights the entire width of a cell). Technically, a cursor like that is something completely different from the hardware cursor, but the function of all kinds of cursors are the same: to show us where the active part of the screen is.

When programs create their own logical cursors, they normally make the hardware cursor disappear, either by deactivating it or by moving it to a position just off the edge of the screen.

Next we want to take a look at how the coding is worked out for attribute bytes which control how text characters appear on the display screen. Although the attributes for the Color Graphics Adapter and for the Monochrome Adapter are quite different, there is a common design that underlies each scheme. Let's start by looking at the common part, and then we'll get into the specifics for both color and monochrome.

The eight bits of each attribute are divided into four fields, like this:

```
7 6 5 4 3 2 1 0
```
B	Blinking (of foreground)
. R G B	Background color
. I . . .	Intensity (of foreground)
. . . . . R G B	Foreground color

As we can see, the rightmost four bits control the foreground color: three bits (RGB) specify the main red-green-blue components of the color, and an intensity bit (I) makes the color bright or dim. The other four bits similarly control the background color, but the bit we might expect to control the background intensity is instead borrowed to control foreground blinking (as we saw in Section 12.1, the PC*jr* is able to borrow it back to make 16 background colors). All possible combinations of bits are faithfully produced based on this scheme. You can demonstrate them all with the program COLORTXT listed in Appendix A. Every combination works—no matter how hard on the eyes or how bizarre. Some color combinations are very pleasing, such as bright yellow on blue (one of my favorites). Others are amazing, such as bright blinking blue on red, attribute hex C9, bits 11001001. If you have a color screen, you can try that combination in BASIC with the command COLOR 25,4.

The Color Graphics Adapter uses these attribute bits exactly as this table suggests. The Monochrome Adapter matches this scheme as closely as it reasonably can. The normal display mode, lit characters on a black background, is coded hex 07 (in bits 00000111), which corresponds to the color attributes of white on black. Reverse video is coded just the opposite, hex 70, the equivalent of black on white. The code for underlined is hex 01, which makes the monochrome underlined attribute equivalent to the foreground color blue. The Monochrome Adapter's invisible or nondisplay mode is coded hex 00, the equivalent of black on black. We might expect that the white-on-white code, hex 77, would give us another invisible mode with the whole character area lit up—but it doesn't. The Monochrome Adapter only has a handful of attribute modes, just the ones listed in Figure 12-3. We don't get all the combinations of the Monochrome Adapter's attributes that we might expect—that's why there is no reverse video underlined mode, for example. The Monochrome Adapter only shows those combinations shown in Figure 12-3.

Even though the Monochrome Adapter has only a limited number of distinct display attributes, it works properly no matter what the setting of the attribute bits is. No matter what attribute bits we set, the Monochrome Adapter produces one of its standard ways of showing characters. In most cases, it shows the characters in the normal way, as if the attribute were set to hex 07. If you have a Monochrome Adapter in your computer, you can see how it responds to all the possible combinations of attribute bits by running the COLORTXT program, the same program we use to demonstrate the Color Graphics Adapter's colors.

The attributes that we've been discussing control how characters appear on the screen, in the terms that we've been discussing: color, blinking, and so forth. What they don't control is the actual appearance or shape of the characters, which is controlled by the display adapter. For more on that, see the sidebar *The Character Box.*

The Character Box

In the text modes, the characters that we see on our computer's screen are drawn by the display adapter, rather than by the PC's software (which is the way they are drawn in the graphics modes, as we'll see in Chapter 13). The quality of the characters that we see displayed varies among the display adapters, because of differences in what's called the *character box.*

The character box is the framework that our PC's characters are drawn in. In every case the characters are drawn from a rectangular matrix of dots, although it's not easy to see that looking at the screen.

For the IBM Monochrome Adapter—and any adapter mode that matches it—the character box is composed of nine dots across and 14 down, which allows a well-drawn character. For the Color Graphics Adapter, the character box is eight by eight, which only allows for a noticeably cruder character drawing. For some of the special modes of the Enhanced Graphics Adapter, the character box is eight by 14, nearly as good as the Monochrome Adapter.

It's relatively easy to observe the vertical dimension of the character box, just by turning up the brightness on our display screens. Because the screen's scan lines don't completely overlap, we can see where they fall. But the horizontal resolution is more difficult to see: the pixel dots overlap and blur together so we can't see any separation between them. It's only by carefully observing and comparing the characters that we can judge how many dots across our characters are.

The character box only defines the framework within which the characters are drawn. Not all of the box is used for the characters themselves—parts are set aside for the space between characters. To see how this goes, we'll use the Monochrome Adapter's character box as an example.

The complete Monochrome Adapter character box is nine by 14. Of the nine columns across, the first and last are reserved for the space between characters, so our characters are actually drawn out of seven dots across. Of the 14 rows down, the top two and the bottom one are similarly used for the space between lines of characters, so there are 11 rows to draw the characters with. Two of those rows are used for *descenders,* as on the lowercase letters *p, g,* or *y.* That leaves nine rows for the main part of the characters. So, the Monochrome Adapter's characters are called seven by nine, referring to the main part of the character box, the part that a capital *X* will fill; the actual working part of the character box, including the descender rows, is seven by 11.

The parts set aside for spacing—one column on each side, two rows at the top and one row at the bottom—only apply to conventional characters. The special drawing characters—such as the solid character, code 219, or the box-drawing characters which we mentioned and demonstrated in the BOXES program—use these parts of the character box, so that they can touch each other without any space between.

The finer a character box is, the more detailed the drawing of a character can be. That's why the Monochrome Adapter's characters are able to have *serifs,* the fine parts on the ends of characters which dress them up, and make them more legible.

That's the main part of what there is to know about the technical details that underlie our PC family's text modes. But there's still more to know, and we'll see some of it in Section 12.3 on text mode tricks.

12.3 Text Mode Tricks

There are special features and tricks inherent in our computer's text modes which can be used to enhance the operation of programs and to produce some special effects. Of course the full range of tricks is only limited by our imagination and cleverness, and I can't begin to discover and explain everything that can be done. But there are some fundamental features and tricks that will help us understand the workings of the text mode, and that's what we'll look at in this section. We begin by considering the uses of excess display memory.

While the Monochrome Adapter has just enough display memory to hold all the information that appears on the display screen at once, the Color Graphics Adapter and the Enhanced Graphics Adapter contain more memory than is needed for one text screen image. That's because the graphics modes that these adapters also provide require more display memory than the text modes require. Rather than let this memory go to waste, it's put to use to hold several independent screen-loads of information. These separate screen-loads are called *display pages.*

Figure 12-5 shows how this works for the Color Graphics Adapter when it's in an 80-column text mode. For 80-column text, only 4000 bytes are needed to hold the display screen information (which is just the amount of memory in the Monochrome Adapter). But the Color Graphics Adapter has 16K bytes of memory, enough for four separate sets of 4000. The Color Graphics Adapter's memory can be divided into four independent display pages.

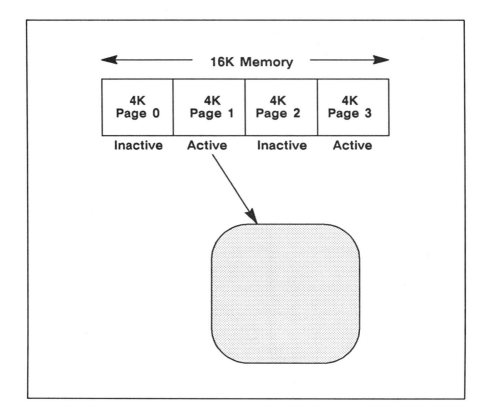

Figure 12-5. Four display pages.

Any one of these display pages can be activated so that its information appears on the display screen. The display adapter is able to switch immediately from one page to another, so that what appears on the screen can be changed without delay. While only one page appears on the screen at a time, our programs always have access to all the data in all the screens, all the time.

That's the point of having and using multiple display pages: while it may take a noticeable amount of time for a program to *generate* information for the screen, the information can be made to appear instantaneously, by switching from one page to another. While we're looking at one screen-load of information, the program can be invisibly building another screen image off stage in another page buffer. When we're ready to have it appear, it can appear without delay.

The number of screen pages available varies with the display adapter and the video mode that we're using. As we've seen, the Monochrome Adapter has only one page, so no page switching is possible (more on this in a moment). The standard Color Graphics Adapter provides four pages for 80-column text, or eight pages for 40-column text. The Enhanced Graphics Adapter, which can be equipped with varying amounts of memory, can have even more pages.

These multiple display pages can be put to any use. They might be used to hold completely new information or slightly changed data. If we built four or eight versions of a character-based drawing, we can rapidly page through them, making them appear in succession creating an animation effect.

Programs switch among the pages by a simple command to the display adapter that tells it to paint the screen image from another part of the display memory. BASIC includes features that let us work with multiple display pages. You'll find them as parts of the SCREEN statement, and you can experiment with them, provided your computer has a Color Graphics Adapter or the equivalent. The third parameter of BASIC's SCREEN statement, the parameter called *apage,* is the ''active page,'' and it controls which page the program is working with (that is, if the program is writing information to the ''screen,'' which screen page is being changed by the program). The fourth parameter of the SCREEN statement, called *vpage,* is the ''visible page,'' and it controls which page image is currently appearing on the screen.

While BASIC provides us with features that do the basic tasks of screen page control, programs written in other languages have to do this themselves, with the assistance of some features provided by the computer's built-in ROM-BIOS. One of the things that the ROM-BIOS will do for our programs is to keep track of a separate cursor location for each page. But, whether our programs take advantage of BASIC's features, or use the ROM-BIOS's features, or do all the screen page control themselves, the multiple-page feature is there to be used.

Few programs actually use the paging feature though, because it's simply not of as much benefit as we might think. For one thing, it's not available on computers equipped with the Monochrome Adapter—and that's been the majority of PCs. If a program has to do without the benefit of the display paging with the Monochrome Adapter, it may not be worth the extra programming effort to have a program use pages with one display adapter and not use them with another.

Even though the Monochrome Adapter does not have multiple display pages built into it, programs can—and often do—adopt the paging idea to make their screen images appear instantaneously. This is done by setting aside a portion of the program's conventional memory as an improvised display page, where a complete screen image is constructed. When the data is ready, it's moved into the real display memory in one quick assembly language operation. The mechanics are different than what's done with true display pages. With true pages, the display data is not moved. Instead, the display adapter switches from looking at one page of memory to another, while with this pseudo-page operation the data is actually moved from another location to the display memory. Moving a full screen-load of data takes such a small fraction of a second that it appears to happen as quickly as true page switching does.

If any of the programs you work with present unusually snappy screen displays, it's likely that they use this "private paging" technique that I've described. My own NU program does as well.

There is more that can be done with the screen display than just moving data into or out of it. It's also possible, with assembly language tricks, to blank out the data that's on the screen, or to change the display attributes, the colors, in a flash. The slow and laborious way to change the data on the screen is to do it a character at a time, changing each position on the screen individually. But there are faster and more efficient ways.

For example, if we want to clear the whole screen, we can do it with just a few assembly language instructions. To blank the screen properly, we'd want to set each data byte to a blank space (code 32, hex 20) and each attribute byte to the "normal" color (which is usually 7, hex 07). We can set the first screen position to blank-normal by using the assembly language instruction that places a two-byte word anywhere we want in memory. The word we'd use is hex 2007, which combines the blank space character (20) with the normal color attribute (07). A variation on the instruction that moves a single word into memory can be used to repeat the operation into successive words of the display memory, so that the same data is propagated over the whole screen.

A variation on the same trick can be used to change only the color attributes, leaving the data unchanged, or vice versa. That's done with the assembly language instructions that "AND" and "OR" data, so that we can just turn on or off the bits we want. Using these tricks, just a couple of instructions can paint a new color across the entire screen, faster than the eye can see.

In addition to the tricks that our programs can perform on their own, the PC's ROM-BIOS contains service routines that will do most of the things that we would like done, including some fancy steps that you'll rarely see used. One of these ROM-BIOS services lets us define a rectangular window anywhere on the screen, and inside that window we can display information and scroll it off the window without disturbing any other data outside the window. That service is among the ones we'll look at in Chapter 17.

But, before we move on to new topics, we have more to explore about our computer's video capabilities. Next comes the graphics modes, a special dimension beyond the text mode we've just seen.

Some Things to Try

1. In BASIC, or any other programming language you use, write a program that prints the 32 ASCII control characters, codes 0-31, on the display screen. See what happens with each, and note which ones appear as their PC characters and which ones work as control characters. Compare your results with the information on these control characters in Chapter 4.

2. Figure out what the memory addresses will be for the four different display pages that a Color Graphics Adapter has when it's working in 80-column mode, and the eight pages in 40-column mode.

3. Why does the Monochrome Adapter have 4,096 bytes of display memory when it only needs 4000? Why might it be risky for a program to attempt to use the left-over 96 bytes in the display memory?

4. If your computer has the Color Graphics Adapter (or any other adapter, including the PCjr's or the Compaq's, that has more than one video page), experiment with text pages using the BASIC SCREEN command to switch pages and the PRINT command to place some information in each page.

13

Video: Graphics Fundamentals

In this chapter we'll take a look at the unique characteristics and capabilities of the graphics modes. We'll begin by seeing what the main features of the graphics modes are, and while we're doing that we'll repeatedly contrast the graphics modes with the text modes, to highlight the differences. Then we'll look at the variety of different modes that are at our disposal. Finally, we'll finish up our discussion with a look at some of the technical details that underlie the workings of the graphics modes.

13.1 Graphics Modes Outline

In each of the graphics modes, our PC's display screen is divided up into a series of dots, called pixels. The pixels are arranged in a rectangular grid of rows and columns, and each pixel can be individually set to show some color, within the range of colors that the particular mode allows. In those respects, the graphics modes aren't fundamentally different than the text modes. And even though there are many more pixel dots in the graphics modes than there are text characters in the text modes—for example, 320 pixels across and 200 down, compared to 80 characters across and 25 down—that's mostly a difference of *degree,* rather than a fundamental difference in kind.

What is really different about the graphics modes is that each pixel on the screen is simply a small splash of light that has no form to it. In the text modes, each position on the screen is a rich entity in itself: it holds a character that has its own unique shape, and the shape is made visible by the contrast between the two colors that fill the foreground and background of the character position. But with the pixels in the graphics modes, we just have a dot of light, with no unique shape and no division between foreground and background. In the text modes each screen position has *three* elements to it. First, there are the two main elements of data (which character is to be shown) and attribute (how the character is to be shown). Then, the attribute part is divided into two parts, the foreground color and the background color, so that we end up with a total of three separate elements to each text screen position. By contrast, in the graphics modes, each pixel has only *one element,* the color that the pixel is set to. In graphics modes, there is no "data" (in the sense that each text mode position has a data element) and there is no background color, only the color of each individual pixel.

If we want to understand the graphics modes, it's important for us to understand the meaning of "background." In the text modes, there really is something called a background color; each character position has one. But in the graphics modes, each pixel simply has a color to it: no foreground, no background, just a single color. What we *think* of as the background color in a graphics mode is just the color that we give to all the pixels that we're not doing something in particular to. The "background color" in a graphics mode is the *default* color that we set all the pixels to, so that they contrast with the color (or colors) that we're drawing with. That's a *practical convention* (and a sensible and necessary one) that has to do with the way we make pictures that people can look at and understand. However, it doesn't have anything to do with the fundamental way the graphics modes operate. In text mode, the background color is something that's a technical reality as well as a visual reality. In graphics mode, the "background color" is just a visual convention that has nothing to do with the technical way graphics modes work.

There is one other thing that the graphics modes give up, compared to the text modes: blinking. In the text modes, we're used to seeing blinking in two things: one is the cursor, and the other is the blinking attribute of characters. The graphics modes don't have either. There is no blinking cursor in the graphics modes, and in fact there is no cursor at all, in the technical sense. (For more on that, see *The Graphics Cursor* sidebar.) In addition, one aspect of the "colors" that are available in the text modes is blinking. Of course *blinking* isn't a color in any real sense, but in the text modes, as we saw in Chapter 12, characters can be made to blink on and off, and the blinking feature is controlled in the same way that true color is controlled—so for the text modes the blinking feature is, in effect, a special kind of color. The normal graphics modes don't provide us with blinking in any form. (There is, however, one exception, which we'll see later, in graphics mode 15.) Software can do almost anything, so our programs can make things blink on and off on the screen simply by changing the screen image on a regular interval. There is no inherent (and hardware supported) blinking feature in any of the graphics modes.

The Graphics Cursor

If we activate BASIC, we'll see on the screen a flashing cursor, of the type we're most used to. If we switch to a graphics mode—say by using the SCREEN 1 command—we still seem to have a cursor on the screen, although if we're observant we'll notice that the cursor appears as a solid block, rather than in the normal flashing form.

What's going on here? A trick!

In the *hardware* sense, there is no such thing as a cursor in graphics mode. The standard flashing cursor—as we saw in Chapter 12—is a designed-in feature of the display adapters, which applies only to the text modes. This hardware cursor flashes and it appears only on just one character space at a time. Normally it just underlines the current position on the screen, and it's created specifically by the display adapter hardware circuitry. Its appearance requires no special effort from our software (other than the occasional command to position the cursor where it's wanted). *That* cursor, the hardware cursor, simply *does not exist* in the graphics modes.

What we see as a cursor in the graphics modes is a software-created effect that serves the role of a cursor (indicating where the active location is on the screen). Functionally it's no different than the hardware cursor, but technically it's a totally different animal, because it's created a completely different way.

When a program—such as BASIC operating in a graphics mode—wants to create a cursor on the screen it simply does whatever is necessary to produce the right kind of effect. Usually that's nothing more than changing the background color where the cursor is to be shown. This same thing can be done in a text mode, to supplement or completely replace the blinking hardware cursor. We're used to seeing this sort of software-generated cursor with spreadsheet programs, which place a cursor on the current cell by making the cell appear in reverse video.

In text mode, programs have the option of using the hardware cursor or creating their own software cursor. In the graphics mode, there's no choice because there is no hardware cursor in graphics mode.

You may encounter the two main conventions for showing a cursor in graphics mode. One, which we see used by BASIC, is the old standard of indicating the cursor location by changing the background color. The other is a newer standard popularized by the Apple Macintosh computer and used more and more in software for our PC family. It shows the cursor as a thin vertical line which may blink (the blinking is a software-generated effect). This line-cursor can be hard to see and use, but it has the advantage of being able to appear anywhere, even *between* characters, not just on top of a character.

No matter what it looks like, anything that acts like a cursor in one of the graphics modes is simply a visual effect created by our software, to serve the same purpose as the text modes' hardware cursor.

Instead, the graphics modes simply have available at their command a palate of colors that each pixel dot position on the screen can be set to. Each graphics mode has its own repertoire of colors—that, and the number of dot positions is what makes up the differences among the various modes. What they all have in common, what characterizes the graphics modes, is the grid of dots and the ability to set each dot to a solid color chosen from a palette of colors.

If that seems remarkably simple and primitive to you, then you are understanding the essential character of the graphics modes. They are at once cruder and more powerful than the text modes. Cruder, because all they can show are colored dots. More powerful, because from those dots we can construct rich and complex drawings that would not be possible to create from the more specialized text modes. The graphics modes provide us with a *rawer material* to work with than the text modes. There is a greater variety of things that we can do with the graphics modes, but getting those things done requires more work, because everything has to be drawn, dot by dot, the hard way, by our software. And that includes, by the way, any text characters that we might want to appear on the screen; they have to be drawn dot by dot as well (see the *Writing Text in Graphics Mode* sidebar).

Writing Text in Graphics Mode

The ROM-BIOS routines that supervise the graphics modes provide services to write text characters on the screen, just as they do for the text modes. The reason is simple enough: if the ROM-BIOS provides character-writing services for any mode, it ought to provide it for *all* modes. There's an important addition to that reason: any part of any program ought to be able to toss an error message on the screen in case it gets in trouble. Having a universal set of text-output routines in the ROM-BIOS, which work in every mode, text or graphics, provides a common way for any program to send up an emergency flare.

In the text modes, programs—including the ROM-BIOS—write messages on the screen by outputting the ASCII character codes, and the display adapter hardware takes on the job of producing a recognizable character. But in the graphics modes, characters can only appear on the screen if they are *drawn* like any other picture.

The ROM-BIOS is prepared to do just that, in a standard way, with a set of little drawing templates, one for each character that it can draw. A table of character drawings is stored in the ROM-BIOS memory area for this purpose. While some of the newer graphics modes, like those provided by the Enhanced Graphics Adapter, may require their own specific drawing tables, a standard table—based on the eight by eight pixel character box used in Color Graphics Adapter's graphics modes—can be found at memory location F000:FA6E in most PCs.

The bits in this drawing table are used to indicate the pixel settings, on or off, used to draw each character. For the standard table, eight bytes represent each character: the bits of the first byte give the eight pixel settings for the first scan line, and so on. In Appendix A you'll find a program called GRAPHTXT, which will decode this table, and display each character drawing in enlarged form, so that we can inspect how each character is drawn. You can use the GRAPHTXT program with any display adapter, because it recreates the drawings with characters, so you don't have to have a graphics screen to use GRAPHTXT to see how graphics characters are drawn.

When our programs use the ROM-BIOS services to display characters in a graphics mode, the ROM-BIOS looks up the character's drawing in this table, and uses the bits in the table as a code to set the appropriate bits in the display memory, so that a drawing of the character appears on the screen. The technique used is roughly the same as our demonstration program GRAPHTXT uses.

In the original PC design, only the first 128 ASCII characters were provided in this table. That covered the most important characters, particularly the letters of the alphabet, but it didn't provide the entire PC character set. Drawings for the upper 128 characters can be provided by our programs, and the ROM-BIOS will use them, provided we tell the BIOS about them by placing the address of the table in the interrupt vector for interrupt 31.

It's common for game programs, and other "light-duty" programs that use graphics, to rely on the ROM-BIOS's services to display any text information that needs to be shown. But "heavy-duty" programs, such as 1-2-3 or Framework, generally paint their own character data when they work in a graphics mode. This is because these programs have their own demanding needs for how characters should appear, and by doing their own character drawing, they can control the size, type style, and features (such as **bold** or *italic*) of the characters that appear. The same is true of word-processing programs that can work in graphics mode.

No matter which approach a program uses—do-it-yourself or leave it to the BIOS—any text characters that appear when our computers are in a graphics mode are drawn on the screen, pixel by pixel, through the work of software, and not, as it is in the text modes, by hardware.

That's given us a basic idea of what the graphics modes are about, collectively. Now it's time for us to consider the range of graphics modes and see what the characteristics and potential of each is.

13.2 A Tour of the Graphics Modes

There are no fewer than 11 graphics modes that we'll be taking a look at, which we saw in the brief summary in Chapter 11. For easy reference, here's a quick recap from Chapter 11 (the mode numbers in the first column of the table, are the numbers used by the PC's ROM-BIOS to identify each mode):

Mode	Type	Color?	Width	Description
4	Graphics	4	320	Medium-resolution graphics, with color
5	Graphics	No	320	Medium-resolution graphics, no color
6	Graphics	2	640	High-resolution graphics, no color
8	Graphics	16	160	Low-resolution graphics
9	Graphics	16	320	Medium-resolution graphics
10	Graphics	4	640	High-resolution graphics
13	Graphics	16	320	Medium-resolution, high-color
14	Graphics	16	640	High-resolution, more color
15	Graphics	No	640	Monochrome graphics, 350 line
16	Graphics	64	640	High-resolution, 350 line
Herc	Graphics	No	720	Monochrome graphics, 348 line

These are the 11 main modes that are available for our PC family. There are other modes, such as the extra-high quality modes provided by the very expensive and very specialized IBM Professional Graphics Adapter, but these 11 are the main ones and probably the only ones that most of us will encounter. In fact, we'll only encounter a few of them at a time, because this full list is provided by a variety of display adapters and we can only have one or two at the most installed in a single computer.

That's the point we should begin with—reviewing what modes are available with what adapters—before we get into the details of each mode. That way, if you are only interested in the modes that apply to your computer, you'll have a roadmap of the ones to pay attention to. And if you're interested in the full range of the PC family's graphics capabilities, you can study them all, and also know what applies to which adapter.

The IBM Color Graphics Adapter—one of the two original display adapters for the PC family—provides us with the first three graphics modes, numbered 4-6. These are the modes that we'll be spending the most time discussing, because they are the most commonly used, and because they provide us with a model for the other modes, which are mostly just a variation on the themes that these three provide. These modes are not exclusive to the Color Graphics Adapter, as we'll see.

The special built-in display adapter in the PC*jr* mimics the Color Graphics Adapter, so it provides the first three graphics modes. In addition, three modes were specially created for the PC*jr*, modes 8-10. These PC*jr* modes are not supported by any other display adapter; they are unique to the PC*jr*.

The IBM Enhanced Graphics Adapter (EGA), like the PC*jr*, covers the three standard CGA graphics modes and also provides its own unique modes, four of them in this case, numbered 13-16. It's important to note that two of these four, like all the other modes we've covered so far, are used with standard RGB or composite monitors. For the other two new modes, one is used with the Monochrome Display and one is used with the special Enhanced Color Display (ECD).

Finally, the Hercules adapter provides one special graphics mode for use with the Monochrome Display. While the other graphics adapters we've been discussing provide a variety of graphics modes, the Hercules only has this one. (It also provides the standard monochrome text mode.)

Now that we know which modes are provided by which display adapters, let's take a look at the particular capabilities of each one.

Video mode 4 is a medium-resolution, four-color mode. It uses a pixel grid of 320 dots across and 200 lines down. All of the standard graphics modes are drawn with 200 lines. The variation in resolution shows only in the horizontal dimension: 160 dots across is called low-resolution; 320 is medium; 640 is high. You might expect that it would not work well to use the same vertical resolution with three different horizontal resolutions, but on the whole it works out reasonably well. In any event, technical limitations largely forced the use of a common 200-line vertical dimension.

Since video mode 4 uses four colors, it works with just part of the PC family's standard 16-color color repertoire. The colors that are made available are a curious combination of free choice and preselection. One of the four colors can be freely chosen to be any of the 16 basic colors. The other three colors are predefined by IBM, but we get to choose from two different sets of three. One set, known as palette 0, includes the colors *green, red,* and *brown* (also known as *dark yellow*); palette 1 has the colors *cyan* (blue-green to those of us unfamiliar with that word), *magenta,* and *white.* We can't mix and match these palettes: they are predefined and fixed by IBM (except as we'll note in a moment). Our programs can, however, freely switch between the two palettes, and freely set the other color to anything, including any of the colors used in the fixed part of the palette.

When a program uses these four colors, it requests them by a number, 0 through 3; 0 selects the freely chosen color (whatever it happens to be) while 1, 2, and 3 select *green, red,* and *brown* from palette 0 or *cyan, magenta,* and *white* from palette 1. One thing particularly worth noting is that these selections are all *relative.* If a program paints a picture using color 0 and then changes the selection of what color *is* color 0, everything that was painted 0 instantly and automatically changes to the new color; the same thing happens if we change our palette selection. This trick can be used in a number of ways to good graphic effect. For example, a drawing can be made to appear and disappear by changing its color to contrast or be the same as its background; or we can make the screen appear to shake violently just by rapidly alternating between the palettes.

You'll see a demonstration of what can be done with color in video mode 4 in the program COLOR-4, listed in Appendix A. (To use COLOR-4 or to experiment with the example given here, you'll have to have a computer equipped for color graphics, of course.)

For a shorter introduction to the color capabilities of video mode 4, try these statements in BASIC: SCREEN 1 will switch you into video mode 4. COLOR, 0 will select the predefined palette 0, while COLOR,1 will select palette 1. These statements demonstrate what happens when we change the one freely selectable color:

```
10 FOR CHOICE = 0 TO 15
20   COLOR CHOICE
30   PRINT "This is color number"; CHOICE
40 NEXT CHOICE
```

The color palettes that we've talked about are predefined and fixed in the ordinary sense. However, two of our display adapters, the PC*jr*'s and the Enhanced Graphics Adapter, have the ability to *remap* the color selection, so that when a program apparently asks for one color—say *red*—another color might appear, say *blue*. This is done through the magic of a hardware register, which allows us to redefine the meaning of the numbers that are used to identify colors. When we can do that, then we can have our own free choice of the four colors that are used in this video mode 4. Instead of being bound by the two standard palettes, we can remap the color numbers so that the standard palettes give us whatever colors we want. This trick only works, however, with those two special display adapters—it doesn't apply to the standard Color Graphics Adapter or any equivalent adapter (such as the Compaq adapter).

Mode 4 provides 200 lines of 320 dots, or 64,000 pixels total. With four color choices for each, we need two bits of memory to record the four possible color choices. That means that this video mode needs 128,000 bits of memory to support it; that's 16,000 bytes. Since the Color Graphics Adapter's display memory provides 16K of memory, there is just enough memory for this video mode. (In Section 13.3, where we dive into more technical details, we'll see how that memory is used.)

Now we're ready to move on to look at some of the other graphics modes. Most of the ideas that we've covered for mode 4 apply to the other modes as well, so we've already covered most of what there is to know about the standard graphics modes.

Mode 5 is a special color-suppressed variation on mode 4. It works just like the two color-suppressed text modes (modes 0 and 2). Mode 5 works identically to mode 4, but the signal coming out of the composite video jack does not have a color signal in it, so that the four colors appear more-or-less as four shades of grey. However, that only applies to the composite video jack; the signals coming out the RGB socket of the display adapter are as colorful as ever. Since this mode is organized just like mode 4, the memory requirements are the same.

Mode 6 is a high-resolution, two-color mode. As a high-resolution mode, it has 640 pixel dots across (and the standard 200 lines down). There are two colors available in mode 6; they are predefined and fixed as the colors black and white. It's debatable, of course, whether or not we should say that this mode has colors; in the technical sense it clearly does: there are two to choose from (just as mode 4 has four to choose from) and they are part of the PC's standard 16-color range. On the other hand, most of us would say that *black* and *white* are ''black and white'' and not a selection of two colors. Call it what you will, as long as you understand what this video mode provides us with: twice the resolution and half the colors of mode 4.

The black and white colors that are used by mode 6 can be remapped, just like the remapping of mode 4's colors when we're using a PC*jr* or an Enhanced Graphics Adapter. This remapping doesn't increase the number of colors that appear at one time, which is fixed at only two for mode 6, but it does permit the use of ''real color'' in place of the colorless colors black and white.

Mode 6 has twice as many pixels as mode 4, 640 by 200 for a total of 128,000. But with half as many color choices to be recorded, only one bit is needed for each pixel in this mode. So, the total memory requirement of this mode is the same as for modes 4 and 5: 16K.

These modes, 4-6, are the main, common graphics modes for the PC family because they apply to every standard graphics display adapter (excluding the Hercules adapter). As a general rule, we find mode 4 used for light-duty programs, such as games and educational programs, while mode 6 is used by heavy-duty business programs such as 1-2-3. Games use mode 4 to gain color, sacrificing detailed picture resolution; business programs use mode 6 to gain high-resolution, sacrificing color. It's a clear tradeoff, but a trade off that isn't necessary in some of the more advanced graphics modes that we'll be covering next.

The next three modes, 8-10, are special to the PC*jr*, and they provide some natural and expected extensions to the basic complement of graphics modes, resolving some of the most obvious shortcomings of the basic set.

Mode 8 is a low-resolution, 16-color mode. It's a bridge from mode 4, in the opposite direction from mode 6. In this low-resolution mode there are only 160 columns of dots across each row, half the number provided by the medium-resolution modes. There are more colors, as you would expect, but not just twice as many, four times as many, 16 colors, the PC's full complement of colors.

Because mode 8 is able to use all 16 colors at once, there are no annoying palette restrictions in this mode. Since this is a PC*jr* mode, and since the *jr* has the ability to remap colors, the colors used in this mode can be altered and tinkered with in many ways. In mode 4, where there is a limited selection of colors, there's a good reason to use this feature; to increase the choice of colors to be used. But in this mode (and mode 9 following) remapping the colors has a less obvious benefit. It can be used, though, for special effects such as making parts of a drawing appear and disappear (by blending in with a same-colored background).

Although this mode does provide more colors than any of the previous graphics modes, the picture quality in this low-resolution mode is so poor that there are few uses for it. If you have a PC*jr* you can see just how poor the resolution is for yourself by using the BASIC command SCREEN 3.

This mode uses just as much memory as mode 4, 16K, because it has only half as many pixels—160 times 200, totaling 32,000—and needs just four bits (twice as many) to specify the colors for each pixel. The four bits per pixel provide 16 color-selecting values. Here we get four times the color choice for only twice the memory. That would be a real plus if this video mode were more useful.

Mode 9 is the second of our special PC*jr* modes; it's medium resolution but it provides the full 16 colors. This mode breaks out of the 16K memory mold, thanks to some special tricks concerning how the PC*jr* manages its display memory. This is one of most satisfying graphics modes, because it combines medium-resolution, 320 dots across, with the full use of the PC's color set. For this mode, 32K of display memory is needed, and any program using this mode must know how to perform some special *jr*-specific tricks to set aside this much display memory. In BASIC we do it by first using the statement CLEAR ,,,32768 to set aside the memory, and then SCREEN 5 to switch to this video mode.

Mode 10 is the third and last of the *jr*-specific modes; it is a variation similar to what mode 9 provides. Mode 10 is high-resolution with four colors. Like mode 9, this mode needs 32K of memory, double the standard graphics 16K. BASIC switches to this mode using the SCREEN 6 statement after CLEAR ,,,32768 to reserve enough memory. Like mode 9, and unlike mode 8, this is a very powerful and useful graphics mode, thanks to the combination of high-resolution and four colors. The four colors for this mode are the same as palette 1 in mode 4: the first color is freely selectable, and the other colors are set to *cyan*, *magenta*, and *white*. But, since this is a PC*jr* mode, color remapping can be used to change the palette to any color selection.

The next set of graphic modes are provided by the Enhanced Graphics Adapter. They provide a variety of special graphics capabilities that span most of what we find available in the other specialty adapters.

Mode 13 is a medium-resolution, 16-color mode. It is essentially the same as the PC*jr*'s mode 9. Like mode 9, is calls for 32K of display memory. (BASIC does not support this mode, or any of the other EGA modes so there's no simple way to demonstrate these modes, even on a computer equipped for them.) The colors can be remapped, as we're used to seeing for anything involving either the PC*jr* or the EGA. *In addition*, if this or another EGA mode is used with the EGA's special Enhanced Color Display, the colors of this mode can be remapped not just into the PC's basic 16-color set, but the ECD's extended 64-color set.

Mode 14 is a high-resolution 16-color mode. It's similar to the PC*jr*'s mode 10, but it goes even further in providing all sixteen colors, not just four colors, in high-resolution. Doing that requires a complement of 64K of display memory.

So far, all the modes we've seen have been intended for the standard types of color graphics display screens used in the PC family: RGB monitors, color composite screens, TV sets, and so forth. The next special EGA mode, though, is intended for use only with the Monochrome Display, the screen normally used with the Monochrome Adapter. This is mode 15, IBM's version of a monochrome graphics mode. It provides a pixel grid of 640 dots across and 350 lines down. The total number of lines corresponds to the total number of scan lines used in the regular monochrome mode, where there are 25 character lines, and each character is drawn with 14 scan lines; 14 times 25 gives us 350, the number of graphics lines in this mode. There is one very special thing about this mode: it provides blinking in a very special way. Each pixel in this mode has four possible attributes: off (black), on, blinking-on, and bright. The main reason for having this unusual combination of pixel attributes is that it allows this monochrome graphics mode to match the features of the standard monochrome text mode (which includes blinking and bright high-intensity features) while it adds a graphics capability. Since there are four possible attributes for each dot on the screen, the memory requirement is two bits for each pixel, 448,000 bits or 56,000 bytes.

The next mode, and the final one of the EGA's special modes, also calls for a special display screen, but this time it's the Enhanced Color Display, a display screen that is able to show a full 64 distinct colors, four times as many as the PC's standard 16. This is mode 16. It has the same extra-high-resolution as mode 15—640 across and 350 down. Each pixel can be set to any of 64 colors, which calls for six bits to support each pixel. This requires a whopping 1,344,000 bits, or 168,000 bytes of display memory. That's a lot of memory! But if we want to have all that color on all those pixels, that's the memory price that has to be paid.

The final video mode that we'll consider is the one provided by the popular, but non-IBM, Hercules graphics adapter. The Hercules adapter pioneered graphics for the Monochrome Display, providing a mode that is similar to what the EGA later provided in its mode 15. There is no IBM mode number for this mode, since it's not IBM supported. For identification purposes, I call it simply the Herc mode. While this mode is similar to the EGA's mode 15, the details are different. It has a small but noticeable increase in the horizontal resolution, 720 pixels rather than 640, and an all but unnoticeable two fewer vertical lines, 348 rather than 350. The figure of 348 is odd because this same adapter has to provide 350 scan lines when it works in monochrome text mode; but that's the way it is. This display mode needs 250,560 bits (one for each pixel), or 31,320 bytes. That is just under 32K of memory. You'll note that the Herc mode provides monochrome graphics as we might expect them to be, a fairly pure form of monochrome graphics that does not have the particular features of the monochrome text mode (that is, it doesn't have either bright intensity or blinking as "colors"). By contrast, the monochrome graphics mode number 15, provided by IBM's EGA board, provides both of those special features.

That finishes our summary of the 11 main graphics modes. What we have left to explore are some details of how the graphics modes use their memory, which is at times peculiar. We'll see that in Section 13.3.

TECHNICAL BACKGROUND ▮ ▮ ▮ ▪ ▪ ▪ ▬▬▬▬▬▬▬▬▬▬▬

13.3 Graphics Details

Now it's time for us to explore the inner workings of how the graphics modes use their display memory. It's substantially trickier than it is for the text modes, both more complicated to understand and for most students of the PC family less important to our overall goal of knowing the main inner workings of the PC.

The layout of the display memory for the graphics modes follows most of the principles that we learned when we explored the layout of the text modes, but some new complications are added that considerably increase the amount of work that a program has to do to place data into the display memory.

The main complication is that while in the text modes the display data is laid out in one continuous lump. In the graphics modes the data is broken down into either two or four interleaved banks.

For example, in video mode 4, the medium-resolution, 4-color mode, the 200 lines of pixels are divided into two banks, consisting of the even and odd numbered lines. The first bank holds the data for line number 0 (the first line), followed by lines 2, 4, and so on to line 198, the last of the even numbered lines. A separate memory bank holds the odd numbered lines, 1, 3, 5, and so on to the very last line, number 199. Figure 13-1 shows how this is laid out.

There are two variations on this banking operation. One divides the horizontal lines of graphics pixels into two banks and the other into four banks. The original three graphics modes, modes 4-6, work in two banks; so does video mode 8, the PC*jr*'s low-resolution mode. The other two PC*jr* modes, numbers 9 and 10, and the Hercules mode divide their lines into four banks. Figure 13-2 summarizes how the lines in the banks are interleaved.

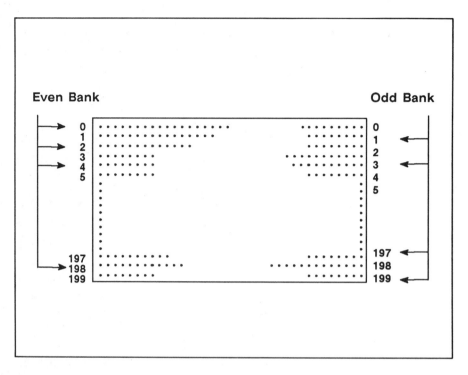

Figure 13-1. Graphics memory banks.

Within each bank, the graphics data is laid out in a direct and compact manner, just as it is in the text modes. The data for the first line in each bank fills successive bytes from the beginning of the bank, and the second line in each bank immediately follows the first, without any gap. However, there is a small gap between the banks, just as there is between the different display pages in text modes. Each bank occupies somewhat less than 8K bytes of storage, and each bank begins on an even 8K address boundary, with a small amount of unused slack space between the banks.

This arrangement of graphics data into banks is done basically for the convenience of the hardware. Since the display screen's picture is painted in two passes, with the lines of each pass interleaved, the graphics memory is laid out in the same fashion, so that the graphics data can be retrieved from memory in a way that's close to the way in which it's needed for the screen. This reduces the overhead involved in painting a graphics picture on the screen.

The flip side to that coin is that the work involved for our software to create a graphics picture is considerably increased, because the address calculations needed to locate each dot are more complicated. The difference

```
Two bank modes:
  Bank 0:  0,      2,      4,      6,      8,   ...
  Bank 1:      1,      3,      5,      7,      9,   ...

Four bank modes:
  Bank 0:  0,              4,              8,   ...
  Bank 1:      1,              5,              9,   ...
  Bank 2:          2,              6,   ...
  Bank 3:              3,              7,   ...
```

Figure 13-2. Bank line interleaving.

isn't enormous: after all, some arithmetic has to be done to calculate the location whether the lines are continuous (as they are for the text modes) or separated into banks (as they are for the graphics modes). However, this bank-separate does increase the amount of calculation that has to be done to work with the graphics display memory.

While the layout of the graphics display memory is essentially the same for all of the modes we've been talking about (modes 4-6, 8-10, and the Herc mode), differing only in whether there are two or four banks on interleaved lines, the composition of the pixel data within the lines has more variation from mode to mode. This is because the different modes need different amounts of data for each pixel. There's also one special complication in one of the PC*jr* modes, as we'll see in a moment.

For the 2-color modes—mode 6 and the Herc mode—there is only one bit for each pixel dot. The data scheme here is as simple as you would expect it would be. Each successive byte in the display memory holds the data for eight pixels; the high-order bit of the byte (bit number 7) is for the first pixel, and so on down the bits. For the standard 4-color modes—modes 4 and 5—there are two bits per pixel. Just as you would expect, each byte holds the complete data for four pixels with the bits taken in pairs: the first two bits of each byte, bits 7 and 6, hold the data for the first of the four pixels, and so on.

But, for the other 4-color mode, the PC*jr*'s mode 10, the bits aren't coded that way at all. Instead, the display memory is used in pairs of bytes, with each pair providing the bits for eight pixels together. The first of the eight pixels gets its data bits from *both* of the high-order bits in the two bytes. The next pixel gets its two bits from the next bit of each of the two bytes, and so on. This curious scheme was worked out so that the PC*jr*'s slower operating speed could keep up with the rapid data demand of this video mode; it works because the PC*jr* has two memory circuits that support every other memory byte. By grabbing and decoding data in pairs of bytes, the PC*jr*'s memory can effectively work twice as fast.

Finally, the 16-color modes, PC*jr* modes numbers 8 and 9, use four bits for each pixel. For these modes, each display memory byte covers two pixels; the four high-order bits provide the data for the first of the two pixels, and the low-order bits the other pixel.

When our software sets to work drawing a graphics picture, it has to not only calculate the memory addresses where the data is stored, but it also has to carefully set the appropriate bits and leave the other bits undisturbed. If the program is painting an entire picture, it could construct the pixel data in groups of 2 or 4 or 8 pixels at a time and simply store the complete data bytes in place—a relatively quick operation. But if the program is controlling the pixels independently, then the data for the pixels that share each byte has to be preserved. The microprocessor's bit-manipulating operations, ANDs, ORs, shifts, and so forth, are used for this. If a lot of bits are being set, the process can become quite lengthy, which is one of the main reasons why graphics-oriented programs run slowly compared to their text-based cousins. The PC's built-in ROM-BIOS provides service routines for manipulating individual pixels, but that doesn't speed the operation up any—it just saves programmers the work of creating these services themselves.

While it's been reasonably easy to make sense out of the graphics modes that we've covered so far, the special modes provided by the Enhanced Graphics Adapter are a world to themselves which is so complicated that it seems to defy description or explanation. If I tried to explain it in a comprehensive way, it would take up about two chapters worth of space here—and when I was done, I'd probably need to be locked up in an asylum: the EGA modes are that complex and perverse. To spare my sanity, and yours, I'll simply summarize what makes these modes so messy.

The first thing is that the special EGA modes require gobs of memory, an amount of memory that can't be fit into the available part of the PC's address space. (The available part is the 64K sized A-block of memory. While there is a 128K total of two memory blocks dedicated to display memory, the B-block may be in use by either of the other display adapters that the EGA works with—so, for its special modes the EGA has to work within the 64K A-block.)

This means that the working display memory has to be switched in and out of the PC's address space, as needed. While normal PC memory, and conventional display memory, is stable in the way it's addressed, the EGA's memory appears and disappears from the address space, so that the microprocessor and our programs can gain access to every part of it, even though there is more than will fit into the allotted space at one time.

214

The matter is further complicated by the fact that the EGA can have various amounts of memory installed in it, unlike the other display adapters, which come with a fixed amount of memory—just the amount that they need and no more. The EGA, on the other hand, can do so many different things that there's no one right amount of memory that it can need. But changing the amount of memory that's installed in an EGA doesn't just change the modes it can use, or the number of display pages that are available in those modes: it also changes how the memory is used and the way it's addressed.

The circuitry of the EGA performs a remarkable juggling act with its memory, adjusting the way the board operates to the amount of memory installed and the video modes that are being used, and making the memory appear and disappear from the PC's working address space as the situation calls for. Any programs that work intimately with the EGA in these new video modes have to be able to perform a dance that matches the skills and peculiarities of the EGA, by giving the EGA commands that control the memory addressing.

If you sensed that it is complicated for a program that uses the standard graphics modes to work out the addressing of the two (or four) banks of lines of graphics data, you can imagine how much more complicated it is to work with the EGA.

Some Things To Try

1. Experiment with the GRAPHTXT program shown in Appendix A. The program stops with character code 127. What happens if it went further? This program assumes that the table it displays is at a certain memory location (F000:FA6E). Can you think of a reasonable way to recognize such a table if we had to search for it?

2. For something more ambitious, try using GRAPHTXT as a starting point and create a program that allows you to create your own character drawings in large scale.

3. Imagine that you are creating specifications for the PC's hardware engineers, and you want to add a cursor and the blinking feature to the *color* graphics modes. How would you have it operate? Can you work out the reasons why the graphics modes don't have blinking or a cursor? Can you think of ways to overcome these problems?

14

Keyboard Magic

ince we've just finished our look at the PC family's display screens, it's appropriate that the next topic be the keyboard—the other half of our interface with the computer. It's mostly through the keyboard and the screen that we interact with our computers, so it's very worthwhile to know the ins and outs of our computer's keyboard.

It should be obvious to all of us that the display screen is a very complex topic—and we've seen just how complex in the last three chapters. Our computer's keyboard, on the other hand, seems like a very simple item—and it is, indeed, comparatively simple. But there are complexities and capabilities just under the surface of the PC's keyboard, complexities that make the keyboard a lot more flexible and a lot more interesting to explore than you might think.

You'll see why in this chapter, and it will make it possible for you to understand how some programs are able to work with the keyboard in some very unusual ways.

14.1 Basic Keyboard Operation

To understand what's going on with our computer's keyboard, we need to understand two key things: *first* that it isn't what it appears to be, and *second* that keyboard information journeys through several layers of transformations, until it emerges as what we thought it was in the first place.

It all takes place through some indirect magic. To make sense out of this, I'll begin by explaining why the keyboard works so indirectly, and then we'll see just how it works.

We expect our computer's keyboard to work in a very crude way: we press the A key, and the keyboard says to the computer ''A''; just that, and nothing more. It doesn't work that way. The reason is very simple. If the keyboard is assigned the task of making the A key *mean* the letter ''A'',

217

then the keyboard is in the business of giving meaning to what we do when we pound away on the keyboard. There are two things wrong with that. One is that it's not the business of the computer's hardware to assign meaning to what we're doing. Hardware is supposed to be like a blank slate—full of potential but with nothing happening. *Software*, on the other hand, is supposed to bring the computer's hardware to life, giving it activity and meaning. So, the first thing that would be wrong with the keyboard deciding that the A key meant the letter "A" is that the hardware would be intruding on a job that should belong to software.

The other thing that is wrong with the keyboard making the A key mean the letter "A" is that that would be inherently inflexible. You and I may say to ourselves that it would be stupid for the A key to mean anything else, but that's not the issue. As much as possible, a computer should be flexible and adaptable; and if the computer's hardware doesn't impose any meaning onto our keystrokes, so much the better.

Those are the ideas that are behind what may seem to be a curious relationship between the keyboard and our computers (and the computer's built-in ROM-BIOS programs).

Here is what happens when you or I press a key on our computer's keyboard: the keyboard recognizes that we've pressed one of the keys and makes a note of it. (The keys are assigned an identifying number, called a scan code, and that's what the keyboard makes a note of—that key number such-and-such has been pressed. You'll see what the identifying scan code numbers are for the standard PC keyboard in Figure 14-1.)

After the keyboard has made a note of the fact that we've pressed a key, it tells the computer that something has happened—it doesn't even say what, it just says that *something* has happened on the keyboard. That's done in the form of a hardware interrupt. The keyboard circuitry gives our computer's microprocessor an interrupt using the particular interrupt number that's assigned to the keyboard, interrupt number 9. That interrupt simply tells the computer that there has been a keyboard action. Interrupts, as we learned in Chapter 6, cause the microprocessor to put aside what it was doing and jump to an *interrupt-handling program*; in this case, one that is an integral part of the PC's ROM-BIOS software.

At that point, the ROM-BIOS's keyboard interrupt handler swings into action, and finds out just what took place on the keyboard. It does that by sending a command to the keyboard to report what happened. The keyboard responds by telling the ROM-BIOS which key was pressed. (The command and the reply work through the PC's *ports,* which we also discussed in Chapter 6. The ROM-BIOS issues its command by sending a command code out to a port address that the keyboard responds to. The keyboard

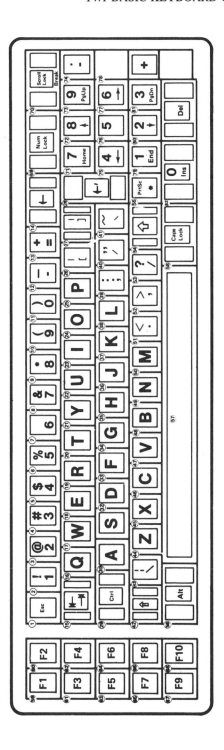

Figure 14-1. Keyboard keys and scan codes.

replies by sending the scan code of the key on another port address, which the ROM-BIOS reads.) In a moment we'll see what the ROM-BIOS does with that information, but first we need to finish up looking at this first layer of operation, that takes place in the keyboard itself.

The keyboard, of course, has to keep track of what key was pressed, waiting until the ROM-BIOS asks for it. (It isn't a long wait—usually about one ten-thousandth of a second; still, for computer hardware, that's a wait.) To do this, the keyboard has a small memory, and the memory is big enough to record 20 separate key actions, in case the microprocessor does not respond to the keyboard interrupts before more keys are pressed; that's rare, but the keyboard design allows for it. After the keyboard reports the details of a key action, it's flushed out of the keyboard's own special little memory, making room for new scan codes.

There are two more things we need to know about the keyboard. The first one is very critical. The keyboard doesn't just note when we press a key—it also notes it when we release a key as well. Either the pressing or releasing of any key is noted in the keyboard, and each separate key action is recorded by the keyboard, turned into an interrupt, and fed to the ROM-BIOS on command. There are distinct scan codes for the press and release of each key, so that they can be distinguished (the press codes are shown in Figure 14-1; the release codes are the same plus 128, hex 80).

That means that the ROM-BIOS is being interrupted to learn about key actions twice as often as we might have guessed. It also means that the ROM-BIOS is able to know whether a key is still being held down or whether it's been released, and that allows the ROM-BIOS to know, for example, if we're typing in capital letters because the shift key is held down.

The other thing that we need to know about the keyboard is that it's the keyboard hardware which makes the repeat-key action work. The keyboard hardware keeps track of how long each key is held down, and if it passes the "repeat threshold" (about half a second) then the keyboard hardware generates repeated key-pressed scan codes at a regular interval, just as if we had (somehow) repeatedly pressed the key without ever releasing it. These repeat key signals appear to the ROM-BIOS just like regular keystroke signals. If it needs to, the ROM-BIOS can distinguish them by the absence of the key-released scan codes in between.

What I've been describing so far is exactly how the standard PC keyboard works, but that's not exactly how the PC*jr*'s keyboard and the AT keyboards work. To learn what the differences are, see the sidebar *Keyboard Differences*. The next thing for us to discover is how the ROM-BIOS works with the keyboard's scan codes and turns them into meaning.

Keyboard Differences

What we've been describing here is the standard PC keyboard, which forms the basis of all keyboards for the PC family. Some models have keyboards that differ from the standard PC one, and they work their way around the differences to maintain full PC compatibility. That's made possible by the modular stages that the computer's keyboard data moves through.

In the case of the PC*jr*, the keyboard has fewer keys and is unable to hold key action data and wait for the microprocessor to request it. The PC*jr*'s keyboard transmits its key actions—with unique *jr* key scan codes—through an interrupt other than the standard keyboard interrupt 9. Since the *jr* can't wait, it signals a key action by a nonmaskable interrupt, number 2. The interrupt handler for that interrupt quickly reads the keyboard data as it is being transmitted, and then translates the *jr* scan codes into the equivalent standard PC scan codes, and *then*—in a final bit of trickery—invokes an interrupt number 9 to pass that to the regular ROM-BIOS routines (or to any program that has interposed itself before the ROM-BIOS and which expects to see standard PC scan codes, rather than PC*jr* codes.)

The PC*jr* goes to great lengths to make its nonstandard keyboard and scan codes appear to work identically to the PC-standard through a quite elaborate and clever set of programming tricks. Other keyboards that differ from the original PCs, such as the ATs, use similar methods although they don't require going to quite such extreme lengths.

In the standard PC keyboard, the two controlling factors of the repeat-key action—the time delay before it begins, and the time interval between generated key strokes—are fixed items. In both the PC*jr* and the AT model they can be changed. In the AT, the repeat-key action is a hardware feature, as it is for the PC; but the AT's keyboard hardware is programmable, so that we can change the repeat-key delay and interval. In the PC*jr*, the repeat-key action is created by the ROM-BIOS software, and it can be changed or even turned off entirely.

When the ROM-BIOS's keyboard interrupt handler springs into action, it receives one of the scan codes from the keyboard, and it has to decide what the key means. The ROM-BIOS quickly goes through several stages of analysis to discover how it should interpret and what it should do to the key action. First, it tests to see if the key action applies to one of the shift-type keys (such as the shift keys on the left- and right-hand side of the keyboard, or the ALT key, or the CTRL key). If so, the ROM-BIOS makes a note of the shift state, since it will affect the meaning of the keys that follow. Next, the ROM-BIOS tests to see if the key action is one of the "toggle" keys (such as the CAPSLOCK key, NUMLOCK, SCROLL-LOCK, or INS). The toggle keys, like the shift keys, affect the meaning of other keys, but the action is different here: the shift keys apply only when they are held down, and the toggle keys apply depending upon whether they are toggled "on" or "off".

For both the shift keys and the toggle keys, the ROM-BIOS has to keep a record of the current state of things, so that it knows what's what. This record is kept in two bytes of low memory, at hex addresses 417 and 418. Each of the bits in these two bytes separately records one part of the keyboard status, either recording if one of the keys is pressed down or recording whether one of the toggle states is on or off. You can inspect and play with these keyboard status bits using the KEY-BITS program listed in Appendix A. KEY-BITS demonstrates how the keyboard status is recorded, and also shows you some surprising things about what information the ROM-BIOS keeps track of. You'll see some things that you wouldn't expect to be recorded—such as keeping separate track of the left- and right-hand shift keys, or noting whether the toggle keys are pressed. Experimenting with KEY-BITS tells you a lot about how the ROM-BIOS works together with the keyboard.

(To help you get the most from KEY-BITS, here are two tips: it takes a bit of time for the program to decode the keyboard bits and display them on the screen. Give it a few seconds to show the results of your key actions. Also, when you're experimenting, remember that the keys interact—if you're in the shift state, pressing the Ins key isn't interpreted as the Ins key, it means the zero key instead.)

After the ROM-BIOS has taken care of the shift and toggle keys, it needs to check for some special key combinations, like the CTRL-ALT-DEL combination that reboots the computer. Another special combination is CTRL-NUMLOCK, which makes the computer pause. See the sidebar *About CTRL-NUMLOCK Print-Screen and More* for more information.

About CTRL-NUMLOCK *Print-Screen and More*

The keyboard ROM-BIOS routines do more than supervise the raw keyboard input and translate it into meaningful key characters. They also oversee some built-in features of the PC family.

The three best-known of the PC's features that the keyboard routines invoke are the system reboot (invoked by the CTRL-ALT-DEL

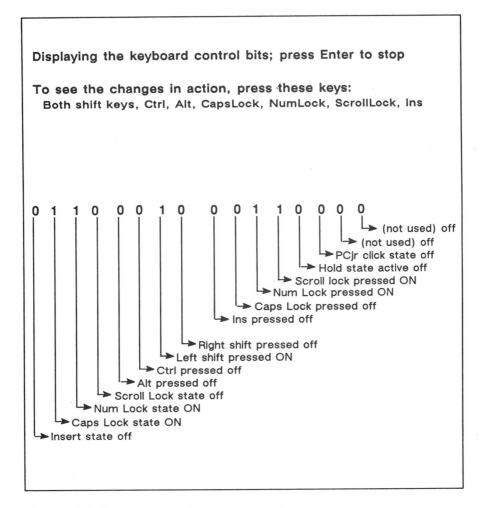

Figure 14-2. Sample screen from KEY-BITS.

key-combination), print-screen (shift-left-asterisk), and system pause (CTRL-NUMLOCK).

In the case of both reboot and print-screen, these are services that are always available to any program that wants to invoke them; print-screen, for example, is simply invoked by issuing an interrupt 5. In the case of these two services, the keyboard routines simply provide us, the user, with a way of getting at a service that normally is only available to a program.

The CTRL-NumLock or pause feature, however, is a special feature peculiar to the keyboard ROM-BIOS. When the keyboard routines recognize this key combination, the ROM-BIOS makes a note of it, and goes into a never-ending do-nothing loop—effectively suspending the operation of any program that is running. When this pause state is in effect, the machine is *not* locked up, and it continues to respond to any hardware interrupts that occur, such as disk and timer interrupts. However, when any of those interruptions are completed, control passes back to the keyboard routine and it refuses to return control to the program that's been suspended. Only when we press one of the PC's regular keys does the ROM-BIOS reset its pause bit, and return the microprocessor to active duty. You'll see the pause bit, which the ROM-BIOS uses to keep track of this state, if you run the KEY-BITS program. However, KEY-BITS can't show the pause bit set, since when it's set, no program, including KEY-BITS, is running.

On some members of the PC family there are other special services that the keyboard ROM-BIOS supervises. On the Compaq models, special key-combinations control the special Compaq display mode and control loudness of the the key-clicking. In the Compaq-286 modes, another key-combination also controls the running speed. And in the PC*jr*, keyboard clicking is also controlled by a key combination.

Finally, if a key action passes through all that special handling, it means that the key is an ordinary one which can be assigned some meaning—that is, if the action is the key being pressed and not released. Releasing a key ordinarily means nothing, if it's not one of the special shift or toggle keys. When we press an ordinary key, the ROM-BIOS can recognize it as it produces keyboard characters in the ordinary sense—such as the A key. To give an ordinary key meaning, though, the ROM-BIOS has to translate the key into its character code. This is the point where the A key becomes the letter "A". In this translation process, the shift-states are taken into account, to distinguish letter "a" from "A" and so forth.

When a keystroke is translated into its meaning, there are two sets of meanings, two types of keyboard characters. The first is the ordinary ASCII characters, such as "A" or Control-A (ASCII code 1) or whatever. The second is for the PC's special keys, such as the function keys. These keys—which include the function keys, the cursor keys, the Home key and so forth—have special codes which distinguish them from the ordinary ASCII character keys.

The ALT-Numeric Trick

There is one more special trick that the keyboard ROM-BIOS routines perform for us that many PC users don't know about, something I call the ALT-Numeric Trick.

Most of what we want to type into our computers is right there on the keyboard, in plain sight: the letters of the alphabet, and so forth. And much of the more exotic stuff can be keyed in by combining the CTRL key with the alphabetic keys; for example, CTRL-Z keys in ASCII code 26, which is used as an end-of-file marker for text files. But we can't key in every one of the PC's character set that way. For example, if we wanted to key in the box-drawing characters that we saw in Chapter 4, we won't be able to do it.

To make it possible for us to key in virtually anything, the ROM-BIOS provides a special way for us to enter any of the characters with ASCII codes 1 through 255. (Oddly though, we can't key in ASCII code 0 this way, or any other way.)

We do it by holding down the ALT-shift key, and then keying in the ASCII code of the character we want; we enter the code in decimal, and we have to use the numeric keys on the right-hand side of the keyboard, not the number keys on the top row of the keyboard. When we key in this special way, the ROM-BIOS makes a note of it, calculates the code number we've keyed in, and when we release the ALT key, it generates an ASCII character, very much as if we had pressed a single key that represented that ASCII character.

To try it yourself, you can use the ASCII code for capital A, which is 65. Hold down the ALT key, press and release 6 then 5 on the right-hand side keys, then release the ALT key. The letter A should appear on your screen, just as if you typed in a capital A.

This special scheme works under most circumstances, but not all. BASIC changes the keyboard operation so it doesn't work when we're using BASIC. And keyboard enhancing programs, such as Prokey, may modify the scheme so it works differently. But, under most circumstances, we have this special ROM-BIOS facility at our command to enhance our ability to enter anything on the keyboard.

To accommodate both the plain ASCII codes and the PC's special codes, the ROM-BIOS records its key characters as a pair of bytes. If the character at hand is an ASCII character, then the first of the two bytes is non-zero and it holds the ASCII character itself. (In this case, the second character can be ignored. It generally holds the scan code of the key that was pressed.) The special PC characters are identified by a zero in the first byte. When the first byte is zero, the second byte contains the code identifying which of the special key characters is present.

BASIC practically gives us access to these two-byte keyboard codes with the INKEY$ function. With it we can inspect the keyboard codes. The little program below shows you how. Just run this in BASIC, and start pressing keys (the Enter key will stop the program):

```
100 FOR I = 1 TO 10 : KEY I, "" : NEXT
110 K$ = INKEY$
120 L = LEN (K$)
130 IF L = 1 THEN PRINT "ASCII character   ";ASC(LEFT$ (K$,1))
140 IF L = 2 THEN PRINT "Special key code ";ASC(RIGHT$(K$,1))
150 IF K$ = CHR$(13) THEN SYSTEM ELSE 110
```

After a "real" keystroke has been recognized and translated into its two-byte meaning, it's stored in the ROM-BIOS's own keyboard buffer. This is the second time that the keyboard information has been stored in a buffer—once in the keyboard's own internal memory and now in the ROM-BIOS's storage area. The ROM-BIOS has a buffer large enough to store 15 characters. If it overflows, the ROM-BIOS issues the complaining beep on the speaker which experienced PC users are accustomed to, and then it throws away the latest key data.

Once our key actions have been received and translated into meaningful characters by the ROM-BIOS, they are available for our programs to use. Our programs can either take them directly from the ROM-BIOS—using the ROM-BIOS keyboard services—or they can get them from DOS—using the DOS keyboard services, which indirectly takes them from the ROM-BIOS. Either way, our programs end up using these keyboard characters that have been constructed from our key actions by the ROM-BIOS.

That, anyway, is the way things work with our keyboards when things are proceeding in a straightforward way. But, the whole elaborate scheme for processing our key strokes that we've been following is intended to allow programs to sidestep the normal keyboard operation and start pulling rabbits out of hats. Next we'll see some of how that is done.

14.2 Keyboard Tricks

The PC's design allows our programs to work with the keyboard in many, many ways. Even when our programs aren't doing anything exotic, they have a choice of two ways of obtaining their keyboard data—either by obtaining it directly from the ROM-BIOS or by getting it through the DOS services. But that certainly isn't the only way that a program can come by keyboard information.

I certainly can't give you an exhaustive rundown of keyboard tricks here for many reasons. One of them is that ingenious programmers are inventing new keyboard tricks all the time. The biggest reason is that the tricks are far too technical for us here. They are really advanced programmer's tricks that have nothing to do with our goal in this book, which is to *understand* the PC family. But, more and more, we all find ourselves using programs that are based on keyboard tricks, and it's very worthwhile for us to know basically how they work, so that we can use them comfortably, and not think that there is black magic going on.

There are a number of ways that a program can respond in unusual ways. One of them is indirectly demonstrated in the KEY-BITS program. Any of our programs can, if they wish, monitor the keyboard status bytes and act accordingly. Here's a crude example of how:

```
10 DEF SEG = 0
20 PRINT "Please press both shift keys at once! "
30 IF PEEK (&H417) MOD 4 <>3 THEN 30
40 PRINT "Thank you! "
```

This allows a program to treat the shift-type keys in some special way. While ordinary programs have no good reason to do something like that, we're not talking about ordinary treatment of the keyboard, but special treatment. Often the designers of game programs will want to do something rather special, particularly with the shift keys. For example, the "Night Mission Pinball" program—created by Bruce Artwick, the same wizard who created the Microsoft Flight Simulator—uses the shift keys to control the pinball flippers. To do that, the program has to recognize when either of the shift keys is held down, which it can do simply by monitoring the keyboard status bits.

One of the most interesting types of programs that we use on our PCs are resident programs like the popular Sidekick program, which sits inactive in our computer's memory until we activate it with a special key combination. Let's see some of the ways that this can be done.

You'll recall from Chapter 6 that the PC has an internal clock which "ticks" about 18 times a second. The clock tick is made audible, so to speak, by a special clock-tick interrupt, interrupt number 8. Normally the ROM-BIOS receives that interrupt and uses it only to update its time-of-day record. But the ROM-BIOS also makes the ticking of the clock available to our programs by generating another interrupt, number 28, which does nothing unless one of our programs has set up an interrupt vector to receive this interrupt. Then, the program will be specially activated 18 times each second.

Let's consider how Sidekick might use this technique to spring into action. The normal signal that Sidekick uses to tell that we want it to swing into action is that we've pressed the CTRL and ALT keys at the same time. One way that Sidekick could do that is simply to use the timer interrupt to give it a frequent chance to check the keyboard status bits to see if we have both keys pressed (similar to the way our sample BASIC program above checks for both shift keys). If Sidekick doesn't find the bits set, it simply returns control from the timer interrupt, and very little time has been wasted. But if Sidekick *does* see the signal bits set, then Sidekick can keep running, performing its special magic.

In this example (which is based on the way I presume Sidekick works) the timer interrupt does *not* involve interfering in any way with the normal flow of keyboard data. Instead, it makes use of the timer interrupt and the keyboard system's willingness to let our programs see the state of the shift keys.

That, however, is far from the only way that a program can make special use of the keyboard. For even more exotic operations, a program can interpose itself into the middle of the keyboard data flow so that it can intimately monitor, and possibly modify, the information. This is what keyboard enhancing programs, such as Prokey and Superkey, do.

If a program wishes to completely take control of the keyboard, or at least have complete access to knowledge of what's going on in the keyboard, it can interpose itself into the path of the keyboard hardware interrupt—simply by placing an interrupt vector pointing into the program in the place of the standard vector, which directs keyboard interrupts to the ROM-BIOS. Then, when the keyboard causes a hardware interrupt, our new program "sees" the interrupt instead of the ROM-BIOS seeing it.

There are two main things that such a program might do. One is simply to take full control of the keyboard data, so that the ROM-BIOS never sees it. This can be done by a program that wants to take ruthless and total control. Most programs which intervene in the keyboard data process, though, aren't interested in stopping the flow of information from the keyboard to the ROM-BIOS—they merely want to monitor it and, when appropriate, modify it, but not stop it. This sort of program inspects the keyboard data as it goes by, but generally allows the normal flow of information to proceed, passing through the normal stages of operation. That's how most keyboard enhancing programs, including Prokey, work. They step in to monitor and modify the keyboard data. To do that job, they may even have to replace the ROM-BIOS processing programs with their own program steps, but they don't stop the processing of the keyboard data in the way in which the ROM-BIOS normally does it.

When we look at the wide variety of programs that are available for our PC family, we'll find many ways that programs treat the keyboard in special ways, and if we look under the surface of them, we'll find different degrees of programming going on. What we've discussed in considering the likes of Sidekick and Prokey represents the extreme case. There are, however, much less radical ways to handle keyboard data in special ways.

To see how, let's consider the example of Framework. Framework makes special use of the so-called grey-plus and grey-minus keys, the plus and minus keys that are on the far right-hand side of the PC's keyboard. For an ordinary program, there is no difference between the meaning of these plus and minus keys and the plus and minus keys that are located on the top row of the keyboard. However, Framework uses these grey keys to perform a special operation, which moves us up or down a logical level within Framework's data scheme. To do that, however, Framework has to be able to recognize the difference between a grey-plus and the other plus key. You might be tempted to think that Framework would have to tinker with the keyboard data (in the manner that, say, Prokey does), but that's not necessary.

As we saw earlier, when the ROM-BIOS presents keyboard data to our programs, it presents it as a two-byte code where the first byte indicates the ASCII code of the character data. If we press the grey-plus key, or the other plus key, this byte of information from the ROM-BIOS will be the same— ASCII code number 43. However, the second byte that the ROM-BIOS makes available to our programs reports the scan code of the key that was pressed, and so it makes it very simple for a program like Framework to tell the difference between when we press the grey-plus and the other plus keys; it can also easily tell when we generate the plus code by using the ALT-numeric scheme that we saw earlier in the chapter.

Framework is able to respond to the special grey-plus and minus keys simply by making *full* use of the standard information that's available, without having to perform any special magic or interfere in the operation of the ROM-BIOS or the flow of keyboard information.

That's an important thing for us to know, because people often assume that it's necessary to use special and potentially disruptive tricks to accomplish special objectives in programs. This example with Framework illustrates that it is possible to get everything done that's needed without trying to break out of the standard conventions that help keep our PC computers working smoothly.

Some Things to Try

1. For the toggle keys, like the CapsLock key, the ROM-BIOS keeps track not only of the current toggle state, but also whether the key is pressed. Even though our programs have no normal use

for this information, there is a simple logical reason why the ROM-BIOS records it. Can you discover why?

2. The scheme used to separate the PC's special character codes from the ASCII codes works quite well, but it has one technical flaw. Can you find it? How could you correct it?

3. There *are* some ways (though devious) for a program to detect the keyboard pause state that we discussed in the sidebar on CTRL-NUMLOCK. Can you think how it might be done?

15

Other Parts: Communication, Printers, and More

I n this chapter we're going to finish our round-up of the PC family's hardware capabilities, by covering a miscellany of parts and hardware capabilities. We'll be looking at the PC's parallel and serial ports, which are used for printers and for remote communications. Then we'll move on to explore the PC's ability to generate sound, to work with mice, to use cassette tapes, and more.

15.1 Printers: The Parallel Port

One of the standard attachments to our PCs is what's called a *parallel port*. It's hard to find a PC that doesn't have one, and most of the option cards that we add to our computers—including the IBM Monochrome Adapter card, many memory expansion boards, and just about every multifunction board—come with a parallel port. In fact, it's so common for the option boards that we install in our computers to have a parallel port that many PCs have two or even three separate parallel outlets even though we have no use for more than one.

A parallel port is a special-purpose data outlet designed for only one purpose: to provide a connection to a printer. There are actually two different ways that we can connect printers to our computers: through a parallel port or a serial port. The parallel port, which is our topic here, is specially designed for printers only; the *serial port*—which we'll be discussing in Section 15.2—can be used for many purposes, and a printer is only one of them.

You'll find that what I'm calling a parallel port goes under several names, and you should know about them so that you don't get confused. IBM usually calls it a parallel printer adapter. It's called *parallel* because of the way it transfers data (more about that shortly). It's called *printer* because that's the only use that it's put to, for passing data to a printer. We can call it an adapter, or a board, or an option, as we choose. People commonly refer to it as a *port* (as I have been here), using that word in the sense of a "data outlet." Here, though, the word *port* doesn't mean the same thing as the ports that we discussed in Chapter 6. Those ports are a particular feature of the PC's microprocessor, which are used for communication between the microprocessor and other parts of the hardware (including parallel printer adapters). Here, when we use the word port we mean it in a more casual sense. Our PC's microprocessor *does* use its ports to talk to this "port," but the two uses of the same word don't mean the same thing. Incidentally, you may also occasionally see our parallel printer port called a Centronix interface, from the name of the company which established this standard way of communicating between a computer and a printer.

This printer interface is referred to as *parallel* because it is designed to transmit data a byte at a time, with all eight bits of the byte passing out to the printer at the same time, moving out through eight separate wires, in parallel.

The interface between the computer and the printer that's used in the parallel port is not a particularly rich or intelligent one, and it only allows for the transfer of a few special status signals between the printer and the computer. Basically the computer can only send out two things: data to be printed, and a special initialization signal that a printer is supposed to use to reset itself. Of course, all sorts of special signals can be buried in the printer data itself. Most printers have an elaborate set of control codes that can be sent to them in the stream of data that's sent out to them. But these control codes are specific to each printer, and they almost exclusively have to do with the formatting of the printed data (such as the selection of wide printing or underlining, etc.). In the design of the parallel interface itself, there is only one special signal that the computer can send to the printer, and that's the *initialization* signal.

Similarly, there isn't a great deal that the computer can communicate to the computer. There are primarily three things. One is simple acknowledgement, which the printer uses to report that data is received properly. The second is a busy signal, which the printer uses to tell the computer to hold up sending more data, until the printer is able to handle it. The third is the only really printer-specific signal (since all the others could apply to any transmission of data), and that's an out-of-paper signal. All standard computer printers have a sensor that recognizes when the printer is out of paper, and the parallel printer interface provides a special channel just for the printer to pass this signal back to the computer. This out-of-paper signal is particular to the parallel printer interface, and it's not available with printers that use the serial port that we'll be discussing in Section 15.2.

The design and capabilities of the parallel printer interface have nothing specific to do with our PC family, because they are designed for and used by the entire information processing world. There is one PC-specific item, though, that we need to know about. The basic architecture of the PC's printer adapters (and the ROM-BIOS routines which support them) allow for up to three completely independent parallel ports to be attached to any one PC computer. No more than three can be added, but there can be as many as three.

This means that our computers can have as many as three parallel printers attached to them at once. With the right software in place, our PC's can drive two or three printers at once, keeping them all busy. That's what we might do if we were using our computers as a sort of print-engine, a central point to bang out lots and lots of printing. That, however, would be a very specialized use of the PC, and that's not the way most PC software, including DOS, is set up. The normal convention for any PC that has more than one printer attached to it is for us to have a choice of printers at our disposal, but for only one to be used at a time. Although it's not too common, some PC users have their systems set up just that way. Typically when that's done, one printer will be quick and crude, used for printing draft copies; the other will be slower and better, used for printing final copies.

Since the topic of multiple printer outlets has come up, it's worth mentioning here—although it has nothing to do with our discussion of the PC's hardware—that DOS provides some ways of switching our standard printer output from one printer to another. The MODE command can be used for part of that, and the PRINT spooling command can direct print to different devices as well.

Most of the printers used with our PCs come set up to be used with the parallel printer interface. However, some come in two models, one for the parallel interface and the other for the serial interface, while a few printers—for example, the Hewlett Packard LaserJet printer—only come in a serial interface model.

While the parallel port that we've been discussing is intended specifically for use with a printer, the similarly-named serial port can be used for a variety of purposes, as we'll see in Section 15.2.

15.2 Communication Lines: The Serial Port

The other main path for our computer's data is what we call the serial port, or serial interface. IBM more formally calls it the Asynchronous Communications Adapter, for reasons we'll see shortly.

The parallel port we discussed in Section 15.1 is basically a one-way path for data to be transmitted to the printer. As we saw, the link isn't exclusively one-way, because acknowledgment, busy, and out-of-paper signals can be sent back. But in terms of sending a full complement of data, the parallel port is outgoing only. The serial port, however, is a fully two-way path, which is the key to the main uses that we put it to.

What we call our computer's serial port or serial interface is based on a standard that is widely used in the information handling industry, called RS-232. RS-232 is a standard convention for transmitting two-way, asynchronous serial data. The path is two-way, so data can be sent back and forth. It's *asynchronous*, which means that the transmission of data is not based on a predefined timing pattern. Instead, it is sent on an irregular catch-as-catch-can timing, with both sides prepared to handle the irregularities. (There are other forms of communication—not commonly used on personal computers—which are *synchronous*, based on a standard timing signal.) The transmission is serial, which means that data is sent a bit at a time. (We'll see the complications that that introduces in a moment.)

While the parallel interface is designed for one simple and fairly well-controlled use, the serial interface is designed for an enormously wide variety of uses. As a consequence, it is very flexible but it also has a confusingly wide range of parameters and variations that can be adjusted to suit many needs. These are called the *communications parameters*, and they are a source of considerable confusion when we try to work with the serial ports.

The communication parameters are a set of specifications which establish how each serial port will work. Any interface, including this serial interface, has two ends to it, and the equipment on each end must agree on the settings of the communications parameters so that they can properly recognize each other's signals. Since our PC's can adjust to any combination of parameters, and since very often what's on the other end of the serial interface connection can't, the job of adjusting and matching usually falls to our computers, or more specifically, us. In principle that's not hard to do, but it assumes that we know what the parameters should be, and that we know how to set them in the first place. That's no technical challenge for an experienced and knowledgeable PC user, but many people who are relatively new at using PCs can be perplexed by the challenge. After all, we don't normally have to tell electronic things how to work—we normally just plug them together and they know how to get the job done. With serial communications that's all too often not the case, which can lead to considerable frustration.

We need to get a little idea here of what the communications parameters are. Digging into them deeply is a technical matter that needn't concern us here—it belongs in a specialized book on communications. But at least we'll see an outline of the basics here.

The serial communications parameters begin with a *baud rate*, which determines how fast the port will run, in a measure called *baud*, or bits per second. Baud rates run from a low of 110 to a high of 9600. The most common rates for PCs to use is 300 (for slow telephone communications) or 1200 (with faster modems). Lower rates are rare, but we may encounter higher. For telephone use, 2400 baud modems are becoming increasingly common, and some printers—such as the Hewlett Packard LaserJet—accept data at a 9600 baud rate. To convert a baud rate into practical terms, we can just knock one digit off and have the approximate data rate in characters (or bytes) per second. That's because transmitting a byte of data, complete with the overhead bits that serial communications adds, normally takes ten bits of transmission.

After the baud rate comes the number of data bits for each data character. There are two choices, 7 or 8. Of course our PC's character bytes are eight bits long, and to be able to transmit the whole PC character set we have to work with an 8-bit character. But most serial communications is done with just the main ASCII characters, which are only seven bits long. That's why much serial communications is done with a 7-bit character.

Next is the *parity*, or error-detection coding. RS-232 communications allows for three different settings: odd or even (two different ways of calculating a parity check bit) or no parity checking (which cuts down on the communications overhead). The parity type is usually noted by its initial letter, so we'll run into mentions of parity setting of E (for Even), O (odd), or N (none). Finally comes the number of "stop" bits. Each character of data transmitted is surrounded by "start" and "stop" bits that bracket and punctuate the transmission of characters. We can control the number of stop bits by specifying either one or two stop bits.

Actually, as you might have guessed, the full range of communications parameters, including the forms of parity, are more complicated than what I've outlined here, but this gives us the main points. The key thing for us to understand is that the communications parameters are rather complicated and messy, but they have to be set just right, so that both ends of the serial connection can understand each other. At times, setting these parameters falls on our shoulders, so we need to be able to at least recognize the names and common values of the parameters to help us deal with them.

There are two main uses that we put the serial port to in our PCs. One, which we've already mentioned, is as an alternative connection to our printers. This, of course, is only done with those printers that are made for a serial connection—which a relatively small proportion of the printers that are used with PCs, though there are still plenty of serial printers.

The other, and by far the greatest use, is for communication as we commonly think of it, connecting our computers to the telephone network. To do that we have to have quite a few other elements besides a parallel port. We have to have a modem, which translates computer signals into telephone signals, modulating (the *mo* of modem) the computer bits into the equivalent of a sound wave, and demodulating (the *dem* of modem) the telephone sound waves into computer bits. We also have to have a telephone line to connect to, and something that knows computer talk on the other end of the phone line—such as a computerized database service (like the Source or Compuserve) or an electronic mail service (such as MCI Mail), or another computer, such as another PC acting as a computerized bulletin board.

Printers and telephones, however, aren't the only things that we can connect our PC's serial port to, they are just the most common. We can also use the serial port to connect our printer to other output devices, such as plotters (which make drawings on paper just as printers type on paper). The serial port can also be used for other forms of input. Some mouse devices (which we'll discuss again briefly in Section 15.4) use the serial port for their input. Also, when PCs are connected to scientific instruments—either to receive data or to send out commands—serial ports are the natural choice, since they're based on a common standard that is easy to design electronic equipment to use.

As we saw in Section 15.1, the PC's basic design allows us to attach as many as three parallel printer interfaces; for serial communication ports, the design limits us to no more than two ports. This is ironic, because the serial ports are so much more flexible and can be used for so many more things. As a consequence, we're more likely to have more need for serial ports than parallel. In practice, though, nearly all PC users find that their machines can accommodate more equipment than they want to connect to it.

15.3 Sound

One of the more interesting things that our PCs can do is make sounds—a surprisingly wide range of sounds. Here's a very simple demonstration of how the PC can play scales:

```
10 FREQ = 130.81
20 FOR OCTAVE = 1 TO 4
30    FOR NOTE = 1 TO 7
```

```
40      SOUND FREQ, 3
50      DIFF = 1.1225
60      IF NOTE = 3 OR NOTE = 7 THEN DIFF = 1.0595
70      FREQ = FREQ * DIFF
80    NEXT NOTE
90 NEXT OCTAVE
```

Trying that simple program on your PC will give you a quick idea of the PC's ability to play just about any musical note that we want. It will also give you an idea of the crude yet effective sound quality of the little speaker that's built into our PCs.

Most of us think of the uses of sound in PCs as mostly belonging to game programs. ''Serious'' PC programs usually don't do anything with sound other than to beep at us when something goes wrong. But serious programs *can* find serious uses for sound. One of the best examples that I know of comes from IBM's TopView program. TopView makes a special use of the Ctrl key to toggle between two modes of using the keyboard. To help us note the difference, TopView makes two different sounds when shifting between the modes: one is sort of a ''boop-beep'' and the other is the opposite, a ''beep-boop'' sound. The effect is striking, and gives us easy-to-understand feedback. It's an excellent example of how our programs can make productive use of more than crude beeps.

Other Uses for Sounds

The speakers built into our PCs can serve more purposes than allowing our programs to make noises at us. They can also be used in support of the hardware.

One example of this is as a ''keyboard clicker.'' The standard PC keyboards that IBM supplies make a very satisfying *click* when we press and release them—satisfying to some folks, annoying to others. This click is what's called an *audible feedback*, a sound that helps us know the keys are working. This clicking can be a valuable unconscious helper, giving a concrete sensual reality to work that otherwise seems very abstract. The clicking doesn't suit everyone, though.

There is nothing that we can do to change a mechanical feature like that on the PCs that have that sort of keyboard. But some members of the PC family don't have noisy keyboards.

The PC*jr* and all the members of the PC family made by Compaq have quiet keyboards that don't make any mechanical noise. Instead, they supply their audible feedback by making a clicking sound on the speaker. It's not quite as satisfying a sound as the mechanical click of the standard IBM keyboards, but it has the advantage that it can be changed.

The PC*jr*'s keyboard clicking can be turned off and on by pressing the Ctrl-Alt-CapsLock key combination. That sets and resets the clicking bit that we saw in the keyboard status bits in Chapter 14. The Compaq models give us an even better control over the keyboard sound: we can adjust the loudness of the sound, using the Ctrl-Alt-Grey-Plus and -Grey-Minus keys. If you're finicky about your sound, that can be a real benefit.

Our computer's speakers serve other hardware purposes as well. For example, during the Power-On Self-Test (or POST routine), the speaker reports any errors found, which can help a lot if the display screen isn't working. Similarly, in the Compaq-286 models, one or two quick beeps are used to signal when the computer shifts into slow or fast mode.

How our computers are able to make sounds is fairly simple. Inside the computer is a small speaker connected to the PC's circuitry. A speaker makes sound by being fed an electrical signal which is changed, or modulated, corresponding to the sound that's to be made. The speaker converts the changes or waves in the electrical signal to matching sound waves, which we hear. In a hi-fi system, the electrical signals are translated from a recording of sounds. In our computers, the electrical signals are generated by the circuitry under the control of our programs.

The PC's circuits tell the speaker to pulse in and out, producing sounds. Our programs control the pitch or frequency of the sound by controlling how rapidly the in and out pulses are sent to the speaker.

There is no volume control in the PC, since it wasn't intended to produce sophisticated sounds. You will notice that the loudness of the speaker does vary, depending on what frequency of sound we send it. You can hear that for yourself by trying the musical scales program above, or using this one, which goes through a wider range of frequencies:

```
10  PLAY "MF"
20  FOR FREQ = 100 TO 10000 STEP 100
30    PRINT "Frequency ",INT (FREQ)
40      SOUND FREQ, 5
50  NEXT FREQ
```

Our programs control the computer's speaker through one of the microprocessor's ports. We got a sneak preview of that in Chapter 6 when we looked at ports. Let's take another look at that program:

```
10  SOUND 500,1
20  X = (INP (97) MOD 4) * 4
30  PRINT "Press any key to stop this infernal noise!"
40  OUT 97, X + 3 ' turn sound on
50  FOR I = 1 TO 250 : NEXT I ' kill time
60  OUT 97, X ' turn sound off
70  FOR I = 1 TO 250 : NEXT I ' kill time
80  IF INKEY$ = "" THEN GOTO 40
```

The speaker is controlled by the two low-order bits of port 97 (hex 61). You'll see the above program reading the data that's currently stored in port 97 (using the INP statement). That's because the other bits of this port are used for other things, and we want to leave them set the way they are.

To turn the sound on, we set the two low-order bits of port 97; to turn it off, we reset them. To make sure that these bits aren't already on, we use the arithmetic MOD 4 * 4 to set them off.

The two port bits that control the sound also control two different aspects of how the sounds are made. The higher bit, the one with value 2, simply turns the speaker on and off. If we cycled this bit on and off, we'd get a sound whose frequency is set by how fast the program pulses the speaker by turning this bit on and off. The other bit controls the real heart of the PC's sound-making ability—it determines if the speaker is fed a signal from the PC's programmable timer.

The PC's programmable timer—the 8253 timer chip we saw in Chapter 5—can be set (programmed) to produce any of a wide range of regularly timed signals. It's actually able to spit out two different signals. One of them is used to generate the "clock-tick" interrupts, 18.2 times a second; the other is used to generate tones on the speaker. To produce a regular sound, we first program the timer chip to produce the frequency that we want, and then we set the bits in port 97 to send the timer pulses to the speaker and also to activate the speaker.

You can see that process represented in the little program above. The line that reads 10 SOUND 500,1 causes BASIC to set the timer frequency (which it needs to do to carry out the SOUND statement). Once we've set the timer frequency, then we can make the sound heard by turning on the port bits. If we only turned on the bit with value 2, we'd hear just a tiny click as the speaker was pulsed on. But when we turn on both bits, the timer's pulses are fed to the speaker, and the speaker is being driven at the frequency that the timer is set to.

A program does not need to use the programmable timer to make sounds—it can generate sounds simply by turning on and off the bit that activates the speaker. Working that way, a program can make very complex sounds simply by varying the time interval between when it pulses the speaker on and off. But doing that requires constant attention from a program, keeping the microprocessor busy. If we use the timer, our programs can start a sound going, and the sound will continue without any further attention from the program; that allows the microprocessor to pass on to other work. Then when the program wants the sound to stop, it can come back and reset the port bits, or change the timer frequency for a new sound. That's how BASIC is able to play music in the "background," music that plays while BASIC goes on with our computations.

The PCjr's Special Sounds

The sound skills that we've been covering in this chapter are the ones common to all the members of the PC family. The PCjr, though, has some special skills that go far beyond that. Since the PCjr was intended to find lots of uses in the home and in schools, where sound is more important, it has a greatly expanded sound capacity.

The core of the PCjr's special skills is a special-purpose chip designed and made by Texas Instruments. This TI sound chip is able to make sounds of greater purity and range than the PC's simple timer circuits can. The main feature of the TI sound chip is that it has three independent "voices," which means that it can generate three separate tones at once permitting a richer polyphonic sound. To make it even better, the TI sound chip has a volume control, so that it can set how loud each of the voices is. Further, the TI sound chip has a "noise" feature allowing it to make many kinds of nonmusical sounds, just the sort of thing that is needed in game programs to make the sound of motors, explosions, and so forth.

The TI sound chip isn't the PCjr's only special sound feature. In addition, the PCjr has a sound "pass through" feature allowing it to combine its own generated sounds with sound-signals from other sources, such as an audio cassette recorder. This feature can be used to add recorded sounds to learning programs; for example, a program to teach us foreign languages could benefit from the combination of a recording of what the spoken language actually sounds like and the computer's ability to repeat and skip around lessons.

15.4 Miscellaneous Parts

We've seen the main parts of the PC in our discussion so far, so we already know the heart of what there is to know about the PC's hardware.

But there are some more items in the PC family's kit of hardware tricks, and we'll finish up this chapter by looking at them.

One thing that will help us understand these odds and ends is to realize that when a computer like the PC is designed, the engineers who decide what features to build into it must do their best to anticipate the future and figure out in advance what we are going to want to do with our PCs. It's an impossible task, of course, and so we find some loose ends appearing. There will be things which the engineers thought would be important that are hardly used. And there are things the engineers didn't anticipate, that get added on later.

Through the course of this book I've made some passing references to things that were designed into the PC that haven't been used as the designers intended. We'll see some of them in this section.

One of the most striking of the unused features of the PC is its cassette tape interface. The PC's designers didn't realize just how seriously the PC would be taken, and they thought that there might be many PCs used without any disk drives at all (as amazing as that must seem to us now). Some of the early, cheap home computers didn't have any disk drives, and they just used cassette tapes to record their programs and data. IBM thought some PC users might want to use their computers that way too, so the PC was designed with a cassette port.

For all practical purposes the cassette interface was never used, and the port connection for it was even dropped from the more advanced models of PC, such as the XT and AT. It was kept in the ill-fated PC*jr*, just in case interest in tape I/O arose.

The cassette port is able to read and write data—in a slow and limited fashion—from a audio tape cassette recorder when it's plugged into the computer with a special adapter. The computer is able to read and write data, and turn the cassette motor on and off, but it isn't able to even do such basic things as rewind that tape—that's because most inexpensive cassette recorders have to be manually switched into rewind. You can see the elements of the PC's cassette feature in the BASIC MOTOR statement and things like OPEN ''CAS1:''.

While the cassette interface has been almost completely ignored, two other features that were included in the original PC design have found their specialized uses, even though they aren't widespread and even though most PC users are as unaware of them as of the cassette port. These are joysticks and light pens.

Joysticks are a special kind of input device for a PC, consisting of a movable rod—the stick—and two buttons—the ''triggers.'' Joysticks are mostly used for game programs, and since the PC isn't a game-oriented computer, few PCs have been equipped with them. Using a joystick with a standard PC requires the installation of a special joystick adapter board as well as the joysticks themselves. Since the PC*jr* model was home- and game-oriented, it had built into it the equivalent of a joystick adapter board, and the back of the PC*jr* has two connectors for joysticks to be plugged in and used.

Figure 15-1. A typical joystick.

The stick on a joystick is able to sense movements in two dimensions, and our programs can read the stick position in the form of *X* and *Y* coordinates to follow the movement of the stick. The trigger buttons can be read as well to sense when they are pressed. You'll see the main elements of how a program can work with a joystick in the BASIC statements STICK and STRIG.

Another little-used feature of the PC is *light pens*. A light pen is a hand-held probe that can be touched to the display screen. Through a combination of hardware and ROM-BIOS software features, the computer is able to sense just exactly where on the screen the light pen is touched.

The name *light pen* suggests that the pen writes information, but it's really just the opposite. It's used to read information, specifically the position on the screen where the pen is touched. Of course, if we combine the pen with some drawing software that follows the movements of the pen across the screen, then it will seem that the pen is writing on the screen. But light pens are really just sensing devices.

Light pens can be used in many ways, but the most common use is with what's called *CAD/CAM*—Computer Aided Design (and its cohort, Computer Aided Manufacturing). Taking advantage of a light pen, a CAD/CAM program can let us draw on the screen, select choices from a menu just by touching the pen to an item, "pick up" and move parts of a drawing, and so forth.

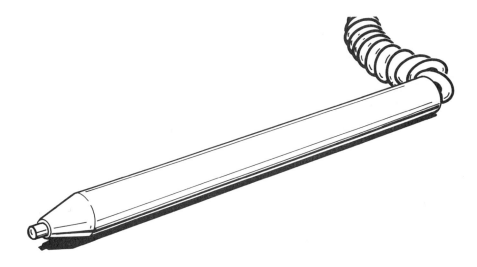

Figure 15-2. A typical light pen.

The PC's hardware and software can only sense where a light pen is being pressed onto the screen if the phosphors that light up the screen flash on and off very quickly. The phosphors used in the IBM Monochrome Display are called "long persistence," which makes them easier on the eyes, but they stay lit too long to work with a light pen. (If you have a Monochrome Display you've probably noticed that it takes a few moments for images to fade from the screen, thanks to the long-persistence phosphor.)

Like joysticks, light pens require the addition of an adapter board to the PC as well as the pen itself, except for the PC*jr* model, which has a light pen adapter built in. The PEN statement in BASIC supports the light pen, and if you study its details you learn the main elements of how light pens are used.

Both joysticks and light pens are special-purpose kinds of input devices that allow us to feed the computer *position* information, rather than the text information that the keyboard provides. There is a term for this general type of hardware: they are called *pointing devices*. Joysticks and light pens are the two pointing devices that IBM's engineers designed into the computer, anticipating that they might become popular. Instead, a completely different kind of pointing device has caught on, the *mouse*.

In an abstract sense, a mouse is no different from a light pen or a joystick. In fact, there is an enormous similarity between a joystick and a mouse, since both have free two-dimensional movement and trigger-buttons to indicate action. But that is like saying that there's no difference between a keyboard that has the keys arranged in the normal order (QWERTY as it's called) and one that has the keys arranged in alphabetic order. Functionally they are equivalent, but the difference is that the QWERTY keyboard is a popular standard.

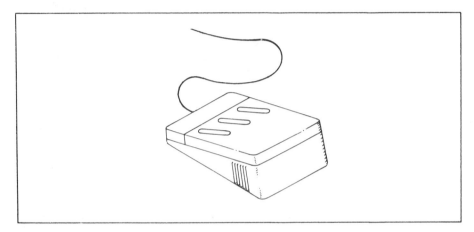

Figure 15-3. A typical mouse.

So it is with the mouse. Despite the fact that there are other pointing devices, and despite the fact that IBM gave its support (in the ROM-BIOS) to the light pen and the joystick, it is the mouse that has become the widely accepted pointing device for use by our programs.

There is a wide variety of types of mouse—some with three buttons or two, some that work optically (and require a special pad that they run over) or mechanically, some that plug into their own adapter boards, and some that work through a standard serial port.

Despite the wide variety—which would tend to work against the widespread use of mice—mice have become very popular, and more and more important PC software takes advantage of mice. (I wrote the text of this book with the Microsoft Word program, which takes advantage of a mouse. After long resisting the use of a mouse, I discovered that it was very handy indeed.)

To use a mouse we have to have, one way or another, BIOS support for it, similar to the device support that's in the ROM-BIOS for other devices. In some cases (for example IBM's TopView) the program that uses the mouse includes the BIOS-type support. In other cases (for example, with the Microsoft mouse) the mouse comes with its own memory-resident program that provides BIOS support for any program using the mouse. The second approach is more in keeping with the general philosophy that BIOS support for a device should be identified with the device and separate from any programs that use them.

And that completes our roundup of the various minor parts of the the PC's hardware. Now we're ready to move on to our next main topic, one we've circled around repeatedly: the PC's built-in ROM-BIOS software.

Some Things to Try

1. Do you think there are any important advantages or disadvantages to using the parallel or serial ports for a printer? Discuss.

2. How many uses can you think of for the serial ports, besides the ones mentioned here?

3. Write a program to experiment with the two port bits that control the computer's speaker. You can use the little programs in this chapter as a starting point. Try to turn the speaker on and off without using the timer bit. See how quickly you pulse the speaker with a BASIC command to make as high-pitched a sound as possible.

16

Built-In BIOS:
The Basic Ideas

n this chapter we're going to begin exploring the software heart of
the PC, its built-in ROM-BIOS. Our task here is to understand the
basic ideas behind the ROM-BIOS, the philosophy of how it is
organized and what it tries to do. That lays the groundwork for
Chapter 17, in which we'll explore the details of the services that the
ROM-BIOS performs.

Before we proceed any further, though, let's note one thing to avoid
confusion. There are two things in our computer called BIOS. One is the
ROM-BIOS, a built-in software feature of our computers; that's the topic
for this chapter and the next. The other is the DOS-BIOS, the part of DOS
that performs a similar service (but on a quite different level) for DOS.

16.1 The Ideas Behind the BIOS

The ROM-BIOS has a clumsy name that only hints at what it's all
about: ROM-BIOS is short for *Read-Only Memory Basic Input/Output System*. Ignore the name and concentrate on what it does for us. The
ROM-BIOS is a set of programs built into the computer that perform the
most basic, low-level and intimate control and supervision operations for
the computer.

Software works best when it's designed to operate in *layers*, with each
layer performing some task and relieving the other layers above of any
concern for the details within that task. Following this philosophy, the
ROM-BIOS is the bottom-most layer, the layer that underlies all other
software and operations in the computer. The task of the ROM-BIOS is to
take care of the immediate needs of the computer's hardware and to isolate
all other programs from the details of how the hardware works.

Fundamentally the ROM-BIOS is an interface, a connector and translator, between the computer's hardware and the software programs that we

run on our computers. Properly speaking, the ROM-BIOS is simply a program like any other. But if we want to understand the ROM-BIOS, we should think of it as if it weren't really just software, but some kind of hybrid, something halfway between hardware and software. Functionally, that's exactly what the ROM-BIOS is: a bridge between the computer's hardware and our other software.

What makes the ROM-BIOS so special? What does it do that makes it seem to be midway between hardware and software?

The answer lies in what the ROM-BIOS has to do and how it does it. What the ROM-BIOS has to do is to directly control the hardware and to respond to any demands that the hardware makes. How it does it is largely by use of the *ports* that we learned about in Chapter 6. For the most part, all of the PC's component parts are controlled by the process of sending them commands or parameter settings, through the ports, with each part of the circuitry having its own special port numbers that it responds to.

Now we already know that there are many important aspects of the hardware that don't work through ports, such as the memory addresses that are used to control what appears on the display screen. Most of the exceptions to the general rule that the hardware is controlled through the ports are exactly the part of the computer which it's OK for our programs to work with directly—that is, exactly the parts that the ROM-BIOS doesn't have to supervise for us.

Now I don't want you to get the impression that the ROM-BIOS only concerns itself with ports: it doesn't. But ports best symbolize what is special about the ROM-BIOS: it's the software that works most intimately with the computer's hardware, and it's the software that takes care of hardware details (like ports) which the rest of our programs shouldn't have to touch.

What's Special About the BIOS

What's special about the ROM-BIOS is that it is written to work intimately with the computer's hardware, and that means that it incorporates lots of practical knowledge about how the hardware works. It isn't always obvious just what that knowledge is.

If we study the ROM-BIOS listings that IBM publishes for the PC, we can readily see the obvious part of what's special about BIOS programming—using the right ports to send the right commands to the PC's circuits. What isn't anywhere near so obvious is that there is black magic going on as well.

Not everything that it takes to make computer circuits work correctly is plain and clear from their basic specifications. There are many subtleties as well, things such as timing considerations or just how errors actually occur in real experience.

For example, some circuits may be able to accept a command at any time, but they need a short amount of time between commands to digest one command before they are ready to take another. In other cases, two separate steps may have to be performed with as little intervening time as possible. Hidden inside the ROM-BIOS are subtle factors like that. We might see a sequence of commands that appear straightforward and simple, but that have a hidden element in them as well—such as carefully worked-out timing factors.

This is a part of what makes BIOS programming so special, and why many programmers think of BIOS programming as something of a magical art—an art that involves not just the logical steps that all programs are built from but also close cooperation between the programs and the computer's hardware.

16.2 How the ROM-BIOS Works

Although the complete details of how the ROM-BIOS works are really only of concern to accomplished assembly language technicians, the basics of how it's organized and how it works is of real interest to us here to help us understand our machines. That's what we'll sketch out in this section.

To start with, we need to see that the ROM-BIOS is roughly divided into three functional parts, diagrammed in Figure 16-1.

The first part of the ROM-BIOS is the start-up routines, which get our computer going when we turn on the power. There are two main parts to the start-up routines: one is the Power-On Self-Test (or POST) routines, which test to see that the computer is in good working order. They check the memory for defects and perform other tests to see that the computer isn't malfunctioning. The other part of the start-up procedure is the initialization.

The *initialization* involves things like creating the interrupt vectors, so that when interrupts occur the computer switches to the proper interrupt-handling routine. Initialization also involves setting up the computer's equipment. Many of the parts of the computer need to have registers set, parameters loaded, and other things done to get them in their ready-to-go condition. The ROM-BIOS knows the full complement of standard equipment that a PC can have, and it performs whatever initialization each part

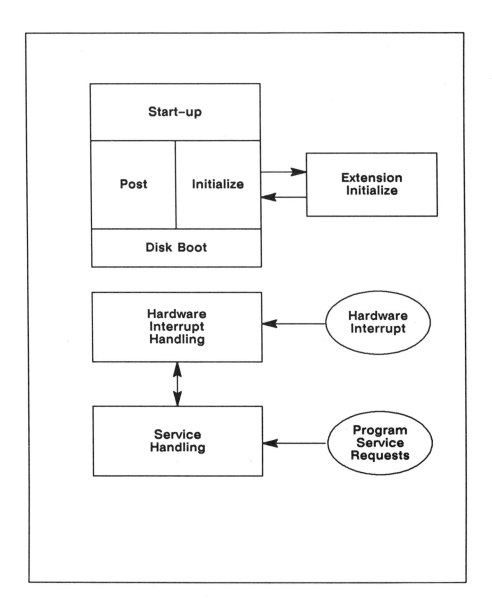

Figure 16-1. Organization of the ROM-BIOS.

needs. Included in this initialization are steps that tell the ROM-BIOS what equipment is present. Some of that is learned by checking switch settings inside the computer (in the case of the original PC model) or reading a permanent memory that records the equipment the computer has (in the case of the AT model). In some cases, the ROM-BIOS can simply find out if equipment is installed by electronically interrogating it and checking for a response. (The PC*jr* model finds out about its optional equipment this way.) Whatever it takes, the ROM-BIOS checks for and initializes all the equipment that it knows how to handle.

Of course, we can add new equipment to our PCs; people do it all the time. Some of this equipment is standard stuff (such as adding more memory or adding serial and parallel output ports) but not all of it is. There is some optional equipment that isn't taken care of in the standard ROM-BIOS routines that needs its own special ROM-BIOS support. To take care of that situation, the ROM-BIOS is prepared to search for additions to the BIOS (see the sidebar *How to Add to the ROM-BIOS*).

How to Add to the ROM-BIOS

The ROM-BIOS in our PCs is a fixed part of the computer's equipment, which leads to a fundamental problem: how do we add support for new options to ROM-BIOS? The answer lies in an automatic feature that allows for additions to the ROM-BIOS—what we call ROM-BIOS extensions.

The scheme is simple: additions to the ROM-BIOS are marked so that the standard ROM-BIOS can recognize them, and give them a chance to integrate themselves into the standard part.

Just as the main ROM-BIOS appears in memory at a specific location (the high part of memory, the 64K byte F-block) additions have a standard memory area reserved for them as well: the C, D, and E-blocks of memory.

Any new equipment requiring special ROM-BIOS support—for example, the XT model's hard disk or the Enhanced Graphics Adapter's special video features—places its read-only BIOS memory somewhere in that block, and includes in it a special marking, hex 55 AA in the first two bytes. The location of the ROM-BIOS can't be just anywhere. It has to be in a unique location that doesn't conflict with any other ROM-BIOS extensions, and it must begin on a 2K memory boundary.

The standard (or we might say, master) ROM-BIOS, as part of its start-up routines, searches the ROM-BIOS extension area for the identifying 55 AA signature. When it finds any, it passes control over to the beginning of the ROM-BIOS extension. That lets the ROM-BIOS extension do whatever it needs to do to initialize its equipment and to integrate itself into the rest of the ROM-BIOS. For example, a ROM-BIOS extension for a new kind of display adapter (such as the Enhanced Graphics Adapter) might change the interrupt vector for video services to direct them to the ROM-BIOS extension rather than to the old ROM-BIOS video routines.

Whatever start-up and initialization work a ROM-BIOS extension needs to do, it performs it when the main ROM-BIOS passes control to it during the start-up procedures. When the ROM-BIOS extension is done initializing itself, it passes control back to the main ROM-BIOS, and the computer proceeds in the usual way. But now, new equipment and new ROM-BIOS support for that equipment has been added.

All this is made possible by the mechanism that allows the main ROM-BIOS to search for and recognize ROM-BIOS extensions.

Incidentally, the software cartridges the PC*jr* uses work as BIOS extensions. They are added to the computer's memory like any other BIOS extension, and they have the same identifying marking that the main BIOS uses to recognize them. The only thing that's somewhat special about them is that they're designed to be plugged in and taken out, while other BIOS extensions are usually installed and left in place.

The very last part of the start-up routines in the ROM-BIOS is the "boot" routine, which tries to fire up DOS, or any other operating system that we have, in our computer. The boot-strap process involves the ROM-BIOS attempting to read a boot record from the beginning of a disk. The BIOS first tries drive A, and if that doesn't succeed, and the computer has a hard-disk drive C, it tries the hard disk. If neither disk can be read, then the ROM-BIOS goes into its non-disk mode (in the IBM models, that means activating the built-in BASIC; with other models, such as the Compaq machines, it means showing a message saying the computer needs a boot-disk).

Normally the ROM-BIOS is able to read a boot record off of the disk, and it hands control of the computer to the short program on the boot record. As we discussed in Chapters 9 and 10, the boot program begins the process of loading DOS (or another operating system) into our computer.

After the start-up routines are finished, our computer is ready to go. The other two parts of the ROM-BIOS form a key part of the running of the computer. These two parts are the *hardware-interrupt handling* and the *service-handling*. They function as two distinct but closely cooperating kinds of routines.

The *service-handling* routines are there solely to perform work for our programs (and for DOS) by carrying out whatever services the programs need performed. We'll see in more detail what these services are in Chapter 17. They are things like a request to clear the display screen, or to switch the screen from text mode to graphics mode, or a request to read information from the disk, or write information on the printer. For the most part, the ROM-BIOS services that the service-handling routines perform relate to the computer's hardware devices—the screen, keyboard, disks, printers, and so forth. These are the basic input/output services that give the BIOS its name. But there are other services that the ROM-BIOS performs as well, which aren't input or output to I/O devices. For example, the ROM-BIOS keeps track of the time of day and one of the services that it performs is to report the time to our programs.

To carry out the service requests that our programs make, the ROM-BIOS has to work directly with the computer's I/O devices, and that's where the intimate and tricky part of the BIOS comes in, including the use, as we mentioned before, of ports to issue commands and pass and receive data with the various devices of printers and disks and so forth. The key job of the ROM-BIOS here is to relieve our programs of the tedious details of how that's done. Our programs don't need to know which port is used to send data to the printer. Instead, our programs just ask the ROM-BIOS to send data to the printer, and the BIOS takes care of the details. That shields our programs not only from the details of how the printer works, but even more important it shields our programs from the very annoying and messy problems of *error recovery*. Surprisingly, the equipment in our computer is often balky, and it will act up temporarily. Part of the job of the ROM-BIOS is to check for errors, retry operations to see if the problem is only temporary (as it often is), and only in the case of stubborn failure report the problem on to our programs.

While some of the hardware parts of our computer only require attention when we want them to do something (that is, when our programs are requesting a service from the BIOS), other parts can call for attention that's completely separate from what our programs are doing. We already know of a few examples of this: we know that when we press a key on the keyboard, it generates a keyboard interrupt that needs attention from the ROM-BIOS. Likewise, the PC's internal clock creates clock interrupts every time it ticks, 18 times a second. There are other hardware interrupts as well: for example, the disks have an interrupt they use to signal when they need attention from the ROM-BIOS. To handle these needs of the hardware there is the final part of the ROM-BIOS, the *hardware interrupt-handling* section.

The *hardware-interrupt handling* part takes care of the independent needs of the PC's hardware. It operates separately, but in cooperation with the *service-handling portion*. In Chapter 14, where we discussed how the keyboard operates, we saw a good example of how that works. The keyboard-handling routines are divided into two separate but related parts that work together. The hardware-interrupt part of the keyboard handling responds to our actions on the keyboard, recording what we do, and holding the resulting keyboard characters ready for use when our programs need them. The service-handling part of the keyboard routines accept requests from our programs for keyboard data, and pass on to them the keyboard characters that the interrupt handler has received. These two parts face in different directions—one to the hardware, the other to our programs—and service different demands. Together, they make the keyboard work for us and our programs.

That captures the essence of what the ROM-BIOS is, and what it does for our computers. With that groundwork in place, we're ready to go to Chapter 17 and see just what sort of services the ROM-BIOS can perform for our programs.

Some Things to Try

1. If you have my Norton Utilities, you can use the SI-System Information program to search for the BIOS signature that identifies additions to the BIOS. Try using it on your computer and see what you find.

2. Analyze how the interrupt-handling and service-handling parts of the keyboard ROM-BIOS routines work with each other. How would you work out the details of how these two parts might interact safely and successfully?

3. What do you think are the special needs and requirements to initialize an extension to the ROM-BIOS? How would an extension smoothly integrate itself into the rest of the BIOS without creating any disruption?

17

Built-In BIOS:
Digging In

I n this chapter we're going to take a more detailed look at what the PC family's built-in ROM-BIOS does for us and our programs. Our main topic is going to be a list of the standard services that the BIOS provides. However, this won't be a exhaustive reference guide— that would make for rather dull reading. Instead, it'll be a guided tour of the powers that the BIOS puts at our command. The point here is to give you a sound feeling for what the BIOS can do for us to serve the overall goal of this book, which is understanding the PC.

Before we begin the BIOS tour, though, we need to look at some of the principles and problems that underlie the services.

17.1 Working Principles and Machine Problems

If you want to understand the workings of the ROM-BIOS and also the list of the BIOS services and comments that follow in Section 17.2, it helps to understand some of the principles that underlie how the BIOS works, how it's organized, and some of the design problems that are inherent in any software as sensitive as the PC family's ROM-BIOS.

The BIOS has to operate in a way that provides the maximum of flexibility, places the least caretaking load on the programs that use it, and works with the highest possible safety (safety against disrupting the working of the computer).

We've already seen some of the way the design of the BIOS works towards these ends, when we looked at one of the BIOS's interrupt handlers in Chapter 6. Part of the design considerations that the BIOS routines have to meet is that they suspend interrupts as little as possible. It's important not to shut down or even hold up interrupts, since interrupts are the driving force that keeps the computer running. To avoid interfering with this driving force, the BIOS must suspend interrupts as little as possible, and, in the dissection of the interrupt handler that we looked at in Chapter 6, interrupts were immediately reactivated. Sometimes this can't be done—sometimes it's necessary to perform a few critical steps free of the possibility of being interrupted, but the BIOS keeps those steps as short as possible.

Since the BIOS performs the bulk of its work with interrupts active, that means other interrupt-driven BIOS service calls can be invoked while the BIOS is in the middle of carrying out an earlier service request. To avoid tripping over its own feet, or confusing the work-in-progress of one service call with another, the BIOS routines must be programmed following a special discipline called *re-entrant coding*. Re-entrant programs, such as the ROM-BIOS, are designed so that all working data and status information that pertains to each service call is kept distinct from the others. This is done by keeping any data either in the stack, or in registers which (by programming convention) will be preserved on the stack if another interrupt occurs.

Although this re-entrant coding is not difficult to do, it must be done carefully, and it places restrictions on the ways that information can be passed between the BIOS and any program requesting services from the BIOS. Much of the detailed design of how the BIOS works and is used all comes from this requirement that it be re-entrant.

As a separate but related issue, the BIOS services need to be organized in a modular fashion. As we'll see in Section 17.2, when we cover the details of the basic BIOS services, they are organized into groups. For example, all the different services for the display screen are grouped together under one interrupt number, but no other BIOS services use that interrupt.

This modular organization by group and interrupt has two obvious benefits. First, for the programs that use the BIOS services, the grouping makes it easier to deal with the complexities of the services. Second, if it's necessary to modify the operation of any particular kind of BIOS service (for example, modifying the video services to accommodate the special features of a new display adapter like the Enhanced Graphics Adapter) then it can be done in a relatively clean and uncomplicated way by simply replacing one interrupt handler.

There is one fundamental complexity and difficulty that has not been dealt with very well in the ROM-BIOS—the problems that are created by the different features of different models of PC (particularly the more exotic ones, like the PC*jr*, the PC-AT, and the 3270-PC) and also by the characteristics of various options for the PC (such as the numerous combinations of display adapters that be used. Each main model of the PC family has its own special variations on the ROM-BIOS services, and much of the optional equipment for the PC family does as well. However, there is no simple, clean, and reliable way for us as PC users, or our programs, as PC software, to adapt to the many possible variations in the BIOS services that come with all these models and equipment.

The matter is made more complicated by the fact that IBM keeps to itself whatever master plan there might be for future additions to the PC family—and allowing for future changes involves a lot of guesswork on the part of programmers. IBM's own *Technical Reference* manuals for the different models of the family add to the confusion, because each is written as if it were for a unique machine. A programmer studying one *Technical Reference* manual can't tell if the services described in that manual apply to *every* model of PC, or the one at hand. You have to cross-check all the manuals to see what's common. Partly for that reason, and partly to avoid getting bogged down in the peculiarities of different models, we'll cover only the universal ROM-BIOS services in this chapter.

On a technical level, there is a great deal more that can be said about the design and workings of the ROM-BIOS, but what we've covered is really the most basic and important part.

In Section 17.2 we'll cover the full list of ROM-BIOS services that are universal to the entire PC family, the PC's basic complement of services. It's a somewhat more technical treatment that some readers may want to skip over, but there are two real benefits of reading through it. First, you will learn just what services the ROM-BIOS puts at the disposal of our programs. This will help you understand how our programs get things done and it may give you ideas for how your own programs can benefit from these services. Second, skimming through the list of BIOS services will give you a feeling for their *level*—that is, an understanding of where they stand in the potential spectrum between very primitive or simple and very rich or complex.

TECHNICAL BACKGROUND ❙ ❙ ❙ ■ ■ ■ ▬▬▬▬▬▬▬▬▬▬▬

17.2 The BIOS Services

Now we're ready to run through a list of the services that the PC family's BIOS provides for our programs. As you can see by the Technical Background head, the material here falls into the advanced category, which may be skipped by readers who are only interested in the broad outlines and main points of the PC. But that doesn't mean that what we'll be talking about here is especially technical or difficult to understand.

257

The ROM-BIOS services are organized in groups, with each group having its own dedicated interrupt In Figure 17-1 you'll find a summary table of the groups. We'll cover them one by one, beginning with the most rich, most complicated, and most interesting: the video services.

Interrupt	Service group
5	Print-screen
16	Video services
17	Equipment list
18	Memory size
19	Disk services
20	Serial port (RS-232) services
21	Cassette port services
22	Keyboard services
23	Parallel port (printer) services
24	ROM-BASIC
25	boot strap
26	Time services

Figure 17-1. The ROM-BIOS service interrupts.

There are 16 separate video screen services in the basic complement of the PC family's ROM-BIOS services. That's quite a number, and it doesn't even include the substantial additions that have been made for specialty models (PC*jr*, AT) or advanced display adapters such as the Enhanced Graphics Adapter. These 16 are the original complement used on the very first PC model, and they form a base for the video services of every member of the family. The services are numbered 0 through 15. We'll go through the entire list so that you can see exactly what kinds of services the BIOS provides.

The first service, number 0, is used to change the video mode. For PCs with just the standard Monochrome Adapter, there's no choice at all. The monochrome mode (identified, as we saw in earlier chapters, as mode number 7) is it. For PCs with the Color Graphics Adapter or its equivalent, there is a choice of seven modes: four text modes and three graphics modes, as we detailed in Chapter 11. This service is used by our programs to switch the display screen into whatever mode is needed. As we'll see later, there is a complementary service that lets our programs learn what the current mode is.

Video service 1 is used to control the size and shape of the cursor. It sets the scan lines that the cursor appears on, which we also discussed in

Chapter 11. This is the ROM-BIOS service that underlies the BASIC program statement LOCATE ,,,X,Y.

Video service 2 sets the cursor location on the screen, corresponding to the BASIC program statement LOCATE X,Y.

Video service 3 reports to our programs where the cursor is located and also the shape of the cursor. This service is the opposite of services 1 and 2 combined. It allows our programs to record the current state of the cursor so that it can be restored after the program is done. We'll see an example of how useful that can be when we discuss the print-screen service.

Video service 4 is the sole service supporting the PC's little-used light-pen feature. When a program invokes this service, the BIOS reports if the pen is "triggered," and where it's touching on the screen. Interestingly, the service reports the pen position in two different ways: the location in terms of the grid of text character positions and in terms of the graphics pixel locations, to make it easy for our programs to interpret the light pen position either way. Less interesting is the fact that light pens never caught on for the PC family.

Video service 5 selects which display page is active (shown on the screen) for the video modes that have more than one display page in memory (see Chapter 11 for more on that).

Services 6 and 7 are a fascinating pair of services that do window scrolling. These two services allow us to define a rectangular "window" on the screen and scroll the data inside the window up from the bottom (service 6) or down from the top (service 7). When a window is scrolled, blank lines are inserted at the bottom or top, ready for our programs to write new information into them. The purpose of these services is to allow our programs to conveniently write out information on just a part of the screen and leave the rest of the screen intact. A wonderful idea, but one that has rarely been used.

The next three video services are used to work with text characters on the screen. Video service 8 reads the current character (and its attribute) off of the screen (or rather out of the screen memory). This service is clever enough, in graphics mode, to decode the pixel drawing of a character into the character code. Video service 9 is the obvious complement to service 8: it writes a character on the screen with the display attribute that we specify. Service 10 also writes a character, but uses whatever display attribute is currently in place for that screen location.

The next three services provide operations for the graphics modes. Video service 11 sets the color palette to be used. Service 12 writes a single dot on the screen, and service 13 reads a dot off the screen.

Video service 14 is a handy variation on the character writing service, number 8. This service writes a character to the screen, and advances the cursor to the next position on the screen, so that it's in place for the next character. (The other services require our programs to move the cursor as a separate operation.) This is a convenient service that makes it easy for our programs to use the display screen like a printer, and just print out information with a minimum of fuss (or flexibility). For that reason this service is called "write teletype."

The final service, number 15, is the inverse of the very first. It reports the current video state so that our programs can adjust their operation to the video mode, or record the current mode to be able to go back to it after changing the mode. This service is the main way that programs determine if the computer is using a Monochrome Adapter or a Color Graphics Adapter, and even those programs that do all their own screen output work use this service to learn which display adapter is in use, so that they know which display memory addresses to place output in.

All these video reading and writing services are the official approved way for our programs to put information on the screen. Using them has the advantage that output heading for the screen is handled in a standard way, which can be automatically adopted to new hardware (such as the Enhanced Graphics Adapter and other new screen options). But many programs do not use these services, simply because there is a disappointingly high over-head involved. Screen output can be performed *much* faster when our programs do it themselves, rather than using these ROM-BIOS services.

That finishes the list of basic video services. There are more, but there aren't any more that are *generic* to the PC family and apply to all the models. The additional extra services that apply just to some models or to some special display adapters are no different in kind from the ones that we've seen. The principles and the general level are the same.

The next thing for us to look at is a quite special service, the print-screen service. This service is different from all the others. The majority of the ROM-BIOS services are used to work specifically with a peripheral device, such as the display screen or the keyboard. The remaining services are basically informational, handling the time of day or indicating the amount of memory installed in the computer. But this print-screen service is a different animal.

The print-screen service is designed to read off the screen the information that's displayed and route it to the printer. We're all familiar with this service because it's directly available to us with a press of the PRTSC key on the keyboard. What makes this service particularly interesting is the fact that it is completely built from other ROM-BIOS services, so that it doesn't do anything unique in itself. It just combines parts that we've already got to perform a new and useful service.

Print-screen begins work by using video service 3 to learn the current cursor position, and service 15 to learn the dimensions of the screen. It saves the cursor position so that it can later restore it to its original position, and then proceeds to move the cursor through every location on the screen, from top to bottom. At each location, it uses video service 8 to read a character off the screen, and a printer output service, which we'll see later, to copy the character to the printer. When this service is done, it restores the cursor to where it was, and then returns control to the program that invoked it.

And that's interesting all by itself. We mostly think of the print-screen service as strictly an adjunct of the keyboard, something that we get by pressing the PRTSC key. Not so. Print-screen is a standard ROM-BIOS service that can be invoked by any program, in the same way any other service is invoked: by issuing an INT-interrupt instruction (for interrupt 5, in this case). What makes the PRTSC key work is that the keyboard ROM-BIOS routines monitor keyboard activity for this key combination. When it's found, the keyboard ROM-BIOS uses interrupt 5 to request the print-screen service. Any other program could do the same. This nifty service can be placed at the disposal of any program to be used in any way that's handy.

Now on to the other services. We'll go through the other device services first, and then cover the information services.

The disk services are invoked with interrupt number 19. There are six basic services, numbered 0-5. The first, service number 0, is used to reset the disk drive and its controller. This is an initialization and error-recovery service that clears the decks for a fresh start in the next disk operation. Related to it is the next service, disk service 1, which reports the status of the disk drive so that error handling and controlling routines can find out what's what.

Disk service 2 is the first of the active disk services. It reads disk sectors into memory. The sectors don't have to be read individually. This service will read as many consecutive sectors as we want, as long as they are all on the same track. Disk service 3 does the same, writing sectors instead of reading them.

Disk service 4 "verifies" the data written on a disk, to test that it is properly recorded. This is the service that underlies the DOS option "VER-IFY ON" that we see in the VERIFY command and the VERIFY feature of DOS's configuration file (CONFIG.SYS). It's commonly misunderstood just what this verification does. It does *not* check the data stored on disk to see that it correctly matches data in memory (data which we might have just read or written). Instead, the verify service simply checks that the disk data is *properly recorded*, which means testing for parity errors and other recording defects. As a general rule, that assures us that our data is correct, but it's no guarantee. If we have the wrong data, but it's properly recorded, the verify service will report that it's all OK.

Disk service 5, the last of the lot, is used to format a track of a disk. This is the physical formatting that underlies DOS's logical formatting of a disk (see the sidebar discussion in Chapter 9). This formatting service is a fascinating business, because it specifies, for each track as a whole, how many sectors there will be, how the sectors will be identified by sector number, the order the sectors will appear in, and the size of each sector. Normally all the sectors on a track are the same size (512 bytes), they are numbered sequentially beginning with 1, and, on floppy diskettes, they physically appear in numeric order (on hard disks, they don't). Modifying some of these standard characteristics is the basis of many copy-protection schemes. Even just changing the order the sectors are written in can be used for copy protection, because the standard DOS COPY and DISKCOPY commands will not transfer the unusual sector order, and a copy-protected program can sense the timing difference that the order of the sectors introduces.

The serial port (RS-232, communications line) services are invoked by interrupt 20. Using the serial port is fairly simple—*everything* is simply compared to the screen and the disk drives—and there are only four services needed. Service number 0 initializes the communications port, setting the basic parameters that we learned about in Chapter 15, the baud rate and so forth. Service 1 is used to write a byte to the port; service 2 reads a byte. Service 3, the last, is used to get a status report, which indicates things like whether data is ready.

Next comes a set of services for the PC's cassette tape interface, a feature of the original PC that has been used little and dropped from the design of the more advanced models of the family. There are four services, in two symmetrical pairs, invoked with interrupt 21. Services 0 and 1 turn the cassette tape motor on and off; services 2 and 3 read and write 256-byte blocks of data. That's all there is to it.

The keyboard services are activated with interrupt 22. There are three of them. Service 0 reads the next character from the keyboard input buffer. The characters are reported in their full two-byte form, as we discussed in Chapter 14. When a character is read by service 0, it's removed from the keyboard input buffer. Not the case with service 1. Service 1 reports if there is any keyboard input ready. If there is, this service also "previews" the character by reporting the character bytes in the same way that service 0 does—but the character remains in the keyboard buffer until it's officially read with service 0. The final keyboard service, number 2, reports the keyboard status bits, which indicate the state of the shift keys and so forth (which we discussed in Chapter 14 and saw in action in the KEY-BITS program in Appendix A). Although we know where to find that information in the low-memory location where the BIOS stores it, this service is the official and approved way for our program to learn about the keyboard status.

The last of the device-support services are those for the parallel printer port, using interrupt 23. There are three simple services: 0 spits out a single byte to the printer, 1 initializes the printer, and 2 reports the printer status, showing things like whether the printer is out of paper.

That finishes off the ROM-BIOS services that are directly used to support the PC's I/O peripheral equipment. It's worth noting that there are two other I/O devices in the PC's standard repertoire the have no support in the BIOS whatsoever: the speaker and joysticks. Joysticks, like the light pen, have turned out to be little used, but it's curious that this device, and the speaker as well, aren't assisted in any way by the BIOS services.

The remaining collection of ROM-BIOS services are used to control information or to invoke major changes in the PC.

Interrupt 17 is used to get the PC's official (and now rather out of date) equipment list information. The equipment list was designed around the facilities of the original PC model, and hasn't been expanded to include new equipment that's been added to the family—largely, I think, because it hasn't turned out to be necessary. The equipment list reports how many diskette drives the machine has (0 to 4), but says nothing about hard disks or other disk types. It reports the number of parallel ports (up to three) and serial ports (up to two). It also reports if there is a game adapter (that is, the option board for joysticks), but nothing about light pens. (That's ironic, since there are BIOS services for the light pen but not for the game adapter.)

A companion service to the equipment list reports the amount of memory the computer has. Officially, it's requested with interrupt 18. The amount of memory is reported in K-bytes.

The third and last of the pure information services are for time-of-day, using interrupt number 26. There are two services: 0 to read the current clock number, and 1 to set the clock. The BIOS time-of-day clock is kept in the form of a long 4-byte integer, with each count representing one clock-tick.

The PC's hardware clock ''ticks'' by generating a clock interrupt 18.2 times a second, and the interrupt handler for the clock adds one to the clock count each time. The clock count is supposed to represent the number of ticks since last midnight. It only shows the right time (that is, the right count) if it has been properly set—for example, by the DOS TIME command or by a hardware real-time clock, like the one built into the AT model or the ones that come with many multifunction boards. When we turn the computer on, the clock starts counting from zero, as if that time were midnight, until something sets the correct clock time/count. DOS converts the clock tick count into the time of day in hours, minutes, seconds, and hundredths of seconds by simple arithmetic. The BIOS routines that update the clock check for it passing the count, which represents 24 hours. When that happens, the clock is reset to 0 and and a "midnight has passed" signal is recorded. The next time DOS reads the clock count from the BIOS, DOS sees this "midnight has passed" signal and updates the record it keeps of the date.

There are, finally, two more quite interesting and quite curious BIOS service interrupts. They are used to pass control to either of two special routines built into the BIOS. One is the ROM BASIC (what IBM calls "Cassette BASIC") and the other is the boot-strap, start-up routines. (Keep in mind, by the way, that only IBM's own models of the PC family have the built-in BASIC; other family members, such as the Compaq computers, do not.) We know the normal ways to activate these two special routines: we reboot by pressing the Ctrl-Alt-Del key combination and we get to ROM BASIC by booting our computers without a disk in the machine. But it's also possible for any program to activate either of these routines by simply invoking their interrupts. There is one special thing about these two routines: unlike the ordinary service routines which do something for our programs and then return processing to the program that invoked them, these two are one-way streets. They take full charge of the machine and control never returns to the program that invoked them.

That completes our coverage of the ROM-BIOS, the PC's lowest level of software support. Now we're ready to move on to the next basic level of software, DOS itself. We'll be devoting the next three chapters to an inner look at DOS.

Some Things To Try

1. What would be the effect of combining all the ROM-BIOS services under one interrupt? Or giving each service its own separate interrupt?

2. Can you think of reasons why the boot-strap loader and the PC's built-in ROM BASIC would be invoked by interrupts? Do you think the reason was to make them available for use by any program, or just easier to use by IBM's own system programs?

3. At the end of Section 17.1 I mentioned that one of the reasons to study the BIOS services is to understand their level. Consider how the *level* of the services might be higher or lower. Take one example from the services and see how you could change its definition to be more primitive or more advanced. Analyze the video services and rank them in terms of relatively high or low level.

18

The Role of DOS

In this chapter we begin a three-chapter tour of DOS, the last major part of the PC epic that we still have left to explore. The next two chapters will investigate how DOS goes to work for us directly and how DOS goes to work for our programs. But before we get into that, we need to set the stage with some background information on DOS, and that's what this chapter is for. We'll start by looking at what operating systems are for in the first place. Then we'll go through the history that shaped the character of DOS and see the ideas that formed the basis for DOS's design. Then we'll see how DOS can be built up and expanded in ways that are internal to DOS (such as device drivers) and ways that are external (such as visual shells).

18.1 What Any DOS is About

The DOS that we use on our PCs is just one example of a class of computer programs that are known as *supervisors, control programs,* or *operating systems.* Operating systems like DOS are probably the most complex and intricate computer programs that have ever been built. The task of an operating system is basically to supervise and direct the work, the operation of the computer.

It's an incredible tribute to the power and flexibility of computers that they are not only able to do computing work for our needs, but they are also able to take on the complex job of looking after their own operation. And it's also a marvelous irony that these most sophisticated programs aren't created to dispatch the work we need done but to take care of the computer's own work. Computers are the most powerful tool that man has ever created. They are so powerful, in fact, that we aren't able to use the tool directly ourselves. Instead, through the intermediary of an operating system we use the computer-tool to make itself manageable enough for us to work with. We give our computers the rather inward looking task of supervising themselves, so that we don't have to concern ourselves with the extraordinary problems that are involved in making a computer work.

When we covered the subject of interrupts in Chapter 6 we got a glimpse of just how demanding the task of supervising a computer can be. Every physical part of the computer's equipment requires some looking after, and some of them demand a lot. For example, the PC's clock, used to keep track of the time of day, demands attention with an interrupt 18 times each second. The keyboard, as we saw in Chapter 14, demands attention every time a key is pressed and again every time a key is released. When I type in the word "keyboard" I've caused the computer to be interrupted 16 separate times, just to note my keystrokes. An enormous, additional load of work gets done after the keystrokes have been recorded.

The task of orchestrating, coordinating, and supervising the breathtaking array of events that take place inside our computers falls to the operating system, which for us is DOS.

So what does the operating system, our DOS, *do*? Essentially, it does three broad categories of things: it manages devices, controls programs, and processes commands.

DOS's work in managing devices—printers, disks, screens, keyboards and more—involves everything that is needed to keep the parts of the computer running properly. On the lowest level, that means issuing commands to the devices and looking after any errors they report. That's exactly the job that the PC's ROM-BIOS performs. In the broadest sense, any operating system that works on our PCs includes the ROM-BIOS as one of its key components. On a much higher level, the operating system performs a major organizing role for the computer's devices. This is particularly evident with the disks. A key, even dominant, part of the operating system's work is to work out the scheme of how data is recorded on our disks: the management of the disk space, the efficient storage of data, and its quick and reliable retrieval.

The second broad job that DOS undertakes is the control of programs. That involves the loading of programs from disk, setting up the framework for a program's execution, and also the provision of services for programs (as we'll discuss in Chapter 20). On more complex and sophisticated computer systems than our PC family, the control of programs that operating systems perform also involves things that aren't possible on our machines, such as setting the limits on what parts of memory and what parts of the disk storage the program can access. Because of the relative simplicity of our PCs, every program has full access to any part of memory and all of the disk storage, but on larger computers that isn't true, and one part of the task of controlling programs on those computers is controlling the limitations and restrictions that programs work within.

The third major job that DOS performs is command processing. That's the direct interaction that DOS has with us, the computer user. Every time we type something in response to DOS's command prompt, A⟩, we are working with the command processing aspect of DOS. In the case of DOS our commands are essentially all requests to execute a program. In more complex operating systems, our commands can take on a wider scope, including things like directing the workings of the operating system itself. Whatever the scope of commands that an operating system provides, a key task for the operating system is to accept and carry out the user's commands.

That, in summary, is the heart of what any operating system, and our DOS in particular, does. Now it's time for us to take a look at some of the history of how DOS came to be like it is, and see some of the ideas that underlie the way DOS works for us.

18.2 History and Concepts of Our DOS

The real history of our DOS begins with the early planning for the IBM Personal Computer and the operating system that had been used with the generation of personal computers that preceded our PC.

The PC was planned and designed at a time when most personal computers used an 8-bit microprocessor, and the dominant operating system for those machines was called CP/M (which stood for Control Program/Microcomputer). Even though IBM was designing the PC to be a much more powerful 16-bit computer, IBM wanted to build on the base of experience and popularity of CP/M machines. Even though the PC was going to be a quite different critter, and even though 8-bit CP/M programs couldn't be directly used on the PC, making the PC's operating system similar to CP/M would make it enormously easier to adapt programs (and adapt user's experience and skills) to the new machine.

Apparently IBM intended to have an updated, 16-bit version of CP/M, which became known as CP/M-86, as the PC's primary operating system, but that didn't work out. See the sidebar *CP/M Crash Lands* for one version of the story why. For whatever reason, IBM decided not to center the PC on a version of CP/M, but instead to have a new operating system created for the PC by Microsoft—that operating system was DOS.

CP/M Crash Lands

There's an interesting story that claims to explain why the PC was introduced with its own new operating system, DOS, rather than with the 16-bit version of the existing and popular CP/M system. Truth or myth, it makes a fascinating legend.

As the story goes, when IBM came shopping for CP/M, Gary Kildall, the man who created CP/M, intentionally kept IBM's representatives waiting, and fuming, while he flew his plane for hours in the skies overhead. Kildall, we're told, thumbed his nose at IBM as a customer, while Bill Gates, head of Microsoft, rolled out the red carpet for IBM. Gates donned his rarely-worn business suits for meetings with IBM to demonstrate that he was serious about doing business with them.

In the 8-bit computer world, Gate's company Microsoft had been dominant in programming languages, and Kildall's company Digital Research dominated operating systems—and IBM was prepared to keep it that way, planning to hire each of them for their specialties. But Kildall played hard to get, even after IBM had Bill Gates plead their case for Kildall's cooperation.

In the end, IBM turned to Microsoft for an operating system as well as programming languages, and Microsoft had to come up with one in very short order. It delivered the goods by picking up an existing but little-known CP/M-like operating system and polishing it to meet IBM's requirements. That operating system became the DOS that nearly every PC user works with.

With DOS as the dominant operating system for the PC family, CP/M's fortunes took a nose dive. Gary Kildall's flight led to a crash landing for his operating system.

Even though DOS was favored from the start, DOS was not the only operating system that IBM introduced with the PC. Two other operating systems, which had their own base of supporters, were also introduced and given official IBM approval: CP/M-86, which we've already mentioned, and the UCSD p-System, an operating system closely tuned to the needs of the Pascal programming language. Nobody wants to use more than one operating system, though, since it's very inconvenient to switch from one to another, and it's nearly impossible to share data, programs, or human skills between operating systems. For practical reasons there could be only one winner in the battle for operating system supremacy and that winner was DOS.

Even though DOS was a competitor to CP/M for the PC—and a competitor which vanquished its opposition—the design and operation of DOS was closely based on the facilities that CP/M provided and the ideas behind them. DOS, as it was initially introduced, had very much the flavor and style of CP/M for an important and deliberate reason: to make it as convenient as possible for computer users who were familiar with CP/M to learn to use DOS, and to make it easy for existing 8-bit CP/M programs to be adapted for the PC.

The influence of CP/M appears from the very first thing we see when we use DOS, the command prompt A⟩. DOS shows the design influence of CP/M in that command prompt and many more things in the way that DOS works with us, the user, and even more in the way that DOS works with our programs.

While experienced eyes can see the similarities between the style of DOS and the style of its predecessor CP/M, the most important ways that CP/M set the style for DOS aren't visible, because they are *ideas*. Foremost among them was the scope and use that was intended for DOS from the beginning. DOS was built with the most primitive concepts of personal computing in mind. This included the assumption that only one person would be using the computer and that the one user would only ask for the computer to do one thing at a time (*not*, for example, printing out one document while computing on something else, which would be performing two tasks at once). DOS was designed to be a single-user system and a single tasking system following the most simple concept of how a computer might be used. It was natural that DOS was designed this way since its roots came from an operating system and a family of 8-bit machines which weren't suited to undertake anything more ambitious.

Our PC family, however, was born to more ambitious goals, and the limitations of the CP/M heritage would have severely restricted DOS's ability to grow with the PC. On the other hand, there was an operating system called UNIX that was widely admired for its broad features, and Microsoft, DOS's builder, had strong experience with the UNIX style from creating XENIX, a variation of UNIX. So, when the time came to make a major revision to the features and internal structure of DOS, many of the concepts of UNIX/XENIX were stirred into the DOS recipe. The result was DOS version 2.0 and all the subsequent versions that we have seen since.

The influence of UNIX is visible to every user of DOS in the sub-directories that we use to organize and subdivide our disks. It shows even more in the internal structure of DOS and the services that DOS provides for our programs. We'll see a very important example of that in Chapter 20 when we look at the two ways DOS provides for our programs to work with files, an old CP/M method and a new UNIX method.

The DOS that we know and use today is something of a blend of the styles and design features of CP/M and UNIX. While DOS contains many of the expansive and forward-looking features of UNIX, it still suffers from many of the limitations of its earliest beginnings. Because DOS originally gave each program that we run total control over the computer and all of the computer's memory, it is difficult for more advanced versions of DOS to impose the limitations that are needed if we want to have two programs actively running in our computer at the same time. Like so many other things, DOS has been able to grow and develop far beyond what it was in its earliest days, yet it still feels the restrictive tug of its beginnings. In Section 18.4 we'll see some of the attempts that are being made to transcend those limitations. First, we need to see how DOS has become a flexible tool.

18.3 Installable Drivers and Flexible Facilities

In its earliest form, DOS was a rigid creation that had predefined into it all of the devices and disk formats and such that it was able to work with. This was release number 1 of DOS, the release that was solely based on the model of CP/M. That version of DOS was not able to adjust itself to changing circumstances, or to incorporate new devices such as new disk formats.

But as the PC family grew, it became important to be able to adjust DOS to the particular needs of each computer and computer user, and it also became important to be able to make DOS accept and accommodate new peripheral devices, particularly the many different kinds of disks that were being used with PCs. So, as part of the major changes that were made with the second release of DOS, version 2.0, which included the changes that added many UNIX concepts, DOS was made adaptable through a facility known as a *configuration file*.

The configuration file is the key to DOS's flexibility and adaptability. When DOS first begins operation, it looks for a file on our start-up disk with the name of CONFIG.SYS. If it finds that file, DOS reads it, and follows the commands in the file that define how DOS is to be configured and adapted. You'll see an example of a configuration file in Figure 18-1; it's the actual CONFIG.SYS from my own computer.

There are two key parts to the way that DOS can be customized, modified, and configured, and I've highlighted them by dividing my own CONFIG.SYS file into two parts, as you see in Figure 18-1. The first part is controlling information that directs things that DOS already knows about. For example, the second line in Figure 18-1 tells DOS how many disk sector buffers to use. Choosing the number of disk buffers involves a simple tradeoff: the more buffers, the less often DOS will have to wait for information to be read in from the disk, but the less memory there will be for our programs to use. On its own DOS would use a very conservative number of disk buffers, around two or three. After some experimentation I found that my computer performed much better when I gave DOS more buffers, 64 in all. This is a perfect example of the flexible facilities that are designed into DOS. If we wish to we can control some of the parameters—like the number of disk buffers—that influence the computer's performance.

```
BREAK=ON
BUFFERS=64
FILES=20
LASTDRIVE=E
COUNTRY=001

DEVICE=MOUSE.SYS
DEVICE=ANSI.SYS
DEVICE=VDISK.SYS /E 384
```

Figure 18-1. A configuration file.

The other key part of DOS's configuration file involves software that can be integrated into DOS, what are called *installable device drivers*. DOS has built into it, naturally enough, program support for all the standard types of peripheral devices that the PC family uses. But we may want to add other, more exotic, components to DOS, and that's what installable device drivers allow us to do.

These drivers are programs that expand DOS's ability to work with the computer's peripherals. The device drivers themselves are written following a strict set of guidelines that allow them to work in close cooperation with DOS, without disrupting any other part of DOS's workings. You'll see three examples of these installable drivers in Figure 18-1. They are identified by the lines that read DEVICE=. For each of these commands, DOS finds the filename that is given in the DEVICE= command and integrates the program stored there into DOS's inner sanctum. You'll see that I have three of them. Two are provided as optional parts that come with DOS: the ANSI.SYS driver, which provides some special screen and keyboard control, and the VDISK.SYS driver, which creates a "virtual" or RAM disk in part of the computer's memory. The third driver which you'll see in my configuration file, MOUSE.SYS, is used to support a truly new item to my computer, a mouse pointing device. The mouse driver is a classic example of how installable device drivers give DOS the ability to work with hardware that was not designed into the basic part of DOS. The other two drivers, on the other hand, illustrate how the installable driver facility can be used to expand the workings of existing parts of the computer.

Whatever purpose and use installable drivers are put to, they provide a way for us to modify, extend, and expand the things that DOS can do, within the scope of DOS's basic design. There are other ways that DOS can be expanded or changed, though, that don't work from within DOS, and that's the subject of Section 18.4.

18.4 Visual Shells: TopView and Others

There are inherent characteristics in DOS that define how DOS looks to us—the sort of face that it presents to the user—and that define what DOS is and isn't capable of doing. As we know from familiar experience, DOS's user interface is based on the simple A⟩ command prompt, and the way DOS accepts commands, which is that we must type them in on the keyboard. We also know that DOS is only able to run one program at a time for us. DOS doesn't give us any way of either having more than one thing going at a time (except for some simple exceptions, such as the PRINT command, which will print away while we run other programs) or of suspending a program in the middle of its operation—in effect putting it on hold—while we run another program and then return to the first one.

However, just because DOS doesn't provide us with a way of doing these things, doesn't mean that they aren't desirable or can't be done. In fact, many of the most talented minds in the PC community have been working hard to provide us with programs that can add fancier facilities *on top of* DOS.

It is possible for us to transform the operation of DOS by using any of a class of programs that are commonly called visual shells (although that only describes some of the things that are performed by this class of program).

Visual shells are programs that essentially wrap themselves around DOS and provide facilities of one kind or another that DOS is not able to do. There are any number of things that such a program might undertake to do, but of the ones that have gotten the most attention from the PC community, two functions stand out. One is providing a more appealing and useful "face," a nicer way to enter commands. The other is some kind of multi-programming that allows us to use more than one program at a time.

The best publicized programs of this type have been IBM's TopView and Microsoft's Windows. I'll discuss them in summary to give you an idea of why this sort of program has been so much discussed and so energetically worked on and also why, so far, they have met with only very modest success. These two will stand as representatives of the whole broad class of shell programs that have appeared and that we can expect to see more of.

One of the reasons why there has been so much interest in the idea of visual shells is that DOS's command interface provides us with so little help in entering our commands. To run a program with DOS, we have to remember the name of the program and type it in, together with any parameters that are needed. Visual shell programs, like TopView and Windows, on the other hand, are able to show us a list of all the commands that we might wish to use, and they allow us to simply select from a list of commands and perform them without having to type the command name in. Using cursor keys or a mouse, we can simply point and shoot, pointing to the command that we want performed and shooting it into action with a single press of the *enter* key or a mouse button.

The command interface can be enriched even beyond that, from the verbal to the visual, by replacing the names of commands on the screen with drawings, called ''icons,'' which represent the function that the command performs. Some of the most advanced visual shell programs work in this way.

But easier or more attractive command entry is not the main reason why there is so much interest in visual shells. Equally important is the ability of some of them to work with more than one program at a time. This can be done a variety of ways, each of which has its own unique technical challenges. Some actually involve having several programs in active operation at the same time—as TopView does—while others involve putting programs on hold while other tasks are performed and then returning to the suspended program without having to start it from scratch.

While there has been a great deal of interest in this variety of program to jump outside of many of the limitations that are inherent in DOS itself, it appears to me that the time has not really come for this sort of program to blossom. The main reason is simply that the PC's main microprocessor, the 8088, does not provide the facilities that allow either DOS or a shell wrapped around DOS to protect itself from being disrupted by ill-behaved programs. On the other hand, the more advanced microprocessor in the PC family, the 80286 that is the engine driving the AT model, does have protection facilities that make it possible for a program like TopView to run any number of programs without any of them interfering with each other, or with TopView, or with the core of DOS. Until we see shell programs of this type, which make use of the 286's inherent protection features, I don't expect that these shell programs, or any similar extensions that might be integrated into DOS, will see widespread use in the PC community. Eventually, though, we can expect something along those lines to become the operating system environment that we all work with.

Some Things to Try

1. Why is it that the PC's main microprocessor, the 8088, can't safely run many programs at once? How can a program like TopView try to overcome some of these problems?

2. If you were designing a "visual shell" for DOS, a new way of making it easier for the PC user to give commands, how would you design it? Work out the best approach that you can think of, and consider what compromises you might have to make, to balance different needs.

19

DOS Serving Us

After beginning our tour of DOS in Chapter 18, we're ready to see what DOS does. In this chapter we'll look at what DOS does for us, in its direct interaction with the user (in Chapter 20, we'll see what DOS does for our programs, in providing services that our programs can use).

We'll begin by looking at how the DOS command processor works. Then we'll see how command processing is enriched and made more complex by batch file processing.

19.1 Command Processing

Of all the things that DOS does in supervising our computers, the one that we're most directly aware of is what's called *command processing*—DOS's ability to accept and act on our commands. As we've seen, the job of command processing falls to the one visible component of DOS's three key parts, the program known as COMMAND.COM.

It's COMMAND.COM that issues the terse command prompt that we're used to seeing, which usually appears like this: A⟩. (For hard disk users it's normally C⟩.) When we see the command prompt, DOS (or more particularly, the COMMAND.COM command processor) is waiting for us to enter a command that DOS will carry out.

Just what is a command? It's really nothing more than a request to *run a program*. The command that we issue—the first word that we type on the command line—is simply the name of a program that we're asking DOS to run. For example, if we issue the command

FORMAT A: /S /V

then we're doing nothing but asking DOS to find a program named "FORMAT" and run it for us. All the rest, everything else that we type in the command line (in this case, "A: /S /V") is simply some further instructions to the program, telling it what to do. Those are parameters that we're giving to the program, and DOS simply passes them on to the program—but to DOS they mean nothing, and the command processor doesn't pay any attention to them.

The programs that the command processor can carry out for us fall into four categories, and it's important that we understand what they are and how they work, because our convenient and effective use of the computer is based largely on how well these commands are put at our disposal. The four categories of commands are *internal* commands, and then three types of *external* commands: *COM* programs, *EXE* programs, and *BAT batch* commands. Let's start by looking at the division between the internal commands and the three other types of external commands.

Mostly our programs—that is, the commands that DOS can perform for us—are separate entities that are stored on our disks in disk files. However, not all the commands that DOS can perform for us work that way; not all of them are kept in their own disk files. The COMMAND.COM command processor includes inside it some of the most important and frequently-used command programs, so it isn't necessary to fetch a program file from disk in order to carry out these commands. These are called the *internal* commands, because the programs that perform the command work are inside COMMAND.COM itself.

The list of internal commands varies from version to version of DOS. Here's a typical list of internal commands: among the more commonly used ones are CLS, COPY, DATE, DEL/ERASE, DIR, REN/RENAME, TIME, and TYPE. Among the less well-known are BREAK, CD/CHDIR, ECHO, MD/MKDIR, PATH, PROMPT, RD/RMDIR, SET, VER, VERIFY, and VOL.

The command processor holds inside it a table of these internal commands and the program code to carry them out. When we give DOS a command, the first thing that COMMAND.COM does is to look the command name up in its table to see if we're asking for an internal command. If so, COMMAND.COM can carry out the command immediately. If not, then COMMAND.COM must go looking on our disks for the file that holds the *external* command program.

The command processor identifies the files that hold external commands by two things: first the filename of the disk file is the name of the command; second, the extension to the filename identifies the file as one of the three types of external commands: a COM file, an EXE file, or a BAT batch command file.

Since the filename of the program file defines the name of the command that the program file will carry out, we have a great deal of freedom to change the names of our commands. We can do it simply by renaming the files (keeping the essential extension name, but changing the filename part) or making another copy of the command file under another name, so that the command is available to us either by its original command name or any other names we want to give it. I do this all the time and find it one of the handiest DOS tricks there is. I use it mostly to abbreviate the names of the commands I use the most. For example, I can invoke the word processor that I wrote this book with either under it's regular name, WORD, or with the one-letter command W.

We can do this with any of the external commands that we have available simply because external commands are based on the names of the files that hold the command programs. We can give our commands any name that's allowed as a filename, and we can give them alias names simply by duplicating the files under different names. We can't do that, however, with the command processor's internal commands (unless we try the relatively radical operation of tinkering with the table of command names inside COMMAND.COM).

Of the three kinds of external commands two—COM and EXE files— are variations on the same principle, while the other, the BAT file, is something else entirely. Both COM and EXE are proper program files that the command processor will load and execute for us.

From the point of view of the user who fires up programs through the command processor, the differences between COM and EXE program files have no practical importance, but it's interesting to us to know what's what with them. Basically the difference is that COM files are a simple, quick-loading format, while EXE files are more complex. A COM file is what's sometimes called an "image" file, which means that what's stored on disk is an exact image of the program as loaded and run in the computer's memory. A COM file needs no further processing or conversion by DOS in order to be run; it's just copied into memory, and away it goes.

You might think that *all* program files were like that, but the fact is that many programs require a small amount of last-minute massaging and preparation before they can start operation. The crux of this load-time preparation is the one thing that can't be known in advance when a program is created: the memory address where the program will be copied into. Generally the various parts of a program are intensely cross-linked. Different sections of the executable code know where each other are (so that they can "call" each other) and the program code knows the memory locations of all the bits of data that come with the program. While any program can know the *relative* location of its parts, no program can know in advance the absolute memory addresses of where those parts will be. After all, where a program is loaded in memory depends on how much memory is being used by DOS and by resident programs (like Sidekick or Prokey) and that can change.

It is possible for a program to automatically self-adjust to adapt itself to wherever it happens to be placed in memory. And that's exactly what COM-type programs do. Using the segment registers and careful programming conventions, COM programs don't need to be adjusted for where they are located in memory. But not all programs are able to work that way. It turns out, when we get into the technical details of it all, that the COM format is rather restrictive and many programs simply can't work that way. For one thing, under normal circumstances, COM can't be any bigger than 64K in size—and that's not enough to accommodate the most sophisticated programs. So the EXE format exists to handle programs that can't simply be loaded as a pure memory image.

When DOS loads an EXE program into memory it performs any last-minute processing that is needed to ready the program for execution. One main part of that preparation is to plug the memory address where the program is loaded into as many parts of the program as need it. To do that, the EXE file format includes a table of which parts of the program need to be modified, and how it should be done. That's not the only special work that needs to be done for EXE programs, though. There are other things, such as setting up the program's working stack (COM programs take care of that for themselves).

There are differences in the ways that COM and EXE programs are loaded, and there are also differences in the way they are written—slightly different programming conventions are used to accommodate the different way they are loaded and run. Also, somewhat different steps are used by programmers to prepare these programs (as we'll see, in outline, in Chapter 21). All in all, though, this is just a technical matter that concerns program developers. From the point of view of the computer user, there is no difference between COM and EXE programs.

When DOS runs our programs, either COM or EXE, the command interpreter finds the program on disk, loads it into memory (processing EXE as needed) and then turns control of the computer over to the program. When the program is finished, it passes control back to the heart of DOS, and DOS reactivates the COMMAND.COM command processor. While the core parts of DOS are permanently held in low-memory locations, most of the command interpreter is kept in high memory, the area that our programs are allowed to use for their data. This is done to avoid permanently tying up much memory for the command interpreter. If a program needs to use the memory where the command interpreter is located, it simply does so (without even being aware that it is overwriting the command interpreter). When a program finishes and hands control back to DOS, DOS checks to see if the command interpreter has been disturbed. If it hasn't, DOS simply starts using it again; if it has, then DOS loads a fresh copy from disk. That's why, for PCs that don't have a hard disk, we sometimes need to have a copy of COMMAND.COM on our working diskettes beside the copy that's on the DOS system diskette that we start the computer with.

That's the essence of how DOS runs programs for us, DOS's own internal command programs, and the command programs—of either COM or EXE type—that are stored on disk. But there is one more type of command that DOS can carry out for us, the batch file command. That's what we'll look at in Section 19.2.

19.2 Batch Processing

Batch files represent a powerful expansion of DOS's ability to carry out commands for us, and they are the last of the four categories of commands that I said DOS performs for us. But properly speaking, batch files are not a fourth kind of program, in the same sense that DOS's internal commands and COM and EXE files are programs. Instead, batch command files are *scripts* of conventional program commands that DOS can carry out for us, treating all the steps in the script as a single unit, which we can ask DOS's command interpreter to perform by entering a single command.

Batch files are identified by the filename extension of BAT. Inside a batch file is simply ASCII data, in the normal format of an ASCII text file. Each line of the text file is a command that the command interpreter will attempt to carry out for us.

The simplest kind of batch file is simply a series of conventional program commands, one after another, which have been gathered into a batch file so that we can conveniently run them in sequence as a single unit. But there is much more to batch file processing than just that.

For one thing, parameters can be used with batch files, just as they can with ordinary programs, and the command interpreter is able to take the parameters that we give with the batch command and pass them on, in whatever way we need, to the programs inside the batch file. But even more sophisticated than that is a whole *batch command language*, which enables the command interpreter to carry out logical steps for us, repeating the execution of programs, or skipping steps depending on errors that happen, or parameters that we give, or whether the files that we need actually exist.

While this isn't the place to go into the full complexities of DOS's batch processing command language, it's worthwhile for us to briefly note that it exists and that it's one of the most powerful tools that is placed into our hands to help us make effective use of DOS. Experienced users of DOS tend to do practically *everything* in their computers through the batch processing facility, simply because it makes it possible to avoid the work of repeatedly entering in a series of commands, or simply type out the standard parameters that a program needs. To give you an idea of how much I use batch files, I just counted the number of different batch files that I've built for myself to use in my own computer—they total an amazing 145 in all! That might be a lot more than you need (I suspect it's more than I really need, too), but it gives you an idea of just how important batch files are to my use of my PC.

If you haven't already mastered the uses of the batch file, I highly recommend that you take the time to do so. I would offer some advice, though. There are advanced parts of the batch command language that can be quite confusing when you first try to study them and figure out how to make good use of them. I'd recommend that you try to learn and take advantage of batch files in an incremental way, first using the simplest features and then, when you're comfortable with them, moving on to see if you have any use for the more advanced ones.

Some Things to Try

1. Using any snooping tool that's available to you (such as DEBUG or my Norton Utilities), browse around inside your computer's COMMAND.COM and find the table of the names of internal commands. Do you find anything unusual? What else, besides the command names, does COMMAND.COM need to hold in the table? (For information on how to use DEBUG or my Norton Utilities, see Chapter 22.)

2. How do you think that a COM-type program can adjust itself to wherever DOS loads it into memory? What are some of the problems that might have to be solved, and how can a program overcome them?

3. If you're familiar with the ins and outs of DOS's batch command language, analyze it to see what you think are the strong points and weak points in it—particularly look for the parts that are awkward to use. Try inventing your own batch language. What features do you think would be the most useful or most powerful?

20

DOS Serving Our Programs

After we've looked at the basic ideas behind DOS and seen how DOS works for us, it's time to see how DOS works for our programs. This chapter is a parallel to Chapter 17 where we covered the services that the ROM-BIOS provides for our programs to use, and here we do the same for DOS. The similarity is strong, of course, but before we progress too far into the subject, we should note the two key differences: one is that, as we saw in Chapter 19, DOS does much to serve us, the computer's users, directly, which the ROM-BIOS does not. The other key difference is that the ROM-BIOS provides services our programs on a very low level, while many of the services that DOS provides for our programs are complex and on quite a high level. That's one of the key themes that will emerge as we tour through the DOS services.

20.1 DOS Services and Philosophy

The services that DOS provides for our programs are subject to a number of conflicting tugs that have pulled them in several directions and which account for some of the contradictory nature that we see in them.

While the ROM-BIOS services that we studied in Chapter 17 were designed in whole, and were created afresh in the best way their designers could manage, the DOS services have had neither the benefit of a single underlying purpose nor of being built in one integrated effort.

Four main influences have shaped the DOS services into being what they are today. Two of the four are other operating systems in whose image DOS has been formed.

The first one, as we learned in Chapter 18, was CP/M. Because CP/M was the dominant operating system for the 8-bit generation of computers that were the PC family's predecessors, and because there was so much CP/M-based software available, DOS was carefully designed to be enough like CP/M to make it relatively easy to adapt old CP/M programs to the PC and DOS. The key to this was having DOS present to programs an appearance very much like CP/M's. The appearance had to include identical or nearly identical operating system services and also a similar philosophy in the design of the disk architecture, so that CP/M programs would not have to be rethought and redesigned from scratch. So DOS's first big influence was the near imitation of CP/M.

The second major influence, which came later, was UNIX. Not long after the appearance of DOS and the PC it became clear that the CP/M framework had too limited a horizon to fulfill the PC's future. The UNIX operating system, on the other hand was highly regarded, and DOS's creator, Microsoft, had deep experience developing their own variation on UNIX called XENIX. When it came time to revamp DOS into something more forward-looking, much of the style and many of the features of UNIX were stirred into DOS. This became DOS's second big influence, mated however well or poorly with the CP/M influence.

Two other factors have played a big part in the character and evolution of DOS. One was the desire to make and keep DOS as hardware nonspecific as possible, to have it be computer-independent and peripheral-device independent. Some of the innermost working parts of DOS must be specifically adjusted to the hardware features of the machines it is working on, but this is isolated to a specifically machine-dependent part, which is called the DOS-BIOS (as distinct from the machine's own ROM-BIOS). Outside of the DOS-BIOS, DOS is basically unaware of the particular characteristics of the computer it's working with. This is beneficial, since it makes DOS and particularly the programs that are designed to use DOS services machine independent. But it also has some important drawbacks, because it tends to remove many of the most useful machine features from the realm of DOS services.

The most painful example concerns the use of the computer's display screen. The services provided by DOS do not give our programs a way to position information on the display screen, so our programs are faced with a choice of either using the screen in a crude teletype-fashion, or of giving up the machine independence that using only DOS services provides. That has prevented us from having a wide range of powerful programs that automatically work on any computer which uses DOS, even computers that aren't fully PC-compatible. In any event, the reluctance to give DOS features such as full-screen display output has been an important influence in DOS's evolution.

The final major influence that has shaped DOS has been the relatively ad-hoc addition of features needed to support the new directions that IBM has taken the PC family in. In general, we can say that rather than being designed in a unified way, features have been added to DOS on an as-needed basis, so that the various parts have not fit together quite as smoothly as they might otherwise have. This ad-hoc approach has brought us versions of DOS which, for example, first had no memory management services at all, and then attempted to add memory management to what had been an unruly every-man-for-himself approach to the use of memory. The same has been true of the services necessary for shared resources and networking and for multi-programming and multi-tasking of programs.

When we stir together these four main influences, out comes the DOS that we know and use in our PCs. Emerging from this DOS stew is the collection of services that DOS provides for our programs to use, which we'll look at in Section 20.2.

TECHNICAL BACKGROUND ❙ ❙ ❙ ▉ ▉ ▉ ▉

20.2 All the DOS Services

Now we're ready to work our way through the main list of services that DOS provides for our programs. As it was in Chapter 17, this section has a Technical Background head that identifies the more technical sections of the book. Read on, though, if you want to get a good impression of what DOS can do for our programs and thus for us. You'll find some of them remarkably interesting. We won't be elaborating on each one individually, because that would make this chapter impossibly long and test your stamina. Instead, we'll take an overview that hits the essence of the services that DOS provides.

The DOS services routines are all invoked by a common interrupt instruction, interrupt number 33 (hex 21), that is used as a master way of requesting the services. The specific services are requested by their service ID number through the simple process of loading the service number in one of the microprocessor's registers, the same way that they are used to request ROM-BIOS services within each service group (such as the video group).

The DOS services are also organized into groups of related services, but in a more informal and less tightly defined way. We'll be covering them in terms of these groups, covering the services roughly in numeric order. One thing to bear in mind is that unlike the ROM-BIOS services— which are *relatively* static—there's a growing list of DOS services, with new ones being added for each release of DOS. That's both good and bad. It's good that new facilities are being added, but it's bad because only a fraction of PC users keep current with the latest release of DOS. This creates problems for programs that want to take advantage of the latest DOS features, since many PCs will be using older versions of DOS. Along the way through our discussion we'll point out the main dependencies in the versions of DOS.

We begin with the most elementary group of DOS services, ones that are designed for what's called "console I/O," or interaction with us, the user. The input services read from the keyboard and the output services display information on the screen, in the simplest and crudest way, treating the screen like a printer, just typing information away on the screen without any sense of position on the screen. These services are a carryover from DOS's predecessor operating system, CP/M. These I/O services are as crude as they are because they are intended to be completely machine-blind, to work uniformly without any awareness of the features of a particular display screen (which is why the screen output services aren't able to position information onto particular locations on the screen).

As part of the CP/M heritage, these services are a screwy hodgepodge. For example, while there is a simple keyboard input service and a simple screen output service, there is also another service that acts as input or output or combines both depending upon which way you use it. All these CP/M-style services were provided to make it relatively easy to translate CP/M programs to DOS with a minimum of difficulty. That was part of an effort to help the PC in its early days when there was lots of CP/M software and little PC software. Now the thinking behind that is long obsolete, but these services remain.

As a part of the same group of elementary DOS services are services that send output to the printer and that read and write data to the communications line (the serial port).

All of the DOS services that fall into this group are matched by similar or in some cases even identical services that the ROM-BIOS provides. Why would DOS duplicate services that the BIOS provides? The answer lies in the theory that programs should turn to DOS for all their services, so that they are not tied to the particular features of one machine. Using DOS services is, in principle, more adaptable and makes it possible for our programs to run on other machines. It also allows for a more flexible handling of I/O, for example, by rerouting data. That's what the DOS MODE command does. It makes it possible for us to direct printer output to the serial port. If our programs used the ROM-BIOS printer services, that wouldn't be possible.

Unfortunately that good principle only works well for very simple input and output operations with the printer, serial port, keyboard, and the screen when we don't care where our data appears on the screen. Most programs have much more sophisticated needs, though, particularly for screen output. DOS lets us down in that regard, for there are no screen-positioning services in DOS's basic complement of services.

While that first group of DOS services provides essentially nothing more than what we already have available from the ROM-BIOS, the next group ventures into the realms that are naturally DOS's—high-level disk services, particularly file input and output.

This group of services is also related to old design features of CP/M, and it's based around an approach that has been obsoleted by new developments in DOS. These older file services are called, in DOS's terminology, the "traditional file services," and they are based on the use of something called a *File Control Block*, or FCB. FCBs are used by our programs to provide the name and identification of the files our programs will work with, and the FCB also holds status information while a file is in use. When our programs use these traditional file services, DOS keeps its records of what's-what inside the FCB, which makes them vulnerable to tinkering by our programs. (Newer file services, which we'll see shortly, hold DOS's control information apart from our programs, which allows for a safer and more reliable operation.)

Let's see the variety of things these FCB-oriented traditional file services can do for us. First, to track down files, there are a pair of services that are used to locate files, which match wild-card filenames that include the characters "?" and "*". One of this pair starts the searching process, and the other is used to continue a search. Our programs can use them either simply to find the first matching filename, or to find the full list of files that match the specification.

Other traditional file services will "open" a file (prepare the stage for reading or writing data) and later "close" it. Then there are services to read or write a file sequentially from beginning to end, or to read and write randomly, skipping to any position in the file.

The console services that we first mentioned and the traditional file services make up the majority of the universal DOS services, the ones that were available in the long-forgotten first version of DOS, version 1.00. There is a small handful of additional services in this universal group, ones that read or set DOS's record of the date and time, one to end a program, one to turn disk verification on and off, and a few others that are less interesting to describe but which perform one technical service or another.

Since these universal services were available from the very beginning, they can be used with every version of DOS. The DOS services that we'll be discussing from this point on have been added in later releases of DOS—mostly beginning with version 2.00—so they can only be used when our programs operate under the appropriate DOS version.

The first of these—and now obviously an essential service—is one that reports which version of DOS a program is running under. That allows our programs to find out if the services that are needed are there. If not, a program can adjust itself to what's available, or at least gracefully exit, reporting that it needs a different version of DOS. Since this service was introduced in DOS 2.00 it would appear that it came too late. Fortunately, thanks to the way that earlier versions of DOS work, if a program uses this service they will in effect report themselves as version number "0"; that's not exactly correct, but at least it properly indicates a pre-2.00 version.

For file operations, DOS 2.00 and all later versions provide an alternative to the FCB-oriented traditional file services. These new file services work with what is called a "handle," which is simply a two-byte number that uniquely identifies each file that is in use by a program. When a program opens a file, using these new file services, DOS gives the program the handle that's used to identify the file for all subsequent file operations until the file is closed. This use of handles allows DOS to keep all critical file-control information safely apart from our programs, which protects it from damage or tinkering. These handle-oriented services provide all the facilities that the FCB-oriented traditional services do, but in a cleaner fashion. Also, our programs are provided with several standard handles—one for writing ordinary information on the display screen, another for error messages (which will appear on the screen, even if the user tells DOS to reroute screen output) and so forth.

In addition, all versions of DOS from 2.00 on provide services that are closely related to the extra structure that has been added to DOS disks: services to create and remove directories, change the subdirectory, move a file's directory entry from one directory to another, and so forth.

There are also services that allow our programs to work more intimately with the computer's devices, without having to break outside of the DOS framework. Previously our programs could either look at devices—such as disks—in a dumb way through DOS or in a smart way entirely on their own. These new device control services bridge the gap. As an example, with these device services our programs can determine whether a particular disk drive is fixed (as a hard disk or RAM disk is) or removable (as a diskette is), and for removable drives, whether the drive can sense when we've switched disks (as the AT model's high-capacity diskette drives can). All this allows our programs to use the computer in a more sophisticated way.

There are also memory services, which allow our programs to work together with DOS in grabbing or releasing the use of memory. Normally each program that runs under DOS has the exclusive use of all of the computer's memory, but these memory services allow a broader sharing of memory.

Also a part of the services provided by DOS 2.00 and later versions are services that allow a program to load and run subprograms and program overlays, and give them a degree of independence from the program that started them.

Most of the additions that have been made to DOS appeared with version 2.00, but other things have been added in later versions. Version 3.00 added extended error codes, which allow our programs to get a much more detailed explanation of what has gone wrong when an error is reported. The main additions that appeared in DOS 3.00 and 3.10, however, concerned themselves with the special problems of using networks. These new services provide the "locking" and "unlocking" of access to all or parts of a file, which make it safe and practical for several computers to share access to the same file (through a network) without interfering with each other. There are similar network-related services that deal with the control and redirection of printer output.

So far, we've just discussed the mainstream of the DOS services, but there are some others that are quite interesting and useful which we don't want to pass over. Probably the most fascinating of all are the "terminate-but-stay-resident" services that allow programs to embed themselves into the computer's memory and remain there while DOS continues to run other programs.

These are the resident programs that PC users have become so familiar with, programs like Prokey and Sidekick, and resident parts of DOS such as the MODE and PRINT commands. There are two stay-resident services that these type of programs use—an old one that's part of the universal DOS services, and a more advanced one that's part of the services introduced with DOS 2.00. Whichever service is used, they make it possible for programs to become resident in a part of the computer's memory that will not be used by subsequent programs that DOS runs.

Related to the operation of these programs is a DOS service that helps a resident program tell if it is safe to swing into operation. In Chapter 17 we discussed the fact that the ROM-BIOS programs must be re-entrant, so that they can be suspended or doubly active without difficulty. DOS, however, does not work in a completely re-entrant way. That means that at certain times if DOS is in the middle of one operation it's not safe for a program to request another DOS service. There is a special DOS service that is used to report whether or not DOS is in that dangerous state. If you use the Sidekick program and have ever had it "chirp" at you, that was the reason why. If we try to activate Sidekick but Sidekick finds that DOS is in its don't-interrupt-me state, it reports this by making a chirping sound on the computer's speaker.

Another interesting DOS service is the one used for country-dependent information, such as the currency symbol (dollar sign, pound sign, etc.) that should be used, or how numbers are punctuated (like this: "12,345.67" or this "12 345,67"), and so forth. DOS is designed to adjust to different national conventions, and it can report the country-specific information to our programs so that they can automatically adjust, if they wish to. Not only can our programs learn the country information from DOS, they can also instruct DOS to change the country code that it is working with.

There are more DOS services that we can discuss here, but what we've seen should give you a sound feeling for the main range of DOS services, as well as a peek at what some of the unusual curiosities in the services are. So, we're ready to pass on to our next adventure, learning how programs are constructed.

21

How Programs Are Built

Among the most fascinating topics that we get to enjoy in covering the PC family is how programs are built. Whether you plan on creating programs for the PC or whether you just use PC programs and want to have the intellectual satisfaction of knowing what's behind your programs, it's just wonderful to know how it's done: the mechanics of creating a program. That's what we'll be covering in this chapter.

Naturally what we'll be doing here is only taking a brief survey of how programs are constructed, so that you can get a feel for what's involved. For deeper understanding of the steps of program building, you can turn to any number of specialty books on programming for the PC family, including my survey book *The Peter Norton Programmer's Guide to the IBM PC*.

21.1 A Little Talk About Programming Languages

In the end, our computers only carry out the instructions that they are given in so-called "absolute" machine language. But people—programmers like you and I—don't write programs in machine language. We write programs in *programming languages*. Programming languages are the tools that programmers use to create programs, just exactly as English and other spoken languages are what writers use to create books.

If we want to understand programming languages, we need to know what they are like and also how they are, one way or another, turned into the machine language that the computer ultimately has to have in order to get anything done. In this section we'll focus on the nature and characteristics of the programming languages themselves. In Section 21.2 we'll consider how the programming languages that humans use are translated into the machine language that the computer uses.

Perhaps the first thing that we need to know about programming languages is the distinction between assembly language and all other programming languages (which are collectively called *high-level languages*).

Assembly language is essentially the same thing as the computer's own machine language, only it's re-expressed in a form that's easier for us to work with. The key thing about assembly language is that a programmer who writes in assembly language is writing out, one-by-one, all the detailed instructions that the computer will follow to carry out a computer program. We've had some brief tastes of assembly language before; for example, in the *Looking at an Interrupt Handler* sidebar in Chapter 6. You'll see some more in Figure 21-1, which shows an assembly language subroutine that I use in my own programs. It's one that will flush the keyboard buffer (an important operation that's needed before a program asks a safety question such as, "OK to delete this file?"; flushing the keyboard buffer protects against a reply being typed in before the question is asked). If you want to know what an assembly language subroutine looks like, complete with all its window-dressing, you can learn a lot just by studying Figure 21-1.

Assembly language is the programmer's equivalent of the computer's own machine language, because each individual machine language instruction can be created with a few assembly language codes. While machine language instructions appear in almost incomprehensible hexadecimal codes, assembly language codes are easily intelligible to experienced programmers. With just a little practice, the rest of us can make sense of at least some of what's written in an assembly language program. For example, the first active instruction in Figure 21-1 is MOV AH,11, which tells the computer to MOVe the number 11 into the register called AH. Now I won't claim that the meaning of MOV AH,11 should be obvious to anyone, but you can see how it shouldn't be too hard to get the hang of reading and even writing this kind of stuff.

To understand what assembly language programming is all about you need to understand that there are essentially three parts to it. The first part is what we mostly think of assembly language as being: individual machine language instructions, written in a form that programmers can understand (like MOV AH,11). In this part of assembly language, each line of program code is directly translated into a single machine language instruction.

The second part of assembly language programming consists of commands that control what's going on, essentially setting the stage for the actual working part of the program. In our example in Figure 21-1, everything before MOV AH,11—for example, the line that reads ASSUME CS:PROG—is part of this stage-setting overhead. In the case of ASSUME

```
; FLUSHKEY - clears DOS keyboard input buffer

;  DOS generic

            PGROUP   GROUP  PROG

            PUBLIC   FLUSHKEY

PROG        SEGMENT BYTE PUBLIC 'PROG'

            ASSUME   CS:PROG

FLUSHKEY    PROC     NEAR

TEST:
            MOV      AH,11      ; check keyboard status
            INT      33         ; function call

            OR       AL,AL      ; if zero
            JZ       RETURN     ;   then done

            MOV      AH,7       ; read one byte
            INT      33         ; function call

            JMP      TEST

RETURN:
            RET

FLUSHKEY    ENDP

PROG        ENDS

            END
```

Figure 21-1. An assembly language subroutine.

CS:PROG, it's indicating what's happening with the CS Code Segment register that we learned about in Chapter 6.

The third part of assembly language programming is a labor-saving device. Whenever a series of instructions is repeated, assembly language allows the programmer to abbreviate many instructions into the form of a "macro instruction," or macro for short. Figure 21-1 doesn't include any macros, but it could. You'll notice that a pair of instructions (MOV AH,X and INT 33) appears twice, with only a slight difference between them (the MOV has a different number in it). These instructions can be replaced with a macro representing the pair of instructions in a single line of code. (The macro facility in assembly language is able to take care of the difference between our two pairs of instructions by substituting a *parameter* with the appropriate number in it; macros can handle this trick and others that are much more elaborate.) In a nutshell, these three elements—program instructions that get turned into machine language code, overhead commands, and macro abbreviations—are the heart of assembly language.

Writing a program in assembly language is an exceedingly long and tedious process. To give you an idea of just how many instructions are involved in a program (not just a brief subroutine, like the one in Figure 21-1), the NU program which is the heart of my Norton Utilities—an example of a *medium*-sized program—has about 20,000 machine language instructions in it. A large and complex program, such as Lotus 1-2-3 or Ashton-Tate's Framework, can easily have over 150,000 separate machine language instructions in it. If any of these programs are written in assembly language, the programmers have to write out that many separate commands to the computer, each of them intricate, each of them a potential "bug" if any detail is done wrong. Think of it; if I write this book and get any of the words speled rwong, it won't destroy the usefulness of the book—but each tiny mistake in a program potentially can destroy the value of the program. And when a program written in assembly language has 150,000 or even 20,000 instructions (also called *lines of code*) in it, the possibilities for error are enormous.

High-level languages—every computer language other than assembly language—are designed to avoid the tedium and error-prone nature of assembly language, by letting the computer do as much of the work as possible of generating the detailed machine language instructions. High-level languages rely on two ideas to make this possible. One is the idea of summarizing many machine language instructions into a single program command. This is the same idea that we've already seen in assembly language macros, but applied in a broader way. The other idea is to remove from sight details that have to do with how the computer operates, but which have nothing to do with the work that we want to accomplish—for example, which registers are used for what in the computer's machine language.

If we want a program to add three numbers together, the program will use one of the computer's general-purpose registers, such as AX, BX, CX, or DX (as we learned in Chapter 6), but it really doesn't have anything to do with what we're trying to accomplish. Assembly language programmers have to concern themselves with pointless details such as choosing which register to use for what (and using it consistently). High-level language programmers are spared that effort. High-level languages are characterized by the fact that they generate lots of machine language code for each program command (a many-for-one saving of human effort, which gives high-level languages their name) and by their avoidance of unnecessary detail (such as specifying which registers and memory addresses are used).

Assembly language and high-level languages each have their own benefits and drawbacks. I've focused on some of the drawbacks of assembly language—mainly that it requires more work to write because it requires more lines of program code to accomplish the same end, and that it's more error-prone because it involves lots of niggling details—and there are others: one important one is that it requires more expertise to write than most high-level languages. However, there are important advantages to it as well: assembly language programs are usually smaller and run faster, because assembly language programmers use their skills to find efficient ways to perform each step, while high-level languages generally carry out their work in a plodding unimaginative way. Also, using assembly language we can tell the computer to do anything it's capable of doing, while high-level languages normally don't give us a way of performing all the tricks that the computer can do. Broadly speaking, we can say that high-level languages let us tap into 90 percent of the computer's skills, while assembly language lets us use 100 percent, if we're clever enough.

So far, I've been talking about high-level languages as a collective category, as if they were all alike. They do have a lot in common, particularly in contrast to assembly language, but there are many important differences among them. Our next step is to look at the varieties of high-level languages, which we can best see by talking about the specific languages that are most important and widely used in programming for the PC family. There are literally hundreds of programming languages, and easily dozens that are used on the PC, but we'll only talk about an important few, BASIC, Pascal, C, and dBASE, using them to paint a representative picture of all high-level languages.

BASIC is the closest thing there is to a universal language for personal computers. Essentially, every personal computer comes complete with BASIC in one form or another, and the IBM Personal Computers even have BASIC built into their ROM programs so that we can use BASIC on the IBM PCs without using disks. You've been seeing plenty of BASIC in this book, since nearly all of the programming examples that I've been showing you are expressed in BASIC.

BASIC isn't a real professional's programming language, but it is good for tinkering around (which is one of the main reasons why we've been using it in our examples) and it's good enough for many program applications that aren't too demanding. For example, two of the programs that I use regularly are written in BASIC: my general ledger accounting program for my business records, and my communications program (PC-Talk) for on-line access.

BASIC's strength is that it is easy to fiddle with, and that it includes features that give us easy access to most of the PC family's special features, such as playing music on the computer's speaker. (Most other high-level languages have only broad general features that can be used on any computer built into them. To use the PC's unique characteristics, programmers using those languages have to use special methods, which usually means tapping into some assembly language. More on that later.) BASIC has some major limitations, which you should know about: it runs much slower than other high-level languages, and it has a severe limitation on how large a program can be built and how much data can be handled. Also, from the point of view of professional craftsmanship, BASIC provides a clumsy set of tools that work against efforts to write well-constructed programs.

In contrast, the Pascal and C languages are very well suited for professional programming. Both languages have the features that are considered to be most useful in helping programmers create well-crafted programs that are reliable and easy to update. To let you see something of what each language is like, I've included two fragments of Pascal and C from my own working programs in Figures 21-2 and 21-3. They'll give you a quick way of getting a feel for what Pascal and C programs look like, and how they are built.

```
{ A Pascal Program to Count Words }

program count (output, input_file);
var
   input_file  : text;
   i           : word;
   thousands   : word;
   units       : word;
   line        : lstring (255);
   alpha       : boolean;
   active      : boolean;

procedure report;
   var
      i, x : word;
   begin
```

```
    write (chr(13));
    if thousands = 0 then
      write (units:7)
    else
      begin
        write (thousands:3);
        write (',');
        x := units;
        for i := 1 to 3 do
          begin
            write (x div 100 : 1);
            x := (x mod 100) * 10;
          end;
      end;
  end;

procedure add_to_count;
  begin
    units := units + 1;
    if units >= 1000 then
      begin
        units := units - 1000;
        thousands := thousands + 1;
      end;
    if (units mod 100) = 0 then
      report;
  end;

begin
  thousands := 0;
  units     := 0;
  reset (input_file);
  while not eof (input_file) do
    begin
      active := false;
      readln (input_file, line);
      for i := 1 to line.len do
        begin
          if active then
            begin
              if line [i] = ' ' then
              active := false;
            end
          else
```

```
                    if line [i] in ['a'..'z','A'..'Z'] then
                      begin
                        active := true;
                        add_to_count;
                      end;
              end;
          end;
      report;
      write (' words.');
    end.
```

Figure 21-2. A sample Pascal program.

```
/* A 'C' Program to Draw a Double-Line Box Outline */

box ()
  {
    drow =  0; dcol = 1; vdup (205,78);
    drow = 24; dcol = 1; vdup (205,78);

for (drow = 1; drow < 24; drow++)
  {
    dcol =  0; vdup (186,1);
    dcol = 79; vdup (186,1);
  }

drow =  0; vdup (201,1);
        dcol = 79; vdup (187,1); ·
drow = 24; dcol =  0; vdup (200,1);
        dcol = 79; vdup (188,1);

if (TEST)
  {
    if (swtchset ("X"))
      {
        int       i;
        unsigned x;
        char s [40];
        int  sl;

        for (i = 1; i <24; i++)
          {
            sl = 0;
```

```
        decint (s,&sl,i,3);
        drow = i;
        dcol = 77;
        vstr (s);
    }

    drow = 24; dcol = 3;

    x = spstart - splowest;
    decint0 (s,x);
    vstr (" ");
    vstr    (s);
    vstr    (" stack used ");

    dcol += 2;
    decint0 (s,poolleft);
    vstr (" ");
    vstr    (s);
    vstr    (" pool left ");

    dcol += 2;
    x = pool - poolsave;
    decint0 (s,x);
    vstr (" ");
    vstr    (s);
    vstr    (" pool used ");

    dcol += 2;
    x = poolends - poolend;
    decint0 (s,x);
    vstr (" ");
    vstr    (s);
    vstr    (" heap used ");
    }
  }
}
```

Figure 21-3. A sample C program.

Pascal and C have many similarities, including the same kind of structural features that assist good programming practices. Both are very suitable for professional use in the building of the largest and most demanding programs. Pascal finds its champions among those who have studied it in school (it is the language most favored for teaching computer science—in fact, it was originally created as a language for teaching, rather than for professional use), and those who have the inexpensive and extremely popular Turbo Pascal compiler. C is favored by programmers who are looking for the utmost in efficiency in a high-level language, and those who want their programs to be in tune with one of the directions in which personal computers are evolving (toward the UNIX operating system, which is highly oriented to the conventions of C).

Personally I have used both Pascal and C in my own programming for the PC family. My popular Norton Utilities programs were first written in Pascal and later converted to C. I am fond of both languages. By itself I consider Pascal to be the better language, cleaner and less error prone; on the other hand, C is particularly good for writing programs that need to be tight and efficient and which work closely with the computer's BIOS and DOS. It's also worth noting that for both the Pascal and C versions of my programs, I had to use assembly language subroutines to perform tasks that couldn't be done in the high-level language. The assembly language subroutine shown in Figure 21-1 is one of those. This illustrates an important point in the creation of professional-quality programs: often the best programming is done primarily in a high-level language (such as Pascal or C), with assembly language used as a simple and expedient means to go beyond the limits of the high-level language.

My own experience points up some of the most important factors in the choice of which programming language should be used to create a particular program. Generally a programming language is chosen on very pragmatic grounds: which languages the programmer already knows (or can easily learn), and how well suited the programming language features are matched to the work that the program has to accomplish. Personal taste, or convenience, also plays a major part in the selection of a programming language—and why shouldn't it?

There is one final group of programming languages that we need to consider, what I will call *application languages*. These are programming languages that are an integral part of major application programs, such as dBASE II and III, Rbase 5000, Framework (with it's ''Fred'' programming language) and so on. This sort of programming language is also sometimes called a *very* high-level language, because it involves a step up in the power of the features that the language provides, thanks to the application (database system or whatever) that it is a part of. Individually each of these application languages is a whole world of its own, with very little similarity between them in their features or programming characteristics. This is very much different from the group of high-level languages which as a whole tend to have a lot of similarity in what they can do and even how they do it.

Probably the most widely known and used kind of application language are spreadsheets, such as the famous 1-2-3 program. Spreadsheets basically *are* programming languages because they allow us to set up and store commands that can be used over and over again—which is the essence of what a programming language is. A spreadsheet programming language is much more specialized than most programming languages: it's more powerful in some ways, thanks to the features that are built into a spreadsheet, and much more limited in other ways, since it has to work within its own spreadsheet context.

In a broad, general way, we can say that application programming languages are divided into two groups. One group, typified by 1-2-3 and other spreadsheets, has a narrow range of uses, restricted to the basic purpose of the application. The members of this group are essentially application programs made partly programmable. The other group, represented by dBASE III or Framework's Fred language, has broader powers, powers that are nearly as general and flexible as ordinary programming languages (like BASIC). The members of this group are essentially full-fledged programming languages that can take advantage of special application features (such as accessing a database).

So far, we've had a short look at the nature of various programming languages themselves. What we need to look at next is how they are implemented, what turns them into usable machine language instructions that our PC computers can carry out. That's what we'll look at next.

21.2 Translating Programs

To make any program, no matter what programming language it was written in, come alive, it has to be translated into the only thing that our PC computers can actually execute: machine language instructions. Our programs are all *translated* from the programming language that the programmer uses into the machine language that the computer uses. There are three main ways that this translation is done. They are called *interpreting, assembling,* and *compiling*. Understanding the basics of each of these three ways of translating programs is important to us, because it helps us comprehend what is going on in our computers, and it helps us understand some of the important limitations of our programs and why some programs run fast and others quite slow.

Interpreting is a special kind of translation, in which our programs are essentially translated into machine language on the fly, as the program is being carried out. It's quite a bit like what's done at international conferences or at the United Nations, where the words of a person speaking are simultaneously translated into other languages.

Basically what happens when a computer program is interpreted is this: the program to be interpreted—we'll call it Program-P—is worked over by an interpreter program, which we'll call Interpreter-I. When we use Program-P, what happens is that the computer is actually running Interpreter-I, and Interpreter-I carries out the steps that Program-P calls for. Interpreter-I scans over the text of Program-P, and step by step, Interpreter-I performs the work that Program-P says is to be done. In effect, Interpreter-I is translating Program-P word by word, step by step, and carrying it out (executing it) on the fly—just the way that simultaneous translators at the United Nations work.

Interpreting is inherently a slow and inefficient process, but a flexible one. It's slow because the translation is being done at the same time the work of the program is being carried out—so time is being taken up performing two tasks (translating the program and doing the program's work) instead of just one. It's inefficient because the translation is done over and over again—not just each time the program is run, but also each time a step of the program is repeated. Since much of the power of programs comes from repeated steps (program *looping* as it's called) there's plenty of repeated translation when a program is interpreted. On the other hand, interpreting is also especially flexible, because an interpreted program can be adjusted, changed, or revised on the fly. Since the translation of an interpreted program is done continuously, changes to an interpreted program can be made on the spot and accommodated immediately.

We have plenty of experience with interpreted programs. The BASIC that we use in our PCs, and practically all the programmable applications—spreadsheets like 1-2-3, and databases like dBASE—are interpreted.

There is an important technical issue concerning interpreted programs that is useful for us to know about. When we run an interpreted program, such as any of the BASIC shown in Appendix A, we think of that program as what's running in the computer. But in a strict sense that's not true. From the point of view of the computer and the operating system (DOS), the program that is being executed is the interpreter (BASIC, or 1-2-3, or whatever) and what we think of as the program is just the *data* that the interpreter is working with. For a BASIC program, the actual program that's running is BASIC.COM, and our "program," e.g., MAZE.BAS is just data for the program. Of course this "data" is a very special kind of data—it's data that *describes the steps that we want the computer to perform*, which is exactly what a program is to us. Under most circumstances this technical distinction is of no importance, but at times we bump into some of its ramifications. For example, because the BASIC interpreter is only designed to work with a single 64K data segment (recall our discussions of memory and data addressing in Chapter 7), interpreted BASIC programs can't be larger than a total of 64K for both the "program" (which is technically data to the interpreter) and the program's own data.

While I've said that BASIC, spreadsheet programs, and dBASE programs are all interpreted, they don't have to be. While the normal form of these languages *is* interpreted, there are some compiled forms as well; we'll come back to this later.

Interpreted programs, as we've said, are translated on the fly, as the program is being run. The other two types of program translation—assembly and compiling—aren't done that way. Instead, they are translated in advance, so that they are permanently converted into the machine language that the computer needs to run the program. Assembly and compiling have more in common than they have differences, so we'll cover that first.

Assembled and compiled programs are translated into the computer's machine language by the program developer, in advance, before anyone uses the program. For these programs, translation is part of the program development process. This means that the user of the program doesn't have to waste time translating the program and also doesn't need to have the translating software. Programs prepared in this way are complete in themselves. In contrast, interpreted programs can only be used if we also have the interpreter as well. We can only run BASIC programs if we have the BASIC interpreter (the program file BASIC.COM).

The people who design an assembler or compiler for any programming language have to make many decisions about how the translator will work. Among the decisions are the exact details of what features the programming language will have. We may think of some programming language—say Pascal—as being just one thing, but that's really not true. To anyone writing programs, a programming language like Pascal is the child of the marriage of two elements: the general form of the programming language (which defines the languages main form, its syntax and principle features) and the specific implementation (which defines the specific features and *modus operandi*, just how it's used). In the example of Pascal, there is a very substantial difference between IBM's own Pascal compiler, and Borland's Turbo Pascal compiler. The differences involve important things such as how the compiler works with character string data (a language feature) and whether programs can be built from separately compiled parts (a *modus operandi* issue).

It's due to these reasons that programmers don't really write programs in some general programming language, they write them using the characteristics of a specific implementation of a general programming language. Programs aren't written in "Pascal" or "C," they are written specifically in Turbo Pascal or Lattice C, or whatever. This is an important thing to know, whether we're setting out to write our own programs, or we just want to understand how the choice of a programming language affects the programs we use.

Most compilers and assemblers for our PC family follow a standard *modus operandi* that was created as part of the overall organization of DOS. In this standard way of operating, the translator converts our programs from the language that the programmer wrote them in, into the computer's machine language instructions, but that doesn't mean that the translated version is just ready to use. Normally it's not. While it has to be converted into executable machine language instructions, the instructions aren't yet fully dressed up for action. We'll see the reason for this—and the additional steps that are needed to get them ready—in Section 21.3. Not all program language translators work that way, however. Some follow their own rules, and have their own conventions for how a program is finally dressed for work. The best-known example of this is Turbo Pascal. With Turbo Pascal, a program can be executed immediately after it's translated. The advantage of this is obvious, but there are real disadvantages as well— translators like that go their own way and don't fit into the DOS world as comfortably as conventional ones do.

In the first section of this chapter we noted the distinction between low-level assembly language and all the high-level languages (Pascal, C, BASIC, etc.). In assembly language a programmer must write out the equivalent of every machine language instruction that the finished program will perform. In a high-level language, the programmer can write a program in terms of larger steps, steps that will be translated into many individual machine language instructions. In keeping with this distinction, the translators for assembly language are called *assemblers*, and the translators for high-level languages are called *compilers*. Depending upon what we can focus on, the distinction is either important or inconsequential. From one point of view, both are the same: they convert the programmer's form of the program (the *source code*) into machine language instructions (the *object code*), and there is no difference between a compiler and an assembler.

From another point of view, a compiler is given the very creative and demanding task of deciding what kind of machine language instructions will be used, and making strategic decisions about how the computer's resources are to be used (for example, deciding what the registers will be used for). On the other hand, an assembler performs a very mechanical and uncreative conversion of the programmer's instructions into the exactly equivalent machine instructions. From this perspective, a compiler is a very complex beast, and there is an enormous potential for differences in the *quality* of a compiler (one compiler might generate very efficient code, while another could produce lousy code), differences that just don't apply to assemblers.

When a programmer works with a compiler or assembler, the programmer's source code is fed into the translator, it's checked for errors, and if it's in workable shape, out comes the machine language object code as a result. You can identify any object code files that you might come across by their filename extension, OBJ. The object code is ultimately for use by the computer itself, to be turned into a finished, executable program. For the programmer's own use, the compiler or assembler spits out any error messages indicating flaws in the program (not logical flaws—bugs— which are the responsibility of the programmer, but syntactical flaws, such as misspelled keywords, or missing punctuation, stuff like that).

Because an assembly language programmer is working very closely with the computer's basic skills (it's machine language instructions), an assembler gives the programmer lots of technical information about the results of the assembly. To give you an idea of what it looks like, Figure 21-4 shows the assembler listing for the assembly language program shown in Figure 21-1. One of the things that an assembly listing shows the programmer is the exact machine language instructions, shown in hexadecimal. Normally a compiler does not give a programmer anywhere near so much technical information—after all, one of the main purposes of using a high-level language is to avoid working with extraneous technical details. But, if a programmer wants to know more about the machine language code that a compiler is generating, most compilers are prepared to print out an assembly language equivalent of the object code that has been created. This object code listing allows an experienced programmer to evaluate the quality of the code that the compiler generates, and it can be helpful in deciding which way of writing a program is most efficient.

Depending on how we look at the process of translating a program from source code to object code, we can think of compilers and assemblers as very different creatures, or two minor variations on the same theme. Either way, compilers and assemblers are charged with the task of converting what programmers write into what the computer can perform. After that comes the final steps of putting a program together into a working whole, and that's what we'll cover next.

```
                              ; FLUSHKEY - clears DOS keyboard input buffer

                              ;  DOS generic

                                      PGROUP   GROUP PROG

                                      PUBLIC  FLUSHKEY

0000                          PROG    SEGMENT BYTE PUBLIC 'PROG'

                                      ASSUME  CS:PROG

0000                          FLUSHKEY PROC    NEAR

0000                          TEST:
0000  B4 0B                           MOV     AH,11   ; check keyboard status
0002  CD 21                           INT     33      ; function call
0004  0A C0                           OR      AL,AL   ; if zero
0006  74 06                           JZ      RETURN  ;   then done
0008  B4 07                           MOV     AH,7    ; read one byte
000A  CD 21                           INT     33      ; function call
000C  EB F2                           JMP     TEST

000E                          RETURN:
000E  C3                              RET

000F                          FLUSHKEY ENDP

000F                          PROG    ENDS

                                      END
```

Segments and groups:

```
             N a m e              Size   align   combine class

PGROUP . . . . . . . . . . . .   GROUP
   PROG . . . . . . . . . . . .   000F   BYTE    PUBLIC  'PROG'
```

Symbols:

```
             N a m e              Type   Value   Attr

FLUSHKEY . . . . . . . . . . .   N PROC 0000    PROG      Global  Length
                          =000F
RETURN . . . . . . . . . . . .   L NEAR 000E    PROG
TEST . . . . . . . . . . . . .   L NEAR 0000    PROG
```

```
Warning Severe
Errors  Errors
0       0
```

Figure 21-4. An assembly listing.

21.3 Putting Programs Together

One of the key elements in practical programming, really like practically anything, is the old principle of divide and conquer—any task becomes more manageable when it is broken down into distinct parts. Programming works that way too, and so the process of program development has been set up in a way that makes it practical to break a program into functional, modular parts, and then piece together the whole program from its parts. That's basically what we have to talk about in this section: the mechanisms that make it possible to put programs together from parts, and how these mechanisms work.

Three things form the center of the idea of divide-and-conquer in programming: *subroutines, linking,* and *libraries.*

Subroutines, as we know, are fragments of a program that are relatively self-contained. They perform some particular part of the work that's to be done, turned into a separate unit as part of the overall design of a larger program. One of the key reasons for creating subroutines is to subdivide and therefore simplify the task of creating a program.

Once we decide to break a program down into logical parts and make those parts separate subroutines, the next logical step is to entirely remove the subroutines from the main program. After all, the point of subroutines is to reduce the logical clutter in a program by isolating work into discrete components, the subroutines. If we're going to sweep part of the program off into a logical corner (a subroutine) to tidy up the design and organization of the program, we might as well move it out of the way entirely. This is done by extracting the subroutine from the body of a program, and treating it as a separate entity. We take the subroutines out of a program, and treat them by themselves—which includes compiling or assembling them on their own. This idea of *separate compilation* is a key adjunct to the idea of creating subroutines in the first place. Since we're breaking down our program into logical modules, distinct components, we might as well make them completely separate by putting the source code (what the programmer writes) into their own disk files, and compiling (or, in the case of assembly language, assembling) them as separate items.

There are two main advantages to separating out our subroutines. The one is that it shortens and simplifies the source code for a main program. The other is that it makes the subroutines easily available for use by any program. If we had to keep our subroutines inside each program, then when we created a new program that could use some of our old subroutines, we'd have to go to the trouble of copying the source code for the subroutines into the new program. By separating out our subroutines (and compiling them separately) we make them available to any program we create. We also save time and trouble by only having to compile a subroutine once and not over and over again each time we create or revise a program that the subroutine is used in.

This whole idea of subroutines separately compiled requires, though, that we have a way of combining the different parts of a program—its separately compiled subroutines—into one piece. This is done in a process that's called *link editing* performed by a program called LINK, which comes as a part of DOS. The process of link editing works something like the way we used to build models cut out of paper—the sort of thing where you fit Tab A into Slot A. A program that needs to use a subroutine named X has in it, in effect, an empty slot marked X; and a separately compiled subroutine has the computer equivalent of a tab marked X. The job of the link-editor program LINK is to fit the two together.

Link editing involves making all the connections between different pieces of a program to make them work as a whole. In the last section, we mentioned that compilers and assemblers generate their machine language instructions in a form called *object code* which isn't completely ready to be run as a program. The reason for this is that object code is set up in the form that's needed for link editing, with all the "tab" and "slot" markings. The job of the link editor, LINK, is to gather together all the parts of object code, make the connections between them, and then spit out the results in a form that finally is ready to be run in the computer. Even when a program doesn't have any subroutine connections that need to be made, standard DOS compilers and assemblers still translate their programs in the object code format, just as a standard way of working.

We can see that creating a program involves two basic steps (besides the little step of our writing the program in the first place): translating the program's source code into object code, with a compiler or assembler, and then converting the object code into a finished program, with the link-editor LINK.

It's worth pausing to note here that we're talking about the standard DOS way of creating programs, which is used by most programming language versions. But not every one follows the DOS standard. For example, the extremely popular Turbo Pascal compiler goes its own way, and avoids the use of object code and linking. Instead, Turbo Pascal (and its cousins) directly creates executable programs, in effect combining compiling and linking into one step. This has the advantage of simplifying and speeding up the process of developing a program, but it also eliminates much of the flexibility that comes with separate compilation and link editing.

If we create lots and lots of subroutines, we can be faced with the problem of having lots and lots of separate object code files cluttering up our disks—which can turn into a real nuisance. There is nothing uncommon about a programmer developing dozens of subroutines, and for a large programming project, or for a programming language that makes liberal use of built-in subroutines, the number can easily grow into the hundreds. For example, my Norton Utilities are built out of approximately 175 subroutines and program modules—that's just too many to conveniently keep track of.

The solution to that practical problem is what are called libraries of object modules. An object library is a single disk file that can contain the object code for any number of program subroutines. After a subroutine is written, the programmer compiles (or assembles) the subroutine into a separate, distinct object code file, and then uses a special DOS program called LIB which takes the object code and stuffs it into a library together with other subroutines. LIB makes it possible for us to gather together the clutter of many subroutine object files into one tidy package, an object library file. You can identify any object libraries that you come across by their filename extension, which is (naturally enough) LIB.

So far we've seen all the pieces that make up the puzzle of how programs are built. Now we will put the pieces together to see them in action. I'll run through a little example from my own programming work to illustrate all the main steps of the process.

We'll begin with the assembly language subroutine that we first saw at the beginning of this chapter, FLUSHKEY. After FLUSHKEY has been written by the programmer (me), the programmer's source code is stored in a file named FLUSHKEY.ASM. Each programming language has its own standard filename extension that's used for source code and for assembly language, its ASM. To assemble FLUSHKEY, we use the assembler program, named MASM (which is short for Macro Assembler), with a command like this:

```
MASM FLUSHKEY
```

That gives us an object file, named FLUSHKEY.OBJ. Next we can add FLUSHKEY to our object library, which I'll call OURLIB just to identify it:

```
LIB OURLIB+FLUSHKEY
DEL FLUSHKEY.OBJ
```

You'll notice the command line for LIB had a plus sign (+) in it. That's our way of telling LIB to *add* FLUSHKEY to the library. There are other operations that LIB can perform for us as well. You'll also see that after adding FLUSHKEY to our library I deleted the object file, since we no longer needed it.

That takes care of how we work with subroutines. The next step is to show you how we compile and link a main program. For our example, we'll consider a program written in the programming language C called NU. The source code file for that program will be called NU.C with the standard filename extension for a C program. For the C compiler that I happen to be using, there are two steps to the compiler, named MC1 and MC2. It's common for compilers to be broken into separate pieces that work in conjunction, and this compiler is one of them. So here is how we would compile my NU program:

```
MC1 NU.C
MC2 NU
```

After both of those compiler steps are finished, we will have a program object file named NU.OBJ. To link edit it into a finished program, we use the LINK program. Our example actually shows both of the two ways that the link editor can find the parts it needs to put together to make the complete program. One way, as we've mentioned, is by using a library (in this case the library OURLIB). The other way is for us to tell LINK the names of some specific object files that it needs to gather together (in this case there will be two of them: one is our NU.OBJ object file and the other is a standard object file used for all C programs, called C.OBJ). So, our link editing goes like this:

```
LINK C+NU,NU,,OURLIB
```

To fully understand what's going on here, you have to know more about all the details of program building. But even in this simple outline, we've seen the essence and all the key parts of how programs are built and put together.

In Chapter 22 we'll get into the business of snooping, tinkering, and exploring, and that includes snooping inside of some of the programs that we use—it's another way of gaining insight into the subject of this chapter, how programs are built.

Some Things To Try

1. In this chapter we briefly mentioned the function of the LIB program. In order to manage a library well, LIB has to have a variety

of skills. What are they? Work up a list of the separate functions that you think LIB needs to perform for us.

2. Batch command files are the key to combining program steps like the ones we've mentioned here for building programs. Try your hand at writing a batch file to assemble a program and add it to an object library. Write another to compile and link a program. If you know how to use batch file logic, make your batch files adjust to any errors that occur.

22

Exploring and Tinkering

On the surface of things there is only so much that we can discover; but when we dig down just a little, we can unearth *wonders*. That's pretty much what this chapter is about: how we can dig into the PC and explore and tinker with it. In this chapter we'll cover the good reasons why it's not just interesting but truly valuable to know how to dig below the surface of our PCs and we'll get acquainted with two of the tools that can be used to do this exploring.

22.1 The Point of Exploring and Tinkering

There are more reasons than you might imagine why it's to our benefit to know how to explore, discover, change, and tinker with our PCs, as we'll be discussing in this chapter. The best reason of all is the reason that doesn't have a direct, immediate benefit: exploring widens and deepens our knowledge of the PC family, and that simply makes us more proficient PC users, better able to use the full range of the PC's powers, better able to avoid problems with our PCs, and better able to deal with problems when they do occur.

Among the things that we can discover in tinkering with our PCs is how the data is organized on our disks—both the structure of the disk itself, and the internal structure of the data files that our programs work with. Similarly, we can discover a great deal about how our programs work, how they manage their data, their use of memory, and other parts of the computer's resources by some hunting and exploring. There are often hidden wonders inside programs—particularly some very interesting messages—that we can unveil.

There are also direct benefits to tinkering, as well. If our disks are damaged, or if the data in a file is "corrupted" so that the program working with that data rejects it, refusing to work with it, sometimes we can use our tinkering skills to repair the damage. This isn't always possible, of course, but sometimes we can hammer things back into shape and carry on.

So whether it's to expand our knowledge, to satisfy our curiosity, or to attempt emergency repairs, the ability to explore and tinker can be quite worthwhile.

There are many program tools that we can use to do our exploring and tinkering, but we're going to focus in on just two, the two that are most widely available and that provide a good spectrum of features: DOS's DEBUG program, and the NU program from my Norton Utilities set.

Of the two explore-and-tinker tools that we'll be looking at, DEBUG is the more powerful and also the harder to use. To a certain extent, of course, those two properties go hand in hand: powerful features almost necessarily are accompanied by complex and harder-to-use commands. But that isn't the only reason why DEBUG is the more demanding one, and we ought to take a moment to see the whys and wherefores of that.

Any program tool—from 1-2-3 to the tinkering tools we're discussing here—is designed to serve some particular need. In the case of DEBUG, the technical needs of advanced programmers was the target that DEBUG aimed for. As a free program that's included with every copy of DOS, DEBUG wasn't intended to be the ultimate programmer's tool, just a good basic tool for programmers. Since DEBUG was targeted to advanced programmers, and since it wasn't planned as a top-of-the-line luxury tool, its features are technical, and its command structure and user interface is crude—but it gets the job done.

While DEBUG is crude but powerful, my NU program is much simpler but also less powerful. NU was designed to be as slick and easy to use as possible for (relatively) nontechnical PC users. I made NU this way because I saw that most programming utility tools were designed by top-flight programmers for other top-flight programmers. The needs of these "high-end " users were being well met, but the utility needs of the rest of us had been neglected—and that's why I focused my NU program on clarity and ease of use.

Together, DEBUG and NU give us a good example of the range of features that we can find in utility programs that allow us to tinker and explore. There are many others available, though, and you ought to know about them in case you want to widen your choices. Among them are Trace-86 from Morgan Computing, IBM's Professional Debug Facility, and Periscope from Data Base Decisions. These three are simply the ones that I'm familiar with and know to be good. A little research on your part (particularly in programmer-oriented sources, such as the excellent PC Tech Journal) will turn up others.

22.2 Working with DEBUG

In this section we'll be looking at the things we can do with the DEBUG program to dig inside our PCs. DEBUG is one of the utility programs included with every version of DOS, so that everyone who has a member of the PC family has a copy of DEBUG to work with.

As I explained in the last section, DEBUG is a tool that is technically oriented, designed to serve the needs of programmers and others who have no difficulty working with the ins and outs of the PC's microprocessor. This includes an assumption in DEBUG that we are comfortable using hexadecimal numbers and segmented addresses. Almost everything that we can do with DEBUG calls for us to specify our commands in hex, and for us to enter and interpret plenty of segmented addresses (also given in hex). Hopefully that's no barrier for you, but if it is you may want to forget about using DEBUG entirely. If it is, skip over this section and pass on to the next, where we'll look at a more civilized tool, NU.

DEBUG is a powerful tool, with many aspects to it, and a great deal more power than we're interested in exploring here. You've already had a taste of some of that with the DEBUG U-unassemble command, which can be used to decode the hexadecimal of absolute machine language instructions into the more intelligible assembly language format. We saw that feature of DEBUG when we looked at interrupt drivers in Chapter 6. There are also features that allow us to do the opposite of that—the A-assemble command, which acts as a crude assembler, turning assembly language statements into machine language—and features that let us trace our way through a program, watching it execute and seeing the results of each step. Those commands and more like them are fascinatingly powerful, but they're more than we can bite off here. Digging into them really belongs in a book on advanced programming techniques.

What we will look at here are some of DEBUG's commands that allow us to snoop and explore. We'll begin with some background on DEBUG.

The DEBUG program works with a minimum of fuss (and a minimum of help to us), which takes a little getting used to. When we fire up the program, with the simple command DEBUG, it responds by just giving us its command prompt, similar to DOS's command prompt. DEBUG's prompt is even more terse: it's just a hyphen:

\-

Whenever we see that DEBUG command prompt, DEBUG is ready for us to give it a command. All of DEBUG's commands are abbreviated into a single letter. We might as well start by learning the command that we use to finish using DEBUG and return to DOS: it's the Q (for Quit) command.

For snooping around with DEBUG, one of the main commands that we'll be using is the D-display command. D tells DEBUG to display some of the contents of the computer's memory. DEBUG shows it in a form that combines hexadecimal and character format. Here's an example of what the D command might show us:

```
2B68:0100  66 7F 06 06 0F 00 00 00-0A 0E 00 00 7F 60 60 60   f............'''
2B68:0110  7E 03 03 63 3E 00 00 00-0A 0E 00 00 1C 30 60 60   ˉ..c)........0''
2B68:0120  7E 63 63 63 3E 00 00 00-0A 0E 00 00 7F 63 03 06   ˉccc)........c..
2B68:0130  0C 18 18 18 18 00 00 00-0A 0E 00 00 3E 63 63 63   ............)ccc
2B68:0140  3E 63 63 63 3E 00 00 00-0A 0E 00 00 3E 63 63 63   )ccc)......)ccc
2B68:0150  3F 03 03 06 3C 00 00 00-0A 0E 00 00 00 18 18 00   ?...(...........
2B68:0160  00 00 18 18 00 00 00 00-0A 0E 00 00 00 18 18 00   ................
2B68:0170  00 00 18 18 30 00 00 00-0A 0E 00 00 06 0C 18 30   ....0.........0
```

This display information appears in three parts: on the left is the memory address of the data that DEBUG is showing us; in the middle is the data in hex format; on the right, are the characters that correspond to the hex information shown. DEBUG "censors" the character data, only showing ordinary text characters. This has its good and bad aspects: it doesn't show us all the interesting characters that lurk in our computer's data, but it does insure that we can copy the data to a printer without accidentally sending a control code that makes the printer act up. (By contrast, the data displays generated by the NU program, which we'll cover in Section 22.3, show every character there is so we can see it all, but we may not necessarily be able to get a printed copy of it.)

DEBUG displays any data that it has in memory, but that can be just about anything. As we saw in Chapter 6, it can look at the beginning of the computer's memory (say to look at the interrupt vectors), or at the higher reaches of memory where the ROM-BIOS routines are stored. We'll take a look at some of those shortly. In the middle, we can display DEBUG ordinary program data area; this is where we have DEBUG load programs from disk, or other disk data, so that we can inspect it.

For example, if we want to use DEBUG to browse around inside DOS's command interpreter COMMAND.COM, we can tell DEBUG to load COMMAND.COM into memory when it starts up, and then display the beginning of the contents of COMMAND.COM, like this:

```
DEBUG COMMAND.COM
-D
```

When we do that, we'll get a display like this (I've skipped on from the beginning of COMMAND.COM to a part that we can recognize):

```
2B82:1180  C4 06 56 8B F2 C7 44 01-00 0D 5E CF 00 00 00 00   ..V...D...^.....
2B82:1190  0D 0A 0D 0A 54 68 65 20-49 42 4D 20 50 65 72 73   ....The IBM Pers
2B82:11A0  6F 6E 61 6C 20 43 6F 6D-70 75 74 65 72 20 44 4F   onal Computer DO
2B82:11B0  53 0D 0A 56 65 72 73 69-6F 6E 20 33 2E 31 30 20   S..Version 3.10
2B82:11C0  28 43 29 43 6F 70 79 72-69 67 68 74 20 49 6E 74   (C)Copyright Int
2B82:11D0  65 72 6E 61 74 69 6F 6E-61 6C 20 42 75 73 69 6E   ernational Busin
2B82:11E0  65 73 73 20 4D 61 63 68-69 6E 65 73 20 43 6F 72   ess Machines Cor
2B82:11F0  70 20 31 39 38 31 2C 20-31 39 38 35 0D 0A 20 20   p 1981, 1985..
```

The DEBUG D-display command, by itself, will just show us 128 bytes from its current work area. If we want it to show us another area, we can give it the address we want it to show, like this: D 1180 (which is what I used to show the part of COMMAND.COM that you see above), or like this: D 0:0 (which is what we'd do to get the very beginning of memory). To have it show more than 128 bytes at a time, we just add the letter L (for length) and indicate how many bytes we want shown, which we have to give in hex. For example, this command D F800:0 L 300 shows hex 300 (or 768) bytes, starting high in memory in the ROM-BIOS area.

All by itself, this D-display command can be used to explore a great deal of the PC's memory and disk data, but there are other DEBUG commands to help us find even more.

One DEBUG command allows us to search through data, which can be very helpful in hunting down messages that we know are stored inside a program. If we know the text of one message, and use DEBUG to hunt it down, we're likely to find the area where other messages are stored, and studying these messages can tell us a lot.

The command that this is done with is the S-search command. Like the D-display command, we enter the search command with the initial letter S, followed by whatever memory address and length we want the search to act over. Following that, we tell DEBUG what we want it to search for. We can give DEBUG that either in hex or, if we're looking for characters, the string of characters enclosed in quotes. To let you see what it's like, here's an example which I'll explain in a second:

```
S F000:0 L FFFF "1790"
```

The use for that interesting little command came up when a neighbor of mine had his PC/AT act up. It started giving him an error message number 1790—but he couldn't tell just what it was for. Since the message appeared when his machine was first turned on, I knew that the message was part of the Power-On Self-Test (or POST) routines that are stored in the computer's ROM-BIOS. To see if we could learn more about what this message meant, I used DEBUG to hunt for where the message was located, with the command you see above, searching through all of the ROM-BIOS area (from address F000:0 for a length of hex FFFF, the full 64K of the ROM-BIOS area) for the text "1790". DEBUG located the message, and told me where it was, with this message:

F000:E3DB

That told me where the message was stored. Then I used the D-display command to see the full message and anything around it. I gave DEBUG a starting address a short ways ahead of where it found the "1790", so that we could see more of the surrounding messages. This is the D-display command I entered: D F000:E390, and here is what DEBUG showed me:

```
F000:E390  72 0D 0A 31 37 38 30 2D-44 69 73 6B 20 30 20 46   r..1780-Disk 0 F
F000:E3A0  61 69 6C 75 72 65 0D 0A-31 37 38 31 2D 44 69 73   ailure..1781-Dis
F000:E3B0  6B 20 31 20 46 61 69 6C-75 72 65 0D 0A 31 37 38   k 1 Failure..178
F000:E3C0  32 2D 44 69 73 6B 20 43-6F 6E 74 72 6F 6C 6C 65   2-Disk Controlle
F000:E3D0  72 20 46 61 69 6C 75 72-65 0D 0A 31 37 39 30 2D   r Failure..1790-
F000:E3E0  44 69 73 6B 20 30 20 45-72 72 6F 72 0D 0A 31 37   Disk 0 Error..17
F000:E3F0  39 31 2D 44 69 73 6B 20-31 20 45 72 72 6F 72 0D   91-Disk 1 Error.
F000:E400  0A 32 01 04 00 00 80 00-00 00 00 00 00 31 01 11   .2...........1..
```

Seeing the full text of those messages, my friend was able to get a clearer idea of just what had gone wrong with his machine.

This is just one real-life example of the variety of things that DEBUG can do for us in exploring our computers.

If you want to learn more about what DEBUG can do for you, you'll have to be prepared to cope with some messy technical details, but DEBUG will reward your efforts with a wealth of information. While we don't have space here for me to explain all the wonders of DEBUG to you, I can help you by listing the DEBUG commands that are most important for exploring and tinkering. We've already seen the D-display and S-search commands. To make changes to data, you'll need to learn about the E-enter and F-fill commands. To read and write data that's stored on your disks, you'll need to learn about the L-load and W-write commands. If you learn the basics of these DEBUG commands, you'll be able to inspect and change, and explore and tinker with, any data in your computer.

Now it's time for us to move on to another tool, one whose powers have a different dimension than DEBUG's, and one that can be quite a bit easier to learn to use.

22.3 Working with NU

NU, like DEBUG, is a program with more than a few aspects, a program that can show you many things about your PC's disk data. One important thing to know, though, is that NU is focused completely on your computer's disks—so it can't be used to explore the PC's own memory, and it doesn't concern itself with the computer's machine language instruction set (the way DEBUG's U-unassemble and A-assemble commands do). But, for telling you things about your computer's disks, NU probably has no equal.

To use NU, if you're not already familiar with it, you simply select from its menu choices by pressing the function or number keys; the *Esc* key is used to jump back to a prior menu. Within a data display, the cursor arrow keys and paging keys will move you around.

While NU, like most programs, has lots of features, the part that's of most interest to us here is found in NU's Menu 2. We'll start by looking at selection 2.2, which displays technical information about any disk. You'll see a sample of it in Figure 22-1.

```
Menu 2.2
                    Display Disk Technical Information
        Drive C:

        Basic storage capacity:
          20 million characters (megabytes)
          17% of disk space is free

        Logical dimensions:
          Sectors are made up of 512 bytes
          Tracks are made up of 17 sectors per disk side
          There are 4 disk sides
          The disk space is made up of 614 cylinders
          Space for files is allocated in clusters of 4 sectors
          There are 10,405 clusters
          Each cluster is 2,048 bytes
          The disk's root directory can hold 512 files

        Press any key to continue...


         Currently selected:  No file or disk sector selected
                    Drive C:  Directory: PROGRAMS
```

Figure 22-1. Sample of disk technical information from NU.

What we see in menu 2.2 is an outline of all the basic information about a disk—its total amount of space (and the proportion that's available for use), plus the logical dimensions that make up the disk, which we learned about in Chapter 8: the size of the sectors, how many sectors per track, and so forth. That's absolute information about the disk. Menu 2.2 also shows the key DOS-related information, such as how big the DOS clusters are (which affects how efficiently the disk is used) and other items such as how many file entries the disk's root directory can accommodate.

Menu 2.2 provides us with a small gold mine of basic information that we can use to discover the dimensions and working of any disk we have, including RAM disks. Using menu 2.2, we can unveil how each disk is structured.

Even more fascinating than the disk technical information is the disk space map, which appears as menu selection 2.3. You'll see an example of that in Figure 22-2.

The disk map gives us a representative drawing of how the entire space on the disk is used. Each position on the map represents a small portion of the whole disk storage space. (On a diskette, or any disk where there are fewer than 500 disk space clusters, each cluster is individually and exactly represented on the map. When there are more than 500 clusters, positions on the map represent approximate fractions of the disk space.) The hatched portion of the map shows the unused free space on the disk, while the small squares show the space that's in use. If the disk has any ''bad-track '' areas, they are shown too, as you'll see in Figure 22-2.

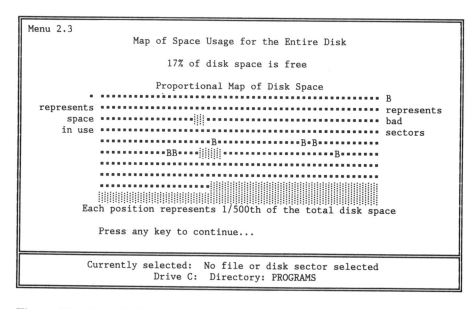

Figure 22-2. Sample disk map from NU.

While the map we've seen shows the status of the entire disk, we can get a similar map that shows the relative location on the disk of each individual file (or subdirectory, since they are stored just like files). These individual file maps can show us where a file is (interesting, but essentially useless), tell us if it's stored all together in one place or scattered over the disk, and also simply give us a quick visual impression of how big the file is. You'll see one of these individual file maps in Figure 22-3.

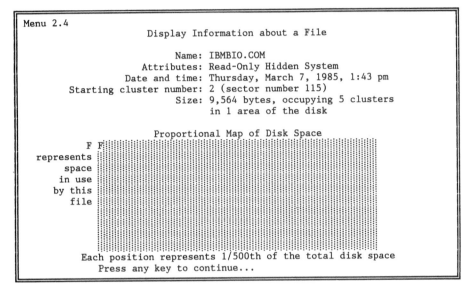

```
Menu 2.4
                        Display Information about a File

                        Name: IBMBIO.COM
                  Attributes: Read-Only Hidden System
                Date and time: Thursday, March 7, 1985, 1:43 pm
      Starting cluster number: 2 (sector number 115)
                        Size: 9,564 bytes, occupying 5 clusters
                              in 1 area of the disk

                        Proportional Map of Disk Space
           F  F
   represents
       space
       in use
     by this
        file




             Each position represents 1/500th of the total disk space
             Press any key to continue...
```

Figure 22-3. Individual file map from NU.

The display of information about a file that shows up in menu selection 2.4 is more than just a map of where the file is, as you'll see in Figure 22-3. It also has listed all the information that's available about the file from the file's directory entry—filename, size, date and time marking, and also some information that's not otherwise readily available, such as the sector and cluster IDs where the beginning of the file is stored.

If we want to take a look at the contents of any file on the disk, or any sector's data (whether it's associated with a file or not), NU will show it to us in menu selection 2.5. You'll see an example in Figure 22-4.

NU can display our disk's data organized in three ways. Figure 22-4 shows it in one of three, a combination of hex and character data, similar to the way that DEBUG displays data. As you'll see in Figure 22-4, the same data is shown twice: in hex format on the left hand side, and in character format on the right hand side. This allows us to inspect data in its most absolute form (hex) and also to easily recognize any text messages that might be lurking there.

The example that I chose for Figure 22-4 is one of my favorites, because it illustrates two of the most interesting reasons for snooping inside files. This data display, which is taken from an IBM utility program called DOS Tree Display, reveals that it's an IBM program and it even shows the name of the author: Robert A. Flavin. If you simply used this program, you won't know who wrote it, or even that IBM owns it—that's never displayed to the user, but it's here for us to see, through the magic of a snooping tool.

```
TREED.COM sectors 27,559-27,562         Cursor at offset 0, hex 0
E9B7020D 0A444F53 20547265 65204469 73706C61 790D0A28 i7...DOS Tree Display..(
63292043 6F707972 69676874 20496E74 65726E61 74696F6E c) Copyright Internation
616C2042 7573696E 65737320 4D616368 696E6573 20436F72 al Business Machines Cor
706F7261 74696F6E 20313938 340D0A62 7920526F 62657274 poration 1984..by Robert
20412E20 466C6176 696E2020 20524942 4F0D0A1A 00770000 A. Flavin   RIBO....w..
00000000 00000000 00000000 00000000 00000000 00000000 ......................
00000000 00000000 00000000 00000000 00000000 00000000 ......................
00000000 00000000 00000000 00000000 00000000 00000000 ......................
00000000 00000000 00000000 00000000 00000000 00000000 ......................
00000000 00000000 00000000 00000000 00000000 00000000 ......................
00000000 00000000 00000000 00000000 00000000 00000000 ......................
00000000 00000000 00000000 00000000 00000000 00000000 ......................
00000000 00000000 00000000 00000000 00000000 00000000 ......................
00000000 00000000 00000000 00000000 00000000 00000000 ......................
00000000 00000000 00000000 00000000 00000000 00000000 ......................
00000000 00000000 00000000 00000000 00000000 00000049 .....................I
6620796F 75207765 72652073 7570706F 73656420 746F2068 f you were supposed to h
61766520 65787465 6E74696F 6E73206F 6E206469 72656374 ave extentions on direct
6F727920 6E616D65 732C2074 68657265 20776F75 6C640D0A ory names, there would..
68617665 20626565 6E206578 616D706C 6573206F 66206974 have been examples of it
20696E20 74686520 444F5320 6D616E75 616C210D 0A245452 in the DOS manual!..$TR
45454420 2D2D2044         Press Enter for help      EED -- D
```

Figure 22-4. Sample of disk data display in hex from NU.

I often find hidden information like this when I go looking inside programs. You'll find all kinds of interesting things. In one case I encountered a salute to the wives of a program's authors. Back to the case at hand, we can see, at the bottom of Figure 22-4, an irritated (and misspelled) message from Bob Flavin, complaining about the use of filename extensions in directory names. Oddly enough, the program never seems to issue this message, but there it is to see.

One of the things that NU lets you do with the data that's displayed as you see it in Figure 22-4 is to make direct changes to the disk data, by just typing right over it—a very convenient way to change data. All we have to do is to move the cursor to the part we want to change (on either the hex or the character side of the screen) and type our changes in. This ability to type changes right over existing data makes NU, and other programs like it, a much more convenient tool for modifying disk data than DEBUG is. This makes "patching" a disk—making changes to the data—quite convenient.

When I first began mentioning the data display in menu selection 2.5, I said that there were three ways that NU can show us a disk's data. One of the other two ways is in pure text file format. That's similar to the character side of the hex-and-character display, but it shows the data divided into lines, just the way it appears in text files—that can be very helpful in trying to make sense out of text data. The third format, which you'll see in Figure 22-5, interprets the data as directory entries. This makes it possible for us to easily decode the information in a subdirectory when we come across it.

```
Sector 84 in root directory shown in directory format

Filename Ext    Size      Date        Time   Cluster Attributes
=======.==  ====  ======  ====  ===========  ======  ======================
PC-TALK                   Sun Jul  7 85 12:02 pm   5,136 Directory
PNCI                      Sun Jul  7 85 12:02 pm   5,282 Directory
PROGRAMS                  Sun Jul  7 85 12:02 pm   5,714 Directory
SYMPHONY                  Sun Jul  7 85 12:06 pm   7,798 Directory
TAPE                      Sun Jul  7 85 12:06 pm   8,500 Directory
ADDRESS            640 Tue Feb 26 85 10:55 am      33
EMPTY                1 Sat Jan  8 83 10:26 am      34
ENDPAGE              2 Mon May 13 85 10:39 pm      35
INFO             4,480 Fri Jun 21 85  1:07 pm      36
MOUSE                     Sun Jul  7 85  9:12 pm   8,618 Directory
FWSPOOL  005   73,779 Fri Jun 21 85  4:52 pm      40
APPOINT  APP      651 Tue Jun  4 85  4:09 pm      77
NORTON   BAK      384 Mon Jul  8 85  9:32 am      22
NORTON   PRO      384 Mon Jul  8 85  9:34 am      24
SOCHA                     Mon Jul  8 85  4:29 pm      23 Directory
WORK                      Tue Jul  9 85  6:58 pm      25 Directory
=======  ===  ======  ====  ===========  ======  ======================

              Press Enter for help
```

Figure 22-5. Disk data display in directory format from NU.

Any data that we look at with NU can be shown in any of these three formats: interpreted as directory data, laid out as text data, or shown in absolute hex and character format. We can inspect the same data all three ways, simply by flipping through the three formats—which gives us a lot of flexibility and power in working with our data.

Using the features of NU to display and change data, we can get into any part of our DOS disks, see what's there and, if we know how, tinker with and modify the data—either simply to change it, or to repair some damage that might have happened to it. I can give you an example of why we might want to do this, from my own experience.

Two DOS programs, called BACKUP and RESTORE, are used to make floppy diskette backup copies of hard disk data. In an early version of DOS, the BACKUP program sometimes recorded one of the backup diskettes incorrectly, with a hex 0 in place of part of one of the filenames. This tiny error made it impossible to restore the data that had been copied to the diskettes—a disaster! Fortunately, when this happened to me, I was able to use NU to browse around on the bad diskette, exploring until I discovered what the problem was. Once I discovered it, all I had to do was to replace the erroneous hex 0 with a proper character for the filename. It was a simple and easy repair job, which would have been impossible without a exploring and patching tool like NU. In that one case, NU saved an entire hard disk's data for me! This is a powerful example of why it can be very worthwhile to have a tool of this kind at hand, and know how to use it.

Some Things to Try

1. Using DEBUG, search through your computer's ROM to find the copyright notice on the ROM-BIOS. Give DEBUG the command D F800:0; then follow that with the command D until you see what you're looking for. If you don't find the message starting at F800:0, try again at F000:0.

2. If you have the NU program, use it to look at the dimensions of each type of disk that you have. What do the figures tell you?

3. Again, if you have NU, make a copy of one of your diskettes, and experiment with making changes to it. Find the diskette's root directory, and change one of the filenames by typing over the name. Test to see if the name got properly changed.

4. Using NU's ability to show the same data in directory and hex format, display part of your disk's directory and then try to find just where each part of the directory (name, extension, date, size) is recorded in the hex part. Changing the hex data and then seeing what changed in the directory display will help you tell what's what.

Program Listings

MAZE—Start-to-Finish Maze (Introduction)

```
1000 ' Little Maze Program, Copr. 1985 Peter Norton
1010 '
1020 GOSUB 2000    ' do set-up work
1030 WHILE NOT.YET.DONE
1040    GOSUB 3000 ' sound tone
1050    GOSUB 4000 ' choose distance
1060    GOSUB 5000 ' move
1070    GOSUB 6000 ' check for end
1080    GOSUB 7000 ' choose direction
1090 WEND
1100 GOSUB 8000    ' report triumph and finish


2000 '
2010 ' Subroutine to do set-up work
2020 '
2030 DEFINT A-Z
2040 KEY OFF  : SCREEN 0: WIDTH 80 : CLS
2050 RANDOMIZE TIMER
2060 NOT.YET.DONE = 1
2070 BOX.FOREGROUND = 0 : BOX.BACKGROUND = 7
2080 CURRENT.ROW = 1 : CURRENT.COL = 1
2090 MESSAGE$ = " Start " : GOSUB 2500
2100 CURRENT.ROW = 22 : CURRENT.COL = 68
2110 MESSAGE$ = " Finish! " : GOSUB 2500
2120 CURRENT.ROW = 2 : CURRENT.COL = 10 : DIRECTION = 1
2130 SOUND.TIME = 100 : PLAY "MB" : SOUND.CANCEL = 1
2140 SOUND.BASE = 50
2150 LOCATE 2,9,0 : PRINT CHR$(204);
2160 COLOR 7,0 : MOVING.CHARACTER = 205
2170 RETURN


2500 '
```

```
2510 ' Subroutine to draw a message box
2520 '
2530 COLOR BOX.FOREGROUND, BOX.BACKGROUND
2540 LOCATE CURRENT.ROW,   CURRENT.COL
2550 PRINT CHR$(201);STRING$(LEN(MESSAGE$),205);CHR$(187);
2560 LOCATE CURRENT.ROW+1,CURRENT.COL
2570 PRINT CHR$(186);MESSAGE$;                    CHR$(186);
2580 LOCATE CURRENT.ROW+2,CURRENT.COL
2590 PRINT CHR$(200);STRING$(LEN(MESSAGE$),205);CHR$(188);
2600 RETURN

3000 '
3010 ' Subroutine to sound tones
3020 '
3030 IF SOUND.CANCEL THEN SOUND 100,0     ' cancel previous
3040 SOUND SOUND.BASE+750*RND,SOUND.TIME ' random tone
3050 RETURN

4000 '
4010 ' Subroutine to choose distance
4020 '
4030 IF DIRECTION = 1 THEN LIMIT = 78 - CURRENT.COL
4040 IF DIRECTION = 2 THEN LIMIT = CURRENT.COL - 2
4050 IF DIRECTION = 3 THEN LIMIT = CURRENT.ROW - 2
4060 IF DIRECTION = 4 THEN LIMIT = 23 - CURRENT.ROW
4070 IF LIMIT < 1 THEN LIMIT = 1
4080 DISTANCE = INT (RND * (LIMIT + 1) )
4090 RETURN

5000 '
5010 ' Subroutine to move
5020 '
5030 FOR I = 1 TO DISTANCE
5040    LOCATE CURRENT.ROW,CURRENT.COL
5050    PRINT CHR$(MOVING.CHARACTER);
5060    GOSUB 5500
5070 NEXT
5080 RETURN

5500 '
5510 ' Subroutine to change to next location
5520 '
5530 IF DIRECTION = 1 THEN CURRENT.COL = CURRENT.COL + 1
5540 IF DIRECTION = 2 THEN CURRENT.COL = CURRENT.COL - 1
```

```
5550 IF DIRECTION = 3 THEN CURRENT.ROW = CURRENT.ROW - 1
5560 IF DIRECTION = 4 THEN CURRENT.ROW = CURRENT.ROW + 1
5570 LOCATE CURRENT.ROW,CURRENT.COL
5580 RETURN

6000 '
6010 ' Subroutine to check for end
6020 '
6030 IF CURRENT.ROW < 22 THEN RETURN
6040 IF CURRENT.COL < 68 THEN RETURN
6050 NOT.YET.DONE = 0
6060 RETURN

7000 '
7010 ' Subroutine to choose direction and turn corner
7020 '
7030 RIGHT.TURN = INT (RND * 2)
7040 RIGHT.TURN = 1 - RIGHT.TURN
7050 IF DIRECTION=1 THEN NEW.DIRECTION=3+RIGHT.TURN
7060 IF DIRECTION=2 THEN NEW.DIRECTION=4-RIGHT.TURN
7070 IF DIRECTION=3 THEN NEW.DIRECTION=2-RIGHT.TURN
7080 IF DIRECTION=4 THEN NEW.DIRECTION=1+RIGHT.TURN
7090 IF NEW.DIRECTION=1 AND CURRENT.COL>75 THEN GOTO 7040
7100 IF NEW.DIRECTION=2 AND CURRENT.COL< 5 THEN GOTO 7040
7110 IF NEW.DIRECTION=3 AND CURRENT.ROW< 5 THEN GOTO 7040
7120 IF NEW.DIRECTION=4 AND CURRENT.ROW>20 THEN GOTO 7040
7130 IF DIRECTION=1 AND RIGHT.TURN=0 THEN TURN.CHAR = 188
7140 IF DIRECTION=1 AND RIGHT.TURN=1 THEN TURN.CHAR = 187
7150 IF DIRECTION=2 AND RIGHT.TURN=0 THEN TURN.CHAR = 201
7160 IF DIRECTION=2 AND RIGHT.TURN=1 THEN TURN.CHAR = 200
7170 IF DIRECTION=3 AND RIGHT.TURN=0 THEN TURN.CHAR = 187
7180 IF DIRECTION=3 AND RIGHT.TURN=1 THEN TURN.CHAR = 201
7190 IF DIRECTION=4 AND RIGHT.TURN=0 THEN TURN.CHAR = 200
7200 IF DIRECTION=4 AND RIGHT.TURN=1 THEN TURN.CHAR = 188
7210 PRINT CHR$(TURN.CHAR);
7220 DIRECTION = NEW.DIRECTION
7230 IF DIRECTION < 3 THEN MOVING.CHARACTER = 205
7240 IF DIRECTION > 2 THEN MOVING.CHARACTER = 186
7250 GOSUB 5500
7260 RETURN

8000 '
8010 ' Report triumph and finish
8020 '
```

```
8030 SOUND 100,0
8040 CURRENT.ROW = 22 : CURRENT.COL = 66
8050 MESSAGE$ = " Finished! "
8060 SOUND.TIME = 2 : PLAY "MF"
8070 SOUND.BASE = 1000 : SOUND.CANCEL = 0
8080 FOR I = 1 TO 10
8090    BOX.FOREGROUND = 7 : BOX.BACKGROUND = 0
8100    GOSUB 2500
8110    GOSUB 3000
8120    BOX.FOREGROUND = 0 : BOX.BACKGROUND = 7
8130    GOSUB 2500
8140    GOSUB 3000
8150 NEXT
8160 BOX.FOREGROUND = 28 : BOX.BACKGROUND = 15
8170 GOSUB 2500
8180 LOCATE 12,25 : COLOR 7,0 : SOUND 100,0
8190 PRINT "Press a key to return to DOS... ";
8200 WHILE INKEY$ = "" : WEND
8210 SYSTEM
```

HEXTABLE—Generate Hex Arithmetic Tables (Chapter 3)

```
1000 ' Hex Arithmetic Tables, Copr. 1985 Peter Norton
1010 '
1020 FOR TYPE = 1 TO 2
1030    GOSUB 2000 ' title
1040    FOR I = 0 TO 15
1050       FOR J = 0 TO 15
1060          GOSUB 3000 ' show the value
1070       NEXT J
1080    NEXT I
1090    GOSUB 4000 ' pause
1100 NEXT TYPE
1110 SYSTEM

2000 '
2010 ' Titles
2020 '
2030 KEY OFF  : SCREEN 0: WIDTH 80 : CLS
2040 LOCATE 3,20 : COLOR 1+8
2050 PRINT "Hex ";
2060 IF TYPE = 1 THEN PRINT "Addition";
2070 IF TYPE = 2 THEN PRINT "Multiplication";
2080 PRINT " Table";
2090 COLOR 7+8
```

```
2100 LOCATE 5,20
2110 FOR I = 0 TO 15
2120    PRINT HEX$(I); "   ";
2130 NEXT I
2140 FOR I = 0 TO 15
2150    LOCATE 7+I,16
2160    PRINT HEX$(I);
2170 NEXT I
2180 COLOR 7
2190 RETURN

3000 '
3010 ' Show the value
3020 '
3030 IF TYPE = 1 THEN X = I + J
3040 IF TYPE = 2 THEN X = I * J
3050 SHOW$ = HEX$ (X)
3060 ROW = I + 7
3070 COL = J * 3 + 18 + (3-LEN(SHOW$))
3080 LOCATE ROW,COL
3090 PRINT SHOW$;
3100 RETURN

4000 '
4010 ' Pause
4020 '
4030 LOCATE 25,20 : COLOR 1
4040 PRINT "Press a key to return to continue... ";
4050 COLOR 7
4060 WHILE INKEY$ = "" : WEND
4070 RETURN
```

ALL-CHAR—Show All PC Characters (Chapter 4)

```
1000 ' Show All Characters, Copr. 1985 Peter Norton
1010 '
1020 GOSUB 2000    ' do set-up work
1030 FOR CHAR.VALUE = 0 TO 255
1040    GOSUB 3000 ' show the character
1050 NEXT CHAR.VALUE
1060 GOSUB 4000    ' prepare to finish

2000 '
2010 ' Subroutine to do set-up work
2020 '
```

```
2030 DEFINT A-Z
2040 KEY OFF  : SCREEN 0: WIDTH 80 : CLS
2050 LOCATE 3,25 : COLOR 1
2060 PRINT "The Complete PC Character Set";
2070 VIDEO.SEGMENT = 0
2080 DEF SEG = &H40 : VIDEO.MODE = PEEK (&H49)
2090 IF VIDEO.MODE = 7 THEN VIDEO.SEGMENT = &HB000
2100 IF VIDEO.MODE < 4 THEN VIDEO.SEGMENT = &HB800
2110 IF VIDEO.SEGMENT <> 0 THEN RETURN
2120 LOCATE 12,25
2130 PRINT "Error: unfamiliar video mode!"
2140 GOSUB 4000


3000 '
3010 ' Subroutine to show each character
3020 '
3030 ROW = CHAR.VALUE MOD 16 + 5
3040 COL = (CHAR.VALUE \  16) * 3 + 16
3050 SCREEN.OFFSET = ROW * 160 + COL * 2
3060 DEF SEG = VIDEO.SEGMENT
3070 POKE SCREEN.OFFSET, CHAR.VALUE
3080 RETURN


4000 '
4010 ' Finish up
4020 '
4030 LOCATE 24,24 : COLOR 1
4040 PRINT "Press a key to return to DOS... ";
4050 WHILE INKEY$ = "" : WEND
4060 SYSTEM
```

REF-CHAR—Characters with Reference Numbers (Chapter 4)

```
1000 ' Characters & Reference, Copr. 1985 Peter Norton
1010 '
1020 GOSUB 2000    ' do set-up work
1030 FOR CHAR.VALUE = 0 TO 255
1040    GOSUB 3000 ' show the character
1090 NEXT CHAR.VALUE
1100 SYSTEM


2000 '
2010 ' Subroutine to do set-up work
2020 '
2030 DEFINT A-Z
```

```
2040 KEY OFF   : SCREEN 0: WIDTH 80
2050 VIDEO.SEGMENT = 0
2060 DEF SEG = &H40 : VIDEO.MODE = PEEK (&H49)
2070 IF VIDEO.MODE = 7 THEN VIDEO.SEGMENT = &HB000
2080 IF VIDEO.MODE < 4 THEN VIDEO.SEGMENT = &HB800
2090 IF VIDEO.SEGMENT <> 0 THEN RETURN
2100 LOCATE 12,25
2110 PRINT "Error: unfamiliar video mode!"
2120 GOSUB 4000 : SYSTEM


3000 '
3010 ' Subroutine to show each character
3020 '
3030 IF CHAR.VALUE MOD 128 > 0 THEN GOTO 3080
3040 COLOR 7 : CLS : COLOR 1
3050 LOCATE 3,25 : PRINT "Reference Character Set ";
3060 IF CHAR.VALUE = 0 THEN PRINT "1st"; ELSE PRINT "2nd";
3070 PRINT " Half";
3080 COLOR 7
3090 RELATIVE.CHAR = CHAR.VALUE MOD 128
3100 ROW =   RELATIVE.CHAR MOD 16
3110 COL = (RELATIVE.CHAR \ 16) * 10
3120 SCREEN.OFFSET = ROW * 160 + COL * 2 + 814
3130 DEF SEG = VIDEO.SEGMENT
3140 POKE SCREEN.OFFSET, CHAR.VALUE
3150 LOCATE ROW+6, COL+1
3160 PRINT USING "###";CHAR.VALUE;
3170 PRINT " ";
3180 IF CHAR.VALUE < 16 THEN PRINT "0";
3190 PRINT HEX$(CHAR.VALUE);
3200 IF CHAR.VALUE MOD 128 = 127 THEN GOSUB 4000
3210 RETURN


4000 '
4010 ' Pause
4020 '
4030 LOCATE 24,27 : COLOR 1
4040 PRINT "Press a key to continue... ";
4050 WHILE INKEY$ = "" : WEND
4060 RETURN
```

BOXES—Box-Drawing Characters (Chapter 4)

```
1000 ' Draw Line Boxes, Copr. 1985 Peter Norton
```

```
1010 '
1020 GOSUB 2000    ' do set-up work
1030 FOR EXPANDED = 0 TO 1
1040   RESTORE
1050   FOR BOX.TYPE = 1 TO 4
1060     GOSUB 3000 ' get drawing data
1070     GOSUB 4000 ' print title
1080     IF EXPANDED = 0 THEN GOSUB 5000 ' draw box
1090     IF EXPANDED = 1 THEN GOSUB 6000 ' draw box
1100   NEXT BOX.TYPE
1110   GOSUB 7000    ' pause
1120 NEXT EXPANDED
1130 SYSTEM


2000 '
2010 ' Subroutine to do set-up work
2020 '
2030 DEFINT A-Z
2040 DIM CODES (6,6)
2050 KEY OFF : SCREEN 0: WIDTH 80 : CLS
2060 RETURN


3000 '
3010 ' Get the drawing data
3020 '
3030 READ TITLE.STRING.$
3040 FOR ROW = 1 TO 5
3050   FOR COL = 1 TO 5
3060     READ CODES (ROW,COL)
3070   NEXT COL
3080 NEXT ROW
3090 RETURN


4000 '
4010 ' Display the title
4020 '
4030 IF BOX.TYPE=1 THEN BASE.ROW= 1 : BASE.COL= 5
4040 IF BOX.TYPE=2 THEN BASE.ROW= 1 : BASE.COL=45
4050 IF BOX.TYPE=3 THEN BASE.ROW=13 : BASE.COL= 5
4060 IF BOX.TYPE=4 THEN BASE.ROW=13 : BASE.COL=45
4070 LOCATE BASE.ROW,BASE.COL
4080 COLOR 9
4090 PRINT TITLE.STRING.$;
4100 COLOR 7
```

```
4110 RETURN

5000 '
5010 ' Draw box - solid
5020 '
5030 SHOW.ROW = BASE.ROW
5040 FOR ROW = 1 TO 5
5050    TIMES = 1
5060    IF ROW=2 OR ROW=4 THEN TIMES = 3
5070    FOR I = 1 TO TIMES
5080       SHOW.ROW = SHOW.ROW + 1
5090       LOCATE SHOW.ROW, BASE.COL+4
5100       PRINT   CHR$(CODES(ROW,1));
5110       FOR J = 1 TO 9
5120         PRINT CHR$(CODES(ROW,2));
5130       NEXT J
5140       PRINT   CHR$(CODES(ROW,3));
5150       FOR J = 1 TO 9
5160         PRINT CHR$(CODES(ROW,4));
5170       NEXT J
5180       PRINT   CHR$(CODES(ROW,5));
5190    NEXT I
5200 NEXT ROW
5210 RETURN

6000 '
6010 ' Draw box - expanded
6020 '
6030 SHOW.ROW = BASE.ROW
6040 FOR ROW = 1 TO 5
6050    FOR TIMES = 1 TO 2
6060       SHOW.ROW = SHOW.ROW + 1
6070       LOCATE SHOW.ROW, BASE.COL+3
6080       IF TIMES = 1 THEN GOSUB 6200
6090       IF TIMES = 2 THEN GOSUB 6400
6100    NEXT TIMES
6110 NEXT ROW
6120 RETURN
6200 '
6210 ' drawn lines
6220 '
6230 PRINT " ";
6240 PRINT CHR$(CODES(ROW,1));
6250 PRINT "     ";
```

```
6260 PRINT CHR$(CODES(ROW,2));
6270 PRINT "     ";
6280 PRINT CHR$(CODES(ROW,3));
6290 PRINT "     ";
6300 PRINT CHR$(CODES(ROW,4));
6310 PRINT "     ";
6320 PRINT CHR$(CODES(ROW,5));
6330 RETURN
6400 '
6410 ' display numeric codes
6420 '
6430 FOR COL = 1 TO 5
6440    X = CODES (ROW,COL)
6450    IF X = 32 THEN PRINT "      ";
6460    IF X <> 32 THEN PRINT USING "###   "; X;
6470 NEXT COL
6480 RETURN


7000 '
7010 ' Pause
7020 '
7030 LOCATE 25,1
7040 PRINT "Press a key to continue... ";
7050 WHILE INKEY$ = "" : WEND
7060 RETURN


8000 '
8010 ' Box character data
8020 '
8100 DATA "All Double Line: "
8110 DATA 201, 205, 203, 205, 187
8120 DATA 186,  32, 186,  32, 186
8130 DATA 204, 205, 206, 205, 185
8140 DATA 186,  32, 186,  32, 186
8150 DATA 200, 205, 202, 205, 188
8200 DATA "All Single Line: "
8210 DATA 218, 196, 194, 196, 191
8220 DATA 179,  32, 179,  32, 179
8230 DATA 195, 196, 197, 196, 180
8240 DATA 179,  32, 179,  32, 179
8250 DATA 192, 196, 193, 196, 217
8300 DATA "Double-Vertical: "
8310 DATA 214, 196, 210, 196, 183
8320 DATA 186,  32, 186,  32, 186
```

```
8330 DATA 199, 196, 215, 196, 182
8340 DATA 186,  32, 186,  32, 186
8350 DATA 211, 196, 208, 196, 189
8400 DATA "Double-Horizontal: "
8410 DATA 213, 205, 209, 205, 184
8420 DATA 179,  32, 179,  32, 179
8430 DATA 198, 205, 216, 205, 181
8440 DATA 179,  32, 179,  32, 179
8450 DATA 212, 205, 207, 205, 190
```

MSG-HUNT—Hunt for ROM-BIOS Messages (Chapter 7)

```
1000 ' ROM-BIOS Message Hunt, Copr. 1985 Peter Norton
1010 '
1020 GOSUB 2000   ' do set-up work
1030 WHILE OFFSET <= 65535
1040    GOSUB 3000 ' test for a message
1050    OFFSET = OFFSET + 1
1060 WEND
1070 GOSUB 5000    ' prepare to finish

2000 '
2010 ' Subroutine to do set-up work
2020 '
2030 KEY OFF  : SCREEN 0: WIDTH 80 : CLS
2040 LOCATE 2,1 : COLOR 7
2050 PRINT "Searching the BIOS for apparent messages"
2060 PRINT
2070 OFFSET = 0
2080 DEF SEG = &HF000
2090 RETURN

3000 '
3010 ' Subroutine to test for a message
3020 '
3030 MESSAGE.$ = ""
3040 COLOR 7
3050 PRINT "Searching at F000: ";
3060 PRINT HEX$ (OFFSET);
3070 LOCATE ,1
3080 BYTE = PEEK (OFFSET)
3090 WHILE ((BYTE>=ASC(" ")) AND (BYTE<=ASC("z")))
3100    MESSAGE.$ = MESSAGE.$ + CHR$(BYTE)
3110    OFFSET = OFFSET + 1
3120    BYTE = PEEK (OFFSET)
```

```
3130   IF LEN (MESSAGE.$) > 100 THEN RETURN
3140 WEND
3150 IF LEN (MESSAGE.$) > 4 THEN GOTO 4000
3160 RETURN

4000 '
4010 ' Print the message found
4020 '
4030 COLOR 7
4040 PRINT "At F000: ";
4050 PRINT HEX$(OFFSET);
4060 PRINT " this was found: ";
4070 COLOR 1
4080 PRINT MESSAGE.$;
4090 COLOR 7
4100 PRINT
4110 RETURN

5000 '
5010 ' Finish up
5020 '
5030 COLOR 1
5040 PRINT
5050 PRINT "Press a key to return to DOS... ";
5060 WHILE INKEY$ = "" : WEND
5070 SYSTEM
```

VID-MODE—Video Mode Demonstration (Chapter 11)

```
1000 ' Experiment with Video Modes, Copr. 1985 Peter Norton
1010 '
1020 ' following step needed for PCjr
1030 ON ERROR GOTO 1130 : CLEAR ,,,32768
1040 GOSUB 2000   ' do set-up work
1050 FOR MODE = 0 TO 10
1060    GOSUB 3000 ' describe mode
1070    GOSUB 9000 ' pause
1080    GOSUB 5000 ' set mode
1090    GOSUB 7000 ' check results
1100    GOSUB 9000 ' pause
1110 NEXT MODE
1120 SYSTEM ' finish
1130 RESUME NEXT

2000 '
```

```
2010 ' Subroutine to do set-up work
2020 '
2030 KEY OFF  : SCREEN 0: WIDTH 80 : CLS
2040 LOCATE 2,10 : COLOR 7
2050 PRINT "Experimenting with Video Modes"
2060 PRINT
2070 PRINT "As we begin the video mode is ";
2080 DEF SEG = 0
2090 PRINT PEEK (&H449)
2100 PRINT
2110 RETURN


3000 '
3010 ' Describe mode to be set
3020 '
3030 PRINT "About to attempt to switch to mode ";MODE;" which is"
3040 ON MODE+1 GOTO
4000,4010,4020,4030,4040,4050,4060,4070,4080,4090,4100
3050 RETURN
4000 PRINT "Color-graphics, text, 40-column, no-color"
4005 RETURN
4010 PRINT "Color-graphics, text, 40-column, with color"
4015 RETURN
4020 PRINT "Color-graphics, text, 80-column, no-color"
4025 RETURN
4030 PRINT "Color-graphics, text, 80-column, with color"
4035 RETURN
4040 PRINT "Color-graphics, graphics, medium resolution, with color"
4045 RETURN
4050 PRINT "Color-graphics, graphics, medium resolution, no-color"
4055 RETURN
4060 PRINT "Color-graphics, graphics, high resolution, two color"
4065 RETURN
4070 PRINT "Standard monochrome text mode"
4075 RETURN
4080 PRINT "PCjr, graphics, low resolution, with color"
4085 RETURN
4090 PRINT "PCjr, graphics, medium resolution, extra color"
4095 RETURN
4100 PRINT "PCjr, graphics, high resolution, extra color"
4105 RETURN


5000 '
5010 ' Attempt to set the mode
```

339

```
5020 '
5030 ON ERROR GOTO 5060
5040 ON MODE+1 GOTO
6000,6010,6020,6030,6040,6050,6060,6070,6080,6090,6100
5050 RETURN
5060 RESUME 5050
6000 SCREEN 0,0 : WIDTH 40
6010 SCREEN 0,1 : WIDTH 40 : RETURN
6020 SCREEN 0,0 : WIDTH 80 : RETURN
6030 SCREEN 0,1 : WIDTH 80 : RETURN
6040 SCREEN 1,0           : RETURN
6050 SCREEN 1,1           : RETURN
6060 SCREEN 2             : RETURN
6070 SCREEN 0             : RETURN
6080 SCREEN 3             : RETURN
6090 SCREEN 5             : RETURN
6100 SCREEN 6             : RETURN

7000 '
7010 ' Check the active mode
7020 '
7030 CURRENT.MODE = PEEK (&H449)
7040 PRINT "The current mode is "; CURRENT.MODE
7050 PRINT "Which is";
7060 IF MODE <> CURRENT.MODE THEN PRINT " NOT";
7070 PRINT " the desired mode"
7080 RETURN

9000 '
9010 ' Pause
9020 '
9030 PRINT
9040 PRINT "Press a key to continue... ";
9050 WHILE INKEY$ = "" : WEND
9060 PRINT : PRINT
9070 RETURN
```

COLORTXT—Show All Text Color Combinations (Chapter 12)

```
1000 ' COLOR-TXT Show Text Colors, Copr. 1985 Peter Norton
1010 '
1020 GOSUB 2000    ' do set-up work
1030 FOR ATTRIBUTE = 0 TO 255
1040    GOSUB 3000 ' show the attribute
1050 NEXT ATTRIBUTE
```

```
1060 SYSTEM

2000 '
2010 ' Subroutine to do set-up work
2020 '
2030 DEFINT A-Z
2040 KEY OFF  : SCREEN 0,1 : WIDTH 80
2050 VIDEO.SEGMENT = 0
2060 DEF SEG = &H40 : VIDEO.MODE = PEEK (&H49)
2070 IF VIDEO.MODE = 7 THEN VIDEO.SEGMENT = &HB000
2080 IF VIDEO.MODE < 4 THEN VIDEO.SEGMENT = &HB800
2090 IF VIDEO.SEGMENT <> 0 THEN RETURN
2100 LOCATE 12,25
2110 PRINT "Error: unfamiliar video mode!"
2120 GOSUB 4000 : SYSTEM

3000 '
3010 ' Subroutine to show each attribute
3020 '
3030 IF ATTRIBUTE MOD 128 > 0 THEN GOTO 3080
3040 COLOR 7 : CLS : COLOR 1
3050 LOCATE 3,25 : PRINT "Text Color Attribute Set ";
3060 IF ATTRIBUTE = 0 THEN PRINT "1st"; ELSE PRINT "2nd";
3070 PRINT " Half";
3080 COLOR 7
3090 RELATIVE.CHAR = ATTRIBUTE MOD 128
3100 ROW = RELATIVE.CHAR MOD 16
3110 COL = (RELATIVE.CHAR \ 16) * 10
3120 SCREEN.OFFSET = ROW * 160 + COL * 2 + 814
3130 DEF SEG = VIDEO.SEGMENT
3140 POKE SCREEN.OFFSET, 88 " letter X
3150 POKE SCREEN.OFFSET+1, ATTRIBUTE
3160 LOCATE ROW+6, COL+1
3170 PRINT USING "###";ATTRIBUTE;
3180 PRINT " ";
3190 IF ATTRIBUTE < 16 THEN PRINT "0";
3200 PRINT HEX$(ATTRIBUTE);
3210 IF ATTRIBUTE MOD 128 = 127 THEN GOSUB 4000
3220 RETURN

4000 '
4010 ' Pause
4020 '
4030 LOCATE 24,27 : COLOR 1
```

```
4040 PRINT "Press a key to continue... ";
4050 WHILE INKEY$ = "" : WEND
4060 RETURN
```

GRAPHTXT—Graphics Mode Text Characters (Chapter 13)

```
1000 ' GRAPH-TXT Graphics Characters, Copr. 1985 Peter Norton
1010 '
1020 GOSUB 2000    ' do set-up work
1030 FOR CHAR.CODE = 0 TO 127
1040   GOSUB 3000 ' show the character
1050 NEXT CHAR.CODE
1060 GOSUB 4000
1070 SYSTEM


2000 '
2010 ' Subroutine to do set-up work
2020 '
2030 DEFINT A-Z
2040 KEY OFF  : SCREEN 0,1 : WIDTH 80
2050 PAUSE = 0
2060 VIDEO.SEGMENT = 0
2070 DEF SEG = &H40 : VIDEO.MODE = PEEK (&H49)
2080 IF VIDEO.MODE = 7 THEN VIDEO.SEGMENT = &HB000
2090 IF VIDEO.MODE < 4 THEN VIDEO.SEGMENT = &HB800
2100 IF VIDEO.SEGMENT <> 0 THEN RETURN
2110 LOCATE 12,25
2120 PRINT "Error: unfamiliar video mode! "
2130 GOSUB 4000 : SYSTEM


3000 '
3010 ' Subroutine to show each character
3020 '
3030 CLS
3040 LOCATE 2,5
3050 PRINT "Displaying the Graphics Text Character Drawings"
3060 LOCATE 5,5
3070 PRINT "For character code";CHAR.CODE
3080 LOCATE 6,5
3090 PRINT "Character"
3100 DEF SEG = VIDEO.SEGMENT
3110 POKE 828, CHAR.CODE
3120 DEF SEG = &HF000
3130 FOR SCAN.LINE = 0 TO 7
3140   BIT.CODE = PEEK (&HFA6E + SCAN.LINE + CHAR.CODE * 8)
```

```
3150    LOCATE  8+SCAN.LINE,5
3160    FOR BITS = 1 TO 8
3170      IF BIT.CODE ‹ 128 THEN SHOW$ = ".  " ELSE SHOW$ = "XX"
3180      PRINT SHOW$;
3190      IF BIT.CODE › 127 THEN BIT.CODE = BIT.CODE - 128
3200      BIT.CODE = BIT.CODE * 2
3210    NEXT BITS
3220 NEXT SCAN.LINE
3230 LOCATE 18,5
3240 WHILE INKEY$ ‹› "" : WEND ' flush key buffer
3250 PRINT "Press any key to stop...";
3260 FOR WAIT.A.SECOND = 1 TO 2
3270    OLD.TIME$ = TIME$
3280    WHILE OLD.TIME$ = TIME$ : WEND
3290 NEXT WAIT.A.SECOND
3300 IF INKEY$ = "" THEN RETURN
3310 LOCATE 18,5
3320 PRINT "Now press any key to CONTINUE...";
3330 WHILE INKEY$ = "" : WEND
3340 RETURN

4000 '
4010 ' Pause
4020 '
4030 LOCATE 18,5
4040 PRINT "Press a key to return to DOS... ";
4050 WHILE INKEY$ = "" : WEND
4060 RETURN
```

COLOR-4—Demonstrate Graphics Mode Color (Chapter 13)

```
1000 ' Color-4: Demonstrate Mode 4, Copr. 1985 Peter Norton
1010 '
1020 GOSUB 2000    ' do set-up work
1030 GOSUB 3000    ' stage 1
1040 GOSUB 4000    ' stage 2
1050 GOSUB 5000    ' stage 3
1060 GOSUB 6000    ' stage 4
1070 SYSTEM

2000 '
2010 ' Subroutine to do set-up work
2020 '
2030 DEFINT A-Z
2040 KEY OFF  : SCREEN 0,1 : WIDTH 40
```

```
2050 DEF SEG = &H40 : VIDEO.MODE = PEEK (&H49)
2060 IF VIDEO.MODE = 7 THEN GOTO 2230
2070 LOCATE 3
2080 PRINT "Color-4: demonstrate video mode 4"
2090 PRINT
2100 PRINT
2110 PRINT "This program works in four stages:"
2120 PRINT
2130 PRINT "Stage 1: Show pre-defined palettes"
2140 PRINT
2150 PRINT "Stage 2: Show selectable color"
2160 PRINT
2170 PRINT "Stage 3: Appear and disappear"
2180 PRINT
2190 PRINT "Stage 4: Rattling the palettes"
2200 PRINT
2210 GOSUB 7000
2220 RETURN
2230 PRINT "This program does not work in monochrome mode"
2240 GOSUB 7000
2250 SYSTEM

3000 '
3010 ' Stage 1 - Show pre-defined palettes
3020 '
3030 SCREEN 1,0
3040 COLOR 1,0 : CLS
3050 FOR C.NUM = 0 TO 3
3060    LOCATE 5 + C.NUM * 5, 1 + C.NUM * 5
3070    PRINT " Color"; C.NUM
3080    CIRCLE (90+60*C.NUM,45+30*C.NUM),40,C.NUM
3090    PAINT  (90+60*C.NUM,45+30*C.NUM),C.NUM
3100 NEXT C.NUM
3110 FOR TIMES = 1 TO 10
3120    FOR PAL.NUM = 0 TO 1
3130       COLOR ,PAL.NUM
3140       LOCATE 2,10
3150       PRINT " Showing palette"; PAL.NUM
3160       NOW$ = TIME$
3170       WHILE TIME$ = NOW$ : WEND
3180    NEXT PAL.NUM
3190 NEXT TIMES
3200 LOCATE 22
3210 GOSUB 7000
```

```
3220 RETURN


4000 '
4010 ' Stage 2 - Show selectable color
4020 '
4030 SCREEN 1,0 : CLS
4040 COLOR 0,1
4050 FOR COLOR.NUM = 0 TO 15
4060    LOCATE 3+COLOR.NUM,2+COLOR.NUM
4070    COLOR COLOR.NUM
4080    PRINT " Selected color ";COLOR.NUM;
4090    NOW$ = TIME$
4100    WHILE TIME$ = NOW$ : WEND
4110 NEXT COLOR.NUM
4120 COLOR 0
4130 LOCATE 22
4140 GOSUB 7000
4150 RETURN


5000 '
5010 ' Stage 3 - Appear and disappear
5020 '
5030 SCREEN 1,0
5040 CLS
5050 COLOR 4,1
5060 PAINT (1,1),1
5070 CIRCLE ( 80, 50),20,0
5080 CIRCLE ( 80,150),20,0
5090 CIRCLE (240, 50),20,0
5100 CIRCLE (240,150),20,0
5110 PAINT ( 80, 50),0
5120 PAINT ( 80,150),0
5130 PAINT (240, 50),0
5140 PAINT (240,150),0
5150 LOCATE 13,8
5160 PRINT " Appear and Disappear! "
5170 FOR I = 1 TO 50
5180    COLOR 3 + I MOD 2
5190    FOR J = 1 TO 250 : NEXT J
5200 NEXT I
5210 LOCATE 22
5220 GOSUB 7000
5230 RETURN
```

345

```
6000 '
6010 ' Stage 4 - Rattling the palettes
6020 '
6030 SCREEN 1,0 : CLS
6040 COLOR 0,0
6050 CIRCLE  (160,100),80,3
6060 PAINT   (160,100),3
6070 CIRCLE  (160,100),60,2
6080 PAINT   (160,100),2
6090 CIRCLE  (160,100),40,1
6100 PAINT   (160,100),1
6110 CIRCLE  (160,100),20,0
6120 PAINT   (160,100),0
6130 LOCATE 13,17
6140 PRINT " Boom ! ";
6150 FOR I = 1 TO 100
6160    COLOR ,I MOD 2
6170    FOR J = 1 TO 50 : NEXT J
6180 NEXT I
6190 LOCATE 22
6200 GOSUB 7000
6210 RETURN

7000 '
7010 ' Pause
7020 '
7030 PRINT
7040 PRINT "Press a key to continue... ";
7050 WHILE INKEY$ = "" : WEND
7060 RETURN
```

KEY-BITS—Display the Keyboard Control Bits (Chapter 14)

```
1000 ' KEY-BITS  Keyboard control bits, Copr. 1985 Peter Norton
1010 '
1020 GOSUB 2000    ' do set-up work
1030 WHILE CONTINUING
1040    GOSUB 3000 ' show the data
1050 WEND

2000 '
2010 ' Subroutine to do set-up work
2020 '
2030 KEY OFF  : SCREEN 0,1 : WIDTH 80
2040 CONTINUING = 1 : LOCATE ,,0
```

```
2050 DIM MSG.$ (16)
2060 MSG.$ ( 1) = "Insert state"
2070 MSG.$ ( 2) = "Caps Lock state"
2080 MSG.$ ( 3) = "Num Lock state"
2090 MSG.$ ( 4) = "Scroll Lock state"
2100 MSG.$ ( 5) = "Alt pressed"
2110 MSG.$ ( 6) = "Ctrl pressed"
2120 MSG.$ ( 7) = "Left shift pressed"
2130 MSG.$ ( 8) = "Right shift pressed"
2140 MSG.$ ( 9) = "Ins pressed"
2150 MSG.$ (10) = "Caps Lock pressed"
2160 MSG.$ (11) = "Num Lock pressed"
2170 MSG.$ (12) = "Scroll Lock pressed"
2180 MSG.$ (13) = "Hold state active"
2190 MSG.$ (14) = "PCjr click state"
2200 MSG.$ (15) = "(not used)"
2210 MSG.$ (16) = "(not used)"
2220 CLS
2230 LOCATE 1,5
2240 PRINT "Displaying the keyboard control bits; press Enter to
stop"
2250 LOCATE 3,5
2260 PRINT "To see the changes in action, press these keys: ";
2270 LOCATE 4,7
2280 PRINT "Both shift keys, Ctrl, Alt, ";
2290 PRINT "CapsLock, NumLock, ScrollLock, Ins";
2300 FOR I = 1 TO 16
2310    FOR J = 1 TO I
2320       LOCATE 24 - I - I \ 9, 5 + J * 2 + J \ 9
2330       PRINT CHR$(179);
2340    NEXT J
2350 NEXT I
2360 FOR J = 1 TO 8
2370    LOCATE 15, 5 + J * 2
2380    PRINT CHR$(179)
2390 NEXT J
2400 RETURN

3000 '
3010 ' Subroutine to show the data state
3020 '
3030 DEF SEG = 0
3040 BITS = PEEK (&H417) * 256 + PEEK (&H418)
3050 FOR BIT = 1 TO 16
```

```
3060    STATE$ = "0"
3070    IF BITS >= 32768 THEN STATE$ = "1" : BITS = BITS - 32768
3080    BITS = BITS * 2
3090    LOCATE 6,5 + BIT * 2 + BIT \ 9
3100    PRINT STATE$;
3110    LOCATE 24 - BIT - BIT \ 9, 5 + BIT * 2 + BIT \ 9
3120    PRINT CHR$(192); "> "; MSG.$ (BIT);
3130    IF STATE$ = "0" THEN PRINT " off"; ELSE PRINT " ON ";
3140 NEXT BIT
3150 WHILE CONTINUING
3160    END.TEST$ = INKEY$
3170    IF END.TEST$ = CHR$(13) THEN SYSTEM
3180    IF END.TEST$ = "" THEN RETURN
3190 WEND
```

B

Narrative Glossary

This narrative glossary is intended to provide a very brief rundown of the most common and fundamental terminology used in discussing computers. You can use this narrative glossary in two ways—either by reading it all, or by skimming through to find the terms you are interested in, and then reading the surrounding discussion.

Numbers and Notation

Computers work only with **binary** numbers. These are numbers made up of zeros and ones (**0**s and **1**s). **Binary digits** are called **bits** for short. No matter what a computer is doing, it is working with bits. Even if the subject matter is alphabetic characters, or decimal arithmetic, the method is binary numbers.

Writing many bits—for example, 0101010011101010101—is inconvenient, so several shorthand notations have been developed. The most common is **hexadecimal**, or base-16, notation. Hexadecimal digits have 16 possible values, from 0 through 15; they are written as **0** through **9**, followed by **A** (representing the value ten), **B** (for 11), and **C** through **F** (with values 12 to 15). Hexadecimal digits, also called **hex**, represent four binary digits, or bits, at a time. (Another notation—rarely used with personal computers—called **octal** uses the digits 0 through 7 and represents 3 bits at a time.)

The bits that a computer uses are grouped into larger units. A group of eight bits is called a **byte**. Since hex notation represents four bits at a time, it takes two hex digits to represent the value stored in a byte (hex digits are sometimes whimsically called **nibbles**, or **nybbles**). A byte can be used to store 2 to the eighth power (2^8) of values—256 different values. The values can be interpreted as numbers or as **characters** (such as letters of the alphabet). One byte can hold one character, and therefore the terms bytes and characters are sometimes used interchangeably. The letters of the alphabet and the ten digits, together, are called the **alphanumerics**, although the term is sometimes used loosely to mean any text data.

When bytes are used to hold characters, some code must be used to determine which numeric value will represent which character. The most common code is the **American Standard Code for Information Interchange** (**ASCII**). In ASCII, the capital letter "A" has the decimal value 65 (in hex notation, 41), "B" is decimal 66, and so forth. ASCII includes codes for letters, numbers, punctuation and special control codes. ASCII proper has only 128 different codes, and needs only seven bits to represent it. Since ASCII characters are almost always stored inside 8-bit bytes, there is room for the 128 ASCII codes, and another 128 codes. The other codes are sometimes called **extended ASCII**. ASCII codes are standardized, but extended ASCII will vary from computer to computer.

Traditionally the principle IBM computers have not used ASCII coding to represent characters. Instead, they use **EBCDIC** (the Extended Binary Coded Decimal Information Code). We encounter EBCDIC on our PCs only in special circumstances—for example, in data that has been transferred from a large IBM "mainframe" computer, or in a few programs that use EBCDIC, such as some versions of IBM's DisplayWrite word processing programs.

ASCII data, or an **ASCII file**, is data which consists of text—that is, letters of the alphabet, punctuation, and so forth—rather than numbers or other data. Sometimes the term ASCII is used loosely to mean any text data. Properly speaking, an ASCII file not only contains the ASCII codes for letters, spaces, punctuation, and so forth, but also contains the standard ASCII codes for formatting, such as **carriage-return** and **end-of-file**.

When a byte is used to represent a number, the 256 different byte values can be interpreted as either all positive numbers ranging from 0 through 255, or as positive and negative numbers, ranging from -128 through 127. These are referred to as **unsigned** (0 to 255) or **signed** (-128 to 127) numbers.

To handle larger numbers, several bytes are used together as a unit, often called a **word**. On different computers different meanings are given to the term "word," but most often it means either two bytes (16-bits) or four bytes (32-bits). For personal computers, like the IBM PC, a word usually means a two-byte, 16-bit, number.

A two-byte word has two to the 16th (2^{16}) power different possible values. These can be used as unsigned numbers, with a range of **0** through **65,535**, or signed numbers, with a range of **-32,768** through **32,767**. You may often encounter these specific numbers when learning about the limits of your programs (such as how many records a database program can accommodate).

Integers, or **whole numbers**, are not satisfactory for some tasks. When fractional numbers are needed, or a very wide range of numbers is needed, a different form of computer arithmetic is used, called **floating-point**. Floating-point numbers involve a fractional portion, and an exponent portion, similar to the **"scientific notation"** used in engineering. To work with floating-point numbers, computers interpret the bits of a word in a special way. Floating-point numbers generally represent approximate, inexact values. Often more than one format of floating-point numbers is available, offering different degrees of accuracy; common terms for this are **single-precision** and **double-precision**. Floating-point numbers are sometimes called **real numbers**.

Due to the nature of computer arithmetic and notation, items are often numbered starting from zero for the first element; this is called **zero-origin**. Counting from zero is especially done when figuring a memory location relative to some starting point. The starting point can be called many things, including **base** and **origin**. The **relative location** is most often called an **offset**. Starting from any base location in memory, the first byte is at offset zero, and the next byte is at offset one.

Computer Fundamentals

All of the mechanical and electronic parts of a computer system are called **hardware**. The programs a computer uses are called **software**.

The idea of a computer starts with the concept of memory or storage. A computer's memory consists of many locations, each of which has an address, and can store a value. For most computers, including the IBM PC family, each location is a **byte**; for others, each location is a **word**.

The addresses of the locations are numbers. The values stored in each location can be either discovered (read) or changed (written). When our programs read or write a value, they must specify the address of the memory location.

Some computers organize their memory storage into large modular units, often called **pages**. The IBM PC does not use pages, but for addressing purposes it does divide its memory into units of 16 bytes, called **paragraphs** (a term that was chosen to suggest a smaller division than a page). The memory addressing mechanism for the IBM PC uses two parts—a **segment value**, which points to a paragraph boundary, and a **relative value**, which points to a byte located at some **displacement**, or

offset, from the segment paragraph. The two values, segment and displacement, are needed to specify any complete address. Together, they are sometimes called an **address vector**, or just a **vector**.

Amounts of computer memory are frequently referred to in units of 1,024, because 1,024 is a round number in binary notation, and almost a round number in decimal notation. The value 1,024 is known as **K**, for **kilo**; 64K is 64 units of 1,024, or exactly 65,536.

When referring to general capacity, **K** almost always means 1,024 bytes. However when referring to semiconductor "chips," **K** means 1,024 bits. When magazine articles refer to 16K and 64K chips, they mean 16K bits (equivalent to 2K bytes) or 64K bits (equivalent to 8K bytes).

A computer has the ability to perform operations on the values stored in its memory. Examples of these operations are arithmetic (addition and subtraction) and movement from location to location. A request for the computer to perform an operation is called an **instruction**, or **command**.

A series of computer instructions which together perform some work, is called a **program**. Programs are also called **code**.

The part of the computer which interprets programs and performs the instructions is called the **processor**. A very small processor, particularly one which fits onto a single computer "chip," is called a **microprocessor**. The development of microprocessors made personal computers possible. Properly speaking, a **computer** is a complete working machine which includes a processor and other parts; but the processor part of a computer is sometimes also called a **computer**.

The memory of a computer is used to store both **programs** and **data**. To the memory there is no difference between programs and data. To the processor, however, only those stored values which represent valid instructions can be a program. The processor reads and writes from its memory both to carry out a program, and to access the data that the program uses.

To help it carry out its work, a computer may have a small amount of very specialized memory, which does not have addresses. This specialized memory is referred to as **registers**. Registers are used to make arithmetic more efficient, or to assist in handling addresses.

Many modern computers, including the IBM PC, use a push-down stack to hold status information. Data is pushed onto and popped off of the top of a stack, on a last-in-first-out (or **LIFO**) basis.

When a computer uses a common **data path**—a special set of circuit wires—to pass data from one part to another, this path is called a **bus**.

The memory and processor are internal parts of a computer. There are many external parts, generally called **peripheral equipment**, or **peripherals**. Most peripherals must be connected to a computer through some supporting electronic circuitry, called an **adapter**. For a complex peripheral, such as a **diskette drive**, the adapter will include some special logical circuitry called a controller. A controller is often a specialized computer in its own right.

Peripherals may be of many kinds, but they fall into a few simple categories. **Storage peripherals** are used to hold programs and data that can be moved into the computer's internal memory. Examples of peripheral storage devices are **"floppy" diskettes**, **cassette tape recorders**, and high-capacity **hard disks**, or **fixed disks**.

Other peripheral equipment is used to communicate with people. The equipment used to communicate between people and computers are usually called **terminals**. A terminal most often consists of a typewriter-style keyboard, and a TV-like display screen, called a **CRT** (for cathode-ray tube). A **printer** of some kind may be used instead of a CRT. A display screen is called a **monitor**, or simply a **display**. A color display may accept its color signal information in a combined form, called **composite**, or separated into its red, green, and blue components, called **RGB**.

Large computers may have many terminals, but small personal computers usually work with only one terminal, which may be built right into the computer system. Having only one terminal is a large part of what makes a personal computer *personal*.

Other kinds of peripherals, besides storage and terminals, are printers and **telephone connections**. Connections between computers and telephones are referred to by the names of some of their parts, such as **modems** and **asynchronous adapters**. All of these terms, in general use, refer to the entire computer-telephone connection, which is generally called **communications**. The most common format for communications connections follows a design standard known as **RS-232**. The **speed**, or **data rate,** of a communications line is measured in **baud**, which is bits-per-second. It takes approximately ten bits per second to transmit one byte per second (including the data bits and some overhead). The most common speeds for personal computer communications are 300 and 1200 baud, which transmit about 30 or 120 characters per second. On personal computers, an RS-232 connection is also called a **serial connection** or **serial port**, since it transmits data one bit at a time. A **parallel connection** can transmit more than one bit at a time; the printer adapter on the IBM PC is a parallel connection.

Computer printers come in many varieties. The most common printer for the IBM PC is a **dot-matrix printer**, which creates its printed results by writing a series of dots. **Letter-quality printers** produce results comparable to good typewriters. Most letter-quality printers use a print element that is either a flat disk, called a **daisy-wheel**, or one that is shaped like a large thimble. There are also many other kinds of printer technologies, including **ink-jet** (which squirts ink onto the page), **thermal transfer** (used in the IBM Quietwriter), and **laser printers** (which print on paper the same way photocopiers do).

An **interface** is a connection between any two elements in a computer system. The term interface is used both for connections between hardware parts, and software parts, as well as the human interface.

Much of the equipment that can be connected to a computer is generally referred to as **input/output** equipment, or **I/O**.

The smallest physical parts that make up a computer may be called **chips**. Chips and other parts are wired together electrically, and held mechanically on **boards**. If there is one principal board, it is called the **system board**, or **mother board**. Openings for the addition of more boards are called **expansion slots**, into which are placed memory boards, disk boards, asynch comm boards (telephone connections), and other **expansion** or **peripheral boards**.

A microprocessor interacts with its world through three means: **memory accesses**, **interrupts**, and **ports**. Ports have a port number, or port address, and are used for passing data to or from peripheral devices. Interrupts are used to get the computer's attention. There are three kinds of interrupts (although all three are handled the same way). An **external interrupt** is from the outside world (for example, from a diskette drive). An **internal interrupt** reports some exceptional logical situation (for example, division by zero). A **software interrupt** is a request from a program for some service to be performed. A software interrupt is an alternative to using a ''call'' to activate a subroutine. Memory accesses are used to read or write from the computer's memory.

The computer's **memory** can be of several types. Ordinary memory, which can be read or written to, is called **RAM** (random-access memory). Memory that contains permanent data is **ROM** (read-only memory). Memory can be dedicated to some use; for example, to hold the data that appears on the computer's display screen. If a display screen uses the computer's memory to hold its information, then it is a **memory-mapped display**.

Programs and Programming Languages

Series of computer instructions are called **programs**. Parts of programs that are partially self-contained are called **subroutines**. Subroutines may be **procedures** if they only do some work, or **functions**, if they also result in a value (''open the door'' is analogous to a procedure; ''tell me your name'' is analogous to a function). Subroutines are also called **subprograms**, and **routines**.

Many subroutines use **parameters** to specify exactly what work is to be done; for example, a subroutine that computes a square root needs a parameter to specify what number to use. Many subroutines will indicate how successful their operation was, through a **return code**.

Computers can only execute programs which appear in the detailed form known as **machine language**. However, for the convenience of people, programs may be represented in other forms. If the details of a machine language program are replaced with meaningful symbols (such as the terms ADD or MOVE), then the programming language is know as **assembly language** (also called **assembler**, **symbolic assembler**, or **macro assembler**).

Assembler is called a **low-level language**, because assembly programs are written in a form close to machine language. Other forms of programming languages are more abstracted, and produce many machine instructions for each command written by the programmer. These are called **high-level languages**; examples are **BASIC**, **Pascal**, **FORTRAN**, **Cobol**, **PL/I**, **C**, and **Forth**. Programs that translate high-level language programs into a form usable by the computer, are called **compilers**; for low-level languages, the translators are called **assemblers**. There is no real difference between a compiler and an assembler—they both translate from a human programming language to a form of machine language.

When a person writes a computer program, the form it takes is called **source code**, or source. When the source code is translated (by an assembler or compiler), the result is called **object code**. Object code is nearly ready to be used, but it has to undergo a minor transformation, performed by a **link editor**, or **linker**, to produce a **load module**, which is a finished, ready-to-use program.

An error in a program is called a **bug**, and the processing of trying to find errors, or trying to fix them, is called **debugging**.

There are usually many ways to accomplish an objective with a computer program. The scheme, formula, or method that a program uses, is its **algorithm**. For many tasks—even as simple a one as sorting data into alphabetic order—there are dramatic differences in the efficiency of different algorithms, and the search continues for better and better methods.

A program works with symbolic entities called **variables**. In effect, a variable is the name of a place that can hold data of some type. Specific data can be moved into and out of a variable, and the purpose of the variable is to provide a mechanism for manipulating data. Variables usually have a fixed type, which indicates what sort of data they can accommodate;

for example, **integer** type, **single** and **double-precision** floating-point, and **string** (a collection of text characters). In a program, a **file** is just a special kind of variable, one that can be connected to a diskette file or some device, such as the display screen.

Human Roles

On a personal computer, one person may do everything that is to be done. However, in traditional, large computer systems, there is a division of labor, separating human involvement with a computer into various roles. Users of personal computers may wonder about the meaning of various job titles used.

The **user**, or **end-user**, is the person for whom computer work is done.

The **systems analyst**, or **analyst**, determines the details of the work that the end-user needs done, and decides on the general strategy of how a computer will perform the work.

The **programmer** converts the analyst's general strategy into the detailed tactics and methods to be used. This usually includes writing (and testing) the actual program. However, actually writing and testing the program is sometimes left to a **coder**.

The coder turns the programmer's detailed methods into the **program instructions**.

The **operator** runs the program on the computer, to produce the results needed by the user.

Data Organization

Data is organized and viewed differently, depending upon who or what is looking at it. To the computer itself, data consists of just **bits** and **bytes**. To programmers who manipulate data, there are some traditional logical boundaries for data. A complete collection of related data is a **file** (as an example, a mailing list file). One complete unit of the information that is in a file, is called a **record**; in a mailing list file, all of the information connected with one address would be a record. Finally, within a record are **fields**, the information of one type; for example, the zip code would be one field, in an address record, in a mailing list file.

The records that a program reads or writes are **logical records**. Logical records are placed in the storage medium's **physical records**—which are the pieces actually read or written to a diskette. A program sees logical records, while the operating system performs any translating necessary between logical and physical records. On a diskette, a physical record is called a sector.

The terms **database** and **database manager** are used, and abused, so widely that they have no precise meaning. When data is large, complex, and spread across several files, it might be called a **database**. A **database manager** is a program—usually large and complex in itself—that can control and organize a database. Full-scale database management is far beyond the capabilities of a personal computer.

Disk Vocabulary

Data on a disk is stored in **sectors**, which can be individually read or written; in the IBM PC family, a standard-sized sector holds 512 bytes. Sectors are the disk's physical records—the units that are actually read or written. A **track** is the collection of sectors that fits into one circle on a disk; for ordinary diskettes, there are eight or nine sectors in a track; on a hard disk or high-capacity diskette, you'll find around 15 sectors per track. If there is more than one surface on a disk or diskette drive, then a **cylinder** is all of the tracks that are the same distance from the center. Sectors that are in the same cylinder can be read without moving the disk drive's read-write mechanism. Moving the read-write heads from one track or cylinder to another is called seeking, and it is relatively slow.

Diskettes may be **single-sided** or **double-sided**, depending on whether they are recorded on one or both sides. Also, diskettes may be either **double-density**, as our normal PC-family diskettes are, or **quad-density** (single-density diskettes are an obsolete type). On a double-density diskette there are 40 tracks of data; on a quad-density there are 80, giving twice the storage capacity; ordinarily double- and quad-density diskettes have the same number of sectors recorded on each track. **High-capacity** diskettes have the same number of tracks as quad density, but they go one step further: they pack more sectors into each track, 15 instead of the customary 8 or 9.

A diskette needs a table of contents for its files, called a **directory**. Some means must be used to keep track of used and unused space on a diskette; it's done with the **FAT** (**File Allocation Table**). The first sector of each diskette is dedicated to holding the first part of the operating system's start-up program, called the **boot-strap loader**, or **boot record**. So, on each diskette there are four different uses for sectors—boot record, FAT, directory, and data space (where files are stored).

A **diskette** is flexible, thus it is called a **floppy**. A hard disk has a rigid platter in place of the flexible plastic of a floppy; the rigid shape allows more precise data recording, and thus higher density and more capacity. The sort of hard disks installed on personal computers today use a collection of methods called **Winchester technology**, so they are also called **Winchester disks**. Because hard disks are fixed in place and not removable (as diskettes are), IBM refers to hard disks as **fixed disks**.

There are also **cartridge hard disks** that can be plugged in and removed nearly as easily as a floppy diskette.

Operating Systems

An **operating system** is a program that supervises and controls the operation of a computer. Operating systems are complex and consist of many parts.

One element of an operating system is its **BIOS**, or **Basic Input-Output System**. The BIOS is responsible for handling the details of input-output operations, including the task of relating a program's logical records to a peripheral device's physical records. At the most detailed level, the BIOS contains routines tailored to the specific requirements of each peripheral device; these routines are called **drivers**, or **device handlers**.

Usually an operating system is organized into a hierarchy of levels of services. At the lowest level, the **device handlers** insulate the rest of the operating system from the details of each device. At the next level, relating logical data to physical data is performed. At a higher level basic services are provided—such as accepting output data from a program to be placed into a file.

Besides device and data handling, an operating system must supervise programs, including loading them, relocating them (adjusting their internal addresses to correspond to their exact location in a memory), and recovering them from any program errors, through an error handler.

Another element of an operating system is the **command processor**, which accepts and acts on commands given by the computer's user. Commands usually amount to a request for the execution of some service program.

C

Products and Trademarks

Numerous products are mentioned in this book and most of the names of these products are trademarked. Here is a list of the products, their producers, the trademark owners, and—for the products that aren't widely available—how to contact the producers.

- IBM heads the list, of course. IBM is a registered trademark of International Business Machines Corporation. Most of the IBM products mentioned in this book are available from any authorized dealer of IBM Personal Computers, including IBM's own "IBM Product Center" stores, ComputerLand stores, and many, many others. IBM also publishes a series of inexpensive PC programs called "Personally Developed Software"; these programs are not available from dealers. To get a catalog of these programs, or to order them, write Personally Developed Software, P.O. Box 3280, Wallingford, CT, 06494, or call 1-800-IBM-PCSW. Other IBM products whose names are trademarks are IBM Personal Computer, Personal Computer AT, PC*jr*, TopView, Displaywrite, Professional Debug Facility, WordProof, and Quietwriter.

- Compaq is a registered trademark and Deskpro and Deskpro-286 are trademarks of Compaq Computer Corporation.

- Data General/One is a trademark of Data General.

- Hercules is a trademark of Hercules Computer Technology.

- Microsoft and XENIX are registered trademarks and Multiplan and Word are trademarks of Microsoft Corporation.

- Periscope (a marvelous debugging tool for PC software) is a trademark of Data Base Decisions, 14 Bonnie Lane, Atlanta, GA 30328. Data Base Decisions also publishes "Peeks and Pokes" mentioned in Appendix D.

- CP/M and CP/M-86 are trademarks of Digital Research.

- UCSD p-System is a trademark of the Regents of the University of California.

- Bernoulli Box—a remarkable cartridge semi-hard disk—is a trademark of IOMega Corporation, 1821 West 4000 South, Roy UT 84067.

- Trace-86, and Advanced Trace-86, software tracing tools, are products of Morgan Computing, 10400 N. Central Expressway, Suite 210, Dallas, TX 75231.

- dBASE II, dBASE III, Framework, and Fred (the Framework programming language) are trademarks of Ashton-Tate.

- Sidekick, Turbo Pascal, and Superkey are trademarks of Borland International.

- Prokey is a trademark of Rosesoft.

- Lotus, 1-2-3, and Symphony are trademarks of Lotus Development Corporation.

- Volkswriter is a trademark of Lifetree Software Inc.

- Multimate is a trademark of Multimate International.

- Intel is a registered trademark and Above Board a trademark of Intel Corporation.

- PC-Talk III is a product of the Headlands Press, P.O. Box 862, Tiburon, CA 94920.

- WordStar is a trademark of Micropro.

- MCI Mail and MCI are registered trademarks of MCI.

- CompuServe is a trademark of CompuServe Incorporated.

- The Norton Utilities is a trademark of Peter Norton.

D

Other Sources of Information

his book is a book of *understanding*, designed to help you comprehend the IBM PC family. To avoid burying you in too many facts, I've left out many details. Here are some sources you can use to find out more about this remarkable family of computers.

The ultimate source of most information about the PC family is IBM's series of *Technical Reference* manuals. IBM has published separate manuals for the original PC model, the XT, the PC*jr*, and the AT. There is also unified *Technical Reference* manual for the PC family's options and adapters. Periodic updates are available for this manual by subscription. There is also a series of *Technical Reference* manuals for DOS and you'll find some specialty manuals as well, such as the one for the PC Network.

For information in greater depth about programming for the PC family, see *The Peter Norton Programmer's Guide to the IBM PC* (Microsoft Press, 1985).

For excellent and easy-to-understand coverage of the details of the PC's 8088 microprocessor, see *The 8086 Primer* by Stephen P. Morse (Hayden, 1980). For greater depth, turn to *The 8086 Book* by Russell Rector and George Alexy (Osborne/McGraw-Hill, 1980).

For specific details on the AT's microprocessor, the 80286, go straight to the source, a series of manuals by the chip's designer Intel: *Introduction to the iAPX 286, iAPX 286 Programmer's Reference Manual, iAPX 286 Hardware Reference Manual*, and *iAPX 286 Operating Systems Writer's Guide*, all available from Intel Corporation, Literature Dept, 3065 Bowers Ave, Santa Clara, CA 95051.

For more on the 87s, the PC family's high-speed math coprocessors, see the book *8087 Applications and Programming* by Richard Startz (Brady, 1983).

For more on assembly language programming see *IBM PC & XT Assembly Language* by Leo J. Scanlon (Brady, 1985) or the really excellent book *Assembly Language Safari* by a very talented PC programmer (and admired friend of mine) John Socha (Brady, 1984).

For an inside view of specialty programming see *Games, Graphics and Sound for the IBM PC* by Dorothy Strickland, Dennis Rockwell and Kevin Bower (Brady, 1983).

Other useful sources are *Expanding Your IBM PC* by Bil. Alvernaz (Brady, 1985); *A Comprehensive Guide to the IBM Personal Computer* by George Markowsky (Prentice-Hall, 1984); *Interfacing to the IBM Personal Computer* by Lewis C. Eggebrecht (Howard W Sams, 1983).

Another nifty and interesting source of information on the PC is *Peeks and Pokes* by Brett Salter, available from Data Base Decisions, 14 Bonnie Lane, Atlanta, GA 30328.

There are many periodicals that provide excellent sources of information about the PC family. Two magazines dominate in providing general coverage of the PC: "PC Magazine" (which features a regular column by me) and "PC World." For more technical information, turn to "PC Tech Journal". For hot programmer's tips, look to "Dr. Dobb's Journal" or the excellent but relatively little known "Programmer's Journal" (P.O. Box 30160, Eugene, OR, 97403). Finally, there is "PC Week" (which also features a column by me), a magazine that serves the needs of PC users in large organizations. PC Week is a controlled circulation magazine, available free only to qualified subscribers (for information write to PC Week, Ziff Davis, 1 Park Ave, New York, NY, 10016).

Index

Related Resources Shelf

Creating Utilities with Assembly Language: 10 Best for the IBM PC & XT
Stephen Holzner

With assembly language as its foundation, this book explores the most popular utility programs for the IBM PC and XT. For the more advanced user, this book unleashes the power of utilities on the PC. Utilities created and discussed include PCALC, ONE KEY, CLOCK, FONT, DBUG SCAN, DSKWATCH and UNDELETE. The author is a regular contributor to *PC Magazine*.

☐ 1985/352 pp/paper/0-89303-584-X/$19.95

Artificial Intelligence for Microcomputers: A Guide for Business Decision Makers
Mickey Williamson

This book discusses artificial intelligence from an introductory point of view and takes a detailed look at expert systems and how they can be used as a business decision-making tool. Includes step-by-step instructions to create your own expert system and covers applications to cost/benefit analysis, personnel evaluations and software benchtesting.

☐ 1985/224 pp/paper/0-89303-483-5/$17.95

Assembly Language Programming with the IBM PC AT Leo J. Scanlon

Author of Brady's best-selling IBM PC & XT ASSEMBLY LANGUAGE: A GUIDE FOR PROGRAMMERS (recently revised and enlarged), Leo Scanlon is the assembly language authority. This new book on the AT is designed for beginning and experienced programmers, and includes step-by-step instructions for using the IBM Macro Assembler. Also included is a library of 30 useful macros, a full description of the 80286 microprocessor, and advanced topics like music and sound.

☐ 1985/464 pp/paper/0-89303-484-3/$21.95

Programmer's Problem Solver for the IBM PC, XT and AT Robert Jourdain

The best complete reference guide to the facts, numbers and procedures needed to control hardware control over the PC family of microcomputers. Designed for the practicing programmer, this exceptional volume contains detail of direct programming of peripheral chips, operating system interrupts and their controllers, timers, calendar chips, and all hardware components in a typical advanced configuration. Sections are also included on disk layout, memory management, and printer control.

☐ 1985/480 pp/paper/0-89303-877-7/$22.95

To order, simply clip or photocopy this entire page, check your order selection, and complete the coupon below. Enclose a check or money order for the stated amount or include credit card information. Please add $2.00 per book for postage & handling, plus local sales tax.

Mail To: **Brady Computer Books, Simon&Schuster, Box 500, Englewood Cliffs, NJ 07632.**

You may also order from Brady directly by calling 800-624-0023 (800-624-0024 if in New Jersey).

Name _____

Address _____

City/State/Zip _____

Charge my credit card instead: ☐ MasterCard   ☐ Visa

Credit Card Account # _____ Expiration Date_____/_____

Signature _____
Dept. Y   D5831-BB
Prices subject to change without notice.

User's Manual

for

the Diskette Accompanying

Inside the IBM PC

Revised and Enlarged

by

Peter Norton

Table of Contents

What's Here

This Diskette contains the program source code listings appearing in *Inside the IBM PC Revised and Enlarged*, plus several ready-to-use programs that will assist you in learning about and understanding your computer.

The files on this diskette are divided into four groups:

1. two help-files that describe and help you use the programs
2. the 11 lengthier programs that appear in Appendix A of the book
3. 17 shorter program fragments that appear in the body of the book
4. four special programs to help you learn more about your computer, including two from the **Norton Utilities** set and two specially prepared for this set.

You'll find a more complete description of each item in the **More Information** section of this manual.

Note: This diskette is intended primarily to make it easier to use and explore the book's program listings. It is entirely unlike the diskette set that accompanied the first edition of *Inside the IBM PC*. The previous set, called the "Access Tools," provided interface subroutines for use by programmers. That set has been made obsolete by subsequent developments for the IBM PC family.

How to Use the Diskette

To use this diskette, you must be familiar with the IBM Personal Computer and its DOS operating system, and you must know how to run DOS programs and BASIC programs.

This program set will work on any model of the IBM Personal Computer family, including all fully PC-compatible computers. The set will work with the most minimal computer equipment: a single diskette drive, 64K bytes of memory, any standard display screen, and any version of DOS.

Copy these program files to other disks of your own and safeguard the original diskette. In order to use the BASIC programs in this set you will need to combine them with the interpreter program for BASIC, named `BASICA.COM`. The four ready-to-use programs, named `CI.COM`, `DI.COM`, `LD.COM`, and `SI.COM`, do not require any other program to be used. You may find that the LD program is handy to you in your everyday use of your computer, particularly if you have a hard disk in your computer. I recommend that you place a copy of `LD.COM` wherever you keep your miscellaneous programs (such as the DOS commands CHKDSK and FORMAT).

More Information

Here is a complete list of the files on the diskette; they are described after the list:

```
READ.ME
DEMO.BAT

MAZE.BAS
HEXTABLE.BAS
ALL-CHAR.BAS
REF-CHAR.BAS
BOXES.BAS
MSG-HUNT.BAS
VID-MODE.BAS
COLORTXT.BAS
GRAPHTXT.BAS
COLOR-4.BAS
KEY-BITS.BAS

CH-03-01.BAS
CH-03-02.BAS
CH-06-01.BAS
CH-06-02.BAS
CH-07-01.BAS
CH-07-02.BAS
CH-11-01.BAS
CH-11-02.BAS
CH-13-01.BAS
CH-14-01.BAS
CH-14-02.BAS
CH-15-01.BAS
CH-15-02.BAS
CH-15-03.BAS
CH-21-01.ASM
CH-21-02.PAS
CH-21-03.C

SI.COM
LD.COM
DI.COM
CI.COM
```

The first two files on the disk, READ.ME and DEMO.BAT, are intended simply to help you use these programs. READ.ME contains a short description of the files. DEMO.BAT is a batch file that will execute, in sequence, the 11 programs found in Appendix A of the book. If you copy this batch file onto a diskette together with the BASIC interpreter, BASICA.COM, and the 11 program files, you will be able to run and experiment with these programs in a convenient way.

The main part of this diskette consists of the 11 program files which appear in appendix A of the book. These programs demonstrate various aspects of the IBM PC family's features and capabilities. Here is a summary of each of these programs.

MAZE.BAS (introduction) This program creates a hunting maze that randomly searches out a path from "START" to "FINISH." It's a whimsical demonstration of the path we take in learning about our computers, and you can use it as your own way of showing others the circuitous route that we sometimes have to take to accomplish our goals.

HEXTABLE.BAS (chapter 3) This program creates two tables of hexadecimal arithmetic, one for addition and one for multiplication.

ALL-CHAR.BAS (chapter 4) This program shows the complete PC character set, together in one screen image.

REF-CHAR.BAS (chapter 4) This program also shows the complete PC character set, combined with the decimal and hexadecimal codes for each character.

BOXES.BAS (chapter 4) This program demonstrates the box-drawing characters that are part of the PC's character set. First it shows what the boxes look like, then it gives the decimal character codes for each character used.

MSG-HUNT.BAS (chapter 7) This program searches through your computer's ROM-BIOS memory for messages that may be interesting. This program takes some time to run, so be patient if you want to see it all. If you wish to interrupt the operation of this program, you can do so by pressing the Ctrl-Break key combination, and then entering the command SYSTEM to finish the program.

VID-MODE.BAS (chapter 11) This program demonstrates all the PC's video display modes, as much as the BASIC language permits. It informs you of which modes can be used on your computer, and lets you inspect the appearance of each one.

COLORTXT.BAS (chapter 12) This program shows the complete set of color (and monochrome) display attributes that can be used with text characters.

GRAPHTXT.BAS (chapter 13) This program shows, in enlarged form, the drawings of the PC's text characters that are used in the graphics modes. This program does not require the graphics mode to work, so it can be used on every PC, including those without a graphics display adapter.

COLOR-4.BAS (chapter 13) This program demonstrates the colors and operation of the PC's four-color medium resolution graphics mode. Using it requires the color-graphics display adapter (or its equivalent) in order to work.

KEY-BITS.BAS (chapter 14) This program displays and demonstrates the bits that control and reflect the operation of the PC's keyboard, showing, for example, whether either of the shift keys are pressed.

The next 17 files contain the source code for the short programs and program fragments that appear in the body of the book. The files are given names to indicate their location in the book. For example, CH-03-02.BAS is the second listing from Chapter 3. In some cases these programs can be usefully employed just as they are; in other cases they simply illustrate how some programming might be done. The last three examples, CH-21-01.ASM, CH-21-02.PAS, and CH-21-03.C, appear simply to illustrate the form and style of the three main programming languages used for the PC: assembly language, Pascal, and C.

The final group of four files contain four ready-to-use programs, two from the **Norton Utilities** set and two specially prepared for this diskette. All four programs can be used to explore and discover more information about your computer. You will find each one discussed in detail in the following pages.

CI – Country Information

Purpose

Lists the country-dependent information that DOS provides to guide our programs.

Format

    CI

Remarks

DOS provides a way for our programs to automatically adjust to the various conventions of different countries. This program displays the information that is available. This country-dependent information is provided in two levels of service. For DOS-2 versions and later, a program may request that DOS provide it with the current country-dependent information. For DOS-3 versions and later, programs can also *set* the country code among the codes known to the particular version of DOS.

This **CI** program displays the current country information and also shows all the codes that your version of DOS supports. Here is an example of how the **CI** program displays this country-dependent information; each item will be explained below:

```
Code D/T Money 12,345 1.0 m/d h:m $1? $1.00 12/24 A,B Rsrvd
   1 USA $        ,      .   -   :  $1   2   12     ,
  31 Eur ƒ     .        ,   -   :  $1   2   24     ;
  32 Eur F           ,   /   :  1$   2   24     ;
  33 Eur F           ,   /   :  1$   2   24     ;
  39 Eur Lit.  .        ,   /   :  1$   0   24     ;
  41 Eur Fr    ,        .   -   :  1$   2   24     ,
  44 Eur £     ,        .   -   :  $1   2   24     ,
  45 Eur DKR   .        ,   /   .  1$   2   24     ;
  46 Swe SEK   .        ,   -   .  1$   2   24     ;
  47 Eur KR    .        ,   /   .  1$   2   24     ;
  49 Eur DM    .        ,   .   .  $1   2   24     ;
  61 Eur $        ,      .   -   :  $1   2   24     ,
```

The first field, `Code`, shows the identifying country code that is used to identify each country. Code 1 is used for the United States.

The second field, D/T, indicates which format should be used to display the date. There are three standard formats: The USA standard shows the date as *month/day/year;* the European standard shows the date as *day/month/year;* the Japanese standard shows it as *year:month:day.* (Close study of the table above will show the Japanese standard used for Sweden.)

The third field, Money, shows the currency symbol used. Where possible, a currency symbol from the PC's special character set is used, such as the British pound, £, and the French franc, *f.* For many countries the currency symbol is represented by conventional letters of the alphabet, such as the Italian lira, Lit., or the Swedish kronor, SEK.

The fourth and fifth fields show how numbers are displayed. Under the heading 12,345 is the punctuation used to separate thousands. Under the heading 1.0 is the punctuation used as a decimal point.

The sixth and seventh fields show how the date and time is punctuated. Under the heading m/d is the symbol used for dates. Under h:m is the symbol used for time.

The next two fields are used for currency. Under the heading $1? is shown whether the currency symbol appears before or after the amount. Under the heading $1.00 is the number of decimal places used with the currency. In the example shown, all have two decimal places except for the Italian lira.

The next field, 12/24, shows whether the time should be shown in 12- or 24-hour notation.

The last active field, A,B, shows the punctuation used to separate items in a list.

In addition to the information shown here, ten bytes are reserved for further fields that can be added in the future. If your DOS reports any information in this area, it will be shown under the heading Rsrvd.

DI - Disk Information

Purpose

Lists and compares the information available about a disk from two sources - the DOS drive table and the disk's own boot record.

Format

DI [*d:*]

Remarks

Programs like my **Norton Utilities**, that need to work intimately with disks, need to find out key technical information about the disk formats that they work with. There are two sources of this information. One is provided by DOS in the form of a drive table entry that describes the disk. The other is embedded in the disk's boot record for all disk formats except those introduced with versions of DOS before version 2.00. This DI program displays the complete information available from both sources for you to study. Where the same information is available from both sources, it is shown for comparison. The following is an example taken from a PC AT's 20-megabyte disk. Each item is discussed below.

Information from DOS		Information from the boot record
	system id	'IBM 3.1'
	format id (hex)	F8
2	drive number	
2	driver id number	
512	sector size in bytes	512
4	sectors per cluster	4
2	reserved sectors	1
2	number of FATs	2
512	root directory entries	512
41	sectors per FAT	41
10,406	number of clusters	
	number of sectors	41,735
1	offset to FAT	
83	offset to directory	
115	offset to data	
	sectors per track	17
	sides	4
	special reserved sectors	17

The `system id` is an 8-byte description of either the disk format or of the DOS version that created the disk format. It only appears in the disk's boot record and, to the best of my knowledge, is not used for anything.

The `format id` is a standard DOS identifier of the disk format. The standard location for this id byte is the first byte of the disk's FAT (File Allocation Table), but it is also duplicated here in the boot record. This format id can be used to identify the disk format, but not every DOS disk format has a unique id byte; some are used for more than one format.

The `drive number` identifies the disk drive - 0 indicates drive A, 1 drive B, and 2, in the example here, drive C.

The `driver number` identifies which software *driver* supports the disk drive. The driver number is an internal item to DOS and has nothing directly to do with the disk or the disk's format.

The sector size in bytes is one of several entries that describe the absolute dimensions of the disk (as opposed to the logical structure that DOS adds to a disk). The other fields that describe the disk's absolute dimensions are the `sectors per track` and the number of `sides`, that appear toward the end of the list.

The `sectors per cluster` indicates the size of the units of space that DOS allocates to our files.

The number of **reserved sectors** is an item of uncertain use. You will often find, as in the example here, a discrepancy between the two sources of this information.

The `number of FATs` indicates how many copies of the File Allocation Table are recorded on the disk. Two is the customary number for physical disks; virtual disks (RAM memory disks) commonly have just one.

The `root directory entries` indicates the capacity of the disk's standard root directory. The physical size of the root directory can be calculated from this, combined with the sector size in bytes and the 32-byte size of the directory entries.

The `sectors per FAT` indicates the physical size of the File Allocation Table.

The `number of clusters` indicates how many units of disk space there are for DOS to allocate to our files. If there are more than 4080, the disk must have a 16-bit FAT format; under 4080, a 12-bit FAT is used.

The `number of sectors` indicates the total number of disk sectors available for DOS to use, including both the system and data portions of the disk. The number of tracks or cylinders given to this DOS disk can be calculated from this number, combined with the sectors per track and the number of sides. This calculation may not yield an integral number of cylinders, as you will find in the example above. This is normally due to the portion of a hard disk that is set aside for a "master boot record," which may be a single sector or an entire track of sectors. Note that while we can calculate the number of tracks or cylinders that the DOS portion of a disk occupies, we do not have the information necessary to determine the total absolute number of cylinders on a hard disk.

Three offset fields, `offset to FAT`, `offset to directory`, and `offset to data`, indicate the number of sectors from the beginning of the DOS portion of a disk to each of these three key parts of the disk. Our programs can use this information to reliably find the disk's FAT and its root directory.

Finally, the `special reserved sectors` normally indicates an offset to the beginning of the DOS portion of a disk. Like the reserved sectors field, the use of this field is somewhat uncertain. In this example it indicates the number of sectors removed from the disk partition for the disk's master boot record.

LD – List Directories

Purpose

Lists all the directories on your disks.

Format

LD [*d:* ...] [/A] [/P] [/W] [/T]

You may specify specific disk drives to search with the *d:* parameters, or use the /A switch to search all drives.

/P pauses when the screen is full. /W lists directories in wide display format; /T lists a total of the number and size of the files in each directory.

Remarks

LD-List Directories provides a complete list of all the directories on your disks. You may list the directories on one or more specific drives, or ask for all your drives with the /A switch.

Tips and Suggestions

The directory list is useful in helping you keep track of all the directories and subdirectories on your disks. It is particularly useful on a hard disk system, that can accommodate many directories.

You can redirect the output of LD into a file, using the standard DOS method for redirection of output. You can then use that file as a convenient starting point in the creation of a batch file that operates on your directories. This is a handy method that I often use.

Just as you can use LD to get a list of your directories, you can use FF-File Find to get a list of your files.

LD-List Directories is one of several of these **Norton Utilities** programs that are particularly useful in helping you manage a hard disk system. Other programs in the **Utilities** set that are especially useful with hard disks are DS-Directory Sort, FF-File Find, FS-File Size, and TS-Text Search.

For example, to print a listing of your directories:

LD   >LPT1:

SI – System Information

Purpose

Displays interesting technical information about your computer.

Format

```
SI [/N]
```
/N avoids the memory test, that can disrupt some computers.

Remarks

SI-System Information discovers and displays some technical information about your computer. You many find this information interesting, and it has some practical uses.

Here are two examples that illustrate the variety of information that SI reports. From an AT:

```
IBM/PC-AT
Built-in BIOS programs dated Tuesday, January 10, 1984
Operating under DOS 3.10
5 logical disk drives, A: through E:
DOS reports 640 K-bytes of memory:
   161 K-bytes used by DOS and resident programs
   479 K-bytes available for application programs
A search for active memory finds:
   640 K-bytes main memory    (at hex 0000-A000)
    64 K-bytes display memory (at hex B000-C000)
Computing performance index relative to IBM/PC: 7.0
```

Here is another example from a 3270 PC:

```
IBM 3270 PC
Built-in BIOS programs dated Monday, November 8, 1982
Operating under DOS 2.10
3 logical disk drives, A: through C:
DOS reports 525 K-bytes of memory:
    25 K-bytes used by DOS and resident programs
   500 K-bytes available for application programs
A search for active memory finds:
   640 K-bytes main memory    (at hex 0000-A000)
    16 K-bytes display memory (at hex B000-B400)
    16 K-bytes display memory (at hex B800-BC00)
     4 K-bytes extra memory   (at hex CE00-CF00)
BIOS signature found at hex paragraph C000
      C800 CA00
Computing performance index relative to IBM/PC: 1.0
```

SI attempts to identify the computer it is working on, within practical limitations. It can recognize specialty models of the PC family, such as the PC*jr* or the 3270 PC, but some other models can't be clearly identified. SI can also recognize some PC-compatibles. When it can't recognize the machine, it will attempt to find and show you identifying marks, such as a copyright notice within the computer.

SI reports the version of DOS being used and the number of "logical" disk drives that DOS has at its command. This is often more than the real number of physical drives your machine has.

SI reports on the computer's memory, using two approaches. The first is based on information that DOS provides. It shows the total amount of memory, how much is taken up by DOS and by resident programs (such as **SideKick** or **Prokey**), and how much remains for use by our application programs.

The second memory report is based on a live test, performed by probing every part of the computer's memory. Some computers will lock up, reporting a PARITY ERROR when the live probe test is done. *This does no harm whatsoever* to your computer, but it does require you to turn off your computer and start it up from scratch. The /N switch allows you to bypass this test if you need to. The live memory test reports three categories of memory: main memory used by our programs, display memory used by the screen, and extra memory used for special applications.

Your computer may have additions made to its built-in control program, the BIOS. If SI is able to detect any of these additions, it reports them; you will see three of them listed in the second example above. This information is of technical interest only.

SI finishes with a computing performance index. This index provides a rough indication of your computer's relative speed in computing and memory access. To figure the index, SI times how long it takes to perform a series of calculations. The index is then scaled relative to a standard IBM PC. An index of 2.0 means that the calculations were done twice as fast as a standard PC would do them. Due to the methods used, the index can vary but it provides a rough-and-ready measure of your computer's speed. This index is based solely on a routine set of calculations. It does *not* take into account disk performance, that is a major factor in the overall capability of your computer.

Tips and Suggestions

SI may prove useful in providing certain key information about the computers with that you come in contact. For any computer that you routinely work with, information about the system memory overhead may be useful in deciding how much memory to devote to disk buffers or keyboard enhancement workspace.

If you are concerned about the accumulative cost of the resident programs or disk buffers that you are using, you can easily monitor how much memory they take up by studying SI's DOS memory report. First look at how much memory is currently being used. Then restart your computer without the programs or buffers. Add them one by one, and examine the cost of each with SI.

For any computer that is unfamiliar to you, SI may be helpful in quickly showing you the number of disk drives, memory available, and relative computing speed.

Fasten your seat belt!

For the serious computer user who wants to soup up his PC—make it faster, more powerful, more fun—the experts at PC WORLD have a fascinating new book and software program that can make your personal computer truly personal.

Called *The Fully Powered PC* with *PC World Utilities Disk*, it takes you under the hood of your PC. It shows you how to construct your own system, how to combine many single-purpose systems, and how to call up a dozen or more applications with little more than a keystroke.

It puts you on the fast track by showing you how to put applications programs into active memory so they run faster, design menus to guide you through systems you've created, even customize your computer to find and dial telephone numbers. It even includes public-domain software that add still more powerful features to your PC.

In other words, *The Fully Powered PC* helps you create a system that performs exactly the way *you* want it to. And isn't that why you bought a PC in the first place?